PRAISE FOR

The Trials of
Lady Jane Douglas

*"Karl Sabbagh has investigated one of the
great British scandals of the 18th Century
and produced a fascinating piece of detective
work. It tells us more about high society
in England and Scotland at the time than
most conventional histories."*

Magnus Linklater,
former editor, The Scotsman

The Trials of Lady Jane Douglas

The Trials of
LADY JANE DOUGLAS

The scandal that divided 18th century Britain

KARL SABBAGH

SKYSCRAPER

Published by Skyscraper Publications Limited
Talton Edge, Newbold on Stour, Warwickshire CV37 8TR
www.skyscraperpublications.com

First published 2014

Copyright © 2014 Karl Sabbagh

A CIP catalogue record for this book is available
from the British Library.

ISBN-13: 978-0-9926270-1-0

Designed and typeset by
Chandler Book Design

Printed and bound in Great Britain
by CPI Group (UK) Ltd, Croydon, CR0 4YY

The Trials of Lady Jane Douglas

by

Karl Sabbagh

CONTENTS

Who's Who in *The Trials of Lady Jane Douglas*

The Douglas Side:

Lady Jane Douglas (also called Jean and Jeanne) – sister of the Duke of Douglas

Colonel John Stewart – husband of Lady Jane Douglas

Archy and Sholto Douglas – sons of Lady Jane and Colonel Stewart

Mrs. Helen "Nelly" Hewit – companion to Lady Jane Douglas

Isabel Walker – maid to Lady Jane Douglas

The Duke of Douglas – premier Duke and richest man in Scotland

The Duchess of Douglas, formerly Margaret "Peggy" Mains

Mrs. Hepburn – sister of the Duchess of Douglas

William Greenshield, butler at Douglas Castle

Lady Schaw – friend of Lady Jane and later guardian of Archy Douglas

Mrs. Napier – friend of Lady Schaw

The Hamilton Side:

The 6th Duke of Hamilton – cousin of the Duke of Douglas, and the second richest man in Scotland

Duchess of Hamilton, formerly Miss Elizabeth Gunning, subsequently Duchess of Argyll

Archibald Stuart, (also Stewart and Steuart) – agent to the Duke of Douglas, and father of Andrew Stuart

Andrew Stuart – tutor to the Duke of Hamilton

James White of Stockbriggs – factor to the Duke of Douglas

William Hamilton – minister at Douglas Town

Baron Mure – guardian to the Duke of Hamilton

The Duke and Duchess of Queensberry – relatives of Archy Douglas, the Duke his guardian

Other participants

In Paris:

Pierre La Marre (also Lamarre, Le Marre, Le Mar, etc) – alleged midwife to Lady Jane

François La Marre – brother of Pierre

Antoine de Sartine – Louis XV's lieutenant of police

M. Buhot – Inspector of Police charged with monitoring foreign subjects in Paris

M. Gilles – Buhot's doctor and friend of M. Menager

M. Pierre Michel Menager – doctor and key witness

M. and Mme. Godefroi – landlords of hotel de Châlons

Mme. Le Brun – alleged landlady at the house where Lady Jane gave birth

Mme. Michel – landlady of hotel d'Anjou

M. and Mme. Pierre Sanry – a rope dancer and his wife

Joseph Sanry – their baby son

M. and Mme. Nicholas Mignon – a glass-blower and his wife

Louis Mignon – their baby son

Abbé Hibert – first told story of a stolen baby in Paris

Dr. Alexandre Cotterel – curé of St. Laurent, told story to Abbé Hibert

Mme. Garnier – childcare nurse

M. and Mme. Maillefer – syndic of Rheims and his wife

M. Duruisseau – police commissioner for St Germain area

Aeneas Macdonald – lawyer for Hamilton side

James Burnet – lawyer for Douglas side, later Lord Monboddo

Alexander Makonochie – lawyer for Douglas side

Alexander Murray – lawyer for Douglas side

Alexander Murray (different from above) – Sir John Stewart's brother-in-law

Francis Garden – lawyer for Douglas side, and pig-lover

William Stewart – friend of Lady Jane

James Carnegy – lawyer for Douglas side

M. d'Anjou – Andrew Stuart's French legal colleague

In Edinburgh

Lord Monboddo – see James Burnet

Lord Dundas – Lord President of Court of Session

Lord Kames – judge of Court of Session

Lord Strichen – judge of Court of Session

James Boswell – lawyer and biographer of Dr. Samuel Johnson

In London

Lord Mansfield, formerly William Murray – Lord Chief Justice

Edward Thurlow – lawyer for Douglas side

James Montgomery – Lord Advocate for Scotland

Charles Yorke – lawyer for Hamilton side

Alexander Wedderburn – lawyer for Hamilton side

Sir Fletcher Norton – Attorney General, lawyer for Douglas side

Horace Walpole – diarist

Lady Mary Coke – diarist

Alexander Carlyle – diarist

John Montagu, 4th Earl of Sandwich, spoke for Hamilton in House of Lords

Lord Camden, Lord Chancellor of England

Ilay Campbell, counsel for Douglas side

Sir John Steuart of Grandtully – son of Colonel Stewart and half-brother to Archy Douglas

Lady Lucy Graham – daughter of the Duke of Montrose, Archy Douglas' first wife

Lady Frances Dalkeith – Archy Douglas' second wife

William Playfair – inventor, and blackmailer of Archy Douglas

Prologue

July in Paris in 1748 was very uncomfortable. The city was hot and smelly and noisy, and infested with insects, particularly in the crowded lodgings that clustered either side of the sewer-like Seine. England and France had only recently been on opposite sides of a war, so British travellers to Paris were not the most popular visitors, although innkeepers and restaurateurs would put purse before popularity and welcome anyone with a few *ecus* to spend. France under Louis XIV was coming to terms with its humiliation at the Peace of Aix la Chapelle, after the so-called War of the Austrian Succession. In spite of the fact that most of Europe had been involved on one side or the other in the War, it was France and England who settled the terms of the peace, greatly to France's disadvantage, so much so that it gave rise to the simile 'stupid as the Peace'.

But Scots visitors, particularly Jacobites – supporters of the supplanted Stuart monarchy – were tolerated because of their opposition to the English government, on the principle of 'my enemy's enemy is my friend.' There was a Jacobite Scots community in Paris which bided its time out of reach of the British authorities until the restoration of a Stuart to the throne.

When a Scots couple, Sir John Stewart and his wife, Lady Jane Douglas, arrived in a hackney carriage on July 4th at the Hotel de Châlons in the Rue St Martin, they were exhausted. They had left Rheims two days ago and travelled over bumpy roads, stopping for the night at an inn in Nanteuil, where the other passengers in the coach saw little of them, as the couple ate in their rooms. Lady Jane's pregnancy was obvious to all and her due date was only days away, so the couple must have been looking forward to the comforts of a well-cooked dinner and a clean bed when they arrived in Paris. They were accompanied by Lady Jane's long-time companion, Nelly Hewit, a bulky, mannish woman who had known her employer since she was a girl and was fiercely loyal to her.

Lady Jane was now forty-nine years old and this would be her first experience of childbirth, so the two Scottish women viewed the next couple of weeks with some trepidation. Colonel Stewart, ten years older than Lady Jane, was perhaps less worried. He was not of a nervous disposition and once he had settled in at the inn, he looked forward to drinking some fine French wine with a few fellow countrymen and playing a game or two of cards.

Before her pregnancy, Lady Jane Douglas was described as a thin and slender woman who "scarce appeared to have any breasts at all." Now, in her ninth month, she had filled out a little above the waist and a lot more below, but was still a small, pale woman who looked fifteen years younger than her forty-nine years. She was "very genteel and very graceful." Her husband, Sir John Stewart, who used the rank of Colonel as a result of a period many years before in the Swedish army, was tall and described as "a prodigious fine figure of a man"[1] but quite thoughtless, a gambler and a spendthrift. The couple had been married for less than two years and in spite of her acclaimed beauty and sweet nature it was Lady Jane's first marriage.

What Lady Jane and her husband did or didn't do over the next two weeks was to be the subject of the most minute scrutiny by some of the leading lawyers in England and Scotland over a period of ten years, in a lawsuit which, said one observer, "by the variety and luxuriance of its branches, was the most complicated (dispute) that ever was brought before any human tribunal." But its complexity did not stop it becoming a topic of conversation, argument, and even duelling, from Buckingham Palace and Windsor Castle down to the tenements of Edinburgh and Glasgow.

Unlike most complicated lawsuits, the question at the heart of the Douglas Cause, as it was known, was a simple one: Did Lady Jane Douglas give birth to twin boys in Paris on or about July 10th, 1748?

The answer to this question was important for a far wider circle of interested parties than Sir John and Lady Jane and their putative offspring. As sister of the Duke of Douglas, Lady Jane was a member of Scotland's premier aristocratic family, and bearing a Douglas child would affect the fortunes of another great Scottish noble family, that of the Duke of Hamilton. And each of these families was linked to other members of the aristocracy by blood or marriage right up to the royal family, in Scotland, England and further afield. But the interest of the case went even wider than that. It was not merely a civil matter, to do with wills and inheritances and titles. For an English and Scottish public experiencing the novelty and excitement of daily newspapers, the deluge of evidence gathered by both sides in the Douglas Cause provided juicy titbits of information about the sexual habits of the aristocracy, Lady Jane's menstrual history, Sir John's gambling habits, forgery of vital documents, and accusations against the married couple of a crime for which they could be executed in France.

In a surprising way, even some of Europe's leading intellectuals became embroiled in the process as it rippled outwards in ever widening circles. David Hume, the great

Scottish philosopher, became a passionate supporter of one side. James Boswell, Dr. Johnson's biographer, an even more passionate supporter of the other. Denis Diderot, originator and editor of the great *Encyclopédie,* was summoned before a tribunal as an expert witness. Voltaire became engrossed by the case and the way it had misused French legal procedures.

And yet, still at the heart of the matter was one question. Whatever happened to Lady Jane, in Paris in 1748?

The question was at the heart of a long-running battle which took place after Lady Jane and her brother had died, and the issue of inheritance came to the fore. Two teams of lawyers drew up a series of claims and counterclaims.

One team acted for the Douglas family, represented by Archy Douglas, the surviving child of the twins Lady Jane brought back from Paris. They claimed that:

- Lady Jane was pregnant between November 1747 and July 1748.

- She gave birth to twins in July 1748 at the house of a Mme. Le Brun.

- There existed a male midwife called Pierre La Marre who assisted at the birth.

- One child, Sholto, the weaker one, was put out to nurse at a village outside Paris until November 1749.

- The other child, Archibald Douglas, stayed with his parents and was now the rightful heir to his uncle, the Duke of Douglas.

On the other side were lawyers acting for the family of the Duke of Hamilton, relatives of the Duke of Douglas, who stood to inherit his fortune if it could be proved that the Duke's sister had died childless. They claimed that:

- Lady Jane only pretended to be pregnant.

- Even if she had been pregnant, she did not give birth to live babies in Paris.

- She and Colonel Stewart abducted the baby son of Nicholas Mignon, a Parisian glass-blower, and his wife in July 1748, and pretended that he was Sholto Douglas.

- She and Colonel Stewart abducted the baby son of Pierre Sanry, a rope-dancer, and his wife, in November, 1749, and pretended that he was Archy Douglas.

The only three people to know for sure what happened, Lady Jane, Sir John, and Mrs. Hewit, told a story that they and their supporters felt should leave no one in any doubt about the parentage of the children they brought back from France. But the Hamilton lawyers didn't believe their story and thought that if they looked long and hard enough at the Douglas account of what happened in Paris in July 1748, they could find evidence to contradict it.

The city was riddled with spies and secret police at the time of the alleged birth, some of whom had the sole job of keeping tabs on the foreigners in the city. Police records show, for example, that there were 61 British subjects in Paris that month, 45 men and 16 women. It seems a very low figure but we have to remember that the recent war had prevented British travellers from visiting France. While there is a reassuring degree of specificity about the numbers given in official documents, obtained by inspectors who regularly visited all the Paris hotels and lodging houses and made notes from the registers, we can be less sure about who these visitors actually were. The inspectors' effort to reproduce unfamiliar English and Scottish names has a rather hit and miss quality about it. We find, for example: Mrs. Lauthalle, Lady Heum, Mr. MacSwiney, Miss Volffington, Mr. Stafert, Mr. Daelly, Lady Longhole, Mr. Macaument, Mr. Aveyry,

Mr. Dune, Mrs. Horsame, Mr. Blaire, Mr. Farel, Mr. Smiche, Mr. Bossoles, Mr. Houstoon, Mr. Brisbanne, Mr. Macohood, Mrs. Keept, Mr. Falleus, Mr. Monson, Mr. Arbret, Father Delle, Mr. Agralt and Mr. Kousing. Faced with a gallery of characters like these it is not surprising that in the months and years to follow there were to be constant arguments over whether hastily scrawled names in dog-eared notebooks were really referring to the people claimed.

All that we know for certain is that Lady Jane and Colonel Stewart were definitely among the foreigners in Paris in July, 1748, and that Lady Jane showed all the signs of pregnancy before July 1748 but those signs had disappeared by July 20th, when Sir John, Lady Jane and Mrs. Hewit left the Hotel de Châlons. On this date they were all staying in another lodging house, the Hotel d'Anjou in the Rue Serpente. What's more, Lady Jane was accompanied by at least one baby at the time, named Archibald after his uncle, the Duke of Douglas.

The first people outside Paris to be told of the birth were two other servants of the couple who had stayed in Rheims. Mrs. Hewit, with a shaky grasp of spelling and grammar, wrote to them on July 22nd, twelve days after the alleged birth. She explained that on the night of the 9th July, Lady Jane had been ill all night but hadn't said anything until two p.m on the 10th. "Then I think she was in soch a way as I could wisht not to a been witness to," wrote Mrs. Hewit, "tho, I do belive, many is (has) been worc (worse) with on (one), and she produced 2 lovly boys. ... they are two lovly creters, but the yongst very small and weakly, so the doctor beght (begged) he might be sent to the country as soun as possible."

Lady Jane herself gave her first written account of the birth on August 7th, when she wrote to her brother, the Duke of Douglas: "Please know, my Lord, that on the 10th of last month I was blessed with two boys, one a promising child; the other, poor thing, so weak, that I fear is little to be reckoned on; God's will be done: the other my hopes centre in, and want but the pleasure of your approving his having your name, with that of Sholto to the younger, to be happy."²

The Douglas Cause was set in motion by people who believed – or professed to believe – that Lady Jane and Mrs. Hewit were lying in those letters and in other accounts of the birth that followed. With limitless funds at their disposal, both sides in the dispute were able to hire the best lawyers in Britain and France to get at the truth, or – some said – to bribe and threaten their way to constructing a version of events that suited their patrons.

In its ramifications, the story of the Douglas Cause is a microcosm of the 18ᵗʰ century. The participants in the drama span all social classes from royalty down; it deals with the great issues of money, sex, class, power, crime and family. But while today we are familiar with such issues in our own society, in the 18ᵗʰ century attitudes to such topics were influenced by different factors. Society put higher value on such concepts as honesty and worth, and paid far more attention to the character of an individual, with the nobility expected to adhere to standards which 'ordinary' folk were not.

In particular, it is the character of Lady Jane Douglas, the beautiful sister of Archibald, Duke of Douglas, which is at the heart of the puzzle. There were some who argued from her noble character alone – as they saw it – that she could not possibly have been guilty of the crime that was alleged against her. There were others who saw her as a woman who would stop at nothing to achieve her ends, even to the extent of swearing a false oath on her deathbed.

But what seemed to be absent at the time was a more modern type of understanding that we can bring to the matter today, living as we do in a society in which a major in the British army can cheat in a television quiz game, kindly GPs can murder hundreds of patients, princesses of the realm can have nine lovers, and lovable eccentric TV presenters can turn outr to be serial child molesters. Today, we would hesitate to rule on whether someone had committed a crime solely on the basis of her sweet nature, or love of children and animals.

It may be surprising today to learn that such a 'parochial' dispute – one Scottish family arguing with another over an inheritance – should have attracted huge public interest in Scotland, England, and even on the Continent, over the course of twenty years. But the issues it raised then were far wider than they might seem now. Jacobitism, the support for the exiled King James and his family as rulers of Scotland, was a lively issue a few years after the second attempt to replace English rule with Stuart kings, known as 'the 45', Whether you believed Lady Jane was a Jacobite (her husband certainly was) affected your attitude to the legitimacy of Archy as heir, even though it had nothing to do with the matter.

The allegations against Lady Jane might well also have awakened memories of an earlier incident, known as the Warming Pan Scandal of 1688, in which it was claimed that the alleged son of the Stuart king, James II, was not his son at all, but smuggled into the queen's bed in a warming pan. Was the Douglas Cause another example of Jacobitism and a supposititious child – as such children are called – in league to steal an inheritance?

But regardless of these factors, the Cause would not have had as much public impact if it hadn't been for the rapid expansion of newspapers and the growth of a print culture in Britain. In addition to reading daily accounts in the Scottish and English press, interested readers could follow aspects of the case through books written by participants and supporters. From James Boswell's lightly massaged panegyrics of the saintly Lady Jane and her son to Andrew Stuart's devastating onslaught on Lord Mansfield, the progress of the Cause was marked by a succession of books which were often snapped up as soon as they were published.

One final factor that may have heightened public interest was the involvement of aristocratic women at the heart of the story. There were the Duchesses of Hamilton and Douglas facing each other on opposite sides of the issue, each able to throw money and lawyers at the various legal proceeding, each desperate to win the suit, when only one could do so. And of course, there was the late Lady Jane Douglas herself, whose life was exposed and discussed in so much detail during court hearings that she became far more famous after death than she ever was in life.

1

Brother and Sister

The first and only Duke of Douglas was the richest man in Scotland. He had no children and his nearest blood relative was his sister, Lady Jane. By law, in the absence of a son his Dukedom died out. But his property remained and at various times during his life he had vacillated about whom to leave it to. By the last change of mind he left his estates and money to whoever was his nearest male heir at his death. If the young Archy Douglas was 'born of Lady Jane's body' he would inherit; if not, the Duke's estate would go to the Duke of Hamilton.

The Douglas family played a long and distinguished part in the history of England as well as Scotland. In the 16th century, an Archibald Douglas and Earl of Angus married the elder daughter of Henry VII of England, sister of Henry VIII.

The family was also interconnected with other Scottish noble families, including the Hamiltons, who, during the Douglas Cause, became their bitter enemies. This connection came about because William, the first marquis of Douglas, was married twice. By his first wife he produced the line leading to the Duke of Douglas and Lady Jane, and his descendants by his second wife included the Dukes of Hamilton. It is this second marriage and its consequences that led to the two families competing for the inheritance.

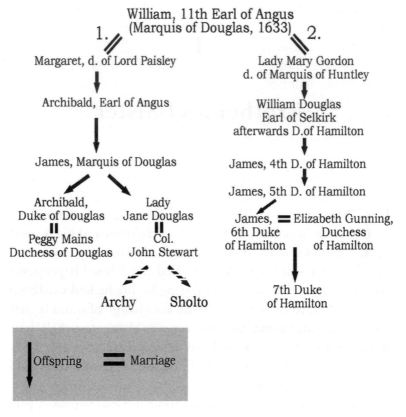

Family tree

Lady Jane and her brother were the children of James, second Marquis of Douglas, who came of age and inherited the title from his father in 1668. He "fell into a Course of low Debauchery", according to one family history, and the friends he made about this time did their best to get their hands on as much of his money as possible. In 1694, his wife, Lady Mary Kerr, gave birth to Archibald, the child who was to become the Duke of Douglas. To protect the interests of his infant son, the second marquis was 'persuaded' by a trio of noble kinsmen, designated as commissioners, to settle his estate on Archibald so that it could not be so easily frittered away. The son, like his father, had a streak of waywardness in him, which was to sour the life of his sister, Lady Jane, born in 1698.[3]

The Douglas wealth was not safe, even in the hands of several noble commissioners. One of them, the Earl of Forfar, "was in the habit of sotting with the Marquis at an alehouse in the town of Douglas, kept by one Simpson, an accomplice in the several frauds practiced upon him." One of these frauds involved a woman called Janet Jack who extracted 50,000 marks from the marquis in return for sexual favours.[4]

In 1700 the debauched marquis died and his son, then aged six, succeeded to the title. Three years later the boy was created first Duke of Douglas, and since it never rains but it pours he was also made Earl of Angus and Abernethy, Viscount of Jedburgh Forest, and Lord of Boncle, Preston and Roberton.

The two children, Duke Archibald and Lady Jane, grew up at a time of rapid political change in Scotland. Although the two countries were ruled by the same king they still had independent parliaments. But in 1707, Scotland was steamrollered by the English monarch, Queen Anne, into full union with England as one nation under the German Hanovers who had been rushed into place to prevent the descendants of James VII of Scotland (and II of England) inheriting the crown. But the Union was not popular in Scotland and there was discontent in all classes at the perceived unequal nature of the "partnership". Members of the Stuart family who were descended from the executed Charles I still had a lot of support. Known as Jacobites, their supporters' restless snapping at the heels of existing British governments occasionally turned to outright rebellion. In 1715 and 1745 (the "15" and the "45"), Stuart pretenders, exiled on the continent, returned to Scotland to raise an anti-English force and take back the crown of Scotland and England. But James Edward, "The Old Pretender", and later his son Charles Edward, "Bonnie Prince Charlie", were rebuffed and returned crownless to exile. At the time of the '45, Horace Walpole wrote to a friend:

"I think of what King William said to the Duke of Hamilton, when he was extolling Scotland: 'My Lord, I only wish it was a hundred thousand miles off, and that you was king of it!'"[5]

As the Duke of Douglas grew up, in the early years of the 18th century, he seems to have acquired no sophisticated habits or intellectual interests. He is described variously as "a person of weak intellect", "liable to sudden outbursts of passion", "proud, ignorant, and silly, spiteful, and unforgiving," and there is even some doubt as to whether he could read or write. He had a tutor who was described as "a young clergyman of uncertain principles ... by no means qualified to raise his mind to those accomplishments proper to his high station – his (the Duke's) talents were therefore permitted to run riot, and that vivacity that proved his ruin, if properly conducted would have added lustre even to the illustrious name he bore; his passions naturally impetuous, never met a check, but were indulged through childhood to manhood."[6]

The Duke's sister, Lady Jane, on the other hand, was beautiful, genteel and well-educated. "Nature was as generous to her as she had been niggardly with her brother," one writer said.[7] While the Duke was running riot, his sister was living demurely with her mother, the Marchioness of Douglas, in Edinburgh at Merchiston House, where a hundred years previously John Napier had invented logarithms.

Like her brother, Lady Jane was taught by tutors, who were closely supervised by her mother, a woman who appears to have experienced "an unhappy turn of mind". There are hints of religiosity in accounts of Lady Jane's mother, and the daughter's purity was guarded by a succession of clergymen and their families, who were friends of her mother's and formed the only circles in which she moved. When she left the house it was only to go to and from church where, we are asked to believe, "her infant beauty which dawned like the first rays of the morning drew on her the eyes of an admiring crowd and she was followed with praises and blessings wherever she appeared."[8]

A certain Mr. Brown, hired by the marchioness to supervise her daughter's education, approved a number of tutors in the face of opposition from Lady Jane's mother, who objected to the fact that they were foreigners and Roman Catholics. But by promising always to be in attendance during these risky sessions, Mr. Brown helped Lady Jane to acquire such a good education that by the age of fifteen "she was believed to be the most accomplished young lady in this or any other kingdom."[9]

These fulsome accounts of Lady Jane's childhood come from a handwritten biography[10], probably written at the time her character was being blackened by the Hamiltons. No author is identified, but, as with many people who came in contact with her story, the writer is clearly smitten with his subject:

"She was rather under what is called the middle size; but the elegance, dignity and symmetry of her figure made her appear not too little, her hair was flaxen and in such abundance, that it was often troublesome to compel it to submit to the barbarity of the then fashion, when she was dressed for Public, but in her common attire it hung round her neck in loose ringlets; her eyes were the most beautiful blue, soft, sweet yet animated and they discovered a soul replete with tenderness and sensibility; the tincture of the lily was not more transparently delicate than the whiteness of her skin, nor did the rose fresh with the morning dew appear more blooming than her complexion, whilst the smiles round her lovely mouth would have subdued the fury of a tigress, her manners were easy, unaffected and gentle, yet never for a moment forgetting the dignity proper for the heiress of the noble house she sprang from."[11]

Such perfection was clearly attractive to portrait painters and, it has to be said, the existing portraits do show a woman of unusual beauty.

Lady Jane Douglas, artist unknown, possibly James Ferguson

We have an account of a sitting by Lady Jane for one painter, James Ferguson, who was a distinguished Scottish astronomer and maker of clocks and orreries, but who also had considerable skills as a portrait artist.

"I drew several pictures of lady Jane," Ferguson wrote, "of whom it was hard to say, whether the greatness of her beauty, or the goodness of her temper and disposition, was the most predominant. She sent these pictures to ladies of her acquaintance, in order to recommend me to them; by which means I soon had as much business as I could possibly manage, so as not only to put a good deal of money in my own pocket, but also to spare what was sufficient to help to supply my father and mother in their old age."[12]

It is hardly surprising that, in spite of her mother's attempt to restrict her movements, she came to the attention of various suitors as she got older. This led to two defining incidents in the lives of the brother and sister, incidents that were referred to by both sides in the later lawsuits, as showing the inherent emotional instability of the two siblings.

One of the themes of the story of the Douglas Cause, seen from a modern perspective, is the unreliability of almost every piece of evidence or testimony offered on one side or the other. A writer trying to retell the story two hundred and fifty years later is faced with confident reports which are so contradictory that, in spite of their verisimilitude, they cannot all be true, which raises the issue, of course, of whether any of them is.

A good example of this is the story of the jilting of Lady Jane by the Earl of Dalkeith. Or, as it may be, the jilting of the Earl of Dalkeith by Lady Jane.

As a starting point I think it is safe to say the following:

Some time in 1720 or 1721, Lady Jane Douglas and Francis, Earl of Dalkeith, contemplated marriage. They did not marry, and Lord Dalkeith went and married someone else. (Understanding this story is not helped by the fact that his new wife was also named Lady Jane Douglas.) After being jilted, our Lady Jane went to France dressed in men's clothes and accompanied by a maid.

Accounts of this event are found in the handwritten biography, lawyers' statements prepared for the courts, memoirs of relatives, memoirs of later figures, and books and articles about the Douglas Cause written later still.

The "General State of the Facts" put before the judges in the Scottish courts says that Lady Jane was the jilter:

"Lady Jane had, in her younger days, been asked in marriage by several persons of high rank; all of whom she refused. Among others, she had been asked by a nobleman of first quality, and possessed of the greatest fortune in Scotland. So advantageous a match was highly agreeable to all her relations: but when it was upon the point of being concluded, Lady Jane made an elopement into France, disguised in mens cloaths. This happened in the year 1721."[13]

It may have been this that led the later writer, Percy Fitzgerald, to write:

"... Lord Dalkeith, whom she jilted on a romantic punctilio concerning one of her former amours..."[14]

The possibility that it was Lady Jane who broke off the marriage is strengthened by "a story ... which was current at the time, that she had owned to the Duke of Buccleuch (as Dalkeith later became) her repugnance, and, throwing herself on his honour, desired to be screened from the anger of her relations."[15]

Here, however, is the handwritten biographer's account of Dalkeith's dealings with Lady Jane, after the two of them became engaged, which has the Earl breaking off the engagement:

"Happening to pay a visit to the Earl of Morton's he found another Lady Jane Douglas, that Earl's sister, who innocently let him into the secret of his own heart at the same time as a tender sigh pronounced how sorry she was he was already engaged. Distracted at his situation he knew not what step to take, but at last resolved on the most extraordinary one that ever entered any man's head. He resolved to make his intended bride his confidant – if she was generous enough to set him at liberty he was happy and would adore her, if not he was resolved to proceed however miserable it was to make him; in this resolution he paid Lady Jane [the Duke's sister] a visit, when throwing himself at her feet, he exclaimed in an agony that he was a wretch that ought to be banished human society for having injured such an angel past reparation. Surprized and confounded at such a prologue to their conversation, she begged he would be composed, be seated, and calmly explain his distress."

As we might expect from the worshipful biographer, Lady Jane the first could not have been nicer about the whole thing and released Dalkeith from his vows. However, the biographer then writes, *"no sooner did she reach her own apartment… than she gave a loose to the anguish of her heart"*[16]

Another account says:

"Circumstances over which Lady Jane had no control, and of which, indeed, as will be shown, she was the victim, had prevented the marriage from taking place."[17]

There is even some doubt in this version of the story, over exactly where the jilting took place. Did the Earl of Dalkeith do the deed in person, at Lady Jane's feet? Or is the correct version that told by the authoritative Sir William Fraser, official biographer of the Douglas family:

"Everything was settled by their mutual friends, and the match ready to be concluded, when Lady Jane, who then happened to be in London, was surprised one day, on her way to Court, by her chair being stopped by a person unknown, who delivered her a letter, written in the name of her lover, signifying that he was under engagements to another lady, of whom he had long been fond, and without whom he could not be happy."[18]

So, faced with these accounts, the most we can be sure of that Lady Jane Douglas and the Earl of Dalkeith nearly got married.

What happened next to Lady Jane is also the subject of disagreement. That she went to France is not in doubt. The male disguise seems to be an indisputable part of the story, too. The writer Horace Bleackley, as a result of his researches many years later, wrote:

"About this time she took part in a strange escapade with a French maid, setting out to Paris in boy's clothes, which adventure her apologists have contended was the result of pique on account of her breach with the Earl of Dalkeith. Henceforth the stigma that must adhere to every Rosalind in real life was responsible no doubt, for her spinsterhood, so unusual in the case of the elegant and accomplished daughter of an illustrious house."[19]

(Presumably, "the stigma that must adhere to every Rosalind" is a reference to lesbianism, although there is nothing else to suggest that this was the reason for her spinsterhood.)

Bleackley must have got the French maid from Sir William Fraser, who wrote:

"In order to prevent discovery she set out privately, and in disguise, attended only by her maid, who was a Frenchwoman, and went to France with a determined purpose of shutting herself up in a convent."[20]

But according to the handwritten biography, she fled with her *Scots* maid, the faithful Mrs. Hewit, who spoke no French:

"…in a few hours she had made up her mind to bear the disappointment but resolved to fly the world, at least for a time, and she engaged Miss Hewit to fly with her to France, where they would shut themselves up in a monastery till the noise of the affair had subsided: Hewit, as young and romantic as Lady Jane, easily agreed to follow her."

I've gone into some detail about these differing accounts, some from near contemporaries, only because they illustrate a pervasive theme in the Douglas Cause, as in many hotly disputed issues – the irreconcilable differences between key points of evidence. This was not peculiar to the 18th century, of course, but perhaps what was different at the time was the greater weight given to the status of a witness in a society where honour and authority were closely linked.

Whatever the reason for the lateness in life of Lady Jane's eventual marriage, she was not short of opportunities during her earlier adult years. When she was in her mid-twenties, she became friends with a cousin of hers, Lord Mark Ker, who sought her hand in marriage. In 1724, he was visiting Lady Jane and staying for a few days at Douglas Castle. This was one of the traditional homes of the Douglas family, who had had a castle on the same site, about 25 miles south-east of Glasgow, since the 14th century. The night before Ker was due to leave, he went to say goodbye to Lady Jane. According to Charles Kirkpatrick Sharpe, who treasured scandalous stories as fodder for his memoirs:

"(The Duke) watched the young man the night before his departure from Douglas Castle so narrowly that he saw him enter Lady Jane's dressing-room in order to bid her farewell, and, fired with the most diabolical rage, repaired to his own apartment and, seizing a pistol, waited till Captain Kerr should return to his chamber and go to bed. The unhappy young man had scarcely done so, when this fiend entered the room, and pulling down the bed-cloaths, shot him in the side with a deep and mortal wound."[21] The killing of Lord Mark Ker was quickly hushed up and the Duke went to Holland to lie low.

Sharpe's suggestion for a motive was that "the Duke ... was as jealous of his sister as if she had been his wife." Sharpe may well be right. The Duke of Douglas was a man who didn't marry until late in life, after his sister had died. During her lifetime he showed alternate bouts of love and hatred for her, something which is at least consistent with an unexpressed attraction to his sister.

When Lady Jane's mother, the Marchioness, was on the point of death in 1736, she said to her daughter:

"Like Moses, you will not see the promised land but will fall in the desert of misery, but your children will support the house of Douglas through many generations."[22] She was right about the misery, but not so accurate about the 'many generations.'

After the death of her mother, Lady Jane set herself up at Drumsheugh House in another part of Edinburgh. She was on reasonable terms with her brother at the time, so much so that he settled on her an income of £300 p.a.

But all that changed when, once more, the Duke's temper got the better of him, and another violent incident occurred which led to a permanent breach with his sister. Writing to a friend in May 1738, the Duke described how he had recently fired a servant, called Will Bayllie of Littlegill:

"You must know that some time ago I dismist Littlegill from my service, for most villanous practices, in the trust he had from me. And because I gave him a very moderate correction, with my whip, which he provok'd me to do, by some insolent answers, it seems this is represented as a most heinous crime..."[23]

However 'moderate' the Duke thought his correction of Will Bayllie, the word got around that, once again, the Duke of Douglas had behaved in an abominable way and there was a good deal of bad feeling about the matter. Some time afterwards, the Duke went to Edinburgh in search of his sister, but failed to find her at home. He then found his own Edinburgh house surrounded by "a great rabble or mob of ruffianish-like people", presumably angered by news of the whipping he had given his servant, and he threatened to shoot them if they didn't disperse.

None of this need necessarily have soured his relationship with his sister. There was no evidence that she was deliberately hiding from him, for example, although that's what he must have thought. But he then received a letter from Lady Jane which 'much enraged' him:

"Dear Brother," Lady Jane wrote, "Being with my Lady Ross at Newbattlechurch I miss'd you when you called here yesterday, and this day I think it is more my duty to write to you, than to come to town to you, being but too well informed that the story of Littlegill had gained the utmost credite above with the great people, in spite of all the pains that was taken to suppress it. And it has had such influence as to bring the old misfortune" (the killing of Lord Mark Ker) "afresh into their rememberance, upon which account they are mightily displeased at present that you are so much seen in Edinburgh, considering it a disregard to the King and a defiance to the Laws. You may be sure this is a powerful subject for me to write upon, but it is what I must doo since this information is not a triffling story but a reality. I therefore intreat you, dear brother, with all dispatch imaginable to hasten out of town, which will make it not appear that you have been in it at all. And it is the reason why I choose, not to come myself to acquaint you with this, since it would have made your being in town too much known, which as things at present stand, is of all things to be shunned. My spirits are depress'd I can write no more. Dear Brother adieu, Jane Douglas."[24]

For the rest of Lady Jane's life, her brother believed that this apparently sisterly advice was motivated by a desire to get her hands on the Douglas fortunes by eventually having him declared insane. According to William Greenshield, the butler at Douglas Castle, the duke had been told that "the mob which had gathered about the lodging ... were hired by Lady Jane, in order to murder the Duke, or carry him to St. Kilda, or some neuter island."[25]

It had been only a few years before, in 1734, that another Scottish aristocrat, Lady Grange, had been forcibly put away as a lunatic on the island of St Kilda, the furthest west island of the Outer Hebrides, by her husband, Lord Grange, a Scottish judge.

In fact, there is no evidence at all that Lady Jane plotted to have her brother certified and put away, on St Kilda's or anywhere else. But the suggestion that she did was just one of many stories against Lady Jane that the Duke heard and believed. And it meant that, for the rest of her life, Lady Jane Douglas was alienated from the head of the noble family whose heir would be her son, if she were to have one.

2

A Foul Conspiracy

The story of the Douglas Cause is a complicated one, and for a modern reader unfamiliar with degrees of nobility and forms of address it can be difficult to keep track of the participants, particularly when their titles change with bewildering frequency. Miss Elizabeth Gunning became the Duchess of Hamilton (in fact Hamilton and Brandon) and then changed into the Duchess of Argyll. The titles of Charles Douglas, third Duke of Queensberry, included Baron Ripon, Marquis of Burnley, Duke of Dover, Earl of Solway, Viscount of Tibberis, and Lord Douglas of Lockerbie, Dalveen and Thornhill.[26]

In trying to tell one Lord from another, there's an extra complication in Scotland, where there was a separate category of person who could call himself 'Lord'. Senior Scottish judges all took the title 'Lord' for the duration of their term. So Lord Grange was, and then became again, James Erskine; James Burnet became Lord Monboddo, and so on, usually taking a name from the place they lived or came from. (One lawyer elevated to the bench came from the village of Woodhead. Deciding that 'Lord Woodhead' would not be a dignified name for a judge, he changed the name of the village to Fountainhall and became Lord Fountainhall.[27])

The competing claimants, the Hamiltons, like the Douglases, were an old-established Scottish family who could trace their line back to the 13th century and fought side by side with the Douglases on various occasions against the Scottish crown, held by the Stuarts. They became more closely linked through the two marriages of William, Marquis of Douglas in the first part of the 17th century.

The Hamiltons had their share of instability in their genes. James, the fourth Duke of Hamilton, was deemed to be one of the handsomest men in Scotland. He had two sons, the elder of whom, James, became the fifth duke, while the younger was named after the monarch, one of his godparents. The fact that the monarch was Queen Anne meant that he went through his life as Lord Anne Hamilton. But such a girly name didn't stop him marrying and having a long line of descendants.

Duke James had a strong temper. In his fifties he became embroiled in a bitter legal dispute with Charles, fifth Baron Mohun. It was a quarrel over an inheritance, a foreshadowing of the Douglas Cause, and the legal proceedings went on for years. During a hearing at Lincoln's Inn in 1712, the duke objected intemperately to one of the other side's witnesses and was challenged by Lord Mohun to a duel with swords, in which – rather incompetently, it seemed – both men were killed. But it turned out that Lord Mohun's second had probably nipped in with a fatal blow to the duke after he was wounded by Mohun. (Lord Mohun's body was taken to his house in Marlborough Street, when the only remark made by his widow was an expression of great displeasure that the men had laid the body on her rather opulent day bed, and stained it with blood.)[28]

The sixth Duke of Hamilton was a gambler, a drunkard and a womaniser. A friend describes drink as having affected the duke's stomach so badly that he vomited blood. "But the instant he recovers a little", says the friend, "he drinks till four, five, or six in the morning." One Mrs. Bell, "a lady of humble rank," summed up his good and bad sides: "He was very debauched in bad women's company," said she, "but among ladies he was one of the politest and best-behaved men in Great Britain."[29] We might not be surprised, therefore, to learn that "the old Duke of Douglas, a man of few affections, loved him as a son."[30]

When Lady Jane Douglas, after a troubled adolescence and a lonely maturity, decided to marry, her choice of husband would have been scrutinised by both linked families, in spite of their own fair share of blackguards on the family tree. But your own blackguards are easier to tolerate than someone else's and if new blood was to be brought into the family, it should at least start off untainted by villainy.

For the Duke of Douglas in particular, there was one form of villainy he would not tolerate. He couldn't stand Jacobites, and it was to turn out that, late in life, Lady Jane chose a Jacobite for her husband.

The Jacobite uprising affected the Duke of Douglas in two ways. For one thing, he resented it because of his loyalty to the English crown. For another, he suffered at the hands of the rebels when they took over his home, Douglas Castle, during their rampage through Scotland. Years later, Archibald Hamilton, the son of one of the Duke's retainers, who had been nine years old at the time, gave an eye-witness account of events:

"The Pretender," he said, "at that time was in very poor health, and had a very odd appearance; he was tall and thin with a blotched face, and inflamed eyes, and his legs very much swelled."[31]

The less than Bonny Prince Charles had turned up at Douglas, with one of his supporters, a man known as the Duke of Perth*:

---

* The Dukedom of Perth was granted by by James II after his deposition, and so was not recognised in England.

"The Duke of Perth several times intruded himself into the Duke of Douglas's presence against his will," Hamilton said, "and endeavoured to persuade him to see the Pretender, or at any rate to say that he was welcome to his House; the Duke constantly refused, and was very much annoyed by Lord Perth's importunity, and at last became so angry, that he (violently) ran at him, and licked him on the shins, with heavy hob-nailed shoes till spots of blood appeared on his white silk stockings."[32]

The Duke of Douglas was never a great one with words, as shown by Hamilton's account of the final insult hurled by the duke at the Pretender.

"When it was announced to the Duke that his unwelcome guests were about to depart, he went with Mr. Hamilton to a window, from where he could see the Gate, and cried out as they were going, loud enough to be heard by everybody 'My Lord Perth I see your friend your Pretender, I say he plays a very poor fiddle.' No notice was taken."[33]

Among the Douglas papers is another small reminder of the havoc caused when the Pretender and his supporters travelled across Scotland. It is a petition written to the Lanarkshire authorities some years later by the duke's butler, William Greenshield, complaining that the rebels 'in ane hostile manner carried away from him 35 shirts 23 pair of stockings 2 new wiggs a pair of boots with some Body Cloths and breeches to the valew of £29 sterling and upwards'[34]

It was unfortunate that, at the time these events were occurring to the great displeasure of the Duke of Douglas, his sister, now about forty seven years old, was was finally beginning to think seriously about marriage, with a man ten years older than her, one Colonel John Stewart, an ardent Jacobite and described by the duke as "a wore out old rake". Even the later printed statement of the legal case for Douglas could not summon up much enthusiasm for the man who became Lady Jane's husband:

"Col. *Stewart* was a younger Brother of the House of *Grantully*; a Man of Family, but no Fortune; of a fine Figure, lively Conversation, and allowed Honour; but, withal, quite thoughtless, and extremely profuse. It was an unlikely Connection for so accomplished a Person as Lady *Jane* to form; A Step, perhaps, fitter to be forgiven than applauded."[35]

How had this unlikely pairing come about?

Whom you married in the 18th century had implications that went far beyond living with someone you like, raising children and generally having a good time together. It was a topic of deep fascination to your relatives, *their* relatives and often to society at large, particularly when large amounts of land or money and the onward transmission of a family name were involved.

In the case of the Douglases, the head of the family, the Duke, had said from an early age that he would not marry, and this placed some pressure on Lady Jane. In spite of the appeals of her early suitors, she claimed to have no particular desire herself, as she described later to a friend in a letter:

"It is mighty certain, that my inclinations were never in the marrying way, and had not I at last been absolutely sure that my brother was resolved never to marry, I never should have one thought of doing it; but since this was his determined unalterable resolution, I judged it fit to overcome a natural disinclination and backwardness, and to put myself in the way of doing something for a family not the worst in Scotland." [36]

Before he took against Lady Jane, her brother was always urging her to marry. The ubiquitous William Greenshield overheard the Duke and his sister discussing the topic:

'I was present at a conversation between the Duke and Lady Jane his sister, in the Duke's lodging at the back of the wall, Edinburgh, when she advised and pressed the Duke to marry, and he advised and pressed her Ladyship to marry, and told her at the same time, it was a matter indifferent which of them married; for if she had children they would heir the estate, and suppose he should marry and have children also, there would be enough for them both, and pressed Lady Jane much to marry, saying, if she married either a nobleman, or gentleman of character, he would give her £300 sterling per annum, to the £300 she then had, and the estate of Dundee; and also, would refer himself to any four noblemen in Scotland, what more he should give her. That at that time they parted in great friendship, as they had always lived, so long as he had the honour to serve his Grace, preceeding that period.'[37]

The writer of the handwritten biography says:

"He pressed her to marry in the strongest terms, prayed her to chuse a gentleman tho' destitute of fortune and he would embrace him as his brother with joy. Willing to oblige him in everything else, she positively refused this. She had conceived an utter aversion to the state. Peevish at her steady resolution, he complained of it to some of his friends and from that fatal moment the arts commenced which in future ruined her."[38]

The financial relationship between the Duke and his sister was a constant factor in their family relationship. It was used at various times as a weapon by the Duke, but initially, when on good terms with his sister, the Duke was keen to be generous and give her a decent income.

How decent that income was is not an easy matter to explain. There is a whole series of calculations to go through before we can translate a sum of 18th century Scots money into an equivalent in today's pounds. In 1736, the Duke gave Lady Jane a bond for 50,000 merks (or marks.) The merk was a Scottish coin worth two thirds of a Scottish pound. The Duke's gift was therefore worth 33,000 Scottish pounds. Then at the Union of the Crowns in 1707, the Scottish pounds were replaced by English pounds at an exchange rate of £12 Scottish to £1 English. So the Duke's bond was worth £2750 English pounds. This bond was used to generate interest for Lady Jane to live on, an amount given in the *Douglas Book* as £138. 17s. 9d p.a. Here is a further complication. This amount is equivalent in today's decimal currency to about £138.88. But that, of course, is not its equivalent in today's *value*. Very broadly, something costing a pound in the mid-18th century will cost just over a hundred pounds today. So Lady Jane was getting the equivalent of about £14,000 from her brother's bond. But because he realised that wasn't enough to live on, he bound himself to make it up to a round £300 a year, the modern equivalent of almost £30,000. Furthermore, if she married the right man he would double that amount, to the equivalent of £60,000. What actually transpired as the relationship soured was a series of deeds and decrees which reduced, withdrew or reassigned the various components of Lady Jane's funds to the point where she was living in penury.

It is time to introduce a new character in the story, a man who would consider himself the true artist of Lady Jane's ruin. Whether it was Lady Jane's refusal to marry that was 'that fatal moment' or her warning letter to her brother after he whipped his servant, the Duke was increasingly persuaded by the poisonous whisperings of a servant of his named James White of Stockbriggs* to suspect his sister of ill-will towards him. Servant he may have been officially but in fact, from the time of his appointment this man held the duke in a psychological grip which tightened over the fifteen years or so that he was in the duke's service.

White, or Stockbriggs, as he was usually referred to, but sometimes 'Stocky' by people who knew him well, was a mason and was initially employed in 1736 as overseer of some building works being carried out at Douglas Castle. He was given the job by Mr. Archibald Stuart, the Duke's agent, and within a year Stockbriggs had become an estates manager, or factor, for some of the Duke's properties. He eventually had such an iron

---

* Sometimes written 'Stockbridge'

grip on all the Duke's affairs that, as one writer put it "(the Duke's) character, during White's ministry, was as little known ten miles from his own house, as it could well be at the Land's End of England."[39] Another observer wrote that "the Duke of Douglas saw with Stockbrigg's eyes, and heard with his ears."[40]

Archibald Stuart, the Duke's agent, clearly had some part to play in this, as Stockbriggs' original hirer: "Extremely sensible of his Usefulness and that his Interest lay in exerting it to the utmost, he made a strict Connection with Mr. White, and found Means to engage him altogether in his Purposes. What those Means were is difficult to trace, after so great a Length of Time, and in the darkness of a foul Conspiracy."[41]

The Duke's agent was also one of a number of people called Stuart or Stewart or Steuart who play a part in this story. In the documents and publications of the time, the name seemed to be spelled indiscriminately in any of these ways, although I will try to be more consistent. It was believed from quite early on that Archibald Stuart, whose son became tutor to the Duke of Hamilton, was acting in the Hamilton interest rather than for the Duke of Douglas.

Many people later saw the story of the Duke's quarrels with his sister, their eventual break, and his continuing hostility as the result of a sustained campaign to obtain the Douglas inheritance for the Hamilton family.

But Stockbriggs was also someone who saw the opportunity to line his own pockets at the Duke's expense, by gaining control of the Duke's affairs. From the moment he became one of the Duke's estate managers he obtained such good terms for himself that he was allowed to manage a rental income of over £1500 a year from some of the Duke's lands without giving the usual securities. He was soon given broader responsibilities, looking after rents of £3,000, and such was his sway over the Duke that there is little doubt that he, and perhaps Archibald Stuart, were the only people who really knew what happened to that money.

"He lived constantly at Douglas," said the writer of the Case for the Douglas side, "and obtained so visible an Ascendancy over the Duke, that it came to be universally observed, the Management of his Grace and all his Affairs was in his Hands: Whoever had Occasion to approach Douglas, must do it by his Means, or not at all; and he judged that his own Influence depended on keeping the Coast as clear as might be, wherefore he discouraged those who were willing to come."[42]

The papers prepared by the Douglas lawyers, printed many years after Stockbriggs' death, are littered with picturesque insults:

"This *White* was a crafty bad Man, who affected Religion to cover his Falsehood, and dissembled Friendship to masque his Malice"[43] ... "a miscreant whom he (the Duke of Douglas) had raised from the dung-hill ... mean tool of avarice and ambition ... malevolence of that wretch's heart, the inconceivable brutality of his soul."[44]

On the whole, this appears to be more than the traditional abuse between antagonists in a law suit. There are eye-witness accounts of Stockbriggs' bad behaviour which have the ring of truth about them. Alexander Carlyle, a young clergyman, observed how free Stockbriggs was with the Duke's money:

"It was the custom at this time for the patrons of parishes, when they had litigations about settlements, which sometimes lasted for years, to open public-houses to entertain the members of Assembly, which was a very gross and offensive abuse. The Duke of Douglas had a cause of this kind, which lasted for three Assemblies, on which occasion it was that his commissioner, White of Stockbridge, opened a daily table for a score of people, which vied with the Lord Commissioner's for dinners, and surpassed it far in wine. White, who was a low man, was delighted with the respect which these dinners procured him. After the case was finished, Stockbridge kept up his table while he lived, for the honour of the family..."[45]

When one of the Duke's Commissioners, trusted with overall supervision of his financial affairs, queried this expenditure in a letter to the Duke, he got a dusty answer – from Stockbriggs: "Lord Haining ... wrote to the Duke, to enquire whether it was by his Grace's Authority that Mr. White was so profuse in entertaining the Clergy at the General Assemblies; which Letter Mr. White kept up, and answered Lord Haining that it was; and if his lordship and the other Commissioners did not like it, they might resign, and he would get others in their Places."[46]

After Stockbriggs died, there were many letters found in his apartment addressed to the Duke, which the Duke had never seen.[47]

According to one of the servants at Douglas Castle, Stockbriggs spread rumours of the Duke's meanness, to deter friends from coming to visit: "He gave out that the Duke would sooner fall upon his fork than give a dinner or a bottle of wine to a friend."[48] And the most extraordinary story of all that Stockbriggs was said to have told about the Duke was that "they were forced to kill a lamb every morning to satisfy his thirst for blood."[49]

Stockbriggs also tried to blacken the names of people who were well-disposed towards the Duke. One of these was William Hamilton, Minister of Douglas Town, who described later how Stockbriggs had told the Duke that he, Hamilton, "thought nothing of reading the news-papers on the Sabbath-day, and of lying in adultery with his cook's wife."[50]

If even half of these characterisations are true, it is easy to see how the Duke, in the grip of this man, could be persuaded to believe anything of his sister. And there were witnesses to Stockbriggs' efforts in this direction. He himself was fond of telling a story of what happened when Lady Jane and a friend, Lady Mary Hamilton, tried to complain about him to Lord Haining. Apparently, Lord Haining defended Stockbriggs (an unlikely event, to start with), at which the two ladies took up a poker and tongs and tried to beat the good lord. According to Stockbriggs, Lady Jane's friend turned to her and said "You should have taken better care of the Duke when you had him in your hands – and poisoned him or carried him off."[51] In a touching afterword, Stockbriggs reported the Duke's reaction on hearing of this dramatic event. "God be thanked, Stockie," the Duke is reported to have said, "that we have got safe off; you, I and Greenshield, might have been all poison'd together."[52]

One scene between Stockbriggs and the Duke is recounted in such eloquent detail that it is either entirely true, or the product of a budding novelist. It relates to an anonymous letter, allegedly written by Stockbriggs, telling the Duke that his sister was planning to get him tried for murder or put in an asylum. A subsequent conversation was said to have taken place between the Duke and Stockbriggs:

"My Lord Duke," Stockbriggs said, "I will stay with your Grace till you have a set of People you may venture to trust for I fear sadly her Ladyship may have made a party in your own house."

"Gracious Heaven," exclaimed the Duke, "what cruelty! What ingratitude! Yet she ever seemed kind, and so gentle too, she would not hurt a fly."

"That is true, please your Grace," Stockbriggs replied, "when she had no design. Yet young and tender as she was, she made no scruple of venturing on a dangerous expedition when she fled from the Duke of Buccleugh."*

"By God!" cried the Duke, starting up, "and I make no doubt all the story she then told in her vindication was a damn'd lie."

"That it was," Stockbriggs replied, "to my certain knowledge her Ladyship is very clever indeed."

* This refers to Lady Jane's former fiancé, Lord Dalkeith.

The anonymous writer of this touching scene continues: "'Oh, damn her! damn her!" cried he [the Duke] in agony, "that ever so deceitful a soul was lodged in so lovely a body, but it's past, never more will I see her, nor think of her, so my dear friend, my only friend.' 'Oh my Lord Duke,' said this artful man, 'Your Grace must not think so – there are your Grace's next heirs, the noble Hamiltons, who all love your Grace as if you was their Father, as to me I am but a poor humble creature of yours, but am ready with my life to defend your Grace.' 'That I make no doubt of' replied the Duke 'so pray take the management of everything yourself, get new servants, and make all safe but never let me see her, nor her handwriting, more; if she writes, return all her letters.' – 'Should her pension be continued?' added this agent of the Devil. 'Yes, yes.' 'May not that assist her plans by having money to bribe with?' 'No, no, let her have it,' for, 'Oh, Jeanie!' said he tenderly, 'wicked as you are I still feel for you a brother's affection.'"[53]

It's hardly surprising that, in this frame of mind, however induced, the Duke of Douglas took a jaundiced view of the man Lady Jane finally decided to marry.

On paper, Colonel John Stewart might not seem a bad catch. He was the son of a baronet, Sir Thomas Stewart, a Lord of Session with the title of Lord Balcaskie, and his mother was the daughter of the Earl of Cromartie. He had an elder brother, Sir George Stewart of Grandtully (pronounced 'Grantly'), from whom he stood to inherit a modest fortune and a title. When Colonel John first met Lady Jane, some time in the 1730s, he was a widower with a very limited income. He was also nearly ten years older than Lady Jane, and when they later decided to get married, he was about sixty and she approaching fifty, a fact from which a later biographer of Lady Jane, Horace Bleackley, draws the rather peculiar conclusion that "Love was out of the question." Bleackley goes on to say:

"Though medical experience did not put aside altogether the chances of offspring, still in the common course such a thing, under such conditions, was looked on as exceptional, and all but impossible."[54]

Colonel John Stewart, husband of Lady Jane Douglas

In addition to being attracted to the possibility, distant but likely, of a useful inheritance, Lady Jane may well have found the Colonel an attractive man. One observer wrote: "This gentleman was far advanced in life but easy in his manner, and genteel in his person, had a never failing fund of wit and good humour, spoke fluently both French and English, had been the greater part of his life abroad, knew everybody, could laugh at everybody's failings, and in his hands, the simplest story became interesting."[55] But this fan of Colonel Stewart's is compelled to continue in a less laudatory vein.

"It is with pain I reverse this agreeable picture. He was extravagant to profusion, which often reduced him to necessities, to relieve which he scrupled not to do the meanest tricks; always in want he ran himself head over heels in debt, and to avoid payment did a thousand scandalous actions. His brother, tired with assisting him, would not now see him, or relieve his necessities which were perpetually craving; to this part of his character Lady Jane was entirely a stranger, and his humour had often diverted her chagrin. She knew he had little fortune but his brother would not live forever, and for the present her own fortune with economy, would do very well."[56]

Colonel Stewart had honed his talent for losing money by participating in the Mississippi Scheme of 1720, buying shares in a company that was set up in France to colonise and exploit the Mississippi Valley and other French colonial areas. Like the South Sea Bubble at about the same time, this bubble burst, in October, 1720, and Stewart was among the speculators who lost everything. He is reported as saying at the time "that he would not again trust in paper though the Pope should keep the bank."[57]

Picking up on the Colonel's impecuniousness, someone later wrote; "Colonel Stewart's property was wholly of the negative kind, dealt with more conveniently in algebraical calculations than in the practical transactions of life."[58]

The clue to his attractiveness to Lady Jane probably lies in his wit. She seems herself to have been a woman of independence and spirit, and a shared outlook on the world that could lead to fun and laughter might have been just what she liked, to enliven the days and weeks in the smoky city of Edinburgh. It is not, of course, difficult to see what Colonel Stewart saw in Lady Jane. He would have known nothing initially of her brother's hostility and seen her as a very attractive solution to his 'negative property' situation, even if she had not been one of the most beautiful women in Edinburgh at the time.

Their early relationship did not always run smoothly. After declaring his love, the Colonel was allowed to pay court to Lady Jane for two years or so. Then, as he described many years later in a letter to his son:

"I met with a strong and unexpected shock from dear Lady Jane, which was, sending me back many trifles she had vouchsafed to receive from me, without giving any reason, and from that time [I] was forbid access, and had no return to letters I sent her begging to know in what I had offended, as I could not accuse myself in thought, word, nor deed. In short, on this unhappy turn, I left Scotland, unable to be where she was whilst banished from her presence. After ten years' absence I was obliged to return on the death of Lord Royston, father of my first wife, as my son succeeded to his fortune. Very soon after, I had the honour of an obliging message from Lady Jane, telling me that very soon after my leaving Scotland she came to know that she had done me injustice, that she would acknowledge it publicly if I chose, as the undeserved shock was known: *enfin*, I was allowed to visit her as formerly, and in about ten months after she honoured me with her hand."[59]

As a member of the Stewart clan, he was a Jacobite and old enough to have fought in the Stuart army in 1715. But his rank of Colonel was gained in the service of Charles XII of Sweden, a man sometimes described as one of the greatest soldiers of all time, who seems to have felt most comfortable when waging war. In his campaigns against Poland, Denmark, Norway and Russia, Charles drew upon the services of mercenaries such as John Stewart, who after the failure of the Stuart invasion in 1715 would have sought employment away from Britain until his misdeeds were forgotten by the English.

The Duke of Douglas knew of Colonel Stewart's interest in his sister, but saw him as entirely unworthy of her. Along with Stewart's Jacobitism was the fact that he was suspected of being a Papist. Under such clouds, if Colonel Stewart were to marry Lady Jane and even to father children who would be Douglases – an eventuality which was perfectly plausible when the Colonel first came on the scene – the Duke would feel his entire family had been disgraced.

But the Hamiltons were also part of his family, and with Archibald Stuart and White of Stockbriggs acting as the promoters of the Hamilton interest in Douglas Castle, the Duke's money, lands and honour could find another home if Lady Jane should disgrace herself by marrying badly.

What is odd, however, is that by setting Lady Jane against her brother, the Hamilton side succeeded in driving her to marriage when she might have chosen to stay single, in which case the Duke's heir would have been a Hamilton, as the handwritten biography points out:

"Here we have strong proof of that watchful Providence which suffers quietly men to prosper in their designs, till they dig a Pitt for themselves; so fared it with these people, had they suffered Lady Jane to remain happy with her Brother whom she fondly loved, her aversion to marriage was their best security, but by driving her to despair they prepared the way to bar their hopes forever; as will appear by the sequel of this little narrative."[60]

3

"Better late thrive"

I f James White of Stockbriggs was the devil in Lady Jane's
life, there's no doubt who her guardian angel was. Mrs.
Helen "Nelly" Hewit was a gentlewoman, five or six years
older than Lady Jane. She lived at Merchiston and became
inseparable from Lady Jane, acting as a mixture of companion
and servant. In those days, to call a woman 'Mrs' meant no
more than 'Mistress' and didn't necessarily mean that she
was married. In fact, there is evidence that at some point
she married a man called Lauchlin MacLean[61] but this was
probably after Lady Jane's death. It is difficult to see how she
would have fitted a husband into her life since she was so
inseparable from Lady Jane.

Mrs. Hewit was no beauty, by all accounts. Her appearance
was "large, tall and masculine."[62] As we've seen, it was probably
Nelly Hewit who shared Lady Jane's flight to France in 1721.
Perhaps her masculine appearance combined with Lady Jane's
'mens cloaths' enhanced the secrecy of their journey.

In all the events that were to unfold as a result of Lady
Jane's marriage, Mrs. Hewit was as guilty, or as innocent,
as Lady Jane. She knew everything that Lady Jane knew.

She was one of only three witnesses to what really happened to Lady Jane, and stuck to her story until the day of her death. For this reason she did not escape the criticism and abuse that the plaintiffs directed at the Douglas party, being described by some as 'a wicked woman.'

She would certainly have known of her mistress's on-off romance with Colonel John Stewart. Lady Jane finally decided to give her hand to him in 1746, and to marry in secret, because of her brother's hostility to the match.

Lady Jane Douglas aged about 40

The ceremony took place in Edinburgh, on the 4th of August, 1746, with the Rev. Robert Keith of the Episcopal Church in Scotland officiating. The bride was almost forty-eight and the groom was fifty-nine. It turns out that, at this time, Lady Jane was still menstruating, according to her doctor, who said later that he was told in 1746 that Lady Jane had had at that time an "uttering haemorrhage, which made it improper for her to take medicines till that was over, from whence it may be presumed, that women in that situation may have children, but that (he) was not informed of the above circumstance relative to Lady Jane by herself, as Ladies seldom talk on such subjects, and Lady Jane was particularly delicate in such matters."[63]

Even more direct evidence came from the lady who did Lady Jane's washing, who said that "before Lady Jane went abroad ... her cloaths had all the marks or symptoms which the cloaths of a woman in the way of having children commonly have."[64]

Before her marriage, Lady Jane had been trying to live on her annuity from the Duke but the lifestyle she kept up in fashionable Edinburgh circles had led her into debt. The Colonel was, as usual, strapped for cash, having little to live on while his brother was still alive, apart from occasional handouts from his son by a first marriage.

This impoverished state, combined with the desire to keep the marriage secret in case the Duke stopped Lady Jane's funds entirely, influenced the important decision the couple made next. They decided to travel to the continent, because, they later said, the costs of living would be less and they hoped to live incognito as man and wife.

A small party gathered at Harwich at the end of August, 1746, ready to embark on a ship for Holland. On the journey from Edinburgh to Harwich Lady Jane had concealed her identity. "I took the name of Grey while on the English road," she wrote in a letter to a friend, "to save expenses; but I did not find I had much less to pay for all that precaution."[65] She travelled from Edinburgh as far as Huntingdon with Mrs. Hewit. Here she stayed a few days at the house of a friend where she was joined by her new husband, and where one of the party saw Colonel Stewart's night-gown and slippers in Lady Jane's bedroom.[66] They then travelled on together to Harwich, armed with a travel document signed in London by the Duke of Grafton, the Lord Chamberlain. The document said: "Pass for Lady Jane Douglas, and

Miss Nelly Hewit, together with their domestics James Ker, John Douglas, Isabella Walker, and Euphemia Caw, to imbark at Harwich and pass, within fourteen days, over to Holland, dated 29th August 1746."[67]

In fact, Lady Jane had no servants called James Ker or John Douglas. "John Douglas" was actually Colonel Stewart, and "James Ker" was a young man known as the Chevalier Johnstone, who was the son of Mrs. Hewit's aunt. He had been in the entourage of Prince Charles Stuart and, with the failure of the '45, like many Jacobites he was wanted by the English. He needed to be out of the limelight and he turned to Lady Jane, whom he had known for some years, and whom he could trust.

Lady Jane offered to facilitate his escape to the continent and he joined the newly-weds at their inn. While they waited for the right wind to carry them to the Netherlands, Johnstone took some dictation from Lady Jane, and wrote a letter to her solicitors in Scotland replying to some demands for money that had been forwarded to her. The letter shows Lady Jane in an unfamiliar light. Accustomed as we are by now to her sweet disposition, gentle demeanour and delicate airs, it comes as a shock to see how peevish she can be when she wants. It appears that some of her creditors have threatened to turn nasty.

"My particular affairs," Johnstone writes, on behalf of Lady Jane, "have taken a most shocking turn, by the impatience and impertinence of some low insects, who unluckily had trifling demands, which I had destined a fund to answer against Martinmas next; but to prevent some demonstrations you mention from happening, I shall remit from Rotterdam, or give you a power to draw for any sum within one hundred and fifty pounds, which I am pretty sure will more than answer. ... And ... I insist my brother may not be applied to at this juncture..."[68]

Clearly, money was a sensitive issue with Lady Jane, and we can see how broke she and the Colonel were by the fact that one benefit of the Colonel and the Chevalier pretending to be servants was that it would save money. The pass for each traveller cost two guineas*, but servants went free. Two guineas was about £200 in today's money, so it was a significant saving to someone in Lady Jane's situation. But Colonel Stewart travelling incognito also helped keep the marriage secret from any passengers they might come across who knew Lady Jane. At the same time Johnstone was desperate to remain unrecognised. Even while at sea, he was on a British ship and the captain could arrest him if he was discovered to be a fugitive.

Both men narrowly avoided getting into trouble on the voyage. One of the other passengers, Mr. John Polson, knew Colonel Stewart and said later in evidence that Stewart asked him "not to take notice of him, or something to that purpose."[69]

Johnstone had some trouble juggling with his role as a footman. He dined with Lady Jane but would have to leap up and stand behind her chair if anyone came into the cabin. There was another friend of the Colonel's on the boat, a baronet, who was clearly allowed to be in on the secret of the marriage because he was invited to spend the evening in Lady Jane's cabin with her and the Colonel. Johnstone, as Lady Jane's footman, was banished to a tiny anteroom which he was told to share with the baronet's footman for the duration of the voyage. There was barely room for two people in this cabin. "When we were in bed," Johnstone said, "our legs were continually striking against each other from the smallness of the space in which we were cooped up. ... Each believing the other to be a footman, our respective observations were delivered in an insulting and contemptuous tone."

It was only at dinner-time, when Lady Jane mentioned to the baronet that her 'footman' was really a man who had been in the service of the Young Pretender, that the baronet

---

* A guinea was a unit of currency and a coin which were eventually replaced by the pound and the sovereign in 1816. But until the 1970s, the word 'guinea' was used to represent a unit of currency with the value of one pound and one shilling (21 shillings).

said that, as a matter of fact, *his* footman was an officer in the Irish Brigade, in the service of France. The two 'servants' were invited in to share dinner and each made 'a thousand apologies' to the other.

After a 24-hour voyage the ship arrived at the port of Rotterdam, in Holland, where the Chevalier Johnstone, only half-awake, rushed away from the boat and set off as fast as he could in case some last-minute hitch led to the captain arresting him. "I could scarcely persuade myself that I was beyond the reach of the English," he wrote, "Lady Jane laughed heartily at seeing me run, and called out that it was entirely useless as I was now out of all danger."

He stayed with the Stewarts in Rotterdam for a week, and then accompanied them to the Hague, "the prettiest village in the world", and on to Utrecht.

For the first few months of their travels, Lady Jane did her best to give the impression that Colonel Stewart was just a good friend, who happened to be staying in the same town, and sometimes the same house, as herself. It's difficult to see how the people they visited or entertained could be taken in by this pose, but the marriage was not openly acknowledged. Nevertheless, rumours reached Scotland, and as late as April, 1747, Lady Jane was writing to a friend to deny them, not, as we can see, for the first time. It is a good example of the sarcasm she can marshall when the occasion demands it:

"The impertinent liberties a great many have taken, in handing about idle stories disadvantageous to me, I am not ignorant of," she wrote, "and my nearest relations, I understand, have been chiefly employed in doing me these kind offices... My cousin, Miss Mally Ker, I hear has taken care to distinguish herself singularly on this occasion... This brainless, bad-hearted woman was the contriver ... of the last story of this kind, which was, for a considerable time, as much believed as this second essay of her abounding good-nature. And I have this thanks to pay her, that the first [husband] she bestowed on me was my good friend Mr. Haldane, a person I have ever honoured and esteemed; and this other, Mr. Stewart, deserves very well, particularly from me to whom he has done abundance of obliging services since I came to this country. When I was at the Hague, he happened to lodge in the same house, at one Dronia's, where there were also fourteen other people, gentlemen and ladies, lodging. This circumstance, perhaps favours the imposition. Many of the too credulous have imposed upon themselves, by too readily believing lies; and will serve, no doubt, to confirm these kind country folks of mine in the construction they are pleased to put upon my actions."[70]

Lady Jane complains about people too credulously believing lies, in a letter where she herself tells lies, and this is a difficult letter to explain away for those supporters of Lady Jane who thought she could do no wrong. Indeed, James Boswell, who became a passionate supporter of the Douglas family, in his collection of Lady Jane's letters published at the time of the Scottish court hearing in 1767, omits the section of this letter containing her denial of marriage.

Elsewhere in this letter she shows that even at the age of forty-eight, she is attractive and flirtatious enough to appeal to the young aristocrats she came across on the continent.

"I have been lucky since I came here in meeting with a great many Scots and English gentlemen. They are indeed chiefly of the younger sort, who chuse this place for their education; but they have so great a share of good sense, and so much wit, they render themselves acceptable to much older people. Amongst the rest, young Lord Blantyre deserves justly the greatest praise. But I am not capable of drawing characters well; the want of which talent I mightily regret, since it deprives me of the pleasure of doing justice to the most promising young gentleman I ever saw in my life."[71]

The young Lord Blantyre was son of Lord Mark Ker, Lady Jane's uncle. He was therefore the brother of the Captain Ker killed by the Duke of Douglas because of his close attentions to Lady Jane, and probably reminded Lady Jane of her former paramour. At almost exactly the same time as Lady Jane's letter, Blantyre wrote to his mother from Utrecht, equally bowled over, and even using the same phrase she did to convey the inadequacy of his descriptive powers:

"The hours which are not devoted to my books I pass very agreeably in the company of a lady, an acquaintance, I believe I may say a relation, of yours, who came here about three weeks ago. If I had any turn for drawing of characters I could have presented you with a very lovely one.... I choose rather to acquaint you that it is no other than Lady Jean Douglas, and by that means I elude a very difficult task – that of painting in their true colours her many lovely qualities."[72]

Colonel Stewart and Lady Jane left Utrecht in April, 1747, to travel to Aix-la-Chapelle. This was a fashionable resort which had its 'season' when the nobility of Europe would gather as spring came to northern Europe. The couple were to stay here for about a year, and, as a later letter from Colonel Stewart makes clear, their lifestyle with its frequent socialising meant that they were continually beset by financial problems:

'In this unhappy situation of her affairs with her brother, wee went together in poor enough circumstances. She had nothing but three hundred pounds annuity from the Duke her brother, and my small patrimony spent long befor; only my son supply'd me with what was of some use at that time, as Lady Jane was in some debt. On this narow bottom wee set owt in a few days after our marriage for Aix-la-Chapelle, where meeting with the Elector and Electrix Pallatine and Princess of Solme, who took particular notice of Lady Jeane, this naturally led us into more expence thane was convenient for our narow funds; she and I both trusting to the kindness of brothers, she, ane only sister, to the Duke, and I, ane only brother, to Sir George Stewart, who had no child, and had ane estate better than £1000, with many woods and other perquisits upon it, to very considerable amount. But it unluckily hapened (that from bad advisers) each of them seem'd to owt-doe one another in unkindness to us; so of course wee came in debt and difficultys which was attended with many unlucky consequences.'

The couple corresponded with friends in Britain, sometimes seeking loans to eke out Lady Jane's annuity. Requests to one friend for £150 in August and to another in September asking for £200 produced no immediate results, and in October, Lady Jane wrote in desperation to a third, for another £200. 'I believe you know I have more relations than friends, perhaps for want of merit in me,' she wrote, and she explained why she needed the money. 'The expense of travelling, imposition of the villanous Dutch, and the extravagant price of all the necessaries here and at Spa, by the neighbourhood of the army, has been so great.'

What she didn't mention was the fact that the Colonel's gambling was making their hardship even worse. One of the other Scottish visitors to Aix, Sir William Stewart, saw the Colonel play cards and lose ten or twelve gold ducats. "I went afterwards to wait upon Lady Jane," he said, "and mentioned to her that Colonel Stewart had lost, upon which tears came into her eyes and she seemed much concerned." Sir William also said that the Colonel had tried to borrow fifty pounds from him and he had said that he would consider money lent to him as 'thrown away money.' "After this," Sir William said, "Colonel Stewart and I were not such good friends as before."[73]

In February, 1748, while Lady Jane was staying in Aix-la-Chapelle, a friend, Lady Crawfurd, died, and her husband's sister, Lady Wemyss, came from Scotland to stay with Lord Crawfurd. Lady Wemyss had heard rumours in Scotland that Lady Jane had married Colonel Stewart, but because there was no acknowledgement of the marriage, and because Lady Jane was still calling herself Lady Jane Douglas, Lady Wemyss decided the rumours were false. Then one day she sent her servant with a message to Lady Jane about the mourning ceremonies for Lady Crawfurd, and the servant returned with some exciting news.

"My Lady (Lady Wemyss) will not believe that Lady Jane and Colonel Stewart are married," the servant said, "but sure I am I saw a pair of men's slippers below Lady Jane's bed."

"You are a fool," replied Lady Wemyss, "it might have been Lady Jane's own slippers."[74]

While the hard-up couple were living quietly in Aix-la-Chapelle, their friends in Edinburgh would have been agog with a rather interesting scandal that was unfolding in the family of Charles, fifth Lord Kinnaird of Inchture. He had been married for eighteen years to Magdalene, Lady Kinnaird, but they had produced no heirs. As things stood, the next heir was Lord Kinnaird's cousin, also Charles. Lady Kinnaird very much disliked this cousin and used to declare that "she would be content to go to hell or do anything rather than he should inherit." Then, in September, 1747, Lady Kinnaird left her home for an undisclosed destination, and two days later it was announced that she had given birth to twins, even though she had shown no signs of pregnancy.

Charles Kinnaird, the cousin, challenged this in court and asked for proof of the delivery and an examination of Lady Kinnaird's body to prove that she had recently given birth. The legal processes began to roll, and the couple were summoned to court in December, 1747, but refused to give evidence or to produce the twins.[75] Shortly afterwards, Lord Kinnaird declared that both children were dead, and the case was closed. On Lord Kinnaird's death ten years later, the cousin became the sixth Lord Kinnaird.

This story would have been followed in all its scandalous details by the Scottish nobility, and Lady Jane and her husband can hardly have been unaware of it in the correspondence they kept up with their friends. And among those friends were Mr. and Mrs. Hepburn of Keith, who had known Colonel Stewart at the time of his first marriage, and met Lady Jane at the Hague in 1747. Now, in March 1748, they travelled to Aix-la-Chapelle to visit Lady Jane, staying for eight or ten days in the town. Remembering this visit seventeen years later, Mrs. Hepburn described how she first made a surprising observation, "that, when she first saw Lady Jane at Aix, she observed a very great difference from the looks she had at the Hague; that her face was very thin; that her belly or waist was very thick; her cheeks thin, and her eyes large; from all which (Mrs. Hepburn) had not the least doubt of her being with child; that she told this to her husband that night, and said to him, that she was sure Lady Jane was with child; that she told the same the next morning to Mrs. Hewit, and said, she took it ill that she had never acquainted her thereof; but Mrs. Hewit said, she wanted to surprise (Mrs. Hepburn) agreeably, and try whether she should find out herself."[76]

If we calculate the time of conception from the date when Lady Jane said she gave birth in July, 1748, it would seem that she conceived some time in October, 1747. But her pregnancy was not really noticed, and eventually admitted, until March, 1748, several months after the Kinnaird business had been stopped in its tracks by the alleged death of Lady Kinnaird's twins.

For some observers of the unfolding of Lady Jane's story, looking back with hindsight at the events of 1747-8, the coincidence in time of the similar Kinnaird story was too close for comfort. It was not impossible that the Kinnaird story had planted the idea in Colonel Stewart or Lady Jane of pretending to be pregnant, with the intention of acquiring one or more babies at the time the confinement was due. On the other hand, there was no doubt in the minds of almost everyone who met Lady Jane at the time that in the months following March, 1748, she showed all the signs of a pregnant woman whose condition became more and more visible with the passing of the days and weeks.

As early as November, 1747, Mrs. Tewis, her landlady, had observed the unmistakable signs of pregnancy in Lady Jane, "by the repeated vomitings and other small indispositions, with which she was troubled in the mornings, and by the particular food she then began to use out of her ordinary course; and the two spouses a few days after requested her, their landlady, to place a second bed in the same room…"

In March, 1748, an Aix friend went to visit Lady Jane. "My husband thought I was pregnant," the friend told her, "and I told him I was too old." Lady Jane responded to this remark by making a sign with her hands, as if to say 'Look at me', by which the visitor understood "that lady Jane Douglas meant to speak of her own pregnancy, and to observe that she was older."[77]

Other friends and acquaintances later said that they had seen various signs which they took to mean Lady Jane was pregnant. The most detailed account was given by Isabel Walker, one of Lady Jane's maids. "Lady Jane was naturally flat-chested," she said, "and very thin, but when with child her breasts rose to a great size." Her later evidence said that "she had occasion frequently to see Lady Jane's naked breasts and belly and that she has had her hands on Lady Jane's naked belly, and found her with live child, and that this she would depone if she was going to step into eternity, whatever wretches might say."[78] … "That as Lady Jane had always said that it was the bile that had come up to her stomach, (Isabel Walker) upon this discovery, told her that now she was very easy about the consequences of the bile, for if it was bile, it was living bile, for that (she) was now conscious she was with child. That Lady Jane was quite bashful, made no answer, but appeared to be angry at her for talking in so free a manner."[79] …

The pregnancy was even apparent to a group of Benedictine nuns whom Lady Jane used to visit at Aix. Although a Protestant, she was suspected by some of having Catholic leanings. The nuns' witness to Lady Jane's pregnancy was later ridiculed by the Hamilton lawyers, but, as one observer wrote "when we consider the strict attention necessarily paid to the conduct of the youngest sisters, it may perhaps be the less surprising that an abbess or prioress of a nunnery should be among the first to notice this alteration in a lady's person."[80]

By April, 1748, it was clear that the marriage and the pregnancy could no longer be concealed, and Lady Jane decided that her brother must be told, in the hope that his heart would soften towards his sister at the news of a possible heir, however much he disapproved of its father.

She asked Lord Crawfurd if he would write to the Duke and break the news, enclosing a letter from her with a more personal plea for his blessing.

Lord Crawfurd described to the Duke how Lady Jane and Colonel Stewart had supported him at the time of the recent death of his wife and went on to say: "During the space of time we have been together, I have ... so far merited my Lady Jane's confidence, as to be intrusted with the alteration there has happened in her state of life, as also the notifying of it to your Grace, by the inclosed..."[81]

Lady Jane's letter has not survived, but we learn something of its contents and the effect it had on the Duke from Mr. William Hamilton, the minister at Douglas Town, who was with the Duke when he opened the letter and handed it to Hamilton to read.

"I'll perhaps say some strong things while you are reading that letter," the Duke said, "but never mind me, go on with it." The letter said that the Duke had often pressed Lady Jane to marry "in order to prevent bad consequences," and now she had complied with his request, and was married to Mr. Stewart, and hoped that these "bad consequences" were prevented. "Your Grace will perhaps think that I have matched far below the dignity of your family," she wrote, "but he is a gentleman related to the best Dukes in France." She went on to say that he was "one of the best beloved gentlemen that ever came from our country; in a word, my Lord, he is a very Titus."

On hearing this the Duke said to Hamilton "I must stop you a little now. Did not you say always to me that Janie was a woman of good sense?"

"I always thought so, my Lord, and I still think so," Hamilton replied.

"Why," the Duke said angrily, "the woman is now mad to give such a character to Stewart, who is one of the worst of men; for he is a Papist, a Jacobite, a gamester, a villain, and he is all the ills in the world!"

The Duke sat down, and asked Hamilton what he should do now, and Hamilton said that the best advice he could give him was that he himself should marry, and this would thwart Lady Jane and Mr. Stewart. The Duke thought this was good advice but then suddenly thought of an objection.

"You know, Sir," he said, "I am an old man, and a goutish man, and I am told that marriage is bad for the gout."

"It is the first time ever I heard it," Hamilton said, surprised, "but allowing it was so, would not your Grace risk a fit of the gout to save your family from sinking?"

The Duke then said, rather sadly, "I once thought that if there was a virtuous woman in the world, my sister Janie was one; but now I am going to say a thing that I believe I should not say of my own sister, that she is a whore; and that I believe there is not a virtuous woman in the world."

"There are thousands of virtuous women in the world," Hamilton said and still pressed him to think of marriage. But the Duke said that he would never marry, because he didn't mind what happened to his estate, and he added that Lady Jane once tried to get his estate sequestrated, and herself put in possession, but she should never have a sixpence from him while she breathed.[82]

According to another writer, the Duke's initial reaction to the news of Lady Jane's pregnancy was rather different:

"At first he seemed much pleased and repeated again and again 'Faith, Jeanie, better late thrive than ne'er do well.'"[83]

However, Stockbriggs and Archibald Stewart were still around at this time, and it would not do to have the Duke reconciled with his sister:

"This behaviour greatly alarmed the associates, who asked his Grace if he did not see the imposition, and that a pretender was intended. They wish'd to God it was possible to be true, but that was not the case, she was several years past childbearing, and no such miracle as a mother at her age was to be seen. They represented the character of Colonel Stewart in its too true colour, nor did they desist, till they had incensed the Duke against his innocent sister so much that he ordered her pension to be stopp'd, and herself to be informed that he would never see her more."[84]

At about this time Lady Jane had her clothes enlarged to accommodate her increasing size. She was now six months pregnant. As arrangements for a Peace Congress at Aix got under way, and inflation in food and accommodation costs hit the town, Lady Jane and the Colonel moved house, to "a burgher's house in mean and strait apartments"[85], and then they decided to leave town entirely and find a cheaper place to live.

Colonel Stewart wanted to go to Geneva, and although Lady Jane was reluctant, she agreed. But then the Colonel changed his mind, thinking that Lady Jane might not be up to such a long journey in her state. On the 15th of May, shortly before they left Aix, the Colonel arranged for a letter to be written to Mr. Andrieux, a wine merchant and agent at Rheims, which was on the direct coach road to Geneva, seeking accommodation for the couple and their servants.

Over the next two weeks, the party travelled from Aix to Rheims, staying over at various towns on the way. The first stop was Liège where Mrs. Hepburn who was with the party later remembered a strange incident. Lady Jane wanted to visit a friend in the town, a Countess, and the carriage stopped outside her house while a servant went to find out if she was in.

"A beggar, who appeared to (Mrs. Hepburn) to have his nose flat upon his face, presented himself before the coach for charity; and to that side of the coach where sir John and (Mrs. Hepburn) sat: that sir John in a violent passion rushed out of the coach, and turned the man about, lest lady Jane, who with Mrs. Hewit sat on the other side of the coach, should see him: that lady Jane asked in a great haste, what was the matter, which (Mrs. Hepburn) told her laughing, saying, that it was a man with a shocking aspect: lady Jane answered, I wonder you laugh, for I think it is the most impious thing I ever saw in my life; and that lady Jane appeared very angry for using the poor man so cruelly, and chid Mr. Stewart for it when he came into the coach extremely; upon which he went out again of the coach, followed the man, and gave him something extraordinary."[86]

From Liege they went on to Sedan, and it became clear that travelling across France was not as quick and easy as they had expected. The journey from Sedan to Rheims, for example, was by a coach that went once a week, and they arrived the day after one of its regular departures. It looked as if they might have to stop in Rheims for the birth, rather than go on to Geneva.

Somewhere on the road – the stories disagree over where – Lady Jane apparently experienced some preliminary contractions, and there were fears that she might be about to give birth before her time. Isabel Walker says she put her mistress to bed and sat up with her all night. It was the eighth month of her pregnancy, and perhaps the long journey along bumpy coach roads was having its effects.

Eventually, on the 7th of June, they arrived at Rheims and put up at the house of M. and Mme. Hibert. It looks as if, even with Colonel Stewart's appetite for drink, they planned to stay there for some time, judging by an order for wine that was found in M. Andrieux' order book, dated 10th of June, 1748:

"Owed by Colonel Stewart, Scots gentleman, and the women who are staying with him in Rheims at M. Hibert's, rue St. Denis, for 104 bottles of Burgundy, at 16 sols. the bottle..............83 liv. 4s.

For eight bottles of white wine, non-sparkling, at 22 sols per bottle

For 22 bottles of ordinary wine at 8 sols per bottle............8 liv. 16 s.

Plus for a barrel I have delivered to contain Sassy water........1 liv. 4 s. "

At Rheims, while helping Lady Jane to dress, Isabel Walker said she saw her in her nightgown and was astonished at how large she had become. She began to think that she must be carrying twins and said so to Mrs. Hewit who told her not to frighten her, as she was already frightened enough for Lady Jane.[87]

Just as she was making the necessary preparations for her lying in, Lady Jane received the news that the Duke never wanted to see her again.

"What could she do?" wrote the anonymous biographer. "Her whole fortune had already been swallowed up by the debts and extravagances of her husband; she had even mortgaged her last half-year's pension, her pride would not let her disclose the situation to any of the English at Aix la Chapelle, who would readily have assisted her, and in this exigency, she took the most imprudent step that ill fortune ever contrived. (But prudence was not among her virtues) and telling her maid Mrs. Crawford that she wished to be under the care of a particular accoucheur at Paris, left her and the footman behind her, and taking places for herself and husband, with Mrs. Hewet in the diligence, privately set off early in the morning for Paris. Where she fixed on her arrival there has puzzled half this kingdom to discover, but in vain."[88]

The remark about the accoucheur, or midwife, could relate to some advice they received while at Rheims. Lady Jane may originally have intended to give birth in the town, but according to some accounts, not long after she arrived Mme Andrieux told Lady Jane that there were no skilled midwives there and that if she had any concerns about the birth she should go to Paris. This was the reason Lady Jane and the Colonel gave later when asked why they had suddenly changed their plans at the last minute, when Lady Jane was uncomfortably near term.

On the 28th June, 1748, while the very visibly pregnant Lady Jane Douglas was resting in Rheims, preparing for the final stage of her journey, a baby boy was born to Mme. Marie Mignon, in the Faubourg St Antoine, a suburb of Paris. The mother was the 37-year-old wife of a glass-grinder, Nicholas Mignon, aged fifty-one, and on July 1st the child was christened Jacques Louis. The mystery of what happened to this child after July 10th, 1748, is at the heart of the story of the Douglas Cause.

4

"Two lovly creters"

Colonel John Stewart was not a homebody. Whether in Edinburgh, London, Rheims or Paris, he liked to socialise. One writer describes him in Rheims as "habitually from home every day in the publick coffee house." It was in this coffeehouse that he met M. Maillefer, a local agent for businessmen in the town, and told him that he and Lady Jane were about to go to Paris. On behalf of the Colonel, Maillefer wrote a letter on the 2nd of July to M. Godefroi, an innkeeper who ran the hotel de Châlons, in the rue Saint-Martin in Paris.

"There is set out today from Rheims," Maillefer wrote, "a Scotch colonel with two ladies, who should arrive on Thursday the 4th at Paris by the Rheims coach. I have directed them to your hotel to alight there. I do not know if it will be for any time; for I believe, that their intention is to have an apartment themselves afterwards. ... As he will have some purchases to make at Paris, I have told him, that he might apply to you, as being a connoisseur in these things, and that you would not allow him to be imposed on. If you have not time yourself to go meet them, engage some one, or your wife, to go thither. I have promised it to them, and they do absolutely expect it."[89]

So began the stay in Paris, at the start of which Lady Jane showed all the signs of pregnancy and at the end of which she didn't. Indeed, in the early phases of the legal process Andrew Stuart, the leading lawyer for the Hamiltons, assembled a large number of witness statements to deny even that Lady Jane was truly pregnant. But a remark he made later suggested that this was more a matter of advocacy than truly reflecting what he believed in his heart of hearts. He said that "he had all the proofs in the world of Lady Jane's pregnancy, but none of her delivery."[90]

The events of the following month can never be known for certain, for various reasons. First and, I would say, most important is the fact that it was only after the death of the Duke of Douglas thirteen years later that any serious attempt was made to pin down the details of those events, through the testimony of people who were being asked to remember what happened on a particular day years beforehand. Some of these people might be expected to remember better than others, since the events were more central in their lives. Lady Jane was dead by the time the case began, but Colonel Stewart and Mrs. Hewit were still alive, as was Isabel Walker, and they were asked to give detailed accounts of the events. But even here, the "wore out old rake" was seventy-five at the time and when he was asked to flesh out the details of the few letters and scraps of paper that had been his only account up till then, his memory was not really up to the task. And people like hotel-keepers and guests, coach drivers and passengers, serving maids, and acquaintances of the couple were even less likely to have clear and accurate memories of times, dates, and places.

The bare bones of the story that the Douglas side put forward were as follows:

Lady Jane and Colonel Stewart arrived in Paris on July 4th, 1748, and stayed at the hotel de Châlons, run by M. and Mme. Godefroi. On July 8th, they paid their bill at Godefroi's and moved to the house of a Mme. Le Brun and her daughter in the

Faubourg St. Germain, where, on July 10th, with the assistance of a male midwife called Pierre La Marre, Lady Jane gave birth to twins, whom she called Archibald and Sholto, two traditional Douglas names. Sholto was very weak and there were fears that he might not live, so La Marre baptised him, and recommended that he be sent out to the country, to gain strength. They had hoped to find a nurse who would eventually travel back to Rheims with them, but failed and put Sholto with a nurse found by La Marre near Paris. The couple and Mrs. Hewit stayed at Mme. La Brun's for ten or twelve days and then, because they were "pestered with bugs" they moved to a third house in the same suburb, the hôtel d'Anjou, owned by Mme. Michel.

From Mme. Michel's, Mrs. Hewit wrote a letter to the two maids they had left behind in Rheims.

"Dear Tiby and Effe," she wrote, "This will be the welcomest leter iver eny of you recved." After describing the birth of the "two lovly creters", she wrote of the search for a wet-nurse for Archy and gave news of Lady Jane's progress.

"Your mr and I had to go not a litell way befor we got a right nurse that we ould pert with him to, at last we got on of the clinest best woman iver you sa, a farmer's wife, so, I hop, he shall do very well; he agreeing so well, we was fond to find the other, who is a very stordy peace [sturdy piece]. Som days after your mr wint out to see him, and found the nurse dronk, upon which he sint the coach for me, and we brought him with hos. We have got a feen milk woman, tell we geet a right norc [nurse], for your mr and mrs is resolved, he shall never go out of ther sight. She is recovering most surprisingly well, not on back-going howr [not a back-going hour]; so soon as the ninth day was over, ther was no confining her longer to her bed, the heat being so vilint."

Baby Archy was at the hôtel d'Anjou for a couple of days and then put out with a wet-nurse on July 26th. Then the family were advised to go to the country to escape the heat of a Parisian August and on the 4th of August the three Scots and the child travelled to Dammartin, a village known to Archy's nurse, who could recommend another nurse to take over the care of the child.

While Lady Jane was at Dammartin, she wrote a letter to her brother. She had written to him in April, finally telling him of her marriage and pregnancy but had had no reply. Now she told him the even more significant news of the birth: "The tenth of last month, I was blessed with twin boys, one a promising child; the other, poor thing, so weak, that I fear it is little to be reckoned on."[91]

The Duke was apparently unmoved and later told Mrs. Hepburn that "he had been informed by Mr. Archibald Stuart and Stockbriggs, that Lady Jane was not in a situation to have children for many years before her marriage with colonel Stewart; and that they said, they had been informed by Mrs. Kerr, who had formerly been housekeeper to the Duke, that a marble table would have a child as soon as Lady Jane."[92]

This Mrs. Kerr was presumably the 'Mally Ker' who told such dreadful lies about Lady Jane travelling with Colonel Stewart to Harwich, (when in fact this was true.)

The issue of Lady Jane's age was to come up time and again, as a reason for doubting that she had given birth to Archy Douglas. Andrew Stuart, the Hamiltons' lawyer, wrote "To have a child at that age is very uncommon. That in her situation with her brother, the Duke of Douglas, it should be a son instead of a daughter, was fortunate; but that two sons should be produced at a birth, where they were so much wanted, and as her first-fruits, in this advanced period of her age, approached so much to the marvellous, as to be in a very high degree improbable. A fact, so circumstanced, as that the history of human nature affords very few if any instances truly similar, must be acknowleged not only to be improbable, but incredible, until it be well attested."[93]

Once again, I think we find Stuart writing as an advocate rather than telling us what he really believes. Long before the era of fertility drugs, it was far from unknown for women in their fifties to conceive. Eighteenth century magazines and newspapers would report such cases on a regular basis in their Births columns, and Stuart must have read them. Here are a couple:

"At Horsham, in the 63rd year of her age, Mrs. Elizabeth Curtis, wife of Mr. Curtis of that place, of Twins, Male, who, together with their mother, were likely to do well."[94]

"At Farringdon in Berks, Anne Painswick, the wife of a labouring man, upwards of 60 years of age, of four children, three boys and a girl."[95]

And we now know that older women who conceive are more likely to have multiple pregnancies – twins or triplets. On January 11th, 2000, the *Associated Press* put out the story of a 54-year-old woman, Aracelia Garcia, in Washington State, who gave birth to three healthy babies, without having used fertility drugs.

None of this proves that Lady Jane's pregnancy resulted in the birth of Archy Douglas, but it suggests that people who first denied that her story could be true because of her age were incorrect. And yet it was the Hamiltons' certainty that Lady Jane could not have conceived that was to be given as the motive for the vast legal process that ground into action after the Duke of Douglas died.

On the 15th of August, Lady Jane and the Colonel left Dammartin with Archy and travelled to Rheims where they were to stay for over a year. During most of this time Sholto, still presumably a weak child, was said to be in the care of a nurse in a village near Paris. In Rheims, Archy was on show to Lady Jane's friends. Mme. Maillefer says that he looked "about six weeks or two months old; that he was of a brown colour, and had large black eyes and brown eye-brows."

Shortly after they arrived, Colonel Stewart received a letter of congratulations from a friend in Aix, M. Obin. The Colonel had ascribed his success in fathering children to the drinking of tar-water, a cure-all that was fashionable at the time, promoted by Bishop Berkeley who wrote a 200-page book on the subject.

"I take a sensible pleasure in the news you have done me the honour to give me," Obin wrote, "of the happy delivery of Lady Jane, your spouse. It must be owned, sir, that the tar waters have had wonderful effects, and I am just begun to take them upon the solicitations of my wife, who has never ceased persecuting me to make use of them, from the moment she heard that my Lady was delivered of two boys. I do not flatter myself, that they will produce such ample and extraordinary effects, in regard to my family; but I hope at least I may arrive at some small share of what they have produced in you, that I may be able, at least, to make my wife the mother of a daughter."[96]

On September 22nd, 1748, Archy was baptised in the Catholic church of St Jacques in Rheims, a ceremony witnessed by several close friends.

Colonel Stewart was happy to invite people to accompany him to see his weaker son on his regular visits to Paris. In October, he went to Paris with a friend, Baron Macelligot, to visit Sholto, although the baron was indisposed and so did not see the child. In November, the colonel wrote to his son by his first marriage, saying:

"My dear Jack, what should hinder you coming here to me where you have hearty welcome to Lady Jane, who wants much to make you acquainted with your brothers, and renew your acquaintance with me. If you have money, a little cannot be better employed; if you have little of that necessary evil, frugality should determine your gratifying me in it, as you cannot possibly live so well and so cheap as with us, where it shall stand you nothing to fare as we do; so, my dear, come."[97]

By the time of Archy's christening Lady Jane was pregnant again – the Colonel obviously couldn't keep away from the tar-water – but at about three months, at the beginning of December, she had a slight accident on her way to visit Lady

Wigton. She slipped and in attempting to save herself she "wrampted her back." When she complained of the pain to Lady Wigton, she was given a drink and sent home in a sedan chair. Nurse Mangin, Archy's wet–nurse, later said:

"...that after laying the whole night in pain, (Lady Jane) miscarried between eight and nine the next morning. She (Nurse Mangin) met Effy Caw upon the stairs with a chamber-pot, who cried out, 'My God, dear nurse, what an accident!' Nurse asked her what she had got there. A miscarriage, answered Effy, of Mad. Stewart. Upon which the nurse had the curiosity to remove what was in the pot, and lifted up a foetus, which she knew to be a male-child, of the length of seven or eight inches. Effy Caw was alone with her at this time, and was the first to throw it into the little-house [lavatory]. Lady Jane kept her bed about ten or twelve days, and her chamber about a fortnight more, without even coming into the nurse's chamber; but the child [Archy] used to be carried in to see her: she was dressed like a sick person, looked extremely pale, and ate scarce anything but a little broth."[98]

There seems to be evidence of at least two later miscarriages in France in the months after this event. It was later written, *a propos* the miscarriage, "...the enthusiastic virility of this middle-aged couple seems to have been beyond all praise."[99]

It was at about this time that the first rumours began to spread amongst Scottish society that Lady Jane's children might not have been 'born of her body.'

Walter Colville, a legal official who was a friend of Lady Jane's, said that he believed these reports to be "a mere farce, and that he never paid any regard to them."[100]

"Jokes on women who are pregnant at an advanced age are no uncommon things," said the Rev. Robert Richardson in his analysis of the case. "Every idle fellow can say 'Miracles are not ceased;' and it happens that Mr. Colvil is not the only person, who informs us, that these reports took their rise from a piece of low humour, which has since appeared to be malicious." A letter of Lord Mark Kerr's describes the duke of Douglas calling the children "in a jocular way Pretenders."[101]

Whatever the rumours back in Britain, the couple and Archy lived a normal sociable life in Rheims, taking all the care that would be expected of normal parents with their growing child. But the most puzzling thing about this period of their lives – at least to modern eyes – is their willingness to leave Sholto with a nurse in Paris for more than a year, rather than bring him to be with them at Rheims.

Colonel Stewart had explained to his friends that Pierre La Marre, the male midwife, was keeping an eye on Sholto and his nurse and sending regular health reports by letter. Such letters later turned up among Colonel Stewart's belongings. One in August, 1749, tells of Sholto's teething; another in September describes the child having a fever and La Marre giving him some rhubarb which seems to have helped. By October, apparently, Sholto was walking and beginning to talk.

In June, 1749, Lady Jane had a letter from a close friend, the Countess of Bassewitz, whose cheeky reference to Colonel Stewart is a further confirmation of the total conviction at the time amongst the couple's friends that there was nothing suspicious about Lady Jane's late-in-life pregnancy and confinement:

"Connected to you, for ever, by the bounds of the most tender friendship, I exhaust myself in wishing for your repose, and the future happiness of the amiable twins, who are the master-piece of the amorous exploits of Colonel Stewart."[102] (The Countess seems to think that the conception involved no amorous exploits at all on the part of Lady Jane, who presumably just lay back and thought of Scotland.)

However well and cheaply the couple lived, they still got into financial straits, and Lady Jane's worries were increased in July, 1749, when the Duke of Douglas finally cut off even the £300 p.a. he had granted her. This was said to be because two of Lady Jane's creditors had laid a claim against her annuity on account of her growing debts.

It may be this blow that finally led Lady Jane and the Colonel to plan to return to Britain. Even though the costs of living were far lower in France, by returning to Britain she could at least plead with the Duke and other relatives in person, since the begging letters she wrote at this time often had no effect. One letter that did work, to Lord Morton, one of Lady Jane's relatives, extracted a loan of £350, enough to cover the costs of paying bills, packing up and travelling to England.

Things then moved fast. Early in November, Colonel Stewart, Lady Jane and Mrs. Hewit set off for Paris to fetch Sholto. Later in the month, they returned with the seventeen-month-old child, now strong and in good health. Then in late November they began their journey to England, via St Omer, Dunkirk, and Margate, arriving in London in Christmas week, 1749.

Lady Jane's aims for the next phase of her life were to find a way of living on a surer financial footing, regain her brother's affections, and see her sons brought into the bosom of their Douglas relatives. But these things were not to be. The Rev. Robert Richardson's account of the case, when he reaches 1750 and Lady Jane's return to England, sees this as the lowest point so far in a life which has had many ups and downs:

"We are now to take a view of a scene of great distress," he wrote, "which would draw tears from many eyes."[103]

5

"An Odious Chimera"

Lady Jane and her husband were to spend the next two years in London, even though her home and family were in Scotland. A month after returning from France, the couple received a nasty shock. Colonel Stewart was arrested and imprisoned for debt in the King's Bench prison in Southwark. It's not clear whether the couple had anticipated this and went back to England partly to face the music, or whether they had hoped to be better off by then, so that Colonel Stewart could pay off the debts that had accumulated while they were on the continent. Although Lord Morton's loan had paid for the journey back from France, once in London Lady Jane had to sell clothes and jewellery just to get money for food and lodging.

Fortunately for the Colonel, debtor's prison in those days was not quite the hardship one might think. Prisoners, on payment of a fee, could live in ordinary houses in an area round the prison, known as 'within the rules of King's-Bench', and about three miles in circumference. In spite of their bankrupt status there were plenty of inmates, including the Colonel, who were willing to pay about four guineas for every hundred they were in debt for the privilege. And even these rather relaxed 'rules' were not strictly enforced. When Lord Ellingborough, the chief justice of the King's Bench, once heard an application for the rules to be extended further than their current limits he replied that he could really see no grounds for the application since to his certain knowledge the rules already extended to the East Indies.[104] Colonel Stewart's residence was just outside the walls of the prison, in the home of a silk-dyer in Blackman Street, but during his two years in the prison he seems to have bent the 'rules' on several occasions to travel much more widely around London.

The first lodging Lady Jane took was at the house of a Mr. Murray, in St. James Place. An early event in their new life was the proper christening of Sholto, who, the couple said, because of his poor health had only had a form of emergency baptism at the hands of Pierre La Marre shortly after he was born. Now, witnessed by a few of Lady Jane's society relatives, Sholto was given a church ceremony in London.

Other relatives were not so obliging. Her uncle, Lord Mark Kerr, wrote her a letter in January, 1750, which took her to task for deeds stretching back thirty years, from the time she fled to France after the jilting episode.

"Your behaviour thirty years ago next month" he wrote, "and four years agone very soon, are both mighty fresh in my memory: so I must tell you plainly, that from henceforward, I give up all correspondence."

And he added a postscript, just to make clear his censure. "NB: Madam, it is all your own doing, with bad advice, too."[105] This was taken to refer to Mrs. Hewit.

With large debts and little income, Lady Jane must have been hurt by this letter. She could not afford to alienate too many relatives, who might be her only source of financial help until her brother mellowed, if he ever did.

Clearly, Kerr was affected by the news of the strange events that had occurred over the last two years and, like an increasing number of relatives, friends and acquaintances, was becoming infected by the anti-Lady Janeites with a suspicion that the children might not be all they seemed to be. Even if he could not believe Lady Jane guilty of deceit, he and others felt she should have been more open about the births at the time she claimed they had happened, when the name and fortune of such a distinguished family were at stake.

The idea of giving birth in a more public way was not as strange as it sounds. Seventy years later, the Duchesse de Berri gave birth in Paris to a boy who was heir to the French throne, and distinguished personages were chosen to be witnesses to the birth. One of them was the Maréchal de Coigny, who was urged by the Duchess — in spite of his repugnance — to pull the umbilical cord to assure everyone that there was a baby attached. Even then, there were those supporters of the rival for the throne who spread doubts about the birth.[106]

As rumours of an imposture by Lady Jane began to circulate, they came to the ears of the servants, including Isabel Walker, who had been left behind in Rheims when the couple and Mrs. Hewit went to Paris for the birth. Walker later described one of the letters that arrived from France from Pierre La Marre some time in 1750, which Colonel Stewart read out to Lady Jane. La Marre asked after the couple and their children, and Lady Jane apparently suggested to the colonel that they take some care of the letter in view of the doubts that were beginning to be expressed. The later legal investigations revealed several more La Marre letters, dated during 1749, when Sholto was said to be in his care, and 1752, inquiring after the children's health.

But it wasn't only the births which people were beginning to doubt. Some people went as far as to suggest that Lady Jane hadn't even been pregnant, and the couple were irritated enough for Colonel Stewart to write to Mme. Tewis, their landlady at Aix who had observed the early stages of Lady Jane's pregnancy:

"You will be much surprised, Madam, to learn that the malice of our enemies, and their assurance, has been such as to dare to insinuate, that our dear children are borrowed, and that my Lady Jane was never with child. This gross and diabolical detraction is incapable to do hurt during our lives; but as the renewing of that odious chimera may possibly give uneasiness to our dear little children when we shall be no more, we have been advised to have the circumstances … as authentically proved as possible."[107]

He asked Mme. Tewis to swear an affidavit that she had observed Lady Jane's pregnancy, which she did in August 1750.

During 1750, Lady Jane's landlord, Mr. Murray, who was aware of her financial distress, suggested that she contact a relative of his, William Murray, who was the King's Solicitor-General, in the hope that he might be able to organise a pension for her. At the suggestion of William Murray, Lady Jane wrote to the Prime Minister, Henry Pelham, and reminded him that her brother had stopped her annuity the previous year:

"Till the Duke of Douglas is set right," she wrote, "which I'm confident he will be, I am destitute. Presumptive heiress of a great estate and family, with two children, I want bread. Your own nobleness of mind will make you feel how much it costs me to beg, tho' from the king. My birth, and the attachment of my family, I flatter myself, his Majesty is not unacquainted with; should he think me an object of his royal bounty, my heart won't suffer any bounds to be set to my gratitude; and give me leave to say my spirit won't suffer me to be burdensome to his Majesty longer than my cruel necessity compels me."[108]

This process of obtaining a King's pension, ultimately successful, took several months, and meanwhile Lady Jane and the Colonel became poorer and poorer. They wrote to each other several times a week, and the letters were often about money, the Colonel seeking it and Lady Jane failing to provide it. "How unhappy, I think myself," she wrote, "that

I can't assist you in money matters; it truly was never less in my power. I really do not know what hand to turn myself to, to get money to pay Murray, and to stay longer than the 2nd of next month, (which I agreed to do) is next to being in the inquisition." Another letter has better news, but only slightly: "You may judge how low money matters are with me at present, by this most scurvy poor half-crown I send you; I'm quite ashamed of it, and, to conceal it from my servants, I have enclosed it well wrapt up in the pretty little money box, which ought to contain gold."[109] She even asked him to send her his cast-off wigs so that she could sell them to shoe-shine boys for polishing boots.

Throughout the correspondence there are little items of news about the children that present a model of parental affection: "Dear little Archy has had a little cold, with a small degree of fever; but, blessed be God, 'tis now in a manner quite over ... I must own when I perceived the child hot, and as I thought, in danger of taking a fever, or the small-pox, I felt a pain and distress of mind not to be expressed."

A letter announcing that the King had agreed a pension of £300 a year came on 3rd August, 1750, and later in the year Lady Jane was presented at Court, where she had a conversation with the King, who asked her if her brother was kind to her. "No, he is not good for much," she said but added, "However, he is a faithful subject to your majesty."[110]

It was clear that nothing could change radically for Lady Jane and her children until she was reconciled with her brother, and the couple's time in London was just a prelude to a return to Scotland to achieve this. But with the King's pension only enough to cover the basic necessities for an aristocratic lady, and with the Colonel in prison and hard up, the family stayed in London.

In September 1751, perhaps to save money, Lady Jane moved from Mr. Murray's house in St James' to lodgings in Chelsea. In a letter to her husband she sounded off about her previous landlord over some slight she had received, displaying the side of her personality that was rarely seen in public:

"As to Murray and his wife's odd behaviour to me, such creatures cannot scarcely raise my anger, far less my resentment. I do indeed exceedingly despise and condemn them and have intirely remov'd any little esteem I had formerly for them and this is all the punishment if it can be called any that I intend for them tho' if it were in my power. I was not I confess quite easy in my mind to be under their roof after I found them out to be very mean interested creatures but now that I am got clear of them I am happy."[111]

Colonel Stewart himself seems to have had rather a good time in the King's Bench prison. He was always fond of carousing and found like-minded companions inside, including a strange character known as the King of Corsica. His name was Theodore, Baron Neuhoff, and had been born in Germany. After service in the French and Swedish armies he wandered around Europe, getting mixed up in various schemes. One day he bumped into some Corsican exiles in Genoa and persuaded them that he could free their island from the control of the Genoese if they made him king. He travelled to the island in March, 1736, was proclaimed King Theodore I of Corsica, and fought the Genoese with some success for a few months, before they regained the upper hand and he fled to the mainland. His seven-month monarchy allowed him to call himself 'King Theodore of Corsica' for the rest of his life, a life spent, like Colonel Stewart's, trying to get out of debt. In fact the two were made for each other. Stewart's rank was gained in the Swedish army, like Theodore's; they both were attracted to rebellions – the Jacobites, in Stewart's case, and Corsica among others for Theodore; and they both had sons who were as impecunious as their fathers.

Theodore's son, Colonel Frederick, used to visit his father in prison from time to time, as a 19th century writer described:

"He used to relate that while his father was in the King's Bench prison for debt, (Colonel) Stewart was a fellow prisoner on the same account. The latter had a turkey presented to him by a friend and he invited King Theodore and his son to partake of it. Lady Jane Douglas was of the party. She had her child, and a girl with her, as a maidservant, to carry the child; she lived in an obscure lodging at Chelsea. In the evening, Colonel Frederick offered to attend her home, and she accepted this courtesy. The child was carried in turn by the mother, the girl, and the colonel. On their journey he said there was a slight rain and common civility would have induced him to call a coach, but that he had no money in his pocket, and he was afraid that Lady Jane was in the same predicament. He was therefore obliged to submit to the suspicion of churlish meanness or poverty, and to content himself with occasionally carrying the child to the end of the journey."[112]

What the Colonel and the King had they shared, but it often wasn't very much. On one occasion Colonel Stewart wrote to his wife to say that he and Theodore had nothing to eat for a week but 'a dish of grey pease'.

But a great falling-out eventually took place between the two friends. In the Earl of Home's papers at the Hirsel there is an angry letter to 'King Theodore', drafted and unsigned but in Colonel Stewart's handwriting:

"Sir," Stewart wrote, "You take strange liberty with me, you have refused to give me an acknowledgement under your hand, for a considerable sum of mony, I generously lent you, in your great misery, even when you was in want of the common necessarys of life, and linnen to cover you: and now sir when I make a demand of the bed, and table linnen shirts handkerchiefs etc, I have too long let you have the use of, you say you will not return them to me, but to my wife. What doe you mean sir by this insult. What is your business whither I have a wife, or not. ... I am sory and ashamed of having been made the Dupe of your forged storys, of your deputys from

Corsica etc, etc, etc, all fals without a shadow of truth; you have now opened my eyes, by artfully triking me out of one hundred and ninety two pounds. I shall ever think and speak of you with abhorrence and contempt, and think no misery can threaten you half so bad as you deserve. If you cannot guess who this comes from, ... I shall be glad of an oportunity of telling you in the plainest terms. I have been too too much, and am now the very reverse of, your humble servant."[113]

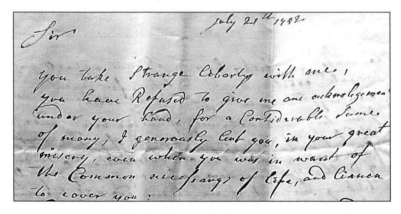

Part of the draft of Colonel Stewart's letter to "King Theodore"

In considering whether Lady Jane was capable of some of the misdeeds she was accused of, we cannot escape the issue of religion and what it meant to her and her husband. Nowadays, it is not easy, even as a modern Christian, to put oneself entirely in the shoes of people for whom the wages of sin were death, hell and damnation. If Lady Jane or the Colonel did what they were accused of, they must either have lived their lives terrified of the consequences to their eternal souls, or unbelievers. But their private correspondence is full of references to God and religion that suggest that their beliefs were genuine. In one letter to her husband, for example, Lady Jane wrote:

"...the paragraph of some of your late letters, and in this last one in particular, upon religious matters, absolutely charm me.

Go on, dear Mr. Steuart, fix your eyes, your hope, and trust above, and all worldly concerns will soon seem perfectly easy, nay, will in reality become so, for God never disappoints those that entirely depend on him, nor will he continue to afflict when we fly to him for succour, and place our whole happiness in his favour alone. Allow me to send you by the bearer a favourite book of mine, *Thomas à Kempis*. Read it, I beg you. In it you'll discover so much heavenly and even worldly wisdom, that it never fails to please both the spiritual and temporal mind, and to instruct both."[114]

The couple's surviving correspondence also supports the genuineness of the parental relationship with the twins. But there were plenty at the time, and later, who were prepared to believe that Lady Jane and the Colonel were engaged in laying down a smoke-screen of innocence, for use in future years if the birth was contested. Percy Fitzgerald puts this idea most strongly:

"...one might think that it would be always easy to prepare such documents in advances[sic] couched in the most affectionate terms, full of conjugal devotion and pious sentiments, and to adopt such a strain habitually and in every communication. To these appeal could be made at the proper moment, and it then might indignantly be asked, Was it at all possible that the writer of such documents *could* be guilty of what was charged? Of course this would be the *haute école* of artifice ..."[115]

This was one of a number of ways by which detractors of the Douglas case, at the time as well as in later years, turned indications of innocence on their head, but of course, without corroboration such claims were impossible to settle either way.

During the two years that Lady Jane and her husband lived in London with the twins, a pair of sisters began to attract the attention of the newspaper-reading public. One of these sisters was to play a major part in the battle for the Douglas inheritance.

Elizabeth and Maria Gunning were Irish girls of no fortune, who had set their minds on marrying titled husbands. So obvious was this ambition that two non-aristocratic suitors played a trick on them by introducing them to a pedlar and pretending that he was a lord. The girls plied him with tea and conversation until the pedlar, who was also Irish, took pity on them, revealed his true identity and proceeded to sell them silk stockings and handkerchiefs.[116]

"The surpassing loveliness of the Gunnings," said one writer, "has almost become a matter of history; nor perhaps is there any instance of mere beauty having excited so extraordinary a sensation as that produced by the appearance in the fashionable circles of London of these two portionless girls.'[117]

During the season in London, the girls were seen everywhere in town.

"I think their being two so handsome, and both such perfect figures, is their chief excellence," wrote Horace Walpole, "for singly I have seen much handsomer than either; however, they can't walk in the Park, or go to Vauxhall, but such mobs follow them that they are generally driven away. ...

They went the other day to see Hampton Court; as they were going into the Beauty-room*, another company arrived; the housekeeper said, 'This way, ladies; here are the Beauties.' The Gunnings flew into a passion and asked her what she meant; 'that they came to see the Palace, not to be showed as a sight themselves.'"[118]

So powerful were their charms that on visiting their brother at Westminster school they asked for, and got, a day's holiday for the scholars.[119]

At some time during their London appearances, Lady Jane Douglas met the Gunning sisters at the house of a friend, and she wrote to her husband about it:

---

* A room containing paintings known as the *Hampton Court Beauties*, portraits of 'the principal ladies attending upon her majesty, or those frequently in her retinue', which were commissioned by Mary II from Sir Godfrey Kneller (c1646-1723).

"They are excessively charming; no wonder they gain the admiration of every body that sees them; ... I do think they don't want a good share of sense; and I don't think they are much affected; I have seen many who have no title to half their charms much more so."

For some time the Earl of Coventry had been in love with the elder of the two sisters, Maria, and then, at the beginning of 1752, the 6th Duke of Hamilton – "hot, debauched, extravagant and equally damaged in his fortune and his person," according to Walpole – met Elizabeth Gunning, dressed modestly as a Quakeress at a masquerade, and fell in love with her. After seeing her on two more occasions, he was so impatient to marry that he summoned a priest one night to perform the ceremony immediately. According to Walpole, the priest refused to marry them without a ring. One was removed from the bed-curtain and they were married at half-past midnight.

"You'll see by the papers," wrote Lady Jane to the Colonel, "that Duke Hamilton is married to the youngest Miss Gunning, she's a charming pretty creature, and generally well spoke of."[120]

The Earl of Coventry was so moved by these events that he married Maria two days later.

"The Duchess was more delicate," wrote Walpole, "with the most beautiful hands and arms in the world, than her sister; but Lady Coventry was still handsomer, had infinite life and vivacity, the finest eyes in the world, nose and mouth, excepting that both had bad teeth."

The new Duchess of Hamilton was eighteen years old. Lady Mary Coke* later said of her that "She had never wished for anything that she had not had,"[121] and she had certainly achieved her most important ambition very early in life. Horace Bleackley, writing in 1907, long after she died, was fulsome, even clairvoyant, in his description of her:

---

* This prolific diarist will feature several times in this book. Her name is pronounced 'Cook'.

"A soft ivory pallor shone in her face, a flush of pink warmed her cheeks, there was a gleam of gold as the sunbeams touched her light brown hair. No less alluring was her character. Truth and loyalty, which were revealed in the grey-blue eyes, ruled all her actions. In the hour of peril, or during the long suspense of sorrow, her fine courage remained undaunted. Endowed with infinite sympathy she was never unmindful of the obligations of gratitude when kindness had been shown to her. Thus loyal, brave, compassionate, she possessed some of the most precious qualities of womanhood. Nor were there many blemishes is this sweet nature. Against her fair fame not a whisper had been breathed."[122]

Two months after their marriage, the Duke of Hamilton and his new Duchess travelled north to their Scottish castles. The stages on their journey were marked by jostling crowds eager to see the beautiful Duchess. In Yorkshire, seven hundred people stayed up all night outside the inn where the couple slept in the hope of seeing the Duchess in the morning; in Newcastle, greeted by an immense throng when she came to enter her carriage, the Duchess stood on the steps of the inn until the Duke came out with a shotgun and threatened to fire on the crowd if they didn't disperse.

Meanwhile, more whispers against the fair name of Lady Jane Douglas were breathed into the ear of her brother, the Duke. In May, Lady Jane received a letter from a friend in Scotland, Mrs. Carse, who passed on some disturbing gossip spread by the wife of Archibald Stuart, Stockbriggs' ally in the campaign against Lady Jane. Mrs. Stuart had apparently told someone that "that great and ancient house [of Douglas], the brag of the world, will be quite extinct. … How, says the person she talked to, has not Lady Jane two fine sons? Ha, says she, they'll never be owned by his grace; and all that's possible to be done against her and hers will soon be put in execution."

Duchess of Hamilton, the former Elizabeth Gunning

This may have been the first that Lady Jane heard of her brother's intention to disinherit her sons. It was the stimulus for a decision to leave London, with the Colonel languishing in jail, and go to Scotland with her boys, with the ultimate aim of regaining the affection of her brother and doing her best to counteract the malicious influence of Stockbriggs that threatened to blight her life and that of her children.

In August, 1752, she went by sea from London to Leith, the port of Edinburgh. For the next few months she mingled in Edinburgh society, catching up with old friends, and trying her best to quash rumours that the boys were not her children. One important fact became clear during her stay there. Although the whole reason for initial suspicions about the twins was Lady Jane's age and the unlikelihood of her still being capable of bearing children at forty-nine years old, the maids and laundresses at the places she visited saw regular evidence of the fact that she was still menstruating at the age of fifty-three.[123]

While in Edinburgh, she tried to visit the new Duchess of Hamilton but was not admitted. She described her attempt in a letter to the Colonel – still in prison but soon to be released – on 5th December, 1752:

"Upon the Duchess of Hamilton's coming to town, I went to pay her a visit, but was refused access, the Duke having wrote to my brother to demand of him, in case I offered a visit to the Dutchess, whether it would be agreeable to the Duke of Douglas, that it should be accepted or not: In answer to which, my brother wrote, that he by no means pretended to dictate or lay down rules to the Duke of Hamilton; but since he intended never to see his sister, he would take it well and kindly, if Hamilton did not see her. Upon which account my visit was not received."[124]

She went to see an old friend and adviser, William Loch, to ask him how best to approach her brother. Loch asked her about the exact circumstances of the birth of the children, and he wrote down what she told him, "that she was delivered in the house of Mad. Le Brun, Sanbourg St. Germain, Paris, the 10th of July 1748; that Mr. Pierre La Marre, a man-midwife, assisted her at the birth; Mad. Le Brun and her daughter were present, a widow lady who lodged in her house, and Mrs. Hewit."[125]

Lady Jane next had a conversation with Lord Prestongrange, a friend and lawyer, and asked him whether he felt she needed to get written evidence of the birth, from Pierre la Marre, the man-midwife, for example, who was still alive. Prestongrange told her that since she and her husband acknowledged the children as their own, there was no further proof necessary and that anyone who challenged the birth would have to prove that they were not Lady Jane's children.

In October, she had a meeting with Archibald Stuart, arch-spreader of rumours, at which no mention was made of any doubts about the children. But he had a motive for not angering Lady Jane – he had been given the task of getting her to hand over some papers she had which were securities for an inheritance from her father, thus putting them under the control of the Duke. At the same time, Stuart assured Lady Jane that he would use his best endeavours to get the Duke to restore to her a gift he had formerly offered of 30,000 marks, along with the £300 a year he had stopped while she was in France. 'Mr. Stuart accepted the papers, laughed in her face, and never came or sent to her afterwards,' says one writer.[126] And the gift and the annuity were never restored.

The Hamilton supporters also claimed that the Duke had received a mysterious letter from someone called Count Douglas, who appeared to be a distant relative of the family, living in France. This letter was said to have carried the news that Colonel Stewart and Lady Jane had bought their children for eight shillings from a hospital in Paris.

As far as Lady Jane's supporters were concerned, the whole 'Count Douglas' letter was a fraud. The original didn't exist and no 'Count Douglas' was ever found who admitted to writing it, but it is clear from the number of people to whom it was shown that there was a campaign to spread as widely as possible something that might pass for actual evidence to support the rumours.

It was clearly time for Lady Jane and her children to meet the Duke face to face and try to counteract the torrent of misinformation. With more flair than accuracy, we have an account of this visit to Douglas Castle from the anonymous biographer.

"With a trembling heart she approached the gate, and was admitted by the porter into the court yard. But as soon as he had informed Mr. White [Stockbriggs] that a lady and two children beg'd admittance, he suspected who the visitors were, and he instantly came to them himself and addressed Lady Jane respectfully, (for fallen as she was no one could do otherwise) but beg'd she would not desire to be admitted as he could not answer for the consequences. She assured him she had no fears, and such was her distress that she presented one of the most humiliating scenes that ever human greatness was reduced to. Lady Jane Douglas by birth, the first woman in the kingdom with her sons, herself the direct heiress of the noble house of Douglas, kneeling before the gates of her ancestors and with streaming eyes and uplifted hands, at the feet of this villain, soliciting admittance: to shock us still more, soliciting in vain. He however pretended he would go and try what could be done, but soon appeared at a window above, begging them to be gone, for that the Duke was going to fire at them with a blunderbuss. Tho' it appeared afterwards his Grace never heard they were there. This frightful sound terrified the maid who screamed and ran to the gate and she frightened the children, who flew, crying round their mother. It was over, she had nothing more to hope or fear, and she solicited no more. But resuming that dignity which better became her station, she took a boy in each hand and with the air of a Princess led them quite round the castle and then retired with them to a little inn in the neighbourhood."[127]

We also have an account from the other side of the castle gate, from William Greenshield, the Duke's butler:

"When Lady Jane came to Douglas castle with her two sons, she look'd in at the little gate as I was passing thro' the court; she called, and I went to her Ladyship, who told me she was come to wait of the Duke, with her children; that I proposed to open the gates, and carry in her Ladyship; but she said she would not go in till I acquainted his grace; that

I accordingly went to the Duke, and told him my message, at which he seemed a little surprised, and stood some time thoughtful, and then, without the least reflection against her, said, he had no room to put them in, and ask'd me where he could lodge them; I answered, there was room enough; but he desired me to call Stockbriggs to speak with him; and when Stockie came, the Duke and him conversed a little together by themselves; that Stockie left the Duke, came to me, and ordered me to tell Lady Jane she could get no access there; and after Lady Jane and the children went away, the Duke asked me if I had seen the children? I told his Grace that I had them both in my arms; that the eldest was black*, and the youngest, Sholto, was as like Lady Jane, as ever a child was like the mother."[128]

Greenshield also used to tell how on the day of Lady Jane's visit, Stockbriggs had locked him and the Duke in a room to prevent the Duke meeting his sister and her boys.[129]

When Lady Jane returned to the inn at Douglas, she sent for a Douglas lawyer, John Anderson, and told him of her distress at not being able to see her brother. She also told him that she had thought of going to Douglas Church the following morning, a Sunday, and sitting in the family pew, but Anderson warned her against this, saying that "the people of Douglas had not seen such a near relation of the Duke in the place for many years; and that considering how she stood with her brother, if she went to church, and became popular in the parish, it would irritate him more and more."[130]

She then sat down and wrote a letter to her brother which William Hamilton, the minister at Douglas, described as "the most moving letter that ever he had heard; and that all the tragedies that ever he had read, or saw acted, never moved him so much; and that it forced tears from his eyes." [131]

In this letter Lady Jane wrote:

---

* I.e. dark complexioned.

"I could not think of leaving this country without making an effort to see you once before I die, to vindicate the cruel, false aspersion that my enemies, wicked and designing people, have as unjustly, as cruelly spoke against me, and which, I am informed, have reached your ears, and that your Grace gives credit to them the thoughts of which pierces my heart, and gives me inexpressible anguish. What then must my sorrow be, and what an additional torment do I now feel when in your house, with my children, come to throw ourselves at your feet! We are debarred access to your presence! recall that cruel sentence, I beseech you, if you don't intend to render me all my life miserable, and to shorten it too, which must be the case; for it is impossible to live any time with a load of such exquisite grief as mine is; all I beg is to be permitted to speak but a few moments to your grace, and if I don't, to your own conviction clear up my injured innocence, inflict what punishment you please upon me, and shall think I deserve your utmost rigour, if I cannot justify myself fully of all that is basely and falsely laid to my charge."

Since this letter would have to go through Stockbriggs to get to the Duke, it is unlikely that Lady Jane's brother ever read her heartfelt appeal. "If the letter had contained proofs of her innocence as strong as Revelation," wrote one of the Douglas lawyers, "they would have been but so many more cogent reasons for not showing it him."[132]

It may seem dramatic licence to refer, as Lady Jane does several times in her letter, to an imminent death. Even with the shortened life expectancy of the 18th century, a disease-free woman of fifty-three would have no reason to think that she might soon die. But if it is possible to die of a broken heart, Lady Jane's 'exquisite load' was to be augmented so much in 1753 by a further burden, that her death in that year may well have been caused, partly at least, by her grief at the events that were now to unfold.

6

The Lady and the Duchess

Within a week or so of leaving Douglas Castle after her thwarted attempt to see her brother, Lady Jane decided to go back to London, leaving the two boys behind in Edinburgh. She presumably saw that there was nothing else she could do to change the Duke's attitude. There was also a complication with her pension from the King, which had only recently started to come through, and might be further delayed.[133]

Furthermore, there seems to have been a worry for some time in Lady Jane's mind that the Colonel was behaving like a loose cannon in London, slipping away from the rules of the King's Bench in order to set up some secret and hare-brained scheme to get money, possibly involving smuggling. She was also clearly irritated by the Colonel's propensity to do favours for some of his cronies when there was so little money to spare for themselves. In a tactful way she said in a letter to him that his good deeds proceeded from "the uncommon goodness and largeness of your own worthy heart which the people in our present trifling age are absolutely unacquainted with; and therefore I'll wave that subject, which is understood as little as *Arabick*." She went on: "Why should we talk of doing great and generous actions, when we're so little capacitated to relieve even ourselves, which we ought to look to in the first place? But don't let this way of arguing perswade you, that I despond; far from it: On the contrary, I expect our affairs will come out beyond even our hopes…"[134]

One reason Lady Jane did not want the Colonel to do anything that might breach the terms of his imprisonment was that there was talk of an amnesty soon that would free debtors from jail. "If my health and happiness is dear to you," she wrote, "let me see your tenderness to me, in taking every proper step that may intitle you to receive all the benefit of liberty must arise from that happy event; and let no dazzling, uncertain scheme allure your thoughts…"[135]

There is evidence at this time that Lady Jane was experiencing stomach pains, and being treated with purgings and medicines. But it didn't stop her setting out on the gruelling twelve-day trip to London by road. She left the two boys behind, because she planned the visit to be a short one. In fact, the stay in London was even shorter than intended. Among the passengers in the stage-coach to London was a friend of hers, Mary M'Crabbie, a milliner. This woman later described how when they arrived in London Lady Jane received a letter from Edinburgh saying that Sholto had acquired a fever on the day she left Edinburgh. Over the next few days, more letters arrived describing Sholto's worsening condition, culminating with the dreadful news of his death, on the 5th of May.

Mrs. M'Crabbie rushed off to see Lady Jane at her lodgings in London and was met at the door by Colonel Stewart and Mrs. Hewit, who told her not to mention the name of Sholto to Lady Jane. "Lady Jane had her clothes on," said Mrs. M'Crabbie, "but was lying above the bed and appeared to be in great distress." Lady Jane asked if Mrs. M'Crabbie had been told not to mention Sholto's name, and then said "Will you indulge me to speak of my son?"

"She cried out with great vehemency, 'Oh! Sholto, Sholto, my son Sholto'", said Mrs. M'Crabbie, "and then she thanked God that her son Archy was alive." Lady Jane apparently then said "What would the enemies of me and my children say if they saw me lying in the dust of death, upon account of the death of my son Sholto? Would they have any stronger proof of their being my children than my dying for them?" According to Mrs. M'Crabbie she then went on to declare "that these children Archy and Sholto were born of her body, and that there was one blessing which her enemies could not deprive her of, which was her innocency, and that she could pray to Almighty God for the life of her other son."[136]

On being told of Sholto's death, the Duke of Douglas apparently said that he wished both the brothers were dead, as he did not believe them to be his sister's children.[137]

Ironically, in the month that Sholto died, the one person who might in the future have confirmed the story of the twins' birth, the man-midwife called Pierre La Marre, also died, in France.

While Lady Jane was grieving for her son, the Duchess of Hamilton and her sister were both enjoying their new baby daughters, born five days apart earlier in the year. Horace Walpole described the domestic bliss of the Hamiltons round about this time:

"Duke Hamilton is the abstract of Scotch pride: he and the Duchess at their own house walk in to dinner before their company, sit together at the upper end of their own table, eat off the same plate, and drink to nobody beneath the rank of Earl – would not one wonder how they could get any body either above or below that rank to dine with them at all?"[138]

Shortly after the dual births, Walpole was lamenting the absence of news in London. "There is no war, no Politics, no parties, no madness, and no scandal," he wrote in a letter to a friend. "Even the era of the Gunnings is over: both sisters have lain in, and have scarce made one paragraph in the newspapers, though their names were grown so renowned, that in Ireland the beggarwomen bless you with 'the luck of the Gunnings attend you!'"[139]

Lady Jane, meanwhile, hurried back to Scotland, to be reunited with her surviving child. She managed to keep up her correspondence with the Colonel, in which she rebuked him for not writing to her, and received a reply which dwelt yet again on how penniless he was and asked her to rectify the situation, a problem which would surely have been pushed to third place for Lady Jane, who was having to deal with her recent bereavement and worsening health. Colonel Stewart explained that an expected source of funding had not materialised but that he was sure that, (Micawber-like), something would turn up soon.

"This sure prospect," he wrote to her, "with the recovery of D.L.J's ["Dear Lady Jane's"] precious health, makes me as happy as it is possible to be, entirely without money, which is my present case: so if my D.L.J. can fall on ways and means to send me a small supply, it would be very convenient; the more so, that I am afraid my friend where I have been in the country is very much drained of cash: A small matter will do, which I will be able in a few weeks to be able to replace with ease."[140]

He did at least, in a subsequent letter, get off the subject of money and offer some advice – bizarre though it was – that he thought might help improve Lady Jane's health. One of her doctors had told the Colonel that it was a shame that the winter weather prevented Lady Jane going riding, which might have improved her health.

"This … must be made up by some other kind of exercise within doors," he wrote, "… Have a deal board laid, the two ends on two chairs, and sit down on the middle of it, and with the smallest effort, you will have the advantage of the most easy trot of a horse, and the same motion as that of a trot, without fatigue or danger of taking cold." He added as a postscript, "N.B. The longer the deal board is that you sit on, the more play it will have, consequently the greater advantage will be found from the gentle exercise. Give some attention to this D.L.J. for I assure you it is almost as good as riding; so do it frequently, and the longer you continue the better. Archy will sit with you, and share of the ride. The greater distance the chairs are set from one another, the better it will be. Care is to be taken that the deal board be firm, so as not to break, which might give a dangerous fall."[141]

But by October when this letter was written, Lady Jane was fading fast, and beyond the benefits of a daily bounce on a long plank, although she tried to get a real ride in now and then. She wrote – but there is no evidence that it was sent – a final letter to her brother the Duke, in which she said: "I am become so ill, that I am now truly an object of compassion, a violent pain in my stomach, to nothing but skin and bone, and withal so weak and feeble that I am unable to walk up my own stair; so that each time I go out to ride, which my physician orders me to do frequently (and which I find some benefit by), I am obliged to be carried up stairs in a chair by two people. I'm still able to walk down, though with great pain and difficulty.

After this description of my melancholy situation, I flatter myself, dear brother, you won't refuse my ardent, earnest request of being permitted to come and pay you my last visit, which I shall only employ in giving you my blessing and best wishes, and to ask your pardon for what has appeared to you wrong in my conduct; and shall not, I do assure your Grace, trouble or take up your time with asking any favour, or making any request." [142]

She still tried to keep up with her religious observances, and had herself carried in a sedan chair up to the communion table at the nearby Church of Scotland. According to the writer of her biography, she did not have enough strength to raise the cup to her lips and so the minister had to hold it for her, "a sight so affecting that it threw the congregation into tears and they sobb'd aloud."[143]

On November 12th, Lady Jane wrote her will, in which she left to the five-year-old Archy: "my gold repeating-watch, with a steel-chain, seals, picture and a locket, a tweezer with blue stones set in silver, a silver tooth-pick-case, a ring with four small diamonds, a ring with two small pictures, a saphire ring with two small diamonds, a plain small gold ring, a small amethyst ring, three little snuff-boxes, a gold horn, two gold small medals, a amethyst buckle, two pair gold buttons, a dozen of silver forks, knives and spoons, and a dividing-spoon." She also left all her best clothes to Mrs. Hewit and her 'inferior' clothes to her servant, Isabel Walker.

Ten days later Lady Jane died. At least two physicians who had treated her in her final months said that she had died of a broken heart.[144] About four hours before she died she asked for Archy to be brought to her bedside. Laying her hand upon his head, she recommended him to God as her son. The biography describes the scene: "'Farewell my child,' said she, clasping him to her bosom, 'I have nothing to leave you, no friend to bequeath you to, all have forsaken thy hapless mother. But remember thou art a Douglas – glory in the name, let it give an edge to thy sword and that shall cut you out a fortune worthy of Douglas – live my child rich in honor and in fame.'"[145]

The heroine-worship of the writer leads him to a touching – if bathetic – description of Lady Jane's actual death:

"'Oh! Father of the Orphan' said she 'and shield of that innocence, that has none to save it accept this precious trust – to thee Oh! Omnipotence I leave him to thee.' She would have said more, by now the obstructing phlegm stopped the passage of her words, yet her eyes tho' sinking into eternal night were still fixed on him with a tender and steady look, till she let his little hand drop from hers with her last sigh..."[146]

In writing to a member of the Douglas family, the Colonel wrote: "The charming Lady Jane is no more! She left this world the 22d November for a better; her own nearest relations broke her dear heart, which occasioned her death. They have a great deal to answer for, for she possessed every good quality, without a mixture of any faults. Her dear son (which is all I now have of her, and is my only consolation) is, I thank God, in perfect health, and in all appearance will be worthy of her, for he has already discovered, on sundry occasions, sentiments worthy of a Douglas…"[147]

Lady Jane had left no money that could pay for a funeral so a lawyer was dispatched to her brother to ask for his help. At first the Duke refused to pay anything towards his sister's funeral expenses, but then he agreed grudgingly to cover the costs, provided it was done as frugally as possible. As the lawyer was leaving the Duke called him back, saying "Remember if either Lord Haining [one of the Duke's advisers] or Mr. Archibald Stuart suffer that boy [Archy] to be present at Lady Jane's burial, it will be the last thing they should do for me."[148]

Four days after her death, Lady Jane's body was buried in the Chapel Royal at Holyrood House in Edinburgh, next to her mother, the Marchioness of Douglas. A later description of the Chapel, written in 1831, says: "She was married in 1746 to Sir John Stewart of Grandtully, to whom she bore Sholto Thomas Stewart, who died in Edinburgh, 14th May 1753, in the 5th year of his age, and reposes by the side of his illustrious parent."

There is no mention of Archy, who, at the death of his mother was penniless and stranded, his feckless father still hatching money-making schemes from his prison in London. A family friend wrote to the Colonel that "Stewarty [Archy] is very well; some ladies here have been making some proposals to Mrs. Nelly [Hewit] about him." Poor Mrs. Hewit, devastated by the death of the woman with whom she had spent the largest part of her life, now saw Archy go into the care of Lady Schaw, a good friend of Lady Jane's but someone who was often heard to say that "she would never see Mrs. Hewit."

On 2nd October, 1754, the victory of Stockbriggs and his pro-Hamilton allies was complete, when the Hamilton family were made heirs to the Douglas estates, by a legal deed whose only witnesses were Stockbriggs, Archibald Stuart, and Stuart's son, a rising young lawyer for the Hamiltons called Andrew Stuart. This deed was followed by a flurry of other legal documents which made explicit the exclusion from any of the Duke's estates of Archy Douglas or any other issue of Lady Jane.

"This perfected the ruin of the defender [Archy Douglas]," wrote a lawyer for the Douglas side. "It became now indifferent to his interests in his uncle's estates whether he were the lawful son of Lady Jane... or bought out of an hospital, picked up in the streets of Paris, or furnished by the disorders of a nunnery; all which stories his enemies had given out."[149] But the lawyer went on to point out how odd it was that, having attacked him as an impostor, the Hamilton party named him as the lawful issue of Lady Jane in the documents that disinherited him.

In 1755, the Duchess of Hamilton gave birth to a son and heir, George-James. In the same year, James White of Stockbriggs died. Unfortunately, the animosity to Archy did not die with him. The Hamiltons, aided by the young lawyer, Andrew Stuart, had begun to take it for granted that they were the Duke's heirs, but they also saw the value of keeping alive the idea that Archy was an impostor, just in case the deeds were successfully challenged.

To counteract the persistent rumours, Lady Jane's friends started to gather evidence that would confirm the facts of her pregnancy and the birth of the boys. In 1756, Colonel Stewart, now released as a result of the King's amnesty to debtors, went to Edinburgh, and Lady Schaw asked a friend, Mrs. Napier, to try to get some facts about the events of July 1748 – dates, times, places, names – out of the disorganised colonel. He was apologetic, saying that "so many years had passed, and so many misfortunes had happened to him, that he could not be so distinct in names as he could wish." Mrs. Napier said that she couldn't understand how that could be, and Colonel John told her that for different reasons, he and Lady Jane "had been obliged to change houses often about the time of Lady Jane's lying in, particularly because one of the houses was full of buggs, and another smoaky, so that he could not say what precise house the children were born in." However, he offered to give the matter some thought over the next few days and write down what he could remember.

Two pieces of paper were produced at the later legal hearings which were said to be Colonel Stewart's summary of the events of 1748 and 1749 in response to Mrs. Napier's questions. These notes were to be scrutinised minutely by both sides when the issue came to court. The more detailed one read as follows:

> "From Aix-la-Chapelle
> To Liege
> To Sedan
> To Rhetelle
> To Rhyms, where wee feard a miscarriage;
> To Paris in the stage-coach.
> LJ brought to-bed of two boys
> July 10th, N.S. in Madame labrunes
> House faubourg St. Germain the
> 20th Removed from that buggy house
> to Madame Michels, house near
> the Pont St. Michell
> then went to Dammartin for
> fresh air where Ly Jean Recovered
> health and strength and so re-turned to Rheims
> in Champagne
> where Ly Jean had a mis-
> carriage and in about 14 months
> after Came to London

N.B. Lady Jean in her Paris expedition took no other designation than Madame Stewart from the poverty wee were in at that time."

Colonel Stewart also mentioned to Mrs. Napier that he had received letters over the years from Pierre La Marre, including descriptions of Sholto when he was under the midwife's supervision. Mrs. Napier suggested that it might be a good idea to produce these letters, and the Colonel said: "Alas, madam, I have been an unfortunate man, have been long in a prison, and all my things tossed about I do not know how or where; but I will seek out these letters and preserve them."

Mrs. Napier then wrote to friends in Paris for their help, sending them Colonel Stewart's scanty information, and received a reply in August, 1756, from the Principal of the Scots College in Paris, John Gordon:

"As to Mr. le Mar acoucheur, I can find no body who ever knew such a person, though I have inquired at several of that trade. I have found out Madame Michelle fauxbourg St Germain. She stays at the *hôtel d'Anjou rue Serpente*; but her information is in no wise satisfactory, not to say quite opposite to information. She says, that about the time you mention, in July 1748, Mr. et Madame Stewart logent chez elle; that Madame Stewart kept her bed on account of her being lately brought to bed, she believes somewhere nigh Versailles; that she had a nurse with her, who is not at present in Paris; but in case she returns, she will get what information she can from her. This is all I have been able to learn about this affair; which is no wise satisfactory. I have heard the nurse is about Madame de Pompadour; if so, I may chance to get some more information; if I do, you may depend I shall acquaint you."[150]

The sixth Duke of Hamilton

In January 1758 the Duchess of Hamilton became a widow at the early age of twenty-four. The Duke caught a chill while hunting at Great Tew in Oxfordshire, and died four days later, as a result, all commentators agree, of the delicate state of his physique because of his dissipated life. The three-year-old son became seventh Duke of Hamilton and when entering his teens was to be the plaintiff, or Pursuer, in Scots legal terminology, in the Douglas Cause. Until he reached the age of majority, his affairs would be supervised by Andrew Stuart and his father Archibald, who saw no conflict of interest in working for the Duke of Douglas and the Duke of Hamilton at the same time.

The only thing now that could stop the Hamiltons inheriting the Duke of Douglas's wealth would be if he married and had children. Stockbriggs and Stuart had advised the Duke strongly against marriage, saying it would be bad for his health. The Douglas lawyers later suggested that another reason for this recommendation was that any woman of honour marrying the Duke would be bound to inquire closely into how it had come about that the Duke's sister had died sick and penniless with her son disinherited, a matter which, at that stage, did not bear close inquiry since there was little or no evidence to support the allegations against Lady Jane.

For the first time, the Hamilton party were to find their advice to the Duke not to marry ignored by him. Against all expectations, the sixty-three year old Duke, considered irascible, mad, and uncouth, even by some of his friends, succumbed to an intensive wooing. The wooer was a distant relative, Margaret Mains of Douglas, known to her friends as Peggy, and sister of Lady Jane's friend, Mrs. Hepburn. When it was mentioned to her that the Duke was a madman, she said that when she pleased she could be as mad as he. Later events were to confirm this.

The story of how Peggy Mains became Duchess of Douglas is part of the folklore of the Douglas Cause. It was told by Alexander Carlyle, who knew her when he was a young clergyman and she was in her early thirties, more than ten years before she married the Duke. According to Carlyle, Peggy was a celebrated wit and beauty "even then in the wane", although her wit struck some people as coarse, even by the fairly basic standards of 18th century Scottish nobility.

Carlyle and a few friends, including Peggy, were having a day in the country when they met up with a friend of Peggy's, another clergyman, with greying hair. Peggy called him a "fusty old bachelor" and he replied "Margaret, you know that I am master of the parish register where your age is recorded, and that I know when you must be with justice called an old maid, in spite of your juvenile airs." "What care I, Tom?" she is alleged to have said, "for I have sworn to be Duchess of

Douglas, or never to mount a marriage-bed."[151]

An account of how she fulfilled this remarkable prediction is given in a document that turned up recently in the Douglas-Home family archives, which has the ring of truth about it, in the circumstantial detail it provides and in its source, which is said to be a diary kept by William Hamilton, the Minister of Douglas at the time.

With Stockbriggs now dead, the diarist writes: "the Duke saw more company, he discoursed calmly and freely, and was found by the generality of people, not to be that frightful and terrible person he was represented to be; for time and experience had softened his temper; and the person who stirred him up being dead, he became quite a different man."[152]

Peggy Mains had a nephew who had been advised to try to meet the Duke, as Chief of the Clan Douglas, in order to advance his career in the army. William Hamilton apparently told the Duke about this young man and added that he had "a bouncing, frolicsome, clever woman for his Aunty" and the Duke suggested that when the nephew visited him he should bring his 'aunty' along with him. Through some misunderstanding – or possibly deliberately – Peggy ended up visiting the Duke without either the nephew or Mr. Hamilton, and the Duke was "so much taken with her frank, easy behaviour, and the turn of her humour, that she became a powerful advocate for her nephew; she used great freedom, and told him among a number of other things, that his Grace seemed to want two things to complete his happiness, – a Duchess, and a young Marquis."[153]

The following day, the Duke sent some ducal silver to Peggy as a present and begged her to visit again. They seem to have competed with each other to accelerate the romance, perhaps because of their advanced ages for the time, and Hamilton's diary next reports that "She went and visited him a few days after that, and lodged in the Castle two nights, when no woman had been for upwards of 30 years, except servants." During this visit a proposal of marriage was made and accepted and the couple were married by Mr. Hamilton on February 28th, 1758.

There is a racy account of the events of the wedding day, in the memoirs of the 19th century antiquarian, Charles Kirkpatrick Sharpe. He describes how, on her way to Douglas Castle in a post chaise with the clergyman, they arrived at a stream in spate, and the coachman refused to go any further. Peggy apparently whipped out a pistol and held it to the driver's head, whereupon he drove on through the rushing stream, soaking her to the knees but getting her to the church on time.[154]

Peggy Mains' appearance on the scene as the Duchess of Douglas promised a change in the fortunes of the Douglas party, since she soon showed that she was a strong supporter of the claims of the ten-year-old Archy to be Lady Jane's son. Unfortunately, the strength and persistence of the Duchess in trying to counteract the years of poisoning of the Duke's mind against his sister soon marred the couple's marital bliss.

Rather like a mariner trying to turn a huge oil tanker, she worked away with little prods and pushes, to turn the Duke by 180 degrees and get him to acknowledge that Archy was Lady Jane's son, and his heir.

Again, like an oil tanker, the Duke for some time resisted the new Duchess's importunings, in spite of her ingenious efforts. In fact, he fought back, with ammunition supplied by a friend of Archibald Stuart's, called Major Thomas Cochrane.

A family friend, Thomas Hamilton, was with the Duke and Duchess of Douglas and four friends at Douglas Castle one day when the Duke took him aside and handed him a letter from Cochrane which he asked him to read out before the assembled company. The letter said that "there was lately a discovery made by Lady Stair: Lady Jane and her two spurious or fictitious children had gone to wait upon Lady Stair; that upon Lady Stair's seeing them, she says, Lady Jane, these will never pass upon the world as twins, the one being much older than the other. Upon which Lady Jane changed colours. Upon which Lady Stair went briskly up to the children, and by looking in their mouths, knew by their teeth that the one was six months older than the other." Cochrane finished by writing "My dearest Lord, I think it is my duty to acquaint you of every thing that may turn out to your advantage; and if ever you find me deviate from truth, may you ever thereafter look upon me as a damn'd villain."[155]

Duchess of Douglas, formerly Peggy Mains

On one occasion when the Duchess tried to persuade the Duke to do something for Lady Jane's son, he resisted at first but when the Duchess threatened to cut her throat with a pruning knife that lay on the table, the Duke reluctantly changed his mind. The following morning, the Duchess came to the Duke's bedroom, fell on her knees and told him that the night before Lady Jane had appeared to her in a dream and told her that the curse of God would fall upon the Duke if he failed to do right by her son, crying out, "Justice, justice, justice, to my innocent child!" The Duke asked whether she had ever met Lady Jane and when Peggy said no, he burst out laughing and asked how she knew it was her. A day or so later the Duchess threatened to throw herself out of a castle window.[156]

In December, 1758, nine months after the Duke and Duchess had married, Douglas Castle burnt down. Some saw a connection between this event and the Duchess's anger with the Duke; others connect it with her desire to move to Edinburgh. It could even have been an accident. The fire may have started in the Duchess's dressing room, but since it destroyed most of the Duchess's valuables – jewels, money and 'rich cloathes' – it is unlikely that she would think it worth paying that high a price to get her own way.

But Peggy continued to keep the pressure up. The most extraordinary scene, if we are to believe the reports of William Hamilton, took place in February, 1759.

The Duke of Douglas had decided to have a few friends to dinner, but the Duchess – presumably out of temper – declined to join the occasion. Halfway through the meal, the diners heard a noise in the next room and asked Hamilton to go and see what was causing it. He was reluctant to do so, probably aware of the kind of thing he might find, but everyone insisted and so he went next door "and found the Duchess lying on her belly on the floor." He remarked that this was not really a posture for a Duchess, but she wouldn't speak to him. Hamilton then tried with the help of one of the Duchess's female companions, Miss Stewart, to lift her and take her to bed, but the Duchess resisted and threw herself on her back. Hamilton "did not think it proper for him to stay any longer in the room with her" and went and told the Duke what was going on.

One of the guests, Lord Shewalton, suggested sending for a doctor, but Miss Stewart said that it was pointless since the Duchess "could not live five minutes."

In fact, the Duchess's life was in no danger and at the end of the meal, she sent Miss Stewart into the dining room to ask the assembled company to come and see her since she had something to say to them all.

"I am going to put a question to you," she said to Lord Shewalton, "and I charge you, as you shall answer to the great God, at the great day of judgement, that you shall answer me, without fear or favour, or respect of persons."

"Madam," said Lord Shewalton, somewhat put out, "That is a way of speaking I am not acquainted with; but pray what is the question?"

The Duchess then said, "My Lord Shewalton, suppose you had a sister that had disobliged you as much as Lady Jane Douglas ever disobliged the Duke, but this sister had a promising young boy for her son, would not you give your estate to this sister's son?"

"I am not obliged to tell to whom I would give my estate," Shewalton answered, "but although I should say that I would give my estate to my sister's son, that is not a rule to the Duke of Douglas; he has his settlements in his own breast, and may give his estate to whom he pleases."

This was clearly not the right answer and so the Duchess turned to Mr. Hamilton, perhaps thinking that a mere clergyman, and a hireling of hers and the Duke's to boot, would be more malleable than a peer of the realm.

But Hamilton said that he had no estate to dispose of, and added bravely that if he had one, he could not give her Grace a better answer than Lord Shewalton had done.

Stopped in her tracks, the Duchess didn't question the other three members of the party, who then left the room.

Lord Shewalton said to the Duchess: "Why in all the world do you tease and vex yourself and the Duke, by pressing him to take proper steps or measures to prove the legitimacy of the defender Mr. Douglas? For if the Duke should grant your desire, it would do the boy much more hurt than good; for it would make many suspect his legitimacy who had no suspicion of it before. The boy is Lady Jane's son, he is the Duke of Douglas's nephew, the law makes him so," he said, and added a phrase which was to be a key legal point in the Douglas case, "for he is habite and repute so."[157]

It was incidents like this that led the Duke to complain bitterly in front of all and sundry about the pressure he was under. One observer says that "in a rhapsody of passion, he threw out reflections all of a sudden against the Duchess, Mrs. Hepburn, (Colonel) Stewart, the Grandtullies, ... and the defender (Archy), damned them all, called (Colonel) John a spendthrift, the defender a spurious brat, and that the Duchess might thank herself for her good advices."[158]

Then, one night, while William Hamilton was in bed at the castle, he received a visit from the Duke who told him that if the Duchess did not stop going on at him about Lady Jane's son he would be obliged to part with her. The Duke said that "he found himself under the melancholy necessity of either living with the Duchess in perpetual torture or parting with her altogether, she having baffled and despised all counsel and advice both from her own and the Duke's friends and relations."

On March 6th, the Duke left the Duchess and decamped from the Abbey at Holyrood House in Edinburgh, where they had been living since Douglas Castle burnt down. He took with him the faithful Mr. Hamilton, to stay with his cousin, the Marquis of Lothian, at Newbattle. Devoid of shame, the Duchess, accompanied by her sister Mrs. Hepburn, followed the Duke and burst in on him while he was in the bedchamber of Lady Lothian who was unwell. As soon as the Duchess entered the room she rushed past several other relatives, flew up to the Duke, threw her arms around him, and kissed him. "My dear Lord," she cried, "why did not you tell me that you was going to Newbattle? Had you told me I would have gone with you."

The group left the Marchioness's bedchamber and went downstairs to the parlour where the Duchess again tried to smother the Duke in kisses. But he held his head away from her lips and said "Madam, I am heartily sorry you have come here this night. I desire you to make no more noise in this House but return immediately to the Abbey, for you and I shall never again lodge under one roof." He then went upstairs and locked himself in the Marquis's dressing-room, while downstairs in the parlour the Duchess pleaded with the Marquis to let her see her husband for a quarter of an hour's conversation "when all would be well." The Marquis told her that her husband didn't want to talk to her, at which she ran upstairs and clung to the door handle, pleading to be let in. Finally, the Marquis ordered his servants to wrest her away from the door and carry her downstairs. She swore that she would die there, hanging from the doorknob, but once her hand was freed she composed herself and walked downstairs to the courtyard. Here, she pretended to faint but soon got up and walked to her carriage, asking only for a drink of water.[159]

The following day, the Duke wrote an official letter of separation to the Duchess with copies to three other Dukes, and their marriage was, to all intents and purposes, over.

7

Two Reconciliations

While the Duke of Douglas's brief marriage was falling apart, the beautiful Duchess of Hamilton was getting her life together, with new suitors to replace her late dissipated husband. She was wooed by the Duke of Bridgewater, and her rejection of him is said to have driven him entirely from the world of fashionable society to take up canal-building as a distraction for his broken heart, thus transforming freight transport in Britain for the next half-century.[160]

In February, 1759, the Duchess married Jack Campbell, a mere colonel at the time, but son of the heir to the dukedom of Argyll.

"It is a match that would not disgrace Arcadia," wrote Horace Walpole, "Her beauty has made sufficient noise, and in some people's eyes is even improved – he has a most pleasing countenance, person, and manner, and if they could but carry to Scotland some of our sultry English weather, they might restore the ancient pastoral life, when fair Kings and queens reigned at once over their subjects and their sheep."[161]

Colonel Stewart, meanwhile, freed from the light constraints of the King's Bench, was in the Isle of Man, still as hard-up as ever and drumming up support for some money-making scheme or other. But he found time to write a letter of condolence to the Duchess of Douglas, suspecting that her support for his son's claims had led to the break up with the Duke.

"It gives great concern to every one that has a heart," he wrote of the separation, "but must be infinitely more afflicting to me, as there is too much reason for my fearing that the generous warm interest your Grace was pleased to express in regard to justice, and my Lady Jean Douglas, ... may in great measure have given a handle to your Grace's enemies to bring about this deplorable misunderstanding, which, I am hopeful, will soon be brought to rights when my Lord Duke comes to think coolly on the step he has been hurried into, by designing false friends about him."

Stewart appears to have heard a version of the door handle-grasping scenes at Newbattle but perhaps not in their full horror:

"My Lady Duchess, the inhumane, barbarous treatment at New battle, though very hard to bear at the time, will, I am convinced, when the Duke comes to the knowledge of it, be the first step to show the monsters, who were capable of ordering and acting in that shocking scene, in their proper colours, and inflame his generous breast with proper resentment; as a lady is ever deemed under protection of her husband, an indignity offered to your Grace is directly done to his Grace."[162]

It was in this same year that a long-awaited event occurred to change the fortunes of Colonel John Stewart. His brother, Sir George Stewart of Grandtully, died, passing on to the Colonel his title and £1,000 a year, a considerable fortune in those days, particularly for a man who had been known to live for a week on a dish of 'grey pease'.

Archy, meanwhile, had been cared for by Lady Schaw at her house in the country, after his mother's death. In a letter to the Colonel, Lady Schaw generously relieved him of any financial responsibility for his son's care and says: "He was extremely cast down for the loss of his dear mother. ... It was mere providence that sent me to this place of the country when my Lady left this world for a better one, which gave me the opportunity to hear of the destitute condition her poor infant was in, whom I brought home, and [it] is my intention to use him as my own child so long as I live; but as I am old, that probably will not be many years. I wish your affairs may be settled, so as to take care of your child at my death; till then, neither I nor none of mine have any demands upon you nor none of yours; and I think myself happy to have it in my power to say that it gives me the greatest satisfaction to show any part of the regard and honour I had for the dear deceased."[163]

Lady Schaw did die shortly afterwards and Archy was cared for by her grandson, Lord Cathcart, who sent him to Rugby to begin an education for the army.

At Newbattle, where he was staying, the Duke of Douglas in spite of everything was beginning to miss his turbulent Duchess. He sent his butler, William Greenshield, several times to see how the Duchess was getting on, and one night had a dream that she was dead, and awoke, crying.[164]

He began to think he might have misjudged her. In the settlement that accompanied the judicial separation, she had accepted much less than she might have been entitled to, and the Duke thought that perhaps she was equally disinterested in her support of Archy's claims. Gradually, pieces of evidence that had seemed to confirm the spuriousness of Archy's birth lost their credibility. In April, 1759, Lady Stair stormed into the Duke's presence. She had just heard about the Cochrane letter claiming that she had doubts about the genuineness of Lady Jane's claims, and she denied every word of it. She said that she had lived to a good old age, and never till now had got entangled in any scandal. Remembering how Cochrane had ended his letter – "if ever you find me deviate from truth, may you ever thereafter look upon me as a damn'd villain" –

she stamped the floor with her staff and called Cochrane "a damned villain" three times, which was strong language for an aristocratic lady in those days, when the word 'damned' was usually printed as d----d.

From this time on, the Duke seems to have mellowed in his attitude to his late sister. "The more he reflected upon the story of Lady Jane, the more reason he saw to believe in it," says the official statement of the Douglas case, "and consequently to observe the reasonableness of such solicitations. He felt remorse too late for his treatment of Lady Jane. It was not too late to repent of his behaviour to the Duchess. Being no longer pestered, as he calls it, he came to himself and sought a reconciliation."[165]

On August 4th, 1759, the Duke settled £1000 a year on the Duchess and they were reconciled. They then turned their minds to the matter of where to live, and planned a new house to replace the castle that burnt down. They knew of a large castle being built for the Duke of Argyll at Inverary under the supervision of the architect John Adam, and the Duke of Douglas insisted that his new castle should be ten feet larger in each dimension than the Argyll pile, which, incidentally, the Duchess of Hamilton would find herself mistress of in ten years time.

A visitor to the Duke at the time, Lord Shelburne, calls him "the last of the feudal lords", and describes being met at the top of the stairs at Holyrood by the Duke wearing his hat and sword and accompanied by his resident historian and poet, John Home, to whom all questions about the history of the Douglas family were referred for an answer. Home's interest in Douglas history had led to him writing a play called *Douglas,* which was first put on in Edinburgh in December 1756, provoking the memorable cry of Scottish pride from a member of the audience: "Whaur's your Wullie Shakespeare noo?" David Garrick, however, called *Douglas* "totally unfit for the stage", although it was eventually put on at Covent Garden in London.

"I told (the Duke) that I had seen a new house he was building in the Highlands," Shelburne said, "He said he heard that the Earl of Northumberland was building a house in the north of England, the kitchen of which was as large as his whole house, upon which the Duchess, an enterprising woman, observed that if the Douglases were to meet the Percys once more in the field*, then would the question be, whose kitchen was the largest? Upon this the Duke nodded to Mr. Home to state some of the great battles in which the Douglas family had distinguished themselves. I told him that I hoped to wait upon him in London. He said he feared not, he was not sufficiently informed to carry any weight there; he could neither read nor write without great difficulty. I told him that many of the greatest men in the history of both kingdoms could do neither, to which he assented."[166]

The seriousness of the Duke's change of heart came when he sent for documents he had signed in 1754 and 1757 making the Hamiltons his heirs, with the intention of revoking them. The events that followed, reported in barely concealed rage in the official Douglas case, show how the supporters of the Hamilton claims were fighting a rear-guard action.

When the Duke called for the will, his lawyer, a man called Andrew Chalmer who was presumably under the thumb of Archibald and Andrew Stuart, refused to deliver them or even to visit the Duke, sending him "two such Letters as never passed before from a Servant to a Master." In these letters, Chalmer explains that there is not time to send them at the moment because he has to go on a journey prescribed by his physician as necessary for his health. He adds that, in any case, he won't send the originals, in case the Duke decides to destroy them, but he condescends to send copies.

"If it be impossible that any Servant should write thus to

---

* The Scots Douglases and the English Percys, the Duke of Northumberland's family name, had been traditional enemies for generations.

his Master," the Douglas case says, "without being corrupted to betray and insult him, it will afford another Proof of the Arts whereby the Duke was incensed; and of the real Opinion those had of Mr. Douglas's Birth, who resorted to such means of supplanting him."

The Duke finally got hold of the originals and "with his own hand" cut off the signatures, thus revoking the will that had made the Hamiltons his heirs. In 1761, the Duke of Douglas wrote a new will, leaving his whole estate first to any "heirs of his body" – which seemed unlikely in spite of his reconciliation with the Duchess – then to "the heirs whomsoever of the body of his father, James, Marquis of Douglas," – which would have included his sister's children – and only failing that, to the Duke of Hamilton and his descendants. At the same time, by another deed, the Duke appointed the Duchess, the Duke of Queensberry and others as tutors and guardians to Archy, and declared that he believed that Archy was indeed the son of Lady Jane and therefore his successor in the estates of Douglas. (Because a Dukedom is only inherited by a Duke's son, Archy would not get the title.)

For more than fifteen years, the Duke had harboured the bitterest feelings for his sister, having previously been as close to her as any two siblings can be. Now, in his late sixties and in failing health, he realised the injustice he had done her, and spoke of his remorse to anyone who would listen.

William Greenshield, the butler, said that he heard the Duke "reflect grievously on himself for the bad treatment he had given to his sister Lady Jane, and prayed to God that he might be forgiven for it, and that the persons who had been the cruel instruments might be forgiven."[167]

The Duchess of Douglas's sister, Mrs. Hepburn, said the Duke had told her about being shown a memoir Lady Jane had written of her early life and that "he would sleep none all night, as the account of his sister's distress had affected him so much. He added that he saw from her memoir that she had certainly been the most injured woman in the world. He said that all that Lady Jane had suffered in her life did not affect him so much as what she suffered at her death. He pressed his breast with his hand and said that his sister had not only been neglected before her death, but after it. The Duke at that time appeared to be much affected, and even shed tears, expressing his regret for the neglect that he himself had shown to Lady Jane."[168]

On another occasion, as his last illness was taking hold, he told Mrs. Hepburn that he "prayed that God might forgive him for what he had done to her, and that God might forgive (Thomas Cochrane) and Mr. Archibald Stuart, for that they and Stockbrigs were the cause of his neglecting his sister. He also said that if he had done injustice to her, he had done ample justice to her son, for that he had given him his whole estate."[169]

The Duke of Douglas died on 21st July, 1761. His funeral was one of the grandest the country had seen for a long time. One witness was a talented footman called John Macdonald who later describes the scene in his memoirs:

"When (my masters) arrived in Edinburgh they had a mind to go immediately to the country," he wrote. "But the Duke of Douglas died, which stopped them for some time, to get all things ready for the grandest burying that had been in Great Britain for a hundred years past. The procession took two days in going from Edinburgh to Douglas Castle. On this occasion there was the greatest feasting and drinking I ever saw. There were about three hundred persons, in carriages and on horseback, and all the family honours."[170]

Among the mourners was Archibald Douglas Stewart, taken out of school to assume pride of place in the funeral procession. Even at the unripe age of thirteen, Archy must have been aware that in spite of the Duke's recent change of heart there might be obstacles in the way of inheriting his uncle's estates. The lawyers were massing. Within an hour of the Duke's death, Andrew Stuart, for the Hamiltons, was in the death chamber along with lawyers for Douglas. Two days later, the lawyers returned and were joined by Colonel Stewart, now Sir John, to open the Duke's archives and begin the first of many legal steps to secure the inheritance.

There were in those days procedures that applied in Scotland when titles or large estates were involved that required proof of the relationship between parent and child. The inheritance had to be ratified by a jury in a process known as a Service. This fairly routine process assembled witnesses and documents to testify to the fact that the person claiming to inherit was truly the son of his parent.

In England, there was no need for such a procedure. A child could be put in possession of an inherited estate as 'habite and repute.' This phrase meant that he had been accepted since infancy by his parents as their child, and that no one who knew the family had seriously questioned the circumstances of his birth. (It could be used about other types of social standing as well – someone could be 'habite and repute' a thief.)

The phrase came up time and again in the Douglas Cause, since it was clear that, both in France and after Lady Jane and her husband returned to Britain with the children, all their close friends and relatives accepted that Archy and Sholto really were her children, 'born of her body'. This judgement was based partly on what Lady Jane and the colonel said at the time and partly on how they behaved towards the children, in every way like doting parents.

Indeed, 'habite and repute' had been the basis of the advice of Lord Prestongrange to Lady Jane when she had consulted him about what to do in the light of the swirling rumours. He knew that the children were generally acknowledged as hers in Scottish society and therefore that would be sufficient, as he thought, to establish any claim.

There is little doubt that, by any ordinary standards, the twins were 'habite and repute' the children of Colonel Stewart and Lady Jane. There is a story of a friend of Lady Jane's,

Lady Lovat, who saw a child at a window in Edinburgh and said to a friend: "If I thought Lady Jane Douglas could be in Edinburgh, I would say that was her child -- he is so like her!" In fact, when she returned home, she found a note from Lady Jane saying that she had just arrived and taken lodgings, in the house where Lady Lovat saw the child. [171]

An indication of how Lady Jane and her children were perceived by Edinburgh society is given in a letter from Lady Jane to Colonel Stewart, written after she attended a birthday celebration for George II in December, 1752, when the children were about four years old.

"Archy and Sholto behaved to a wonder, and were caressed beyond measure. I thought the people would have eat them up; and very many that I did not know complimented me upon their account, and upon my being returned to my own country."[172]

But whatever the uses of habite and repute in England, the formal process of a Service was essential in Scotland before Archy could inherit. This meant that witnesses and documents should be presented that confirmed the facts of Archy's birth. At a hearing at the Court of Session in Edinburgh in September, 1761, the lawyers for Archibald Douglas assembled proof of Lady Jane's pregnancy, including a witness statement by Mrs. Hewit that she had been present at the delivery of the twins and had "received them both into her lap"; a witness statement by Isabel Walker, Lady Jane's maid, saying that "Lady Jane was naturally flat-breasted, and very thin, but, when with child, her breasts rose to a great size"; and evidence of habite and repute.

As part of the preparation for the Service, a trunk of Lady Jane's was opened and inspected by lawyers for both families, and twenty-seven letters selected as backing the claim. Among these were four letters from Pierre La Marre to Colonel Stewart which were to play an important part in the later steps to challenge Archy's claim.

After the evidence was presented to the court, the officials asked three times whether anyone wanted to raise an objection to the claims of Archibald Douglas being granted, and when neither the Duke of Hamilton nor any other of the Duke's relatives made any objection, Archy was pronounced his uncle's heir, or to put it more accurately, he was "on a brieve mortancestry served nearest and lawful heir of tailzie and provision in general to the said deceased Archibald, Duke of Douglas, his uncle in virtue of the disposition and tailzie of the dukedom of Douglas and others."

Within a few days of Archy being granted the inheritance, his father married again, nine years after Lady Jane's death. Sir John's new wife was the Honourable Helen Murray, daughter of Lord Elibank, and one of her brothers wrote in great excitement – and somewhat unflatteringly – to another:

"I presume You have not heard of Madam Nelly being married to the Famous Sir John Stuart known by the name of Collonel Stuart who married Lady Jane Douglass and begot two boys on her in her 51 year, one of which is heir to the Duke of Douglass, his birth was proved clear they pretend, tho' both father and mother were remarkable fair his twin is black, yellow skin'd like a savoyard. Sir John Stuart of Gairtilly [sic] our brother is 75, deaf, blind of an eye and his estate is sequesterated for his debts which are about six thousand pounds, he has another son and many Grand children..."[173]

At the time of the Duke of Douglas's death, the seventh Duke of Hamilton was six years old, so he was under the supervision of guardians who had been appointed to look after his affairs until he came of age. As the guardians read for the first time the details of the evidence that had been offered at the Service in support of Archy Douglas's claim, they began to think that there might be a way to challenge the inheritance, so that it came to the next heir, the Duke of Hamilton. But to challenge or 'reduce' the Service the Hamilton side would have to prove that the evidence offered in support of Archy's claim was false.

This would require someone to take on the considerable task of investigating the alleged circumstances of the birth, and proving them false. Who should that be?

One of the guardians, Andrew Stuart, described the thinking among the Duke's advisers at the time:

"The point of greatest difficulty, as it appeared to these guardians, was, to find out a person proper to be trusted with a commission of such importance: One, whose proceedings and report might give to the world, and to the guardians themselves, a reliance on the result of his inquiries, whose situation and character might remove all suspicion of any thing improper, who would be equally responsible with themselves, for every step of his conduct, and who could embark (on behalf of) the guardians on no measure of which he must not share the dangers and difficulties, as much at least as themselves."[174]

But where could they find such a paragon – "a person proper to be trusted with a commission of such importance"? Step forward – Andrew Stuart.

Andrew Stuart, lawyer for the Hamilton family

There is no one in this story who comes over with a greater sense of his own importance than Stuart. This may be an unjust characterisation. It is possible that in a tavern with his friends, late at night and away from public view, he was the most charming, humble, and modest of companions. Possible, but unlikely. From what he wrote and from his public behaviour, he was pompous, self-important, obsequious to nobility and increasingly obsessed with getting the better of Archibald Douglas and his guardians.

In 1761, Andrew Stuart was a 37-year-old lawyer. His father, Archibald Stuart was the man who had conspired with Stockbriggs to turn the Duke against his sister, while being paid as a lawyer to the Hamilton family as well as the Duke of Douglas. There is no doubt, from the occasions on which he helped his father, that Andrew Stuart believed Lady Jane to be a scheming liar, even before he read any of the details of the birth story. Now, with witness statements, dates, addresses, letters and other documents to go on, there was something to get his teeth into.

In describing the Hamilton guardians' objectives, Stuart took pains to suggest that it was purely in the interests of truth that he embarked on what turned out to be a Sisyphean task. "It was their duty to establish the facts about the birth, even if the researches showed the truth of the confinement."[175]

"...At last, after due deliberation," Stuart wrote, "the request of the other guardians, supported and enforced by that of the person then at the head of the family, as mother of the young Duke of Hamilton, made the hard lot of undertaking this task fall upon me alone. ... The matter was brought to such a point, that it became impossible for me to decline this task, without incurring the imputation of too little concern for the interests of the Duke of Hamilton's family; ... and without at the same time incurring the further imputation of too much selfish attention, if I suffered myself to be deterred by any apprehension of the difficulties or hazards, which might possibly attend this undertaking."[176]

In August, 1762, Andrew Stuart set sail for France. "It was my first excursion beyond the limits of this island," he later wrote "... and undertaken by one who at that time had not a single acquaintance at Paris, – who carried out with him no letters of recommendation to any person that could assist him, – who was then possessed of very little knowledge or experience of the French language for conversation – and who did not carry along with him from Britain any person to assist him in this business."[177]

In the light of these drawbacks, and the fact that Stuart was setting out to investigate events that took place fourteen years beforehand, it is astonishing what he, and the lawyers who eventually joined him, claimed to discover.

8

To Paris

I n the epic struggle that was about to begin, although the lawyers were the most visible and audible representatives of each side, it was the two duchesses, of Hamilton and Douglas, who were the real protagonists.

There was no love lost between them, although the Duke of Douglas had rather a soft spot for the former Miss Gunning. A newspaper report in 1752 said that he presented her with a draft for £10,000 when she married the Duke of Hamilton. However, once Peggy had seized the reins of the Douglas Cause, she saw the Duchess of Hamilton as her enemy. But the social niceties had to be observed, and there was a day in 1762, as the Hamiltons were beginning to think seriously about challenging Archy's inheritance, when Peggy paid a call on Elizabeth. She found her lolling on a settee, and when Peggy tried to start a conversation, the former Duchess of Hamilton, now Argyll, drummed her foot on the floor, perhaps as an indication of boredom. At last, the Duchess of Douglas had had enough.

"I looked her in the face," said Peggy, "and thought to myself – Ay! play awa' with that bonny fit! Play awa' and show

your leg and what a bonny ankle ye hae! Gif my Duke were
alive it micht cast dust in his e'en, but troth! I am a woman like
yourself, and I'll gar ye rue your wagging your fute at me!"[178]
(This is believed to mean: "Play away with that attractive foot!
Play away and show your leg and what a pretty ankle you
have! If my Duke were alive it might throw dust in his eyes
but, upon my word, I'm a woman like yourself, and I'll cause
you to regret wagging your foot at me.")

Emotions ran as high among the lawyers as they did
between their employers.   One of the Douglas lawyers
wrote: "It demanded strong Proof to maintain that a Woman
of remarkable Delicacy and Honour, highly born, religiously
educated, and possessed of the general Esteem, should plunge
at once into a Scene of Falsehood, Baseness, Guilt, and Shame;
to spend the whole Residue of her Life in the hourly Practice
of hateful Dissimulation: Nature, Conscience, Pride, every
just and every noble Sentiment, of which Nobody had more,
constantly revolting."[179]

To find this "strong Proof" was the task Andrew Stuart
had set himself. At the beginning, his investigations were not
carried out as part of any formal legal process. As far as the
Hamilton camp was concerned, this was just an attempt to
decide whether they had a case or not and so there was no
obligation to tell the Douglas lawyers what was being done.
But Stuart's trip to France was seen by the Douglas camp as
the first step in a systematic campaign to exclude them from
the investigative process until the Hamilton side had had a
chance to find and interrogate possible witnesses.

And Stuart didn't have much to go on. "The only lights
which I carried with me to France," he wrote, "for assisting
me in the whole of the investigations relative to the Delivery,
were the date of the event, and the names of Pier La Marre
and Madame Le Brun."[180]

Clearly, finding the man-midwife and the woman in whose
house Lady Jane had been brought to bed would confirm the

Douglas case and knock on the head any Hamilton claim. But Stuart and the other guardians believed that these people were fictitious, something which was much more difficult to prove. At what point in his searches for them would he be able to say "we have looked and found no evidence, therefore they do not exist"?

In fact, there was a surprising amount of detail available in official records about people who were in Paris fourteen years before 1762. France under Louis XV was a police state, with a formidable system for monitoring the comings and goings of different categories of suspicious people, including foreigners, by regular inspections of capitation books which listed – or were meant to list – every house owner or resident in Paris.

In charge of this process was Antoine de Sartine, Louis XV's lieutenant of police, with the status and power of a minister, directly consulted by the king on matters of state security, and in charge of the vast regiment of regular police, spies and informers. His interests were wide, from receiving regular reports on the activities of the Marquis de Sade, to monitoring the publication of the *Encyclopédie* of Diderot (and secretly protecting it from those who wished to suppress it as injurious both to religion and to royal authority.)

So when Andrew Stuart turned up friendless in Paris he went straight to the top, to Sartine, and told him and his assistants a story of a Scottish woman who had pretended to give birth to twins in order to inherit the fortune of a nobleman, her brother. Since this deception – if it had occurred – would have been a capital crime in France, the police were happy to help. It must also have been apparent that such a crime, centreing on what was called a supposititious child, would have involved the acquiring of someone else's baby, possibly by criminal means.

"M. de Sartine had the goodness to interest himself very actively in an investigation which was so important for justice and truth," Stuart wrote, "and once he had been presented with a report on this subject he put matters into the hands of one of his principal police officers, ordering him to give all possible attention to this affair and to cooperate with Mr. Stuart in taking all the steps necessary to uncover the truth."[181] (Stuart sometimes wrote about himself in the third person.)

Sartine designated a certain M. Buhot to help Stuart in his quest. Buhot was Inspector of Police for the faubourg St. Germain, where Col Stewart and Lady Jane stayed in July, 1748, and where the birth had been alleged to take place. He was a senior figure in the Paris police and a former major in the French army. There were twelve inspectors of police to cover the whole of Paris, and each area generated revenue for the office-holder. In Buhot's case, the revenue was £300 to £400 a year and it was his for life. He could also sell it, and pass it on to his heirs.[182]

For two months, while Stuart was staying in comfort in the Hotel de Tours, the second most expensive hotel in Paris, he and Buhot scoured the books kept by hotels, boarding houses and landlords for evidence of Mme Le Brun, in whose house the birth was claimed to have occurred. They found many people called Le Brun but none of them fitted even the few scraps of information about her that had been given in the Service. They also looked in official registers of medical men for any sign of a man-midwife called Pierre La Marre, again without success.

But then M. Buhot, through his own physician, M. Gilles, found one M. Pierre Michel Menager. Both Gilles and Menager claimed to have been familiar for twelve years with a surgeon and midwife called Louis Pierre La Marre, who had died about ten years previously. Menager told Stuart that La Marre had described "bringing to bed a lady of distinction" and looking after her sickly child, and that, if the child survived it would be worth a great deal to him. Menager also said that this delivery had happened seventeen or eighteen years ago, i.e. about 1745. In describing this meeting with

Menager and Gilles, Stuart says that he deliberately didn't give any details of Lady Jane's delivery, wishing to see if they might come up spontaneously with something that showed that the delivery they spoke about was really Lady Jane's. Stuart said later that they came up with nothing specific. He also said that he didn't reveal whether he was for or against the delivery in question, and that as he slipped more descriptive details into the conversation, Menager 'remembered' that Pierre La Marre's story had indeed fitted that description. Stuart also brought out copies of the letters said to have been written by La Marre to Colonel Stewart, letters which, as we will see, were written in atrocious French and with bad spelling, and Menager said that Pierre La Marre was "a remarkable bad writer and speller."

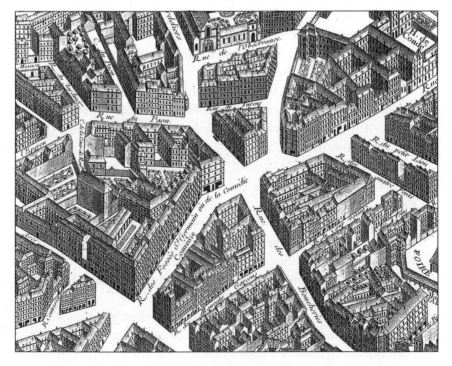

The area of Paris scoured for Mme. Le Brun's house

Stuart says that he asked Menager if he knew of a Mme. Le Brun who assisted his friend and he said he did not. Stuart therefore did not place much credence on Menager's story, and decided that, for the time being, he would ignore it. He later said that this conversation convinced him that "this was an absurd, strange, rattle-headed being."[183]

(Clearly, if Stuart had been acting for the Douglas side, such an intriguing story as Menager's would have been vigorously pursued, as the first mention of a key figure in the Douglas story. Stuart, however, obviously wouldn't want to find a Pierre La Marre who could be placed firmly between Lady Jane's legs on July 10th 1748.)

In October, to counteract the worrying possibility that the midwife actually existed, there was better news, as Stewart related to a French legal colleague: "We happily discovered how Colonel Stewart and his wife had put people off the scent. At the time of the alleged confinement they were actually in very good health and staying in Paris in a secluded quarter and, under borrowed names, lodged with a woman whose name had no resemblance at all to Le Brun. The house where they stayed was discovered only a short time ago, and happily the landlord and his wife who kept the hotel in 1748 are still alive and remember the circumstances that led to the dénouement of this affair."[184]

This was actually the hôtel d'Anjou, discovered by the Principal of the Scots College in Paris, John Gordon, in 1756, after Mrs. Napier had followed up Colonel Stewart's handwritten notes. These had said that he and Lady Jane had arrived there some ten days after the birth, when he wrote "20th Removed from that buggy house to Madame Michels, house near the Pont St. Michell."

Now, Stuart and his police colleague thought they had caught Sir John out. They had visited M. and Mme. Michel at their hotel and asked for their guest register for 1748, fourteen years before. By a miracle of bookkeeping the book was produced. Turning to the month of July, 1748, Stuart found the following entry:

M. Fleuralt Ecossois, et sa famille, entré huit Juillet 1748, i.e. "Mr. Fleuralt, Scotsman and his family, entered the eighth of July 1748." This was two days before the alleged date of the birth, when Colonel Stewart and Lady Jane claimed to be at Mme. Le Brun's. Asked if they remembered this Scotsman and his family, the Michels said that indeed they did, very well, "as if they were standing in front of them at this very moment." They described them as a man and two women, with one woman being the wife of the man and the other her companion, and said that the companion didn't speak French at all, but the gentleman spoke it very well and his wife passably. The man was about sixty, the wife was slim and pale, and the companion large and strong. They couldn't remember the names but said that it could be found in the register, where "it seems to me," said M. Michel, "the man wrote himself what you see there. As for the date you can be sure that it is accurate, because it was written within a day or two of their arrival, and even if the gentleman wrote it two or three days later he would have to put the correct date because our books are often inspected by the police."

Stuart then asked how long the 'Fleuralts' had stayed at the hôtel d'Anjou and was told five or six weeks. "And was it in your hotel that the woman gave birth?" Stuart said. "Certainly not," replied Mme. Michel, "she had given birth some time before she came here. Because I remember very well that a few days after they came here they said they had to make a short trip to a village near Versailles to collect a child they had left there, and they came back from the trip the following day or so, bringing with them a child."[185]

With what must have been growing excitement, Andrew Stuart turned to the book and inspected the entry closely. Sure enough, Stuart said, it was in a handwriting he was beginning to recognise, the handwriting of Colonel Stewart.

To preserve this valuable piece of evidence, the book was deposited with the Paris police, where it was examined by the police commissioner for the area, M. Duruisseau, who said that the writing appeared to be different from other writing on the page, that it was well-formed and that the official marks of the local police inspector before and after the entry suggested that the date was correct.[186]

Stuart must have been very pleased to have solved the case within weeks of arriving in France. He now had proof that Colonel Stewart, Lady Jane and Mrs. Hewit were all liars, assuming that the 'Fleuralts' were the Stewart party, who all said that the birth had taken place on July 10th. It seemed obvious that they were the people in the register of the hôtel d'Anjou and that on the 10th they were already ensconced at the hotel with Lady Jane not giving birth to anyone.

Furthermore, since the party had clearly left Rheims on July 2nd on a two-day journey to Paris, arriving on the 4th, it is very unlikely that Lady Jane would have been able to give birth somewhere else in Paris between the 4th and the 7th and turn up fresh as a daisy at the Michel's on the 8th, showing no signs of just having produced twin boys.

There was one other fact worth following up in the Michels' account of their visitors. Madame Michel remembered that the gentleman had told her that his head was almost broken with the noise he had had to put up with for four days at another hotel where he had stayed before coming to the hotel d'Anjou, and that she thought he had mentioned the hotel de Châlons.

Stuart and his police colleague hurried off to find this hotel, and spoke to its landlord, a man called Charles Godefroi. It seems that, at that time, November, 1762, Godefroi remembered nothing about the British party (who actually had been staying there). If he had, Stuart would have mentioned it in his report to French counsel, but all he says is that "we still don't know where the couple stayed for the four days before going to the hotel d'Anjou."

In spite of the slight problem with Menager's La Marre, and the vagueness of events at the hotel de Châlons, Stuart was bubbling with excitement. For him, the evidence of the Michels was so strong that he decided it was time to take the next step, and on November 17th he wrote a "most secret and confidential" letter to Baron Mure, another of the Duke of Hamilton's guardians.

"Be assured that I am now master of facts which must convince even the Adherents of Mr. Douglas that the whole story of his Birth is an iniquitous daring Imposture, tho' he is innocent. The supposed father and mother with their Assistant Mrs. Hewit have been guilty of a crime of the deepest dye. You may believe that nothing but a thorough conviction in my own mind would make me venture to pronounce so boldly. It is the more remarkable as you know the byass of my opinion was in favour of the reality of his being Lady Jean's son. ... The Researches after the Accoucheur and the imaginary Madam Le Brun have consumed me much time but at length I have found out where they really did live, that it was in the House of one whose name bears no resemblance to Le Brun, that they were in that house the very day of the pretended accouchment as well as before and after that date, that there was no delivery at that time nor the appearance of a person either with child or newly delivered, that during their short residence at Paris they made an excursion to some place in the neighbourhood for one day or two and brought with them to their Hotel a child farther advanced than was possible for any child born after their leaving Rheims and that this was the child carried with them to Rheims who is now the present Competitor."

In his letter, Stuart asked Baron Mure to arrange for Sir John Stewart to be examined as soon as possible, before he or any of the Douglas party got wind of Stuart's discoveries. He emphasised the need to keep his findings secret at this stage, because he feared that once the Douglas supporters heard about the Michels they wouldn't hesitate to try to bribe them and other witnesses to change their stories.

While this letter was sitting in Stuart's room, awaiting collection by a messenger who would take it to London, Stuart's French legal adviser came to call, with some advice which Stuart added in a postscript to Mure.

"His idea is that there should be a suit instantly commenced here against the actors in this horrid Scene. And as the Supposition of a Child is in France a Capital crime and that crimes fall to be tried in the place where committed It is competent for the opposite party to give in an information of the facts to the Criminal Judge."[187]

One advantage of charging Sir John Stewart and Mrs. Hewit with a crime in France was that Andrew Stuart and the other Hamilton lawyers could start gathering evidence from witnesses straight away, before they died or were got at by the Douglas side, without waiting for the approval of the Scottish court.

The time came, however, when Stuart's activities could no longer be kept a secret from the other side, and two days after writing to Baron Mure, Andrew Stuart heard that two Douglas supporters in Paris had received an express letter telling them what the Hamilton side was up to. These were Alexander Murray, who was Sir John Stewart's brother-in-law, and Sir William Stewart, the friend of Lady Jane's who had fallen out with Sir John over his gambling habits. Murray had been heard to say that the midwife who delivered Lady Jane's children was still alive and, indeed, that he had received a message from him. Andrew Stuart decided to invite them to visit him.[188]

They met on November 21st, 1762, at the hôtel de Tours, and it turned out to be an uncomfortable meeting for both sides.

"My sole object in coming here," said Andrew Stuart, "was to discover the truth. If the facts could support me in it I am equally determined to make a Report in favour of Mr. Douglas as against him."

This may have surprised Stuart's visitors, but what he said next was even more surprising.

"The bias of my opinion on arriving here and at the time of undertaking this expedition was in favour of the truth of the proof brought on Mr. Douglas's side," he said. "I have made all possible search after the persons who were said to know the facts here without being able to find them. On the contrary I have found many things to render the facts asserted at least extremely suspicious."

Sir William later remembered that it was during this conversation that Andrew Stuart admitted that "he had all the proofs in the world of Lady Jane's pregnancy, but none of her delivery."[189]

Stuart offered to disclose the contents of the journal he had kept since arriving and the report he had written about his discoveries – on one condition. He wanted Murray to reveal all he knew about the midwife.

Murray had apparently said to friends in Paris that he was "possessed of the certain knowledge of the facts, that would make the affair as clear as the sun at noonday." Stuart was now calling his bluff.

"If this is the case," Stuart said, "you have a very short method of getting the truth of this affair forever established. If you will show me the accoucheur or any person who was either present or at the delivery or had particular access to know it, I will instantly write the strongest letter that can be devised to any person either in England or Scotland that you shall name ascertaining the truth of Mr. Douglas's being the son of Sir John Stewart and Lady Jane Douglas. This shall be done at your sight and at the sight of Sir William Stewart whom you have brought here alongst with you and of any other person at Paris that you choose to add. My object in coming here is answered by bringing the matter to a certainty either on the one side or the other and you shall find me equally ready to certify for as against him."

Since Stuart had written to Baron Mure only three days before saying that "The supposed father and mother with their assistant Mrs. Hewit have been guilty of a crime of the deepest dye," it is difficult to believe in the sincerity of these apparently heart-felt protestations. And certainly Alexander Murray was having none of it.

He first said he would have the midwife taken before a magistrate to swear an affidavit, that he might read the affidavit to Stuart but not tell him the name of the midwife without Sir John's permission.

"You have been here for three or four months without telling us of your errand here," Murray said, "so I feel bound to keep what we know concealed from you."

At this point, Sir William Stewart stepped forward and said to Murray, rather unhelpfully, that Andrew Stuart's offer seemed reasonable to him, and he ought to accept it. But Murray brushed the suggestion aside.

Stuart went on to point out that the fact that he had carried out his investigations in secret did no harm to Archibald Douglas.

"As the story must either be true or false," Stuart said, "Mr. Douglas, in the case of its being true, can suffer no prejudice by the enquiry's being made in a private manner since my report in that case will do him the fullest justice, even more than any proof brought by his own friends. But if it is false, then there is the utmost reason for conducting the researches in such a manner as Sir John Stewart shall not hear of the progress of any discoveries made, because it cannot be doubted that the same person who could be guilty of such a horrid imposture would certainly not hesitate at the next piece of infamy, the corrupting or abstracting the witnesses."

Stuart had one other reason for keeping his discoveries as private as possible, a reason he did not tell Murray or Stewart at this meeting. Since he had asked Baron Mure to find a way of interrogating Sir John Stewart as soon as possible he didn't want anything to leak out about his discoveries until Sir John had given his own answers, in the hope that there would be inconsistencies that he, Stuart, could exploit.

Murray continued to refuse Stuart's offer to exchange information, and started talking about all the 'great personages' he knew in England and France, and threatening to tell them to ignore Andrew Stuart's findings.

"At last our Conference grew a little warm and I told him he might do what he pleased," Stuart wrote a couple of days later, to William Johnstone, a lawyer friend in Scotland. Later in the same letter, he told Johnstone of the recommendations of the French lawyers that they start a criminal prosecution of Sir John Stewart in France as soon as possible, in parallel with the Reduction of Service the Hamilton side was initiating in the Scottish court, and he pleaded with Johnstone to come out to France to help ease the burden of work. He also said that he had no doubt that the Douglas side were even then writing letters to Scotland to mobilise their legal team to come over and carry out their own researches into the events of July, 1748. [190]

On December 7th, 1762, lawyers for the Duke of Hamilton told the Court of Session in Edinburgh that Archibald Douglas was an impostor, and they asked that the proceedings that had served him as heir to his uncle should be declared null and void.

Ten days later, without telling the Douglas lawyers, Andrew Stuart put before the French parliament charges against Sir John Stewart and Mrs. Helen Hewit for the capital crime of fabricating the birth of a child in order to bring about an illegal inheritance.

The stage was set for a contest that was to last four and a half years and generate four thousand closely printed pages of legal depositions, arguments and testimony before being finally resolved.

9

More Discoveries

With hindsight, Andrew Stuart's decision to take the advice of French lawyers and start criminal proceedings against Sir John Stewart and Mrs. Hewit in France was not a very sensible move. He did it to maximise the advantage for his client of finding and interviewing witnesses without having to disclose their evidence to the other side. Who knew what the Douglas party would do to the Michels, for example, by way of bribery and corruption, or to other witnesses who might have a story to tell that contradicted the version of events given by Colonel Stewart and Lady Jane? Many of these potential witnesses were poor working-class Parisians – innkeepers, maids, stage-coach drivers – whose heads, and stories, could be turned by Douglas money. And even the better-off witnesses, people like the 'rattle-headed' Menager, might succumb to the Duchess of Douglas's riches to produce a Pierre La Marre who fitted the story better.

The criminal charges drawn up by Andrew Stuart and his French colleagues against Sir John Stewart and Mrs. Hewit were contained in a Memorial, a kind of legal memorandum, which presented the story, as fact, of a faked pregnancy and simulated birth in Paris in July, 1748. According to French legal procedure, this Memorial would then be read over to witnesses who were asked to tell what they knew of the events set out there. Their evidence would be written down and from that day on, they would be legally required to tell exactly the same story, on pain of being punished themselves if they changed it. There would be no opportunity for lawyers for the other side to challenge statements, point out mistakes or contradictions, or detect falsehoods.

The choice of witnesses was also in the hands of the Hamilton lawyers, so, of course, they only called witnesses *against* the pregnancy and did not call the thirty or so witnesses later found by the Douglas lawyers who remembered Lady Jane's advanced state of pregnancy very distinctly. For the next few months, witnesses were conveyed in batches in front of the Paris criminal court, known as the Tournelle, which operated in a very different way from the English or Scottish criminal justice system.

The Douglas lawyers were outraged. One of them described the Tournelle as "that great Engine for the Manufacture of Witnesses"[191] and in his view the Hamilton team had chosen that method as an efficient way to destroy the Douglas/Stewart story of Archy's birth.

But what was that story? So far, there had been only one account of the actual birth by an eye-witness, the faithful Mrs. Hewit. She had given a statement shortly after the Duke of Douglas's death, in 1761, as part of the Service proceedings in front of the Court of Session.

This large mannish woman was no ignorant servant. In later years, when her evidence was questioned, many came forward to testify to her honesty. She was "an excessive sensible, honest woman"[192], "a woman of truth and veracity, and a sincere conscientious woman"[193], "a woman of probity and veracity."[194]

In her testimony at the Service she said the following:

"That upon the 10th of July Lady Jane was delivered in Paris of two sons, and that she was present at their birth, and received them both into her lap, when they came into the world; that the eldest, whose name is Archibald, was a strong healthy child, but the other, whose name was Sholto, was so weakly, that it was not believed he would live above twelve hours, and for that reason the man-midwife, whose name, she thinks, was something like Le Marr, but cannot be positive as she does not understand French, immediately christened him; that their landlady and her daughter were present at the birth, but she does not remember any of their names, as they were French; that they staid in that house for ten days after the delivery, when they were obliged to transport Lady Jane to another house, on account of buggs; that they remained in Paris altogether about three weeks..."[195]

This was the story Andrew Stuart had to discredit, and as he had recommended in his letter to Baron Mure, Sir John Stewart was swiftly brought before the Scottish court to be interrogated. Normally, a witness was entitled to fifteen days notice but even that was too long for Stuart to wait, so he got his father Archibald to swear that Sir John was planning to flee from justice. In fact, in the decrepit state he was at the time, Sir John would have had difficulty fleeing from his chair to the drinks cabinet. He had gout and an inflamed stomach and had to be man-handled into a sedan chair. In the court he was propped up in his seat, with someone standing by to catch him if he leaned too far and fell over.

Nevertheless, according to Sir William Fraser, official historian to the Douglas family, "Sir John is said to have behaved throughout the whole of his examination with extraordinary spirit and vivacity."[196]

His 'judicial declaration'[197] as it was called was an expansion of the notes he had supplied at the request of Mrs. Napier in 1756, and was given as a series of answers to written questions submitted by the lawyers, known as interrogatories.

Sir John said he and Lady Jane had gone to Paris at the end of June or beginning of July, 1748, and stayed at the house of M. Godefroi, in the rue St Martin. (This was the hotel de Châlons, named by Mme. Michel to Andrew Stuart only the month before.) Because of the 'inconveniency' of the house, presumably the noisiness Mme. Michel mentioned, they moved after a couple of days, on the recommendation, he thought, of Godefroi, to the house of Mme. Le Brun, in the faubourg St Germain, in a street whose name Sir John couldn't remember. It was here, he said, that the twins were born. The witnesses to the delivery were Mrs. Hewit, the man-midwife Pierre La Marre, the landlady and her daughter, and a widow who was staying in the same house. The birth took place in the morning, or at least before Sir John had dined, and Lady Jane was not long in labour.

He was asked to remember events that took place over fourteen years beforehand and wasn't always able to. "Can you describe the size and ages of Mme Le Brun and her daughter, and of the widow-lady who lodged in their house?" he was asked, and this is the answer he gave:

"All three appeared to be middle-sized, none of them appearing to be remarkably little or remarkably tall. Mme. Le Brun was rather meagre than fat and rather black than fair, as few French women are fair."

He was seventy-five at this time and perhaps this explained his vagueness, tending towards confusion, as the examination continued over three days, and he contradicted himself on various points. He withdrew the suggestion of a widow at Mme. Le Brun's, for example, and said that he was getting mixed up with a widow who was staying at Michel's. On the other hand, even allowing for the fact that the birth of his sons was one of the most important days of his life, remembering the shape, size and colouring of people one last met fourteen years ago is not easy for anyone. There is also the fact that, if these people didn't exist, Sir John had nothing to lose by describing them in great and colourful detail and at least appearing to have a good memory.

He told the court that the family stayed at Mme. Le Brun's for ten or twelve days and then, because of bugs, moved to the house of Mme. Michel, which he found by walking the streets. He was asked if he always took the name of Stewart and he said he did, and that Lady Jane went by the name of Mrs. Stewart.

The most significant part of Sir John's testimony for the Hamilton team was the story of Pierre La Marre. Unfortunately for them, they couldn't entirely ignore the accounts of Menager and Gilles, both of whom knew a man who shared a name and certain other characteristics with the person named by Sir John early on in the whole process. Now they heard a much more detailed account of how Sir John had come across Pierre La Marre and why he had employed his services for the birth of his children.

Sir John told the Court that in 1721, he had passed the winter at Liège and through an old friend, Colonel Fontaine, he had become intimately acquainted with a Walloon, a French-speaking Belgian, called Pierre La Marre, an army surgeon who also practised as a man-midwife. Twenty-seven years later, in May or June, 1748, while on a brief visit to Paris, Sir John bumped into his old friend who had come to town on a rather delicate mission, *une affaire epineuse*, which he didn't elaborate. Sir John described La Marre as about sixty, thin, with a dark complexion. It occurred to Sir John, a month away from the expected birth of his child, that he would need the services of a midwife and, ever a man with an eye for saving a penny, he explained that "my finances being in bad order, this was a good opportunity of being served cheaper than by seeing a first-rate man-midwife."

This encounter took place in the Tuileries, the public gardens near the Louvre, and when Sir John suggested that he might need La Marre's services, the midwife said he was happy to oblige. But he declined to give his address, because of the 'delicate mission' Sir John assumed, and said that he could be found most days at certain times either in the Tuileries or in Luxembourg Gardens. When asked how he was expected to find La Marre in an emergency, Sir John said that he supposed he would have had to find another midwife if necessary.

On the day of the birth, La Marre happened to stop by and, seeing that Lady Jane's confinement was near, he stayed on to assist.

Sir John came up with many other interesting details about La Marre: how they met regularly for coffee at Peletier's coffee house; the names of others at the coffeehouse who might have known him; how the two men had long discussions of Lady Jane's condition at an inn called the *Source de Bourgogne*; and how they corresponded while La Marre was supervising the care of Sholto and after Lady Jane and Sir John had returned to England.

This correspondence was of particular interest to the Hamilton legal team, because it took only a cursory inspection of the letters, retrieved from Lady Jane's trunk at the time of the Service, to realise that they were so bad that they could not have been written by a Frenchman. Sir John himself must have realised this too, because under questioning he said that these were *copies* of the letters, made by a clerk who spoke no French and prepared for Lady Jane when she wanted to show them to people at the time the rumours were beginning to circulate. If he thought that was enough to clear up the matter, he was underestimating the abilities of the Hamilton lawyers to make the most of any suspicious circumstance in this case.

Andrew Stuart hoped that this three-day interrogation would come up with enough detail about Sir John's La Marre to prove that it couldn't be the same La Marre known to Menager and Gilles. In that, his hopes were fulfilled, as he was later to lay out in scathing detail in the case made to the Scottish court. Meanwhile, Sir John's evidence was ordered to be sealed up until the court agreed that it could be revealed.

"Only the counsel and agents for the parties, with clerks and other officers of Court were present, and even they were expressly prohibited to take any notes of what passed."[198]

This doesn't seem to have stopped the contents being leaked to Paris within days. On Christmas Day, 1762, Andrew Stuart was handed an account of Sir John's judicial declaration. He would have been particularly interested in Sir John's mention of Godefroi. When he first met the landlord of the hotel de Châlons, Stuart could get nothing out of him about a mysterious group of foreigners who stayed there in July, 1748, and said as much in his first report to a French legal colleague.

But Sir John Stewart said that he and Lady Jane had stayed there, from July 4th, so Godefroi needed to be made to cudgel his brains a little harder. He couldn't come up with a hotel register, but he did have a collection of loose papers, sometimes referred to as his book, from 1748 in which he kept accounts of how much his guests spent, on food and drink. One entry referred to a party of three, but no name or sex was given of these visitors. In a dramatic example of 'recovered memory syndrome', Godefroi said that he now remembered that these three people were Colonel Stewart, Lady Jane and Mrs. Hewit. The Douglas lawyers pointed out that these accounts contained no charges for tea or sugar, which Lady Jane and Mrs. Hewit were known to consume in quantity, and no charges for postage even though Colonel Stewart had a number of letters left at the hotel. They also noted, less plausibly, that three bottles of Burgundy a day was rather more wine than the three of them could have wanted, and, in any case, on another occasion at the same hotel Colonel Stewart "indulged his palate with three sorts of wine in two days: and this company never varied their wine in nine days."

Further diligent research by the French lawyers for Hamilton came up with an entry in police records for the area saying: "12th July, at the hotel de Châlons, Monsieur Stewart, Scots gentleman with his wife."

For Andrew Stuart, this was another triumph. It seemed that the couple were in Godefroi's books until the 12th and yet they were at Michel's from the 8th, giving rise to what the Hamilton lawyers called the 'double logement' theory. Clearly, to throw future investigators off the scent Colonel Stewart had moved his party back and forth between hotels.

There was a further problem for the Defenders, as it is appropriate to call the Douglas side, caused by the Pursuers, the Hamiltons. The story being presented to the Tournelle was based on records that were not available to the court. The hotel registers had been concealed by Andrew Stuart and his team, to prevent the Defenders getting their hands on them. The Hamilton lawyers were the only people to have access to these papers, which meant that the only account of the 'Fleuralt' signature and the July 8th date of entry to Michel's, along with Godefroi's expenses book, was based on the Hamilton lawyers' testimony plus a sworn statement by M. Duruisseau, arranged by the police working for Andrew Stuart.

The day after Christmas, 1762, the first of the Douglas lawyers from Britain arrived in Paris to begin the counter-attack. He was 26-year-old Alexander Murray. (Murray is another of those names, like Douglas, Stewart/Stuart, and Hamilton that are borne simultaneously by a confusingly large number of people in this story. This Alexander Murray was different from the Alexander Murray, Sir John's brother-in-law, who had the argument in November with Andrew Stuart.)

Murray soon met with Scots lawyers in Paris who had been trying to follow in Andrew Stuart's footsteps and check up on what he might be discovering. Neither side had yet discovered a Mme. Le Brun who fitted the bill but in the search for Pierre La Marre, a wife and brother had been found of the La Marre described by M. Menager.

Over the next few weeks, it was to become increasingly clear to the Hamilton lawyers that Menager could be a danger to their case, since he appeared to be in the hands of 'the other party'.

"...It is a very puzzling situation," Andrew Stuart wrote in a letter to Scotland in March, "especially as the Witness we are to adduce [Menager] is entirely at their devotion and will second any game they have to play."[199]

Menager failed to keep appointments to give a statement before the Tournelle, and when he did agree to turn up and give testimony, Stuart suspected that he was just saying what the Douglas lawyers had told him to say:

"When I sent my servant yesterday morning to Mr. Mconachie" (one of the Douglas lawyers) "with a letter, he found Mr. Menager in the room with him and another person. It is not impossible that being Sunday Mr. Menager was employed in getting his questions or responses by heart..."[200]

In the face of increasing Hamilton activity in Paris, the Duchess of Douglas soon arrived to run the investigation on the spot. With her entourage she took over the comfortable lodgings that Murray had rented, and rolled up her sleeves. This was a battle she was determined not to lose, and she summoned reinforcements from Scotland.

Mr. Francis Garden was sent for, a lawyer with "a strong hale body and an easy benevolent mind (which) gave him a particular taste for social hilarity; they suited with the period, and he accordingly became the prince of jolly livers."[201] Part of his jolly living involved a love of pigs. At home in Scotland, a piglet had grown attached to him and followed him everywhere, even sharing his bed. As the pig grew to maturity, this habit became inconvenient, but Garden was still fond enough of the animal to let it sleep on the floor of his bedroom, using his clothes as a bed. Garden said he liked it because it kept his clothes warm till morning.[202] When he took on the task of arguing in front of the French courts he "astonished all present by his legal knowledge and fluency in the French language."[203]

The Douglas team was also joined by Alexander Makonochie, the spelling of whose name varies more than usual throughout the paperwork of this case. The story is told of a social occasion at the house of the Duchess of Queensberry when he was introduced to the company, and Lord Pembroke whispered to the hostess to ask what his name was: "'I told you,' she said, 'Mackonochie.' 'God save us – Mac-a-hon-kock-a-hock-a! Pray, Madam, how may it be spelt.' 'Why,' says she, 'Let me see, I'll tell you this moment — M-a-c-k-o-p-q-r,' and so went on with all the letters of the alphabet, counting them on her fingers …"[204] If his name gave some trouble to Lord Pembroke, what must it have done to the French?

Also in March, the faithful Mrs. Hewit knew that she was not long for the world and wrote a letter to her minister correcting a matter that had been on her conscience. She began "As I find myself very weak, and am told I am letly to dey," and went on to point out that, in the testimony that she had given at the time of the Service she had said that Lady Jane had left Mme. Le Brun's on the tenth day after the birth. But in fact, she now remembered that it was six days afterwards. She explained her mistake as follows: "… I persisted Lady Jane when she insisted to be removed from the bogs [bugs], that it was not possible for her to move tell the tenth day at sounest, for it wou'd kill her, but away she would be, and said any chance was better than staying to be eat up alive by the vilest of vermin. And it being the tenth day of our being in la brouns hous that we left it, might help to make the tenth roun in my mind." She went on to say that "all I declared on my examennation is trou, but that mistak of the day of liven la brouns hous, which I thought trou when I said it, and this I declare to you Sir was I to stap into etarnity this moment."[205]

One of the Duchess of Douglas's early steps as her team assembled was to get to know M. Menager, and Menager, of course, was only too pleased to mingle with the British aristocracy. By this stage, Menager's La Marre was gaining flesh on his bones, as members of his family turned up and were pursued by both sides. His brother, François La Marre, met with Andrew Stuart and his French colleague M. D'Anjou in April and came up with some facts which didn't suit the Hamilton case at all. According to a note Andrew Stuart wrote at the time, which was not revealed till later, when asked if his brother was acquainted with a Mme. Le Brun, François La Marre "told us immediately, and without hesitation, that he was acquainted with a Mad. Le Brun a midwife, who lived in the rue du Seine, Fauxbourg St. Germain; and that he, François de La Marre, also knew her, and that he had often seen her in her house in the rue du Seine and that the house was about the middle of the street."[206]

It would obviously have weakened the Hamilton attack if the Douglas lawyers had heard this, but at a second meeting with François La Marre in May, the two Hamilton lawyers were pleased to hear that when La Marre saw two Douglas supporters about the same time he had not told them about Mme. Le Brun. These people were Alexander Murray and a friend, Robert Douglas. But *they* later described how, in fact, during this meeting François La Marre *had* spoken in exactly the same terms about his brother's friendship with a Mme. Le Brun. (La Marre also apparently tried to get them to pay his expenses for an errand he had carried out for Andrew Stuart and not been paid for. They politely refused.)[207]

There was a further twist later when François la Marr was called as a witness under oath for the Scottish process and denied knowing anything about a woman called Le Brun who was a friend of his brother's. Significantly, at least it seemed so to the Douglas lawyers, La Marre refused to sign his testimony, saying that he had already dealt with the matter in another court.

Both sides eventually came up with a list of Mesdames Le Brun they had found independently of anything François La Marre might have said, but none of them could be identified absolutely with the one mentioned by Sir John.

While the Douglas lawyers were trying to gather evidence for the birth in Paris, the Duchess of Douglas decided to find witnesses to Lady Jane's pregnancy in Rheims. Landladies, English and Scots expatriates, clergymen and nuns, all came to the Duchess's headquarters to tell her how sweet, virtuous and pregnant Lady Jane had been during the weeks and months before she left for Paris. They confirmed the testimony that had been given at the Service by Lady Jane's maids and others that her breasts increased in size, her abdomen got larger and her movements were slower and more laboured.

Then, satisfied that the pregnancy was easy to substantiate, and armed with a Pierre La Marre that she, at any rate, believed in, the Duchess of Douglas went in search of the nurse who was alleged to have taken care of Sholto at the request of La Marre. Menager seemed to think the child had been looked after by a woman in the village of Menilmontant, then just outside Paris, but now part of the much larger conurbation. Spreading the word among local curates, the lawyers found a Mme. Garnier who lived near enough to Menilmontant and who told them that she had nursed a foreign child for Pierre La Marre, a child who was occasionally visited by a foreign gentleman, and that she had the child for about eighteen months.

By May, 1763, the grounds for the Hamilton attack on Archibald Douglas's inheritance had hardly changed over the previous six or eight months. At the heart of it was Andrew Stuart's belief that Lady Jane had not given birth to anyone in Paris in July, 1748, and that the various inconsistencies he had found in hotel records showed deceit by Sir John Stewart in an attempt to cover up the absence of a birth. He also believed, or persuaded others that he believed, there was no such person as Mme. Le Brun and that Menager's friend Pierre La Marre was a red herring.

Even if this story, presented to the Tournelle, was true it was not strong enough either to get Sir John convicted of a capital crime or, if put before the Scottish court of session, to get Archy stripped of his inheritance. There was still a major unanswered question. If Archy and Sholto were not Lady Jane's children, whose were they?

On May 9th, 1763, Andrew Stuart opened a letter from Rheims, which was to inject new life into what was a rather moribund case for the prosecution. It carried news of the child of a poor French couple which had been taken away by a foreign man and woman some thirteen years ago, in the autumn of 1749.

10

The Rope-dancer's Child

Most of the papers containing the story of the Douglas Cause were prepared with some kind of audience in mind. Some were official legal papers to be read out in court or submitted formally to judges; others were legal memoranda between colleagues; some were notes for the files of what took place in meetings; others were letters written from one person to another. As a result, they are all biased, designed to persuade the reader or listener to take one view or the other of the behaviour of Lady Jane Douglas and her husband.

But one document, recently discovered tucked away in the files of the Earl of Home at the Hirsel, shines out as an honest account of the complex and messy process of investigation that took place in France as the evidence slowly piled up on both sides. It is a daily journal by a fifty-year-old Scotsman, James Carnegy of Boysack, who was sent to France to work for the Duchess of Douglas as part of her growing team of lawyers. His journal had no legal function. Indeed, there is no evidence that anyone at the time other than Carnegy knew of its existence, or that anyone else read it through from the time of Carnegy's death until I opened its faded pages, some of them almost illegible, in the summer of 2003. If Carnegy's journal had been circulated during the legal process of disclosure by which each side tried to get sight of their opponents' paperwork, it would have produced a series of bombshells, since it is full of Carnegy's honest views of witnesses, Hamilton lawyers, other Douglas lawyers and, in particular, his employer the Duchess of Douglas, whom he came to loathe so much that he eventually had to ask to be released from her service.

James Carnegy of Boysack joined the circus of lawyers in France just at the time Andrew Stuart received a letter from Rheims with the first firm evidence of a stolen baby. In fact, four days before Stuart opened the letter and less than a week after starting his journal, Carnegy wrote that he too heard an interesting rumour:

"…a story which the Abbé Hibert told us immediately upon his coming in yesterday, that L'Abbé [blank space] here a man of consideration had told in a public company here that the Curé of St Laurent near to Paris had told him that a stranger gentleman and lady had come to a woman in his parish and offered her 50 Louis d'or for a child of hers, the woman at first refused, but tempted by the sum at last consented and gave them the child. She afterwards repented and went in search of them but they were gone. He then told the story of a servant that had been with Sir John and Lady Jane who had been attacked lately by a woman near Sedan, who upon seeing him cried 'What have you done with the child you took from me 14 years ago?

As I know the last story to be absolutely false; the other is of the same stamp, contrived to prejudice the witnesses that have been examined or any other persons knowing something of the matter whom we might find out and in general to raise the cry."[208]

Two days later, Carnegy was questioning Mme. Maillefer, wife of the syndic of Rheims, a business agent who had got to know Colonel Stewart and Lady Jane during their stay in the town.

"Her husband," Carnegy wrote, "by what I can learn, is a little *bavard* [babbler] and I believe has had some hand in propagating the idle story of the Abbé and le Curé de St Laurent near to Paris, as likewise the story of the woman crying after Sir John's servant when she saw him this winter."[209]

The parish of St. Laurent was then a suburb of Paris but today it is swallowed up in the streets around the 19th century Gare St Lazare and Gare de l'Est.

The letter that Andrew Stuart opened two days after Carnegy's journal entry was from an acquaintance in Rheims and told essentially the same story, about an story that came originally from the Curé of St Laurent:

"An English gentleman and his wife came to establish themselves in his fauxbourg, and after having captured the good will of the curé with some alms, they imparted to him the intention they held, of undertaking the education of the son of some poor person of his parish, and even taking him with them. The curé indicated to them a poor shoe-maker, who had six children, among whom they chose, one, whom they took and forthwith disappeared..."[210]

The irony of this event, a defining moment in the unfolding investigation, is that the Abbé Poule who let slip this story in conversation was to become a good friend and supporter of the Douglas lawyers and was mortified when he saw how Andrew Stuart and his team took hold of this rumour, discounted at first by Carnegy, and turned it into a pillar of their case against Sir John Stewart. Two months later Carnegy writes: "... the man [Abbé Poule] seems much touched with his innocent indiscretion at Rheims and can scarcely speak to me without tears in his eyes."[211]

But the cat was out of the bag, although whether it was a real cat or not was one of many points to be argued about all the way up to the House of Lords.

Once Carnegy, Murray, Makonochie and the other Douglas lawyers saw how seriously Andrew Stuart took this story, they needed to match any witnesses he might find with other witnesses who could show that, whoever did take a child from a poor French couple in the parish of St. Laurent thirteen or fourteen years ago, it wasn't Colonel Stewart and his wife.

This search was one of many threads that ran through Carnegy's journal, during the fifteen months he kept it up. From Carnegy's account, it's easy to see why in real terms this was one of the most expensive lawsuits ever. Each lawyer living away from home had to be paid fees and living costs; there were many ancillary employees, from copying clerks to investigators and messengers; travelling costs between Paris, Aix la Chapelle, Rheims, Dammartin and further afield. And when the most exalted figures were involved, the two duchesses and their entourages, no hotel was too expensive, no dinner too lavish. According to Horace Walpole, the Duchess of Douglas was the last of the nobility to be escorted on her travels by halberdiers. It is said that whenever she stayed with friends, she left one of her dresses behind – intentionally.

In the offical papers prepared for the judges there are copies of extracts from another journal, a document which Andrew Stuart claimed to have kept at this time. These extracts were described by one of the Douglas lawyers as possessing "strong Marks of having been drawn for other Purposes than those of meer private Memory and Inspection." At the very least, Andrew Stuart is likely to have chosen with care which extracts he put before the court.

As the events of the next few months unfolded the two journals, Carnegy's written for himself alone, and Stuart's extracts chosen for the courts, gave a picture of the frenzied activity carried out on both sides by dozens of people, both Scots and French.

The available extracts from Andrew Stuart's journal begin at the point where he set out to gather as much detail as he can about the story of the abducted child. Two days after opening the crucial letter, Stuart visited M. D'Anjou, a French lawyer who became closely involved with the Hamilton side. They went off immediately to find the curé of St. Laurent, Dr. Alexandre Cotterel, who told them enough to convince them that the 'English gentleman' was Sir John Stewart. The abduction had taken place late in 1749, meant that it must apply to the weakly twin, Sholto, who appeared in public then for the first time. Over the next few days Stuart and D'Anjou tried to extract more details from the curé and discovered that he had reported the matter to the police at the time. He also said that he had been approached by 'the other party' (the Douglas lawyers) with some questions about a possible wet-nurse in his parish who might have suckled one of the children and when he told them "the singular adventure of the child carried off out of his parish: That that person seemed to give little attention to it; and to say, That that story had *rien de commun* with theirs."[212]

Andrew Stuart was eager to know who the parents were of the abducted child so that he could get some sort of description of the abductors and pin down the date of the event, but the curé was reluctant to pass on this information. Nevertheless, Stuart managed to extract some valuable information from the reluctant curé:

"That he had not only spoke with the father and mother, but had got the act of baptism of their child that was carried off from them: That he had been born or baptized upon the 19th March 1748, and was carried off from them about the age of eighteen or nineteen months: That they had acquainted him of the auberge where these strangers lived: That in consequence he had made search for the aubergiste, who still lives, and whom he expects to be with him to-morrow: That the father and mother give a description of the gentleman who took away the child as a man about sixty; and say, that at the auberge there were two ladies whom they took to be English, one of whom was very pale; and that he had further learned, that that foreign gentleman had been in several other houses searching for children."

It can only have gladdened Andrew Stuart's heart to hear this. "About the age of eighteen or nineteen months", "a man about sixty", "two ladies whom they took to be English, one of them very pale," who else could it be? The one fact that could destroy the usefulness of this information would be the exact date on which the child was taken. They were pretty sure of the movements of Sir John and Lady Jane in the autumn of 1749 – they spent most of their time in Rheims – and to be useful to their case this abduction had to have taken place at a time when Sir John and his two ladies could plausibly be spending a few days in Paris.

When the full story was put together, with the help of interviews with the landlord of the inn where the foreigners stayed, inspection of the police records, and an eventual meeting with the family of the missing child, the following facts emerged about an event which both sides accepted had happened:

Some time in the winter of 1749-50, a gentleman and two ladies came and lodged at the *Croix de Fer* inn, run by a widow, Mme. Selle. The hotel register, in which the gentleman wrote his name, was missing but since the details were copied into police records, it was possible to discover that the foreigner claimed to be "Duvernés, gentilhomme de Korgue en Irlande avec sa femme et sa soeur."

"Duvernés" went to the curate on a Sunday or a feast day and asked for a list of the poor of the parish, to dispense some alms, but the curate refused. The man then went to a local convent, the Sisters of Charity, who introduced him to several people including a family called Sanry. After several visits the Sanrys were persuaded to part with their youngest son, Joseph, aged nineteen months. He was taken to the inn, accompanied by his father and mother, who went to see their child the next day. The day after that the strangers had left with Joseph Sanry, and the parents never saw him again. Ten days later, the father set out on a journey to look for his son, and travelled for six months around northern France without success.

This sad story was corroborated from police records, by an entry on January 10th, 1750, which reads "A letter from the curate of St. Laurent, on the subject of one called Duvernay, who has carried away the child of one Sanry, under the pretext of putting him in the hands of a lady of condition, who would educate him. He gave a false address."[213]

For Carnegy and the Douglas team, the story seemed very bad news on the face of it, and they tried to find out as much as possible. They went to see the curate on June 8th and tried to get the name of the parents of the abducted child but he refused. They then returned on the 9th:

"Mr. Garden, Mr. Hay, Mr. Murray and I went to visit the Curé of St Laurent who told us a very pointed story," Carnegy wrote. "Afterwards we saw and conversed with the father and mother of the child said to be taken away." (So the curé had succumbed to the pressure to give their name.)

Andrew Stuart's journal entry for the same day says:

"Went at seven to Mons. Danjou's, from thence to the curé de St Laurent's, whom we met going out in his coach near his own house. He stopped it for a minute, told us ... that *toute l'Angleterre* had been with him yesterday and this day... He told us, That our *partie adverse* had been with him. The persons who had come to the curé this afternoon, were Mr. Garden, Mr. Murray junior, Mr. Hay, and Mr. Carnegy. They ... insisted upon his giving them the names of the father and mother; which at first he declined; but their insisting so earnestly made him at last give way to it, upon condition that he should be at liberty likewise to give us the names and address of these persons... We sent first to Sanry's house, to know when and where he might be found; and were told in the neighbourhood, that they were not expected home till about eleven; but that their son might be heard of at Nicholet's, *danceur de cordes* [rope dancer] au Boulevard. Dispatched my servant Le Tour to Nicholet's, to desire young Sanry to come to us. The answer was, That the first act only was over, and that he could not come till the end of the whole performance."

To fill the time until the Sanrys might be home, Andrew Stuart and D'Anjou went off to talk to Mme. le Gris who had accompanied "Duvernés" on his search for children. Then, returning to the Sanry's house about eleven at night he was startled to discover the Duchess of Douglas's coach parked outside, flambeaux ablaze. The four Douglas lawyers had got there first, and were actually in the house, also awaiting the return of the Sanrys.

"The first thought of Mons. Danjou and me," Stuart wrote, "was to go into the room where these gentlemen were, and so to be present at their first interview with these people; but, upon second thoughts, I told Mr. Danjou, that I thought it would be the more convincing to them, and the stronger in their favour, if we allowed these gentlemen to have the first interview with Sanry and his wife, free from interruption."

The following day it was Andrew Stuart's turn to meet the parents and hear the story he had been waiting for. He wasted no time in sitting down and writing a letter to Baron Mure about the findings of recent days.

"At present the dénouement of the piece hastens so fast to a conclusion, that I seize the opportunity to give you the first accounts of some interesting particulars," Stuart wrote. After giving a detailed account of the comings and goings between the curate's house, the Sanry family, the *Croix de Fer* inn and the police department, he wrote: "The account which all the persons who had access to know of this singular event concur to fix the theft of the child, the time and place, and the various circumstances which show that it was done by Sir John Stewart, Lady Jane, and Mrs. Hewit, and by no other persons. Besides the persons above mentioned, I have found out the garçon of the auberge at the time of the event, and his wife, who served in the house at the same time, and several other persons who had particular access to know the carrying off of the child. I imagine this last incident will soon open the eyes of all the adherents of the other party. It has come like a thunderbolt upon those concerned for them here; and I imagine you will soon see the effects of it."

Andrew Stuart was right about this. At about the time Stuart was writing his letter to Mure, Carnegy wrote in his private journal: "From June 9th to the 14th we were all taken up about this distressing affair, which indeed from many circumstances has a very gloomy aspect. The house during this time was in the utmost hurry and confusion and for two days dismay and grieff painted on all our countenances."[214]

Stuart's letter continued: "The story is deeply impressed in the memory of the whole family. The eldest sister fell-acrying yesterday when she talked of it; saying, That she had a particular affection for that child; and that he was one of the handsomest boys that could be seen. As to the pedigree and occupation of the family from whence Sholto sprung, I can scarcely mention it to you seriously. The father has passed the greatest part of his life in quality of buffoon to a rope-dancer; and one of his sons, he who resembles Sholto the most, is at present *sauteur* under Nicolet, the famous balance-master and rope-dancer at the Boulevard. ... These circumstances are so ludicrous, that they are enough to discompose the gravity of judges, in a matter otherwise so serious.

When the whole progress of this affair, from first to last, comes to be known, and the singular manner in which the most important of the discoveries have been made, it will be allowed to be one of the most celebrated of the *causes célèbres*. ... This late incident cannot fail to make a noise soon in Edinburgh. The other party know it since last Thursday. It makes a great noise here; where this cause has been much a topic of conversation, from the sovereign downwards. It will be some satisfaction to observe numbers of converts this summer after all the toils and anxieties we have had in this affair."[215]

Since it was impossible for either side to keep their discoveries secret, there were many opportunities – for those who chose to take them – for witnesses to be bribed or threatened to change their stories. Most of those who could corroborate one or other side's story were poor working people, and it would be a strong pauper whose head would not be turned by the purses of Scotland's two richest families.

Early on in the search for evidence of Pierre La Marre, the Hamilton lawyers had come across his widow and her sister who had nothing to offer to support the story of the late midwife's delivery of twins born of a foreign aristocrat. But in June when Andrew Stuart saw her, a week after both sides' lawyers descended on the curate of St. Laurent, Mme. La Marre was much more disposed to confirm that her late husband had delivered a noble foreign lady of twins. She even reported a story told by her sister about once taking a walk with Pierre La Marre after his marriage in 1747, and him telling her to wait a moment: "I am going to see a child," he said to her, "who will one day be one of the richest in the kingdom, whose nurse's month [salary] I am going to pay."[216] The widow also said that after Pierre La Marre's death she burnt "several useless papers" in which there was something to do with the name of Stewart.

Andrew Stuart was horrified by Mme. La Marre's *volte face*, but knew exactly why it had happened:

"The whole tenor of her conversation showed us, that she had been gained over by the other party," he wrote on June 16th, "so we set about finding out what persons of the other party she had seen. At first she denied having seen any person of the other party, or that any of them had come to her home; then she said, that she heard that the relations of the child were here in Paris, and that she even heard there was a Duchess here on that side. Thereafter, in the course of the conversation, it came out, that not only she knew there was a

Duchesse de Douglas here, but that this Duchess had sent for her; and that she had been twice at her house; and that she had one of these times had the honour to dine at table with the Duchess in her house, when her sister and several others were present; and that the Duchess had been very civil to her. This woman La Marre remains yet much captivated with this honour of dining at the Duchess of Douglas's table; shewed some touches of vanity, by telling, in the course of her narrative, that she knew very well how to present herself before the best of company upon occasion; and that she had dressed herself well, and had dined at the Duchess's own table that day that she was asked, and had been very obligingly received. When the Duchess spoke to her, it was always by the assistance of an interpreter, as she did not speak French."[217]

There is no evidence at all that Mme. La Marre had any midwifery skills of her own but it is interesting to note that a few years later, in 1767, Giacomo Casanova, the Italian roué and memoirist, was writing of the young wife of a disgraced friend of his giving birth in Paris at the hands of "Madame Lamarre, a midwife, who lived in the Faubourg St. Denis."

The Duchess of Argyll, formerly Hamilton, was soon made aware of the letter from Andrew Stuart to Baron Mure, brimming with discoveries that were bound to devastate her rival, the Duchess of Douglas. It was time to join the fray, and the Duchess of Argyll set off for Paris to meet her team in their moment of triumph.

The news of Andrew Stuart's 'discovery' of Sir John and Lady Jane's crime rippled through the higher levels of British society. In a letter to the Duke of Portland, Viscountess Weymouth wrote at the time: "The Duchess of Hamilton has triumphed over the Duchess of Douglas at Paris and has proved that the boy that goes for Lady Jane Douglas's son was son to a mason in a village in France which she took at six months."[218] (In fact, if the Sanry child was either of the twins, he was Sholto not Archy.)

Although there was a long way to go before Hamilton triumphed over Douglas, Andrew Stuart's confidence was at its height. The discovery of the parents of one of Lady Jane's children spurred them on to find the parents of the other. And to do that, the French lawyers suggested a new weapon, which was to generate as great a howl of anguish among the Douglas lawyers as the Tournelle. It was called – a Monitoire.

11

The Monstrous Monitoire

I n March, 1762, a prominent merchant of Toulouse, Jean Calas, was executed for the murder of his son, Marc-Antoine. Calas and most of his family were Protestants, although one son had converted to Catholicism, and it had been suspected that Marc-Antoine was thinking seriously of doing so, too.

The young man had been found hanging in his father's warehouse in October 1761, and a rumour swept through the crowd that gathered that he had been murdered by his father to stop him converting. Members of the family were arrested and Marc-Antoine was hailed as a martyr by the largely Catholic population.

In order to gather evidence, a "Monitoire" was ordered. This was a statement about the crime, to be read from every pulpit and nailed up in churches, that was designed to uncover any witnesses who might have something to contribute. The wording of the proclamation that was read out in church was a description of Marc-Antoine's death based on the presumption that it was a murder carried out by the father. The theory that Marc-Antoine might have been about to convert was presented as fact; and there was no mention of the possibility that he might have committed suicide or indeed been killed by anyone other than his father.

The religious status of a Monitoire was such that any person who had information that supported the case and didn't come forward could be excommunicated. Furthermore, since issuing a Monitoire was such a public affair, it provided an opportunity for people who thought they had something to contribute, however mistaken or tentative, to step into the limelight and, perhaps, be rewarded for their good churchmanship. These were reasons to criticise such a one-sided procedure, along with the fact that someone who had evidence that differed from the official statement of the circumstances of the crime might be intimidated from coming forward with an alternative version of the facts and daring to contradict such a solemn ecclesiastical proclamation.

In the legal process that followed the arrest of Jean Calas, the members of the family were unable to give a coherent account of themselves, and the Parliament of Toulouse, by a vote of 8 to 5, condemned Calas to the triple punishment of torture, being broken upon the wheel, and finally being burnt to death. The sentence was executed the following day.

The writer and philosopher Voltaire, a virulent anti-Catholic, befriended the family and took up their cause. He attacked the verdict and the process that had been used to support it, the Monitoire. "These Visigoths," Voltaire wrote, referring to the Parliament of Toulouse, "take as their maxim that four quarters of evidence, and eight eighths, make two complete proofs, and those quarters and eighths can be just rumours and hearsay. What do you say of this manner of reasoning and judging? Can it be possible that the life of men is dependent on such absurd people?"[219]

While Andrew Stuart and his colleagues were considering how to deal with the new discoveries, the Calas case was still fresh in the public mind. It was a year since Calas had been executed, and the campaign of Voltaire and others was under way, centreing on an attack on the Monitoire as a means of gathering evidence.

But the French lawyers, who knew the system, felt that a Monitoire would be the best way of bringing the search for Archy's true parents before as wide a public as possible, particularly among the class of people who might not read newspapers, or read at all. On July 2nd, the French parliament issued a ruling that on the next three Sundays a Monitoire consisting of a 2,500-word statement of the Hamilton case against Archibald Douglas should be read out from pulpits and pinned up in churches throughout Paris.

James Carnegy first heard of the Monitoire, or 'monitory' as he called it, the day it was issued, on July 9th, 1763:

"...the Parlement has given an *arrêt* [ruling] whereby the Archbishop of Paris is ordered to publish a monitory enjoining all persons that know anything of a child or children being carried away to declare the same to their parish curé... It's thought that the monitory may be published Sunday next. They will endeavour by this monitory to find out a mother for Mr. Douglas as they say they have done for Sholto in the parish of St Laurent."[220]

Carnegy was assured by his French colleagues, the day before the Monitoire was first read in Paris churches, that it would be of very little use to the Hamilton case: "Mr. Covin etc think the Monitory very little material, as Monitorys, say they, are never asked but when there is great penury of other proofs."[221]

How wrong they were was to become apparent within a week. But meanwhile, Carnegy had other things on his mind. His stay in France was not going well. He had been away from wife and home for three months and the work was getting him down, even though the Duchess tried to provide her lawyers with recreational activities. One evening, for example, she took them to the Royal Chapel to see the relics, including

"Charlemagne's head, his sword, a part of the real cross, our saviour's belt, an arm of Charlemagne, part of the reed which was given to our saviour when in derision he was hailed king of the Jews…"[222]

Such excitements were not enough to compensate for the depressing daily grind. Carnegy disagreed strongly with his Scottish legal colleagues, and considered one of them to be mentally ill. There were arguments with the French lawyers and assistants, most of whom seemed to want to do the minimum work for the maximum pay. He was disappointed that so many potential witnesses who might have supported the Douglas case were dead or untraceable. The Sanry evidence had clearly been a shock.

After a brief reference on July 26th to the Monitoire – "read what I had seen of the Monitory which is now in all the streets of Paris" – and a couple of lines on the next two days, this section of his journal ended in the middle of the page, and he wrote no more until he returned the following year. But, intriguingly, there is a loose sheet of paper in the journal which, although undated, may well apply to this time. It describes his depressed state and his desperate wish to go home. After mentioning yet another tussle with the grasping French lawyers he wrote:

"In short the pain which these things gave me, joined to many others that would fill a small volume, made such an impression upon me that for the first time in my life I found low spirits approaching with a hasty pace. My health was hourly declining and I am fully persuaded that had I stayed a few days longer at Paris I should have been confined to my bed and rendered useless both to myself and everybody else. … Having applied both to Mr. Garden and Mr. Burnet to facilitate my getting home for a month or six weeks only, and having told Mr. Garden that it was necessary and what I was determined to do and finding that neither of them would give any ear to my proposals nor smooth the way with the Duchess and knowing the Duchess's temper too well not to see that to get her consent and to bid her formally adieu was a thing impracticable, I with the utmost reluctance took leave of her Grace by a letter at which I am well informed her rage had no bounds."[223]

Carnegy was not to return to Paris until early the following year, by which time the conduct of the case had moved in a new and dramatic direction. Far from it being "of little use in the case", the Monitoire would strike gold for the Hamilton team.

As in the case of Calas, the text of the Monitoire left little room for more than one view of the events. At every point, sly digs were made against the Douglas story. When Mrs. Hewit was referred to she was described as "calling herself [Lady Jane's] companion" and later "this supposed companion" [prétendue]. It is stated as fact that Colonel Stewart and Lady Jane "contrived the scheme of procuring supposititious children, with a view to impose heirs upon one of the greatest and most illustrious houses of Great Britain."[224] The messy data from the books of the Michels and Godefroi were transformed into a firm and factual account of obvious deception. "…on the 4th of the said month of July 1748, they arrived at Paris, and alighted at the Hotel de Châlons, rue St Martin, where they remained privately till, and including the 14th of the said month; and in which interval, they, on the 8th of the said month, took another lodging, under a feigned name, at the hotel d'Anjou, in the Rue Serpentes, and lived there in a mysterious manner, from their entry to it, until the end of the said month, that they went away from Paris."[225]

The Monitoire also said, inaccurately, that "it is beyond all probability that a woman so far advanced in years should become pregnant, for the first time." It indicated that Archy, the child first seen in July, 1748, had not yet been connected with any specific abduction but told the story of the revelations by the Sanrys and left no one in any doubt that this had been proved to refer to Colonel Stewart and Lady Jane, and that the missing Sanry child was Sholto.

The proclamation finished with the stirring exhortation: "We order you to admonish all and singular, who have seen, heard, perceived, or have any knowledge of the facts, circumstances, or any part thereof above set forth, or who were present, aiding or assisting thereat, in any manner of way, to appear, and make revelation thereof, and make satisfaction by themselves, or others in their name, in three days after publication of these presents, otherwise we will use the censures of the church against them, even to excommunication itself, in the forms prescribed by law."

This device of using a quaint French ecclesiastical device to winkle out witnesses infuriated the Douglas lawyers, as they indicated in a Memorial attacking it:

"The Monitoire, which is not an equal and judicial state of the case, formed upon the information and evidence of both parties, but is a most partial libel, drawn up by the operators for Duke Hamilton, in an inflammatory stile, was not only posted up through Paris, but actually put into the hands of persons who are to be witnesses, and dispersed into remote parts of the kingdom, where certain of the witnesses reside... It may even tend to excite and encourage false evidence from low people, who will naturally expect mighty advantages to themselves, from pretended or partial discoveries, in a matter of such important consequence."[226]

The Monitoire was ordered to be read on three successive Sundays, starting on July 24th. Two days after the first reading, Andrew Stuart took his Duchess to show off some of his discoveries. They visited the curé of St Laurent, who was asked for the umpteenth time to narrate the story of the abduction of the Sanry's child by the three foreigners. Stuart wrote in his journal that the curé "read us a letter he had got from the Abbé Poule, who foolishly regrets his ever having given any hint that had led to this discovery. We left with the curé some copies of the Monitoire, which he had not yet seen. He is to be in town before next publication."

On the very same day, Pierre-Antoine Baudouin, a man described in the official documents as a salt-officer, was reading a copy of the Monitoire which was fixed to the gate of the church of the Nazareth Fathers, near the rue St. Denis. He had seen the Monitoire the day before, but there was such a crowd that he couldn't get near enough to read all of it. He now read enough to be reminded of something that had happened to his mother-in-law's sister some years beforehand. This sister was Mme. Marie-Nicole Mignon, a laundress and wife of a glass-blower, Nicolas Mignon. Events then moved quickly: Baudouin told his mother-in-law, she went off to tell her sister about the contents of the Monitoire, and Mme. Mignon came hurrying back to hear more details from Baudouin himself. "After having caused acquaint her," says his witness statement, "he judged from the surprise which she testified, and even from her tears, that no body had spoke to her of this affair."[227]

Mme. Mignon then went to see her curate, M. de Beaureceuil, at the church of Ste. Marguerite, as she was required to do by the terms of the Monitoire, and tearfully told him a sad story. In the summer of 1748 she had given birth to a son and when he was thirteen or fourteen days old a woman living in the same lodgings, Mme. Guynette, told her of a foreign gentleman who was seeking to acquire one or two babies. He had said his wife had recently given birth to twins who had both died and that he wanted to borrow two children to console her. Mme. Guynette encouraged Mme. Mignon to give her new-born baby to this man, "if she inclined to make her child's fortune." Mme. Mignon replied that if the gentlemen went to the foundlings' hospital he would find babies of all colours. But she agreed to go and talk to her husband about it. He was rather more positive about the idea and said "If it could take me away from my work, which is very severe, and do good to my child, I will see to it."

As the distressing story unfolded, the curate, obviously taken aback, tried to quell the woman's tears with a jovial remark:

"These people who have taken your child didn't want to do him any harm," he said, "As you see, they have made him a peer of Scotland, with three or four hundred thousand livres a year."[228].

(Whatever the intended consequence of the curate's remark, so early in the revelation of the Mignon's story, it surely alerted the Mignons to the value of connecting their lost son as closely as possible with the mysterious – and apparently rich – strangers.)

The remark suggests that the curate wasn't taking the matter too seriously. He did not immediately pass the news on to the procurator-general, preferring to wait until all three readings of the Monitoire had taken place, but did raise it at a meeting of curates at the house of the Archbishop of Paris on August 5th.

It happened that M. D'Outremont, a senior French lawyer who was helping Andrew Stuart, was visiting the Archbishop of Paris that day, perhaps suspecting that a gathering of curates would be a good place to check on any responses to the Monitoire. What he heard there sent him hurrying off to Andrew Stuart's hotel. It was clear that they had to get to the curate of Ste. Marguerite and make him tell them his story as soon as possible.

The following morning, August 6th, Andrew Stuart and M. D'Outremont set off to see the curate. M. de Beaurecueil was wary. He had not yet got round to sending his report to the Procurator-General and he didn't want to do anything that might lead to the Mignons changing their story. But he outlined what the Mignons had told him. The Hamilton lawyers asked for the address of the couple but the curate refused. He did however relent a little and read the Mignons' statement out loud, saying later that "he does not know whether

Mr. Stuart may have taken notice of the house, and kept in his memory their places of abode."

The Hamilton team now rushed off to break the news to the Duchess of Argyll and one of her sons, Lord Lorne, who were on the point of leaving Paris. "(Their) post-horses were in the court for their setting-out this day for London," wrote Stuart in his journal that night, "but upon this news, and our representing to them that it might be highly proper to continue here a day or two longer, until we could see further into this affair, they delayed their journey till Tuesday next."

Stuart knew that, with the Douglas lawyers constantly on their tail, it wouldn't be long until they too learnt of the existence of the Mignons and tried to get to them. Each side accused the other of bribing and corrupting witnesses, so the earliest version of any story was considered most likely to be nearest the truth.

Stuart and D'Anjou started their search at Mignon's workplace, a glass factory in the faubourg St. Antoine, an eastern suburb of Paris, beyond the Bastille. When they arrived, it was clear that the news of the Mignons' revelations had spread throughout the area, since there were crowds gathered at the factory gate and in the house of the gatekeeper. He offered to bring to them Marie Guynette, the daughter of the woman who had first been approached by the foreign gentleman. Mme. Guynette was now dead but she had often told her daughter the story of the events that had followed the approaches to her of a tall foreign gentleman in the summer of 1748, and told it again to Andrew Stuart and M. d'Anjou. The gatekeeper also found M. Mignon and brought him to meet the lawyers, so that the whole story could be laid out for them. It was an affecting story, told as vividly as if it had happened the previous day, and d'Anjou put it all down in his report:

"That in the month of July 1748 a man whose language was foreign addressed himself to the Widow Guynette, seller of bread rolls at the door of Notre Dame and asked her if she knew some people who could give for some time two young children newly born in order to present them to his wife who had given birth to twins who had then died, saying that this woman would be so afflicted if she learnt this that he would fear for her life if he did not use this means of making her believe that they lived and that it was for this reason that he wished to obtain two children for some time or at least obtain one in good health which would keep her happy until he was able to tell her that the other was too weak to present to her.

That this gentleman asked for blond children with blue eyes who as far as was possible resembled each other.

That the Widow Guynette promised to look for them and actually made the proposition to two women, the first called Marie Destampes, wife of the named Charlan, and the second the wife of the named Mignon, worker at the glass factory, living in the same house as the Widow Guynette.

These two women having listened to the proposition, the Widow Guynette arranged a rendezvous at Notre Dame where she had her stall selling bread.

That Marie Destampes, wife of Charlan, arrived there first with her child which she didn't want to give away.

That the wife of Mignon was also there with her child aged then 15 days or three weeks and reassured by the explanations that she was given by the stranger who promised her money for herself, security for the child and an assurance to do good to him in the future, she agreed to trust him with the child and fixed a meeting for the following day in the house of Madam Hédouard who then sold books at the door of Notre Dame.

That the following day Mignon and his wife came in the afternoon and found the stranger who appeared to both of them a man of about 55 or 60 years old wearing brown garments without gold or silver and a plain hat, that's to say without braid trimming, having with him a woman who was quite large, dressed in a white robe with furbelows or decorations.

That this stranger spoke good enough French apart from the accent of his country but that the woman didn't speak it at all and that they didn't hear her say anything other than Le joli petit garconnat!; that the two people spoke a foreign language between themselves that the other people present didn't understand.

That they went, all of them, to the house of Madam Hédouard who lived near Notre Dame and arriving in her bedroom they found a very clean layette for the child.

That the child was undressed and inspected naked; and that after seeing that he was healthy and had no defect, and, indeed, after praising him very much, the woman who was with the stranger dressed the child with the help of his mother in new clothes."

D'Anjou's account described how he expressed surprise that Mignon had handed his child over to a complete stranger and Mignon said that he himself had been equally surprised, and afterwards distressed but that "he had been blinded."

Within moments of the couple taking the child away in their carriage without leaving an address, Mignon set off after them.

"He had run from street to street following the carriage," D'Anjou reported, "to a road by the side of the Pont-Neuf, (this must be the Rue Mazarine); where having seen the carriage stop he had entered a tavern immediately, to drink a half septier* of wine at the bar (i.e. at the door) because of the fatigue he now felt, not losing sight of the carriage; but when, during the time that he was drinking he had seen the empty carriage disappear, he had guessed that the foreign man and woman had passed with the child into the Rue de Seine via a tennis court which crossed from one street to another.

That he had taken the same route via this tennis court but that he subsequently saw neither of them and after looking

---

* A *septier* or *setier* is given as two gallons.

fruitlessly he had returned to his house to tell his wife of his suspicions, his concerns and his grief.

That after this time he and his wife had scoured all the streets of the Faubourg St Germain as being the neighbourhood where the carriage had taken the strangers but that he had never been able to discover any trace of where they lived or of his son whom he had never seen again."

Mignon invited the Hamilton lawyers to meet his wife if they had any doubts about his story, because she would confirm it.

"The wife of the aforesaid Mignon," D'Anjou said, "(was) very surprised to find so many people come to speak to her, (and) made first of all the most humble excuses for the state in which she appeared.

She was effectively in work clothes – she is a day worker at a laundry. Her face appeared to us as good and as open as that of her husband; the face a little wide, brown eyes, skin darkened by the sun, tired features, but well enough preserved to make us believe that in her youth she had had an agreeable enough appearance.

After having reassured her, we announced the subject of our visit and her husband having told her that he had related everything to us and that we came to hear confirmation of the story, she in effect repeated it to us in the same manner but with more vehemence and feeling, appearing very concerned that we would suspect her of having sold her child and begging us to believe that she was incapable of it, confirming the sincerity and the simplicity of her speech by the natural tears of a true mother.

She told us that among the new clothes that (the foreign couple) had given her son, after having taken off those which he wore, she had rejected as inadequate and dangerous a type of linen wrap instead of a quilted swaddling-cloth, (i.e. two or three-layered cloth) which is usually used for babies; and that she had wanted them to keep his quilted swaddling-cloth, as likely to support his back more firmly than the simple cloth that they wanted to substitute. She also kept his bonnet, since the headwear that the foreigners had brought had no strap to be held under the chin of the child. …

That she had gone to mass at St Esprit the very day before taking her child and that since the loss of her child she had arranged for several masses to be said at St Esprit and elsewhere; that she had visited midwives and that several times she had stood on the steps of the Pont Neuf to see if she could recognise the foreigner passing by, in view of the fact that the Pont Neuf is the most widely-used route in Paris to go from one part of the city to another."[229]

The two men convinced themselves that Mme. Mignon's features resembled Archy's and, when they met her two sons, that one of them was so like him that they had the idea of commissioning a portrait of Archy to bring to Paris on another occasion to show her.

D'Anjou then added, presumably for public consumption, a rather pious sentence that was designed to forestall the constant allegations of bribery of witnesses made against them by the other side:

"And then we left these poor people, saying to them that we were very angry that the laws of France which didn't allow us to show any gratitude to witnesses, gave us no freedom to do good for them; upon which we owe them the justice to attest that they appeared indifferent to this compliment in spite of their poverty."

The next person on the list for the Hamilton lawyers to see was the Widow Charlan, another woman who had been suggested by the Mme. Guynette as a possible child-seller. She lived nearby, in a street already thronged with people who were obviously waiting for the excitement to begin and, with one voice, told Andrew Stuart and d'Anjou where her house was.

In front of "ten or a dozen curious people" they questioned Mme. Charlan:

"She told us that she had gone to Notre Dame ... found in the church a man of the same size, face, age, speech and clothes as the man described by Mignon and his wife (except that she thinks this man had under his outer garments a jacket trimmed with braid). That he proposed to her that she lend him her child for the purpose described by the Widow Guynette, but that on her asking him his name and address and on her being unable to persuade him to tell her them, she had refused to lend her child and had left, having nevertheless received an ecu from him which he had given to pay for a cab."

Clearly it was going to be important to pin this abduction on Colonel Stewart by getting as exact an idea as possible of the date of these events. The ins and outs of the registers of the two hotels would constrain the times and dates when the Colonel could have slipped away to do the deed.

"Neither of them was able to be absolutely definite;" wrote d'Anjou, "but Mme. Mignon said to us that as well as she could remember, it was about eight days before the feast of St Clair, which is on July 18th, and which fixed the period for her because it is the feast of the mirror-makers and glass-workers, the profession of her husband, so that it would have been July 10th.

They say they are very sure that their child was kidnapped before this feast of St Clair but they are not quite sure whether the thing happened eight days or fewer than eight days before the feast.

There is reason to believe that the kidnapping could hardly have happened before the 10th July because it was the mother who brought the child herself from the faubourg St Antoine to the porch of Notre Dame and since her confinement was so recent (since it was on the preceding 30th June) it is hardly likely that she was recovered and in a state to go out earlier than the 10th July. Thus all that is certain concerning the precise date of the kidnapping is that it happened between the

10th and the 18th July, the day before that on which the husband and wife assert they lost their child."

The final visit by the Hamilton lawyers, in a very active and productive couple of hours, was to the bookseller, Mme. Hédouard, at whose house near Notre Dame the foreign gentleman had been shown the Mignon baby.

"This Dame Hédouard is a woman of sixty-seven to sixty-eight years old who appeared to us quite decrepit and unfortunate, to judge by the furnishings of her very small room in which there were two beds without curtains, several chairs, and a commode, with books spread all over the place, very likely forming the basis of her very mediocre business.

This woman, whose memory seemed fairly shaky, could at first remember only the main fact, although she did so very promptly, that Widow Guynette had asked her to lend her room for the examination of the child and that there he was undressed and examined in the presence of a man who had come there. And afterwards she had learnt that the mother had lost this child and greatly lamented her loss.

On being questioned, she remembered that there had been a woman with that man, and often repeated in quite a confused manner that she believed that the mother of the child had been presented in order to be the wet-nurse.

But since her surprise at our number, as well as the weakness either of her age or her mind, had rendered her circumspect or timid we believed it was appropriate not to tire her with long questions, having learnt enough from the memory that she had very clearly of the principal event, which accorded perfectly with what we had just learned from other people."[230]

Whatever the objections to the use of the Monitoire, its results had clearly given a huge boost to the pursuers, who now appeared to have in place the major elements of the story. Andrew Stuart had managed to build a circumstantial but detailed description of when and where the heir of Douglas and his brother had been wrenched by Colonel Stewart from their true parents. What remained to be done was a lot of legwork, interviewing and inspection of records to check and flesh out the story, as well as the preparation of paperwork for two legal processes, the French Tournelle, for the crime of supposition, and the Scottish Court of Session, to challenge the inheritance of Archibald Douglas.

But some of Andrew Stuart's luck was about to run out. By starting the Tournelle and using the Monitoire, Stuart thought he could gather evidence away from the scrutiny of the Douglas team which he could then use in the Scottish court. He was soon to find out that much of this work had been in vain, as Douglas supporters in high places in England and Scotland began to realise what he was doing.

12

Lawyers and Legwork

Once the Douglas lawyers had got wind of what was going on in France, they decided to find a way to stop it, or at least to reduce the head start Andrew Stuart had contrived for the Hamilton side. On March 8th, 1763, they handed in a petition containing an official complaint to the Court of Session in Edinburgh about the Hamilton lawyer's use of the French criminal law and the actions they were taking to build a case.

The petition said:"…that, for some months before the plainte was given in, Mr. Andrew Stuart was employed in going about in Paris, and other parts of France, assisted by one Buhot, who is an officer of the lowest character, employed by the Lieutenant du Police in Paris in the same kind of work as the thief-catchers are by Sir John Fielding in London; that, with his assistance, he has procured some witnesses of the lowest rank of the people, such as barbers, inn-keepers, cooks, etc. who have been examined upon oath, and he is still going on to get more examined; that this inquisition, according to the form in that country, is conducted with the greatest secrecy….nor can the person accused [Sir John Stewart] get any information of what is said against him, not so much as a copy of the plainte."

In no more temperate language, James Boswell, among other Douglas supporters, described what was wrong with the Tournelle:

"This process," he wrote, "was in reality an insult upon justice. It was a mock accusation as it related to two British subjects who were not under the jurisdiction of France, and therefore could not be punished by the courts of France. The real intention of it was to obtain partial depositions in support of the plaintiff's cause from witnesses examined in a private manner, at the instance of one party without the knowledge of the other, and to deter Sir John Stewart, or Mrs. Hewit, from going to Paris to give assistance to the defendant, since however innocent, if they had varied from the Tournelle depositions they would have been put to torture."[231]

The Douglas petition to the Court of Session went on to ask the court to force the Hamilton layers to provide a copy of their charges, the plainte, and to stop the French proceedings immediately. This request was considered as part of a broader hearing to decide what to do next about the Hamilton request to reduce the Service of Archibald Douglas.

On July 5th, just about the time the Mignons were telling their sad story to the curate of Ste. Marguerite, both sides assembled in the Court of Session in Edinburgh to present their arguments for and against the Reduction of Service and to settle the matter of the validity of the Tournelle. "The house was crowded," said the *Scots Magazine*, "there was a great number of ladies in the galleries. The speeches were very long: the Lord Advocate spoke nearly four hours." And this, remember, was just a preliminary skirmish between the two sides over a legal technicality. Yet it lasted three days and at the end of it the court ordered both sides to produce memorials and condescendences, documents that set out in exhaustive detail the arguments.

What a Douglas lawyer described as a 'monstrous waste of paper'[232] was gaining momentum.

The Hamilton 'Condescendance', given in on July 19th, set out the story so far, including the recent discoveries relating to the Sanrys' child, but with nothing about the Mignons, since that drama was unfolding in Paris at exactly the same time as the court proceedings, and Andrew Stuart had not yet told his colleagues in Scotland. (His first letter bearing the news to Scotland seems to have been on August 11th). The other side argued that the whole French process was illegal and therefore none of the information gathered by Andrew Stuart over the last nine months should be available to the Scottish court. The witnesses were 'led' by having a biased account of the events read out to them; there was no Douglas representative present; and the oath sworn by the witnesses bound them to the testimony they gave at that time, with no possibility of revising their testimony in the light of new information or any other change in circumstances without being prosecuted for perjury.

On July 27th, the judges issued their ruling. They decided that a commission of both parties should set out to gather evidence and question witnesses according to Scottish law and to present it at some future date to the Court of Session. They were critical of the Tournelle and said that although they did not wish to bar witnesses in the Tournelle from being examined again by the Scots commission, they would reserve judgement as to their credibility until the evidence was all gathered together as part of a Proof.

Andrew Stuart was a man who fired with both barrels when he felt criticised. As a lawyer, he might have become accustomed to the fact that every lawsuit has two parties that disagree with each other, and therefore one side was always likely to attack and be attacked by the other. But Stuart had a strong sense of honour, at least of his *own* honour, and he seems to have taken this early ruling of the Scottish judges, and the pleased reaction of the Douglas side which followed as a personal attack, although in an address to the judges he wrote as on behalf of his whole team.

"... They have been attacked, and almost overwhelmed in this country by a tumultuous tide of clamour and obloquy, which has been excited to such a height, that one would be tempted to believe, that the feelings of mankind were in this instance perverted; and that it excited in them a sensible and cutting regret, that a complicated scene of fraud was happily detected, and that the true heirs of the first family in Scotland were soon, by your Lordships' justice, to enjoy the inheritance of their ancestors, in place of its being carried of by a supposititious child. ... But so unaccountable is popular prejudice, and so many arts have been used to excite and support it, that ... the minds of men seemed to be actuated by a species of infatuation which overturned every sober reflection, and, like an inveterate jaundice, gave its own tincture to every fact and every argument."[233]

One result of these first legal skirmishes was that Andrew Stuart was required to unpick the Tournelle process, and seek the French king's permission to abandon the prosecution of Sir John Stewart and Mrs. Hewit. From now on, the gathering of evidence would proceed by Scottish rules, with much more disclosure between the two sides.

Andrew Stuart tried to put a brave face on what must have been a severe setback, in a letter to Baron Mure:

"... the necessity imposed upon us of applying to the Parliament and to the King and Council for the cancellation of communication of the Tournelle Depositions was unlucky in one respect that it has lost us a great deal of time and occasioned infinite trouble, yet in another respect I think it fortunate that it has given occasion to placing in a just light the conduct of both partys ... Depend upon it all the efforts of the other party will be used to protract the Cause, this is now their great object they see that when once the proof is taken they are undone, if they can protract it some time they have the chance of some essential witnesses dying, every delay is favourable to them and as they possess the rents of the estates in the interval this increases their desire of catching at every handle of delay...."[234]

Back in Paris, the Enemy were dogging Andrew Stuart's footsteps at every turn. To confirm the Mignon story required Stuart and his growing team of assistants to seek out and visit anyone who might have been a witness or participant in July, 1748, as well as revisiting the people at the centre of the story, the Mignons and their friends and relatives, who found themselves the subject of almost daily visits, from lawyers and helpers for both sides.

On August 15th, Mme. Mignon was visited at about nine o'clock at night by three gentlemen, one dressed in black with a long nose, who questioned her closely about the abduction. The long-nosed man said to her "If you are the mother of that child, you are a very barbarous mother, *maratre*,* to want to deprive this child of the three hundred thousand francs of income that he enjoys." Mme. Mignon replied: "He came from my insides and nothing will stop me reclaiming him." She had also been frightened by a fellow-laundress, a woman who did the washing for the State Prosecutor's wife, who had been told by her employer that the Sanrys had been sent off to prison for propagating the story of their own child's abduction.

At the same time as the Douglas team appeared to be indulging in 'dirty tricks', they were also trying to get evidence of dubious behaviour by Andrew Stuart, suspecting him, among other things, of spiriting away the alleged midwife, Mme. Le Brun, to keep her out of the Douglas lawyers' hands.

Shortly after the Mignon revelations, the Douglas lawyers sent a man called Michel Brisseau to visit Denis du Rocher, a police inspector, to see if he would carry out some detective work for them. There were four tasks, on a piece of paper

---

* Figuratively, a wicked stepmother

headed *Things which must be learned, and of which exact information must be got.*

Item 1 asked "What is become of one Mme. Le Brun... There are good reasons to believe that this woman has been carried away or secreted. She must be discovered at any price."

Item 2 sought information in the registers of the foundlings hospital that might show that Jacques-Louis Mignon had actually been taken there after his birth, rather than stolen by foreigners.

Item 3 set the task of finding out who the Duchess of Argyll's coachmen were so that they could be asked if they had driven her or her lawyers to the house of the Mignons before the Monitoire, which would have suggested that that the whole Mignon story was a put-up job.

The last task which M. du Rocher was asked to perform was to find out if the agents of the Duke of Hamilton had "seduced by promises or gained by money the witnesses who depose against Mr. Douglas."[235]

Du Rocher told Brisseau that he would have to pass the list on to his colleague, M. Buhot, who had been appointed by the lieutenant-general of police to carry out research into the case. Brisseau seemed unperturbed by this, clearly not knowing that Buhot was effectively working for Andrew Stuart and therefore was unlikely to take on the task of uncovering his misdeeds, and nothing more was heard of the list.

The Duchess of Douglas had been in Scotland for the Court of Session hearings and now headed back to London, to collect Archy and take him on to Paris after the Westminster term was over. A brief handwritten note in the Westminster School records notes that "Douglas was remarkable for the worst penmanship in the school. His favourite exercise was in Tothill Fields from whence returning one day very late he instantly conceived and executed some verses that were the best of the day..."[236] It is possible that the Duchess took him to Paris to confront him with his alleged mother and brothers, perhaps to show how unlike them he was.

Archy Douglas, in his teens

On September 7th, the curate of St. Laurent's told Andrew Stuart that he had been visited by four lawyers from the other side, who made him go over his story yet again. The following day, when Stuart visited Mme. Hédouard, the bookseller near Notre Dame, she told him that several people had been to see her on three different occasions, asking the same questions each time.

Clearly, the ordinary people of Paris were becoming fed up with the constant attentions of lawyers. They were also beginning to realise that this case involved a lot of money. Perhaps some of it could be spread in their direction? Marie Guynette, daughter of the woman who led the foreigner to the babies, told Andrew Stuart that she had lost a lot of time and work as a result of this business, and hoped some consideration would be given to that fact. "We told her," Andrew Stuart wrote in his journal, "that it was not in our power to give her any thing, as she was to be heard as a witness in this cause; and that we could not even promise her any thing hereafter; but that as she would be heard before a judge, who was to examine her as a witness, she might upon that occasion state her case to the judge, so as he might consider it in the sum that would be taxed to her."

By early September, Archy and his aunt were in Paris, staying in the hôtel de Modene, and on the 10th the lawyers, taking Archy along with them, drove out to the suburbs to confront Mme. Mignon. She was not there but her neighbours later told her that four gentlemen, including the heir of Douglas, came in a coach. She rushed off, distraught at the missed opportunity to see the boy she believed to be her son, but when she arrived at the hotel, the Douglas party was not there. She cried for several days afterwards.

It was a bewildering time for the sad laundress. She must have been visited by more upper class strangers in the last few months than she had met before in her life. And she didn't even know their names. When she tried to find Andrew Stuart to tell him of yet more harassment, she went to his hotel and realised that she didn't know whom to ask for. "I want to see the gentleman that belongs to the Monitoire," she said to the porter.

With Archy now in Paris, members of the French team for the Hamiltons were able to compare him with his putative mother. M. Buhot of the Paris police saw him at the theatre one day and was struck by the resemblance.

The Sanrys, too, at this time were receiving mysterious visitors. According to their son, two or three people had come to visit his mother and said they were surprised to see her so ill-dressed. They said they had expected to see her dressed in silk and asked her what had happened to the hundred guineas the curate of St. Laurent had given her.

Day after day, Andrew Stuart and his team added details to the story of the two abductions which only grew stronger as they probed it more deeply. But it was not all hard graft. He had time to enjoy himself with some of the English and

Scottish community who were to be found in Paris at the time. They included the philosopher, David Hume, who was lionised by Parisian society, as Stuart described in a letter in December, 1763, to Baron Mure:

"All ranks of people, courtiers, ladys old and young, wits and scavants vye with one another in the incense they offer up to the *celebre* Mr. Hume. Amidst all this intoxicating worship he preserves his own natural stile and simplicity of manners and daigns to be chearful and jolly as if no such things had happened to him, his manner tho' differing in some respects from the French does not faill however to succeed with them. It must be owned that some of the admirers of his works were at first a good deal surprised at the largeness of his figure. They had generally in idea cloathed him with a person very little encumbered with matter. Diderot amongst others was in this mistake and told Mr. Hume at their first interview that in place of taking him for the author of his works he would have taken him for a *Gros Bernardin bien nourri**.

The Duchess of Douglas continues still in this place. I hear she waits letters from Scotland to determine her motions whether to transport herself there, or to remain here. She continues in the same stile of abusing me from morning to night but has rendered herself so ridiculous by this and other things that I fancy she will think of decamping."[237]

On January 27th, 1764, James Carnegy of Boysack returned to Paris to help the Duchess of Douglas and her lawyers to deal with a rapidly worsening situation. All Andrew Stuart's main objectives seemed to have been achieved – deceit proved in Paris, parents found for both Lady Jane's twins – and, in spite of his personal acceptance that Lady Jane had probably been pregnant, Stuart had done his duty to his client by assembling a number of witnesses from Aix and Rheims who could not remember seeing any signs of pregnancy. The Douglas team,

---

* "A well-fed Benedictine monk"

meanwhile, had failed to produce a Mme. Le Brun or her house, and were burdened with a decidedly shaky Pierre La Marre, partly because Colonel Stewart's testimony and the accounts of the rattle-headed M. Menager disagreed at a number of points.

Both sides were now convinced that the other was indulging in dirty tricks to nobble witnesses. Carnegy wrote in his journal a few days after returning to Paris:

"Have dined with M. Guillemin [secretary to M. Sartine] who appears to have the same good intentions to be serviceable as ever. A story he told to Mr. Makonochie within these few days is an odd one – that he received an anonymous letter in the evening telling him a person would come to him next morning who would communicate to him something of great importance. That accordingly next day about ten o'clock, a man dressed in black with a two-tailed wig, aged about forty, came and said that he was well-informed, that he had been active and serviceable in this cause, and that if he was disposed to render the same services to the other party, he had in his pocket a thousand louis to give him. That he refused the offer and that the person went away and that he would hear from him again. Mr. M. suspects some man that writes and translates for A. Stuart. For my own part I cannot help suspecting this story."

It may have been Carnegy's honesty, combined with his willingness to think objectively about his own side's case, that led to murmurings against him in the ear of the Duchess of Douglas. He was barely back in the saddle before the following occurred:

"Was informed by Mr. Makonochie in the morning but under promise of secrecy, that the Duchess had received the night before a letter from C.--- M—y.* Though he is here every day he says he chose that method to communicate to

---

* Believed to refer to 'Count Murray'.

her his sentiments, in which he says that his regard for her Grace, the Douglas Cause, and the great love he bears to Sir John Stewart and his sister obliges him to acquaint her with the danger in case such a man as I should be trusted in her absence. ... It is a most pitiful case that a cause of such importance should be connected with such people, whose very names are sufficient to cast a slur upon it and whose being employed must give the worst impressions, besides the real hurt they do in hindering others from meddling, who would willingly and honestly do all the good in their power."

After noting that Mr. Hay, Carnegy's colleague in the Douglas cause and a good friend, had decided to go back to Scotland he continued: "... so in all probability I shall be left here quite alone, sure and certain after having used all the diligence and care I can be capable of and even if I should be so lucky as to do some essential service, never once to be thanked for it, and to have all the blame, not only of what may be ill done, but likewise be regarded if any cross thing should happen, as in May and August last, as the cause of it, and as we are not yet at the end of our journey, we may very possibly still meet with some bad steps in the road."

Presumably, Carnegy had suffered from the Duchess's anger at the Sanry and Mignon revelations, which took place in May and August, 1763.

From, now on, we have no more access to Andrew Stuart's journal. Much of his time was taken up with attending the hearings of the commission and seeing how his witnesses' stories stood up to questioning from the other side. Carnegy, meanwhile, was continuing in the search for Mme. Le Brun. He and the Douglas lawyers were convinced that she existed, but with Le Brun being such a common name, and a profusion of Mme. Le Bruns available dead and alive, it was difficult to settle on any one who might have been the woman in whose house the twins were born.

On Thursday, February 9th, Carnegy wrote:

"Early this morning Mr. Hay and I went to Mr. Guillemin and gave him a note 1st with respect to a Mme. Le Brun who lived *dans la rue des Amandiers* who is dead, but whose daughter went into a religious house in Paris; 2nd with regard to a Mme. Le Brun whose name appears in the coach register from Paris to Rouen."

Some days later, he wrote:

"…I begin to be afraid that our researches will be fruitless. …I really believe them to be vain and chimerical and that our Mme. Le Brun must have been some other person than any of these we have yet heard of."

This man Guillemin was a particular thorn in Carnegy's side. Any task he was given seemed to take so long that Carnegy and Hay, his main contacts, ended up doing it themselves. And when he did come up with new information, it was often so implausible or incredible that Carnegy discounted it. And it was usually of the sort that would enhance the Douglas case, and Guillemin's own usefulness to his employers.

For example, he told a story about some discoveries concerning Mme. Mignon which would have been very helpful to his employers – if they had been true.

"The most material thing that passed today with Guillemin," Carnegy wrote on February 20th, "was that he thinks he will be able to prove that La Mignon said that the pursuers had assured her that she should live at her ease the rest of her days, that they would establish her eldest son as a wine merchant in Paris and give him stock sufficient for the first year, and that they would put the other, who is an *Ebeniste**, into a shop where he should learn his trade. For my own part having been so often flattered with evidence which in the end landed in nothing, I shall say nothing of this till we shall have seen the people to whom Madame Mignon said this."

---

* A cabinet-maker.

Three weeks later, Carnegy wrote:

"As to the evidence which M. Guillemin flattered us with concerning the promises made by the pursuers to Mignon and his wife both Mr. Hay and I are now of opinion that it will turn out to nothing. He says these people are put on their guard not to speak nor drink with any body and that they say they are afraid to be poisoned in their drink. They have gone from their old house into another in the same street and do not want that the neighbours should tell where they lodge. They say that two gentlemen sent for them lately to come to a cabaret but that they would not go. All this is what Guillemin said to us."

Then there was Guillemin's mysterious story of the man in the two-tailed wig. By April, Carnegy was having severe doubts about that too:

"In going to dinner, we met Guillemin accompanied by one of his friends. We told him that we had frequently been calling for him, he said that he had been mostly in the country. I could not help at the time thinking of the man with the two-tailed wig, that had offered him a thousand Louis d'ors in order to withdraw his assistance from Mr. Douglas. It must be owned that the Duchess and Makonochie have a wide throat to swallow such incredible stuff and it may likewise be owned that Guillemin could never have ventured to tell a story so absurd, had it not been to a person that he easily perceived was equally unacquainted with persons and things. For my part I can as easily believe any story in the Arabian Nights Entertainment – that the Fairy Peribanou's brother was a foot and a half high and his beard thirty two feet long."

After solemnly noting down another Guillemin 'success' – that he had discovered from one of the many Mme. Le Bruns that she had suddenly remembered that she once let a room to a stranger woman who could not speak French – Carnegy wrote: "I am really tired writing such stuff."

And while he was sifting through the information provided by the irregular army of helpers, Carnegy was also visiting people himself, who might have anything to say on either side, about the deeds of the Colonel and Lady Jane. In the first month or so after he returned to the fray, these are some of the visits he made and people he saw:

Every hostelry in the suburb of la Villette that received carriages, chaises, etc.

The landlady of an inn called the St. Laurent.

A widow who kept a brewery in the Faubourg St Lazare and thought she had seen the foreign gentleman who took Sanry's child.

The glass factory to see M. Mortier, Director General.

Two glassworkers, M. Boucault and M. Pinard, to discuss the character of Nicolas Mignon.

M. Ramper, the gate-keeper of the factory.

Mme. Flon, who lent her baby to Mme. Mignon to be suckled after her child had been taken.

Mme. Clavet, a midwife who had been twice asked during her working life to procure children for other people.

M. Vasson, a male-midwife, who was believed to know about children being obtained from the local Foundlings' Hospital.

Mme. Cochart, a midwife who told Carnegy that she frequently had offers for children.

Mme. Beaujeu, yet another midwife, who was an intimate friend of La Marr's, but never heard him speak of the birth of twins to a foreign lady.

M. Dumesnil, innkeeper at the *Croix de Fer* who had seen the Duvernes party and said that both the ladies with Duvernes spoke French like foreigners.

Mme. de la Garde, a seventy-year-old woman who said she was extremely intimate with one of the Mesdames Le Brun.

Mme. Trenelle, to find out where Sanry's house was when she met there with a nun who had brought the foreign gentleman to look at children.

M. Benoit, an architect who was Sanry's landlord.

Mme. Selle, landlady at the Croix de Fer who told Carnegy that she neither saw the ladies nor the child at the *Croix de Fer* and the gentleman only in passing.

M. Canivet, a bookbinder, who knew one of the Mme. Le Bruns, and told Carnegy that she died of erysipelas

This time of year, February and March, 1764, was not a good time to be trudging about the streets of Paris, trying to find some of the 'low people' of the city. And when Carnegy went further afield, in what was a pretty raw winter that year, the drudgery of the work was exacerbated by the weather conditions.

"In the morning," Carnegy wrote on March 5th, "Mr. Hay and I went to Courcy, two leagues from Rheims with a foot thick of snow in the road. We returned to Rheims about five o'clock. Both of us weary with wet feet and very hungry."

Three days later, still at Rheims, Carnegy and Hay were surprised to find one of the Hamilton lawyers, Aeneas (or Angus) Macdonald staying at the same inn. They were even more surprised to find that Andrew Stuart was staying there too, since he had given out in Paris two weeks ago that he was going to London. He was clearly taking his time, and revisiting Rheims on the way. After dealing with his correspondence, Carnegy was visited by Macdonald who said that "A. Steuart was with him and if not inconvenient would come and pass an hour with us, which they did."

It can be surprising to the non-lawyer how people who are at each other's throats one minute can be quaffing claret together the next. This was something Carnegy's employer, the Duchess of Douglas, was to have difficulty with too. But during this sociable evening, both sides were savvy enough not to let anything slip about their own discoveries or tactics, while trying their best to winkle what they could out of the other party. On the following morning, Carnegy and Hay returned the compliment by joining Stuart and Macdonald for breakfast. But James Carnegy's socialising with the Hamilton lawyers in Rheims was to have unfortunate consequences.

Another Douglas helper came in for some scathing comment about this time. The Abbé Garden (nothing to do with the pig-loving Scots lawyer) had been asked to find a particular baptismal certificate and was taking so long about it that Carnegy went and found it himself. "Surprising that the wise Abbé Garden could not find this," he wrote, "when I am sure the shoe black boy in the house could have done it with ease."

Two weeks after the convivial meetings with Andrew Stuart, Carnegy heard that news of them had reached a member of the Scots community in Paris, via another of the Douglas hangers-on.

"Abbé Crookshank told Principal Gordon but in a great secret that Mr. Hay and I had met with A. Stewart and Angus Macdonald at Rheims. – That we had got drunk together and laughed heartily both at the Duchess of Douglas and Duchess of Hamilton, and added 'Mon Dieu, they are in the right'. He is really an honest man of great veracity."

There are signs in Carnegy's private journal that his old depression was returning. He wrote about "the general conduct of this whole affair from the beginning, people employed and only half trusted, different people employed whose aims could never coincide and who had no communication with one another. In short it seems to me impossible with the greatest art and industry to have conducted and managed any affair so ill as this has been in all its branches. If it succeeds surely it is not owing to the prudence nor capacity of the directors."

One of these "people whose aims could never coincide" was a certain Mme. Rose who had been brought into the affair by Lady Stewart, Sir John's third wife. Her spurious discoveries – as Carnegy believed them to be – drove him to use the sort of language gentlemen would never normally use about a lady:

"Mme. Rose has wrote a letter to Lady Stewart setting forth her great services, how ill she has been rewarded for them, and telling that she has found a Pier La Marre who was in Paris in 1748 and that she can prove by twenty witnesses that he then delivered a stranger lady of twins but that she will disclose this important discovery to no person whatever excepting to Lady Stewart, Mr. Burnet or Mr. Garden. This I could depone is the most abominable rascally nonsense that can be imagined but no more than what people that ever could have any dealings with such a bitch as Mme. Rose deserve so I leave this with this reflection made only to myself, that if Lady Stewart, Mme. Rose's correspondent, had never come to France and if Mme. Rose and others of such a stamp had never been either listened to or employed, things could not have failed to go better, and the foundation of Mr. Douglas's cause, though perhaps narrow, yet could certainly have been more solid and his friends who really wanted to have served him would have known better what they were about and what they had to trust to.

In place of which there seems to all appearances that matters will go on as they began – idle and ignorant people, and which is still worse, knaves and rogues employed and trust and dependance given to idle lies and ridiculous stories. Till the proofs come to be taken which will come like a thief in the night and all these chimeras and phantoms will vanish in smoke."

This day's journal entry ends with a cry of frustration and disgust:

"O, how hard a case to be engaged in such an affair with such people and yet not to know, without coming to extremities, how to get your head out of the noose. And that is even when you see that you are not to be trusted and that in all probability the people by whom you are employed would be greatly pleased to be free of you. Many a man and wife would gladly part, and keep only together on account of what the world might say."

On April 1ˢᵗ, perhaps in an attempt to lift their spirits, Carnegy and Hay went out from Paris for the day, to see a much-heralded eclipse of the sun, but the attempt failed:

"It was a dark cloudy day and rained a little sometimes," Carnegy wrote. "I could not perceive the least appearance of an eclipse…"

Adding to Carnegy's gloom was his perception that the Duchess of Douglas was ignoring any discoveries that might support the Hamilton case. The lawyer in him bridled at this:

"I know the Duchess well enough, by sad experience to be sensible that she detests nothing so much as such discoveries and that in order to please her you must find out stories that appear favourable to her views, though they be never so vain and illusory. In this it happens unluckily that Mr. Hay and I are not people fit for her purpose…"

His dislike of the Duchess was growing. Added to her contempt for the proper legal process was her disorganisation. She had returned to London, and Carnegy received a letter from Makonochie, who was with her:

"…he informs that the Duchess, like Volcius in *The Rehearsal*, has one boot off and another on, or in other words that she does not know whether to go to Paris or Edinburgh, so possibly she may be here in a day or two. What she is to do when she comes I do not know and am certain she does not know herself."

Part of the general frustration at this time may have been caused by the continuing uncertainty about how the next stage of the process was going to proceed. The Hamilton lawyers had appealed to the House of Lords against the Court of Session's dismissal of witnesses approached after the Monitoire and as part of the Tournelle. The appeal verdict was expected some time in April.

On April 10th, Carnegy wrote;

"This is now the day the appeal is to be heard. I heartily wish us success for if Mr. Douglas lose the points he has appealed and the pursuers gain their appeal, without being a prophet I may venture to say we will in the end lose the cause."

On Friday April 13th, the House of Lords produced some good news and some bad news for each side.[238]

The Lords rejected the Court of Session verdict that all Tournelle witnesses and all witnesses who came forth after the Monitoire should be banned from giving testimony in the civil action in Scotland. The Hamilton side were pleased at this, since they would have had a very difficult time proving that Col. Stewart had stolen the Sanry and Mignon children, without that testimony.

But they ruled against Andrew Stuart by confirming the order to abandon the pursuit of Sir John on a criminal charge through the French courts, and hand over to the Douglas lawyers copies of all papers, memorandums or depositions gathered as a result of the Tournelle and the Monitoire.

Finally, the Lords gave the order for a new commission to be organised. This would require representatives from both sides to call witnesses, examine and cross-examine them and eventually prepare Memorials that would state each side's case before the court.

"One thing seems certain," Carnegy wrote, on reading the verdict, "that nothing can be done here these three months." Unfortunately, there was enough administrative work, for Carnegy to have to stay in Paris and become ever more enraged by the erratic behaviour of his employer, the Duchess of Douglas.

13

In the Company of
a Bedlamite

With legal activities intensifying in the courts in Edinburgh and London, the battle between Douglas and Hamilton was attracting increasing public attention. The speeches and memorials of the lawyers for both sides were full of juicy details that supporters and detractors of the two families could mull over. The dirty deeds the late Lady Jane Douglas might or might not have done sixteen years beforehand were counteracted by the villainous activities of the Hamilton lawyers in secretly using the unBritish Tournelle and its evil partner, the Monitoire.

For some members of London society it was all just too much. Horace Walpole wrote, at the time of the House of Lords ruling:

"I have been as indifferent about points, of which all the world is talking, as the restriction of franking*, and the great cause of Hamilton and Douglas."

---

* 'Franking' was the practice by which a distinguished person such as a peer or an M.P. could sign a letter which would then be carried free of charge. Blank sheets could be signed in this way and then handed out to friends who didn't qualify so that they didn't have to pay postage on their own correspondence.

On May 25th, 1764, Andrew Stuart packed his bags for a trip to London. With some chagrin, Carnegy noted in his journal how luck had played into Andrew Stuart's hands during his time in Paris:

"A thing comes in my head which I have thought and probably wrote before – that supposing A. Steuart should succeed in gaining this process, he has little or no merit in the affair, though he will have the whole praise of it. He was here in Paris near six months before he began his criminal process with money at command, nobody to oppose him and fully assisted by the police in making all his researches. Yet even after his process before the Tournelle had been commenced five months it's a most certain truth that all the proofs he could have brought would not the least have been regarded, not only in Scotland and England but nowhere in the world. Chance wrought for him what he all his lawyers and all his Inspectors of Police could never have done. The Abbé Poulle, by clattering overly at table (for which he has since wept bitterly to me) made the discovery of a child's having been carryed away from the parish of St Laurent in 1749. Without this evidence of a child's being taken away it is most certain that the parliament would never have ordered a Monitoire and without the Monitoire the carrying away a child in July 1748 never could have been heard of, these people living in a remote corner of this vast Metropolis and the Curé of the Parish never having been informed of the matter."

Carnegy was also worried about the state of the Douglas defence and the performance of his own colleagues. He was critical of Alexander Makonochie, who was in London when he was needed in Paris and who, in any case, spoke French inadequately:

"It is time he were (here) as the process in all appearance may begin sooner than our people seem to expect. If they do not besides send over some knowing prudent man who speaks French, affairs must go wrong, for I foresee a terrible weight of evidence against our own evidence, at least Sir John's is the worst thing against us, neither can we give the least account of ourselves either in the 1748 or 49, but such a one as is worse than saying nothing. When the process draws near, all the idle stories with which people have been amusing themselves with the police and imaginary witnesses to prove the existence of persons that never did exist and facts which never happened, together with ridiculous hearsay stories, will vanish and what has some appearance at least of solidity and reason can only be attended to, as I neither can nor will go about among the underlings of the police."

The French lawyers and assistants, too, continued to exhaust Carnegy's patience:

"(Desjobert) is a most impertinent scoundrel, horribly ignorant, with a great opinion of his own talents and knowledge. It requires more than Job's patience to have to deal with such a low fellow."

For Andrew Stuart, now that the air was cleared – not entirely satisfactorily – by the House of Lords, there was a major campaign to be planned. With the criminal case abandoned, his lawyer's mind could concentrate on framing one case rather than two – a civil case that Archy Douglas should be deprived of his inheritance because he was not the son of Lady Jane.

There were some who thought that the case was entirely unnecessary, that Archy's right to the inheritance didn't really depend on providing meticulous and irrefutable proof that he had been born of his mother's body, but that it was enough for his parents to acknowledge him as their child. This was known as the principle of filiation, and at an inn in Utrecht, on his way back to England, Andrew Stuart bumped into a young lawyer, James Boswell, who adhered very strongly to this principle.

Boswell at this time was a 23-year-old Scotsman, embarking on a legal career and with great ambitions to make a mark on the world, although, as he had said to David Garrick the year before, "I am much afraid that this blossom will never swell into fruit."[239] He was eventually to bear fruit, not through his legal skills but as a result of a chance meeting with Dr. Samuel Johnson which led to Boswell's unique biography of the writer.

Someone said of Boswell that "it was impossible to look in his face without being moved by the comicality which always reigned upon it."[240] Since, by all one can gather about Andrew Stuart, he seems to have been rather a cold fish, the two men might not have been expected to hit it off particularly well. Combine that with Boswell's growing support for the young Archy Douglas and it is likely that the time they spent together, sharing a coach on the journey from Utrecht to Rotterdam, was not spent in fruitful conversation about the Cause.

Boswell's views were summarised by his leading biographer, Frederick Pottle:

"The 'principle of Family' is a complex of so many passions that the outcome of its application to cases is unpredictable. The House of Douglas, in spite of its late sorry representative ... was the proudest house in all of Scotland. The very mention of the name caused Boswell's knees to slacken and he oftener than not wrote it in the oversize characters he otherwise reserved for the Deity: DOUGLAS. Boswell did not want the great House of Douglas to be submerged in the House of Hamilton. To him, the boyish figure of Archibald Douglas was a symbol of Family itself, fighting for its life in a degenerate world."[241]

Pottle, the twentieth century American historian, knew more about Boswell than any other man. But he seems to have felt that James Boswell and his life and work were not looked on as suitable subjects of study for a serious academic. In a letter to Lillian de la Torre, author of *The Heir of Douglas*, he wrote: "In the academic world, particularly in that portion of the academic world that does not engage in original scholarship, the term 'Boswell scholar' is irresistibly ridiculous.

It carries about the same connotations as the phrase 'eminent proctologist'. To consider proctologists funny is unjust, for surgery of the anus and rectum qua surgery, is just as difficult and laudable as surgery of the chest.* But it will never seem so to people in general; nor will the literate public ever cease to feel that serious scholarship devoted to James Boswell is, in its first aspect, ridiculous."[242]

For the duration of the Cause, Boswell – sometimes deserving the label 'ridiculous' – was to wave the flag for DOUGLAS, at times putting himself in jeopardy of the law. He published a number of letters between Lady Jane and Colonel Stewart, written between 1748 and 1753, and wrote of this correspondence: "I entreat my readers may peruse these moving letters, and I know how their honest breasts will feel for much injured innocence. In reading that correspondence, it is just as if two alledged confederates in crime were overheard talking together in the very next room; and when we hear them breathing such strains of truth, shall we not believe them? Nay, it is as if we saw into the very bottom of their hearts; and what do we find there but the sincerest parental affection?"[243] To make doubly sure his readers knew what a sweet and fragrant creature Lady Jane was, Boswell removed her occasional peevish or derogatory remarks from the letters.

Often given to breaking out in verse, Boswell wrote several poems about the Cause, some published at the time, some discovered in his papers after his death.

Two verses of one poem about the deeds of Andrew Stuart in Paris will suffice to give the flavour, with a translation for English readers:

---

* I can't help noticing that 'Boswell' is almost an anagram of 'bowels' and wonder if this influenced Pottle's choice of analogy. Come to think of it, Pottle's a pretty excretory name, too ...

Gif ye a dainty mailing want
And idleseat prefer to working,
Ablins ye'll get it by a plea
That far aff owr the seas is lurking.
Gang ye your ways to Paris town,
Blow in the lug o' lown and sorner,
And Ise be caition yese bring hame
An enlèvement frae ilka corner.

Translation:

If you want a nice farm
and prefer idleness to working,
Perhaps you'll get it by a law-suit
that is lurking far off over the seas.
Go your way to Paris town,
whisper in the ear of ragamuffin and sponger
I'll guarantee that you'll prove an abduction
from every corner.[244]

While Andrew Stuart was in London and Scotland, planning the next phase of the Hamilton campaign, Sir John Stewart was on his last legs at the family seat of Murthly Castle. When James Carnegy heard this he made an astute observation:

"Mr. Brown says Sir John Stewart is just dying and that he is going to Murthly. I make no doubt if Mr. Brown arrives in time but Sir John will emit a proper death bed declaration. It would be the devil to eat the cow and worry about the tail."

This remark, to me, hints at a belief in Sir John's guilt, a belief built up over months of disastrous discoveries by Andrew Stuart and his team, which were boxing in the ability of the Douglas lawyers to make a strong case for their client. "Eating the cow" is presumably doing the deed in the first place, in which case, why worry about "the tail", the small matter of a telling a lie in your deathbed declaration?

In fact, on June 7th, Sir John duly fulfilled Carnegy's prediction, with his usual shaky spelling:

"Having lately had some sever fitts of the goutt in my stommach," he wrote, "with my health in other respects much impaired, these, with my great age, going seventy-six, make it apear incumbent on me to make the following declaration, as aspersions have been thrown out by interested and most malitious people as to the birth of Ladie Jean Douglas her children, in order to robb the surviving child, Archibald, of his birthright, by making his parents, Lady Jean and me, apear infamous, to make him illegittimat.

I, Sir John Stewart of Grandtully, do sollemly declare, before God, that the forementioned Lady Jean Douglas, my lawfull spouse, did, in the year 1748, bring to the world two sons, Archibald and Sholto, and I firmly believe the children were mine, as I am sure they were hers. Of the two sons, Archibald is the only [one] in life now. I make this declaration, as stepping into eternity, befor the witnesses aftermentioned: James Biset, minister of the gospel at Caputh, and James Hill, minister at Gurdie; John Stewart of Dalgoos, Esq., Justice of Peace; Joseph Anderson, tennent in Slogenhole.

(Signed) "Jo. STEWART.[245]

A week after writing this, he was dead.

For Boswell, the deathbed declaration of Sir John, adding its weight to similar declarations by Lady Jane and Mrs. Hewit, clinched everything. There no longer could be any doubt about the legitimacy of Archy's inheritance, as he wrote in his epilogue to the correspondence between Lady Jane and her husband.

"It remains candidly to inquire what weight these Declarations should have with the rational part of mankind. I own they have very great weight with me. ... The heavy charge now brought against them in a volume of circumstantial and *most suspicious* evidence, has been positively contradicted by all of them when stepping into eternity. Let us lay our hands, upon our hearts, and judge as we would wish to be judged."[246]

Meanwhile, in Paris, the "bitch" Mme. Rose was up to her tricks again. She was still offering to deliver a living Pierre La Marre, for a suitable fee. "My opinion," wrote Carnegy, "is that neither Makonochie nor anybody else will ever see him." Mme. Rose also launched an attack on Carnegy and John Hay, in letters to her friend, Lady Stewart, Sir John's wife, "filled with the most incredible and abominable stuff I ever read," Carnegy said. "Though she does not name Mr. Hay and me yet she says plainly that we are sycophants and rogues and gives more than a broad hint that the last journey we made to Rheims was in order to have a meeting with A. Steuart and Angus Macdonald in order to betray Mr. Douglas."

Even the best lawyers in the world need a good case to work on, and Carnegy was becoming convinced that the Douglas lawyers didn't have one. "I am sorry to say it even to myself that when the foundation is false it is a difficult matter to raise a superstructure that is good and honest and of which the different pieces tally and correspond."

The Douglas team's strongest asset at this stage in the investigation was Pierre La Marre. Although Mme. Rose couldn't produce her La Marre, the widow of Menager's La Marre was still alive and being courted by the Duchess for any information she could give that would corroborate the circumstances of Archy's birth. But Carnegy was dubious:

"This forenoon," he wrote on July 4th, "for the first time visited Mme. La Marre with Mr. Makonochie who invited her to dine with the Duchess on Sunday next. For my part I cannot see what use this woman can be of, for though she was married to La Marre more than a year before the date given for Lady Jane's delivery she never heard one word of any such thing. It's true she has a sister whom I never saw, who, it's said, remembers that her brother in law had the care of a child at nurse about that time somewhere towards where the woman lives to whom we gave the name of Sholto's nurse. There is indeed in La Marre's account book which I saw last year and which is ill wrote and seems to have been very irregularly kept, the name of a Madame Le Brun as debitor. This book is at present in the Tournelle in the hands of the clerk and cannot be seen."

Menager was another of the Duchess's regular dinner guests. While the Duchess and Makonochie saw him as an asset to the Douglas case, Carnegy thought he was more of a liability, and wrote in his journal an account of one of the Duchess's dinners:

"I am now ... more convinced if possible that Menager is a rascal than ever. The instant supper was done or rather before it, he went out, and whispered to a woman they called their neighbour so we were left with the wife and this woman, two ugly and fat bitches. ...The woman then produced a watch which she said was of infinite value but as she knew the English were fond of curious things it was better bestowed upon them than her and that she would part with it to any of us for £1800 livres. It possibly might have been worth £800. Then Menager's wife said 'nothing would give her greater pleasure than to have a good English watch and chain'; in short the whole plot was most visibly either to get money or presents or promises of them. Makonochie, who did not understand the tenth word of what passed and has no notion of such things, was not in the least sensible of the thing. I wish he may not in like manner be deceived by others with whom he has dealings here, I can scarcely doubt that it must be the case. We met Menager himself in the court as we came away who pretended he had been abroad, though I am fully persuaded her had never been out of the house."

Makonochie was clearly a source of continual worry to Carnegy at this time. For all his doubts, as a good and honest lawyer Carnegy wanted to do the best for his client. But Makonochie was the senior Scots lawyer in France, and in fact stayed with the process longer than anyone else. However, Carnegy saw him day after day being hoodwinked and scalped by witnesses, French lawyers and the police, and felt that he really didn't have much of a grasp on the case. Guillemin seemed to have a particular contempt for Makonochie, as Carnegy witnessed over dinner one evening: "(Guillemin) told him that he spoke excellent French, when I could not comprehend what he said." Carnegy also saw how Guillemin cheated Makonochie by selling him bottles of liquor at three times the going rate and shoddy clothing that he pretended was made of the finest cloth:

"Guillemin has by way of favour given him (Makonochie), at an exorbitant price, ugly old-fashioned silk for his suit of clothes which he says he got wrought on purpose at Lyons, though I know they are Tours manufactory. People that use such little tricks to me will always be suspicious."

One of the tasks keeping Makonochie busy at this time was the search for the real Mme. Le Brun. Dozens of women with this name had been traced and rejected. Now, in July, another one popped up. This search was triggered by the discovery in police records that on August 3rd, 1748, an English couple, Mr. and Mrs. Soulard, had lodged at the house of a Mme. Thonne. This was really clutching at straws, in the hope that Soulard was a misreading of Stewart. As Carnegy wrote drily: "This landlady's name is Thonne, a short name like Le Brun, according to our ordinary sensible interpretations." But Makonochie's hopes were dashed when it turned out that Mrs. Soulard had not given birth and had not even been ill in the house, and was therefore certainly not Lady Jane Douglas.

The Douglas team were also spending time trying to knock holes in the Mignon story. Guillemin had produced evidence of a number of male children abandoned in Paris in 1748, who were taken into the Foundlings Hospital, presumably suggesting that the Mignons' lost child might be one of them. But for Carnegy, the Mignons' story rang true:

"I know that upon conversing formerly with the witnesses in that affair, the story appears so connected that it was impossible for me, or indeed, I believe, anybody else to doubt that Mignon and his wife actually did give away a child to a gentleman and lady in July 1748 and that they received money for it."

What also supported the Mignon story was corroboration of their claim that on the day they gave away the child they arranged for a mass to be said at the church of St Esprit for the child. "We actually find," wrote Carnegy, "that on the 15th of July, 1748, a mass was said for Jacques Louis, the name of Mignon's child, and the pursuers will be able clearly to prove that on the 18th of said month Mignon and his wife made merry at a cabaret with the money they had got."

In Scotland, meanwhile, the Douglas lawyers had argued successfully for a Commission to begin gathering evidence in France as soon as possible, although Carnegy was all for delaying the process in the hope that witnesses favourable to the Hamilton case might die or the costs rise so much as to cause them to rethink.

In a letter on August 19th, Carnegy wrote:

"For my part I think the managers for Mr. Douglas in Scotland are absolutely infatuated. They have really cooked an excellent dish of fish. I wish them joy in the eating of them. The Duchess whose folly and ignorance is past comprehension understands not one word of the matter and has been singing all day."

The following day, Carnegy and Makonochie went to see M. de la Combe, the French lawyer who had recommended procrastination, to break the news that the Commission was to go full steam ahead.

"It's impossible to conceive the astonishment and vexation he was in upon reading the Interlocutor and still the more when I told him that it had been chiefly obtained by our means. He thinks that now there is no back door left and that the proof will go on without obstacle or difficulty. He has a very mean opinion of the capacity of Mr. Douglas's council and managers in Scotland and said *Il faut que les gens la soient bien bêtes ou au moins infideles.** The latter, I told him. 'They were not,' he says, 'they are very generous to raise out of the mire their enemies of whom they complain so loudly and who, without the aid we have given them, might have remained in the mire nobody could tell how long.' It is really a terrible shock and what is the worst, past remedy – the most decisive judgement in this great cause, and which a child may see, entirely against the defender."

Carnegy's second spell in the service of the Duchess of Douglas had now lasted more than twice as long as his visit the previous year. Once again, family business was pressing, and he was eager to get back to Scotland. But there were three other reasons why he wanted to put France and the Douglas Cause behind him – the conduct of his colleagues, the weakness of the evidence in favour of Douglas, and, perhaps more pressing than the others, his growing detestation of the Duchess of Douglas.

"I am really impatient to see what is down in Scotland in order to get out of this disagreeable situation, of living in the house of an outrageous woman who every hour exposes herself and who, though she pretends to be extremely civil I know believes firmly, ever since Mr. Hay and I were at Rheims, that we betrayed her."

Like many members of the aristocracy in those days, Peggy, Duchess of Douglas, was a tyrant when it came to relationships with subordinates, which category effectively encompassed everyone without a title. The legal team were at her beck and call, carrying out her requests however stupid or ill-informed. In a way, it was fortunate that she distrusted Carnegy. It meant that she gave her attention to Makonochie, Burnet and the other more favoured lawyers, who were also required to dance attendance on her more often. Nevertheless,

---

* "These people must be stupid or at least disloyal."

on too many occasions for Carnegy's liking, he was invited to dine with the Duchess and 'no' would have been a very inappropriate answer to such an invitation.

It was on these occasions, when the Duchess usually let her hair down, that Carnegy found her most loathsome, as shown by a succession of journal entries scattered throughout the period of his stay in France in 1764.

"As Mr. Makonochie is not well, though I keep away from the Duchess as much as possible yet I am obliged to be with her at the time of meals, and really the lies and nonsense that she speaks quite stupefies me. She is certainly the most terrible woman I believe ever existed."

"This day and yesterday the Duchess has rather been more ridiculous and madder than usual. She really behaves in so shocking a manner that scarcely any mortal comes near her."

"This day the Duchess very outrageous. Dinner began by her damning, cursing and spitting, and ended in rank gross bawdy. It is well she only exposes herself to her own family and servants as no mortal has eat with her since she came last here. How she exposes herself to any company comes in the afternoon I know not as I never eat my food in her drawing room but when forced to it."

These remarks were made in June, and, interestingly, there is independent corroboration at this time of rumours about the Duchess's behaviour as leader of the Douglas team. On June 22nd, David Hume wrote from Paris to Baron Mure, co-tutor with Andrew Stuart of the Duke of Hamilton.

"A few days ago," Hume wrote, "I din'd with the Dutchess of Perth which was the first time I had seen that venerable old lady, who is really a very sensible woman. Part of our conversation run upon the Douglas affair. There was present a gentleman, an old friend of yours, a person of very good understanding, and of undoubted honour who laid open to us a scene of such deliberate dishonesty on the part of her Grace of Douglas, and her partisans, as was somewhat new and surprising. I suppose it is all known to poor Andrew whom I heartily love and pity. Hay, the Pretender's old secretary, the only man of common honesty among them, confessed to this gentleman, that he has frequently been shocked with their practices, and has run away from them, to keep out of the way of such infamy, tho' he had afterwards the weakness to yield to their sollicitations. Carnegy knows the roguery, as well as all the rest; tho' I did not hear anything of his scruples."[247]

Baron Mure himself was no favourite of the Duchess's because of his strong role in organising the Hamilton campaign. "Ah, that Baron Mure!" she is supposed to have said while out walking in the Tuileries Gardens, "if I cotch him, I'll mak him as barren a muir as ony in Scotland!"[248]

Occasionally in his journal, even though it is clearly private, Carnegy uses dashes to dilute the impact of the stronger language. When he means 'bitch', he writes 'b---h', for example. There's one intriguing entry where the word he means is not at all clear, but probably refers to a part of the Duchess's anatomy: "She is really a dreadful woman," he wrote, "her folly is possibly greater than her ――."

It is difficult to know quite what the Duchess's problem was. She was obviously a high-spirited woman, as the circumstances of her courting of the Duke revealed. But she was also not particularly well-educated and may well have felt out of her depth as the legal processes unfolded. Carnegy thought the Duchess was ignorant of the significance for the Douglas case of many of the discoveries being made almost daily while she was in Paris, but it is just as likely that she knew only too well how harmful they were to the cause of her nephew, and was trying to ignore this. She was certainly a very emotional woman at this time, as another journal entry shows.

"It is two o'clock and the Duchess still abed," Carnegy wrote, "This probably will be one of her low sullen days. She got up to dinner in high spirits and before it ended she was weeping bitterly, for what neither she nor anybody can tell."

He then made a remark that implied, not for the only time, that she was mad. "There are many people lodged in certain places who have not so good a title to be there as she has," he wrote.

More bad behaviour was apparent in July:

"This day the Duchess most outrageous at dinner, cursed and damned her sister, called her bitch, whore and liar and ordered her out of doors. Now all this from beginning to ending is as false as hell and in this way does she go on every day and can, with as much care as I can take a pinch of snuff, forge a lie to murder the reputation of any person whatever. I feel often the same symptoms as in the fit of an ague when in her company."

The Duchess was also a vain creature, and resented the fact that her rival was such an acknowledged beauty. One night at dinner in Paris she described how the Duchess of Hamilton had behaved seductively in front of her husband, the Duke of Douglas. She had laid herself down "on a sopha in order to let the Duke of Douglas get a full view of her legs and thighs which he did, that she saw them likewise but was not afraid as her own were ten times handsomer and more tempting. On the Duchess of Hamilton's way to Douglas the people had gone out to see her but that she [the Duchess of Hamilton] was terribly mortified to hear the whole of them cry out 'our own Duchess is fifty times bonnier than her.'"

By August, Carnegy's comments on the Duchess's mental stability are more frequent, and shared by others.

"Makonochie now thinks she is mad and that it will soon break out throughly."

"The Duchess very high and mad this night."

"The Dutchess this night so mad that at supper, she said that she had right to be a queen and ought to have been one, that she would go to Berlin to see the K. of Prussia who only was worthy of her. That she would put herself at the head of the vassals and followers of the House of Douglas and with the sword in hand drive her enemies off the face of the earth.

All this time her hands and feet beat time to her words, which were so loud that they might easily have been heard in the street. It is really an agreeable thing to be confined to the company of such a Bedlamite."

The Duchess of Douglas even occasionally invented a language of her own. "This morning Lord Allfort came to visit the Duchess," Carnegy wrote. "She entertained him first about Sir John Stewart that he had always a very bad memory. That even in his young days he had an *Ethururial one*. Whenever she is in high ceremony she has a hundred such words. ... Dined at the Scots College and in the evening the Duchess outdid herself in lying, evil speaking and nonsense in so much that when I came to go to bed I was quite stupefied."

"The Duchess all this day in outrageous high spirits, clapping her hands, roaring, laughing, lying and speaking nonsense. She told at dinner that she never had but two dangerous distempers in her life, that in both, high fevers, she had been given over by all her physicians, the one occasioned from the sight of a mouse, the other of a rat."

By mid-August, Carnegy had asked Makonochie to break the news to the Duchess that he had to return home. On August 23rd, he met her to discuss the matter: "In the forenoon she at last spoke to me of my going away, told me what a loss it would be to her affairs, fell acrying, tears she has at command, in a quarter of an hour afterwards she was roaring and singing. I told her that though my own affairs and my mother's health were out of the question, that she knew herself I could not stay along with certain persons that were to come over*, though she knows that the thing is certain and determined and I believe is exceedingly well pleased yet I must lay my account to suffer much grimace and many theatrical performances. However, ten days I hope will now put an end to my sufferings."

---

* James Burnet, whom Carnegy disliked.

But he had to suffer one more encounter with the Duchess, perhaps the most offensive, at dinner on August 25th:

"Last night she was more ridiculous and more insupportable than can be conceived. In complaining to Mr. Strange of the dearness and badness of the inn where she lodged at Dover she said the service was so bad and the people so dirty – that 'they did not teem* her pot but left it full both of thick and thin'. Let anybody consider what a figure I make as part of such a woman's family."

Three days after learning about the Duchess's nocturnal toilet arrangements, James Carnegy booked a place in a coach for St Omer, on the road to Calais. A week after that, on September 4th, he left Paris, and the 'family' of the Duchess for ever.

James Carnegy of Boysack was to lose a daughter later that year, who died in childbirth, and he himself only lived another four years, dying of "a putrid fever" at Sancerre in France, in 1768.[249] But he left us, unwittingly, a rare and vivid glimpse into the extraordinarily shambolic goings on in Paris as the two teams of lawyers pitted their wits against each other.

With a pessimism born of a detailed knowledge of the evidence, Carnegy must have thought the Douglas Cause all but lost as he crossed the border into Scotland.

But locked up in the coffers of the Tournelle, to see the light of day for the first time the following year, was a hotel register that was to provide a very unpleasant surprise for Andrew Stuart.

---

* Pour out (Scots)

14

A Setback for Stuart

Whatever had been learnt by questioning witnesses inside and outside the Tournelle during 1763 and 1764 now had to be revisited for the Commission set up by the Court of Session. The ordinary people of France who had played bit parts or starring roles in the meanderings of Lady Jane and Colonel Stewart from 1747-9 now had to tell their stories all over again. The Mignons, the Sanrys, the Michels and the Godefrois must have wondered what they had got themselves into.

We now know, but it was surely suspected then, that repetition of half-remembered events consolidates them in the mind until they become cast-iron certainties, so vivid before the mind's eye that it is no longer possible to doubt them. Accusations of perjury and corruption flew around between the two sides, as witnesses changed their stories or disagreed with each other, but some inconsistencies in testimony, at least, were just as likely to be due to the imperfections of memory, the intimidating circumstances of the Commission hearings, or the desire to say something rather than nothing.

The taking of evidence began in October, 1764, at the

Hôtel d'Artois in Paris. Each witness 'deposed', and a statement based on that deposition was taken down in the third person.

As attackers of the Douglas claim, Andrew Stuart and his colleagues concentrated on assembling witnesses to prove four key facts:

- That Lady Jane only pretended to be pregnant.

- That she did not give birth in Paris.

- That she and Colonel Stewart abducted the Mignon's baby son in July 1748.

- That she and Colonel Stewart abducted the Sanry's baby son in November, 1749.

The Douglas team assembled its witnesses to prove the following five facts:

- Lady Jane was pregnant between November 1747 and July 1748.

- She gave birth to twins in July 1748 at the house of Mme. Le Brun.

- There was a male midwife called Pierre La Marre who assisted at the birth.

- One child, Sholto, the weaker one, was put out to nurse at a village outside Paris until November 1748.

- The other, Archibald Douglas, stayed with his parents and was now the rightful heir to his uncle, the Duke of Douglas.

As it turned out, both sides produced reams of evidence to support all nine of the above 'facts'. But by today's standards, both the nature of the evidence and the way it was obtained meant that it was often unreliable. There were many examples, on both sides, of dredged up memories and reports of conversations that had taken place many years before, that were thrown into the pot in the hope that some of them would support or contradict the claims made by Archy Douglas about his parentage.

A week into the hearings, the Mignons' turned up at the Hôtel d'Artois to tell the story, probably true, of the time they sold their baby to a stranger. They were followed by Marie Guynette, who said how she had heard "more than a hundred times" the story told by her mother of the day a stranger came up to her at her bread stall outside Notre Dame and asked her to find him some babies.

Another piece of the story was filled in on November 5th by Mme. Anne Garnier, a quarryman's wife, who lived on the road from Paris to Menilmontant. She told of being brought a sickly child to nurse by a man-midwife, Pierre La Marre, some time in the summer of 1748. From the child's dress she imagined "he was not a child belonging to this country, as his clothes were quilted and after the English mode, and the headdress and caps being edged with lace which she believes to have been English." She said that two gentlemen, who spoke French with a foreign accent, came twice to her house to see the child, and that she looked after the child for about eighteen months until he was taken away by Pierre La Marre.

(This piece of evidence, if true, could refer to Sir John bringing his son or a friend to meet Sholto, as he had mentioned he might do in his letters, something which couldn't have happened, of course, if Sholto was really Joseph Sanry.)

The day after Mme. Garnier's deposition, it was the turn of Pierre Menager to step into the spotlight. Both sides hoped to use him to support their case. Andrew Stuart was by now convinced that the late Pierre La Marre known to Menager and married to the still living Mme La Marre was different from the Pierre La Marre described by Sir John in his testimony to the Court of Session, and he hoped to use Menager's testimony to prove that. On the other hand, for the Douglas lawyers it was a matter of any port in a storm, and they felt they could deal with any inconsistencies by skilful argument.

By all accounts Menager was a self-dramatist, and probably enjoyed his time in the spotlight. As we've seen, Andrew Stuart suspected that he was working to a script supplied by the Douglas lawyers. For those in the Hamilton team who had come to believe that Menager was a fantasist, it rather confirmed that view when he described in his testimony how he came to meet the Duchess of Douglas. "I was at the Prince of Turenne's," he said to the commission, "where we were reading *Hippolyte, Comte de Douglas*, and I recounted what I knew of the affair (of the Hamilton/Douglas lawsuits)." *Hippolyte, Comte de Douglas* was a romance written by Mme. Marie-Catherine D'Aulnoy in 1690 which, in fact, had nothing to do with the current Douglas family, and included one of the very first fairy tales ever published. The following day, Menager continued, the Comte de Murray came to visit the Prince de Turenne and mentioned that the Duchess of Douglas was then in Paris. The Prince apparently said "There is no one who can give you better information about the affair than my surgeon, M. Pierre Menager," and the relationship – along with the detailed account of Pierre La Marre, perhaps – was forged.

The story Menager related to the commission was just what the Douglas team wanted to hear, at least as far as the details of the birth were concerned. It featured the man-midwife, Pierre La Marre, whom Menager had known and worked with for seventeen years, Mme. Le Brun, and her daughter and her furnished rooms, along with "a lady of great family" aged about forty-eight, and two boys, one of whom was weakly and put out to nurse in the neighbourhood of Menilmontant. But there were a lot of inconsistencies to be explained.

Sir John Stewart had described Pierre La Marre as a Walloon, a French speaking inhabitant of Belgium; Menager's friend was not. Sir John described him as having been an army surgeon in 1721, when Menager's La Marre was only ten years old. Menager's La Marre could not have delivered twins in 1748 because he was apparently away from Paris in the army.

Then there was the fact, mentioned in one of the letters allegedly from La Marre to Sir John, that he had spent some time in Naples. Makonochie had arranged for enquiries to be made in Naples in 1763, although in fact, Pierre La Marre's widow said he had never been to Italy. Andrew Stuart taxed Menager with this mystery.

"The answer he gave after thinking a little," Stuart later wrote, "was, that his friend was very much of a *libertin*, and that he had often suffered by the *maladie venerienne;* and that as that disease in France often goes under the name of the *maladie de Naples*, from whence it came, La Marre, by the *voyage de Naples*, had probably meant to intimate to his correspondent, that he (Delamarre) had lately *passé le grand remede pour la maladie venerienne*. This answer was so remarkable, made such an impression on me and on Mr. Buhot, who was also present, and shewed us so completely the disposition and character of this man, that it was impossible for us ever to forget it."[250]

The Douglas team had had no success in finding their Mme. Le Brun. The best they could do was to bring before the commission in December another Mme. Le Brun. She had the mellifluous maiden name of Pelagie Prissette, and the Douglas lawyers were keen for her to tell the story she told only a few days before, the day before Christmas Eve, to Mr. Makonochie, M. Guillemin, and an army officer, M. Jean Valfort. On this occasion she said that nine years ago a friend, Mme. Fontaine, had told her about another Mme. Le Brun who witnessed the birth of twins to 'a stranger lady of great distinction' seven years beforehand, making this event occur in 1748. And she even recalled the name of the accoucheur, a man who was paid fifty guineas for his services. Makonochie and the others must have been delighted to learn that she remembered his name as

La Marre. According to M. Valfort she also said that "when she should appear before the judges, and if God himself should descend from heaven, she would say nothing else."

This Mme. Le Brun was therefore rushed into the schedule of witnesses on December 27th, and the Douglas lawyers must have sat back in eager anticipation of the effect her statement would have on Andrew Stuart and the Hamilton team. They can only have been dismayed, therefore, to hear her say under questioning by a Douglas lawyer that her friend Mme. Fontaine never spoke to her of a man-midwife called La Marre, nor had she told her that a stranger-lady gave birth to twins in the house of a person called Le Brun. She also said that "what she has at present said upon oath is the pure truth."

The author of one account of the case, wrote: "We see, that in only four days this woman is transmuted by some secret chemistry from a strong witness for Mr. Douglas, to a very artful agent for the pursuers."

The Hamilton lawyers were ranging widely in their selection of witnesses and experts, some would say unnecessarily so. One issue, for example, was the exact status of the letters that Colonel Stewart said he had received from Pierre La Marre. Although he claimed to have had a long correspondence over several years with the man-midwife, only four letters survived, three at least admitted by Sir John to be 'copies' and all of them described by Andrew Stuart as forgeries. It has to be said that a schoolchild with elementary French would be able to pick out the errors in these letters, and be pretty sure that they were not written by a Frenchman.

One, for example, in which he describes his trip to Naples, begins as follows:

"Paris Jain le 9 ume 1752

Monsieur J'ay recut la ooke ili a quilque temps par la quille Je suis bien aise d'aprendre que les francs jumaux dout J'avois le bon heur d'heureusement accoucher Madam votre chere Epouse 10ieme Juliet 1748…"

This was probably the most significant of the letters, since if its contents were genuine, it confirmed Archy's inheritance unequivocally. A rough translation of the core of the letter is: "I am glad to learn that the twin-brothers, of whom I had the good fortune to deliver Madam, your dear spouse, on the 10th July 1748, are well; especially the youngest, Sholto Thomas, for whom there was so much fear, having come into the world so weak, that I was obliged to perform also the office of the priest..."

Whatever the source of the contents of these letters, the Hamilton team said – and the Douglas team grudgingly had to accept – that they were unlikely to have been written by an educated Frenchman, and any French person off the street could have testified to that effect.

Andrew Stuart, however, wanted the biggest gun he could find and he turned to the originator and editor of the 28-volume *Encyclopédie*, Denis Diderot. Diderot was a friend of David Hume's and so it is likely that Hume suggested to Andrew Stuart that he show the La Marre letters to the eminent encyclopedist. Although he couldn't speak English, Diderot could read it very well. "I am reading the maddest, the gayest, the wisest of all books," Diderot wrote to his mistress, Sophie Volland, while engrossed in the first six volumes of Tristram Shandy.[251]

Now, on May 14th, 1765, one of France's greatest intellects appeared before the commission and solemnly picked his way through the errors in the four La Marre letters. "From the style, the phrases and the idioms of these letters," he said, "I do not believe they can have been written by a Frenchman, unless that Frenchman had been at pains to write them in the English idiom." Diderot quoted a number of phrases which seemed to be word for word translations of English phrases into French. *"Pour quelque temps passe il a beaucoup soufert"* was one, and *"Je suis tres perswade que vous serez tres satisfait en le voyant; ce que vous nous faites esperer bientot."*

"Amongst all the faults which one might fall into in writing the word *persuadé*," Diderot said, "the only one which could never be committed by a Frenchman is to put in a *w*, a letter which is almost not of any use in the French language." He also pointed out that where there were French words that ended *re* with an English equivalent ending in *er*, such as lettre/letter and fièvre/fever, the English word was often used by the writer of the letters.

The Douglas lawyers tried, without success, to get Diderot to agree that there were different dialects of French and that, perhaps, in a town like Montreuil sur Mer, where La Marre hailed from, they did things differently there. There was also the matter of the signatures to these letters which struck a French reader as odd since they included La Marre's full name, *Pier La Marre,* and occasionally even *Peir la Marr*, where a Frenchman would write just *La Marr.*

However humble his contribution, it is possible this experience whetted Diderot's appetite for more information about the strange story of the birth of Archy Douglas. Later the same year, in a letter to Sophie Volland, he complained about how busy he was, saying that there were on his desk a comedy, a tragedy, a translation, a political work, a report, and a comic opera:

"The report," he wrote, "to which I will give all my time and knowledge because its object is worth it, concerns a Scotsman called Mr. Stuart who is contesting the award of a great title and an inheritance of many millions to a supposititious child whose parents are intoxicated with 'posterity mania.' It is a cause that requires the judgement of a geometer as much as a lawyer, one where a man who knows how to calculate probabilities will have plenty of scope."[252]

Around this time the parliament of Paris announced that it considered Jean Calas, who was executed three years before, as innocent of the murder of his son. This was the culmination of the campaign by Diderot's great foe, Voltaire, against the legal process, including the Monitoire, which led to Calas' trial and condemnation.

By now, with the bulk of his case assembled, Stewart must have thought that things were going pretty well. The witnesses called before the commission were merely telling the story that Stewart and his team were increasingly confident was true, the story told in the Monitoire, that began with the first remarkable discovery that Colonel Stewart had signed a false name at the hôtel d'Anjou where he and Lady Jane were staying when they claimed that she was giving birth to twins at Mme. Le Brun's.

The only problem was, this discovery – the one that started the two lawsuits, the reduction of service and the Tournelle – was incorrect. The fulcrum of the Hamilton case against the Douglas story began to crumble as the Michels and the Godefrois gave evidence in June 1764.

Andrew Stuart believed that Sir John and Lady Jane had registered at Mme. Michel's hotel on July 8th, under a false name, and that, since Lady Jane had clearly not given birth at Michel's on the 10th, but was in possession of a baby soon afterwards, the baby must have been the Mignon's child, which the parents believed had been abducted round about the middle of July.

On April 12th, 1765, the commission heard testimony from the lawyer, Pierre Duruisseau, who had made a written statement about the Michel's hotel register, lodged in the Tournelle since 1762. What he said backed up Andrew Stuart's original account of the register. Duruisseau testified that: "the article concerning *Monsieur Fluratl*, a Scotsman, and his family, entered the 8th July 1748,* did not appear to the deponent any way suspicious; ... That the deponent remembers to have asked at Michelle, Of whose writing was

---

* The name was 'Fleuralt' in Andrew Stuart's original account of the discovery, but 'Fluratl' in Duruisseau's deposition.

the article of Monsieur Fluratl? And that Michelle answered the deponent, That this article was neither of his writing, nor that of his wife; and that he presumed that it was of the person who called himself *Fluratl*."[253]

But a few days later, Mme. Michel testified to the Commission that, as far as she could remember without seeing the actual register, the 'Fluratl' entry was written by her maid, Marie, who wrote a number of the other entries on the same pages. This matter – the confusion of signatures and dates between Duruisseau and Michel – could be settled in only one way.

Alexander Makonochie wrote to Andrew Stuart asking to see the original books of Godefroi and Michel, to confirm some of the testimony that was being given. Stuart said he could not supply them and that the French court would not release the books until all the witnesses in France had given their testimony. It was only in July, after the commission had finished hearing the last batch of witnesses, in Rheims, that both sides could inspect the books.

Robert Richardson, a clergyman who wrote a detailed analysis of the case a few years later wrote:

"As the proof stood on the 3d May 1765, it appeared plain, that sir John Stewart and lady Jane came to Michel's on the 8th of July; that they brought the child thither on the second or third day after their entry; all which was easily ranged in such a manner as to coincide with the day on which the Mignons lost their child, Thursday the 11th of July. Such a rare coincidence of two independent events, proved by witnesses who had no connection with each other, could not but strike every rational mind, and assure success to the pursuers.

What must be our surprize to find, that a cold and chilling frost came in this month of July 1765, from what quarter we cannot tell, to blast these laurels?"[254]

The 'frost' that Richardson referred to crystallized around a word and a number on one page of the register of the hôtel d'Anjou. On July 12th, both parties were finally able to inspect the books, and in particular, the page of Michel's register that showed the 'Fluratl' entry. So important was this page that an engraving was made for inclusion in the legal papers.

The entry for 'Fluratl' in the register at the hôtel d'Anjou

There are two things apparent even to the uninformed eye. First, contrary to Duruisseau's sworn deposition, the writing of the 'Fluratl' entry is *similar* to that of several other entries on the page, so it was unlikely to have been written by Colonel Stewart. Second, although the date says "Le 8 juillet 1748" the entry comes just after an entry for July 10th, suggesting that the 8th was a mistake and should have been the 18th.

The Godefrois also spoke before the Scottish Commission about the visitors who stayed at their hotel from July 4th to 8th. They argued convincingly that their memory of the entries in their expenses book demonstrated very clearly that the visitors were Colonel Stewart and his wife. But along with the Michel's register, newly released from the Tournelle's archives, was the Godefroi book in question which showed serious discrepancies between the confident story of the Scottish gentleman and two ladies told in the Godefroi's testimony, and the scrappy and inconclusive nature of the actual entries which were said to provide an account of the group's consumption of food and drink over a period when they denied staying there at all.

One of the Hamilton side's own supporters wrote:

"I have considered the evidence of this man Godefroi, and of his books, and I confess I never saw such a Burlesque upon evidence. An inn-keeper swearing at the distance of eighteen years to the particular days of the week or month when a person or company entered to his house, what rooms they occupied, and how many days they staid, is such a memory as never was heard of before."[255]

Richardson wrote at the time: "As for the credit and conclusiveness of the article in Godefroi's household-book, it amounts to this; that someone once owed him something..."[256] And he attacked the confidence placed by Andrew Stuart in the various hotel registers by saying: "If a man goes to a gaming-table, and after changing the dice three times finds, that he can still throw nothing but deuce-ace, he must be void of reflection, if he does not begin to suspect, that all the dice in that house are loaded."[257]

Now that the books themselves were available, there were several conclusions to be drawn. First, Duruisseau must have committed perjury. Second, it was likely that, far from being an invented name designed to disguise the identity of the couple, Fluratl was a misreading by the maid Marie, "a woman addicted to drunkenness", of the name 'Stewart', given to her on a piece of paper by Colonel Stewart. His signature found on the bottom of letters could easily be read in that way.

Why it ever occurred to anyone that, in search of a pseudonym, a Scotsman called Stewart would light on *Fluratl* rather than a name like Donaldson or McTavish defies belief. Third, it was likely that Colonel Stewart and Lady Jane had entered Michel's on the 18th July, just about when they said they did.

Looking at the events of July, 1748, in the light of a detailed examination of the books of the Michels and the

Godefrois, it seemed probable that Colonel Stewart, Lady Jane and Mrs. Hewit had travelled from Rheims to Paris, and stayed at Godefroi's from July 4th to some time before the 10th; that they had been somewhere else between the 10th and the 18th – the Douglas team would say at Mme. Le Brun's – and then arrived at the Michels' hotel, on the 18th and not the 8th. If this was the case, there was ample time for Lady Jane to have given birth to twins between the two hotels

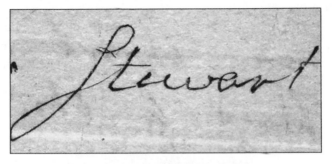

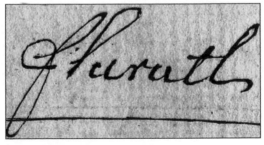

Sir John Stewart's signature, compared with the 'Fluratl' signature.

After nearly three hundred witnesses had given evidence and many hundreds of thousands of words been transcribed, it was finally time for the two legal teams to prepare their Proofs, the collections of all witness statements, and head home.

The Duchess of Douglas took a while to pack her bags and assemble her entourage, but by September 11th she was on the road. On that day, Horace Walpole happened to be travelling in France, and on arriving at a hotel in Amiens, discovered that the Duchess was staying there too.

"We are not likely to have an intercourse," he wrote to a friend, "or I would declare myself a Hamilton." The following day he discovered that she had left the hotel, to continue on her way home.

"You will not guess what she carries with her," he wrote. "One of her servants died at Paris: she had him embalmed, and the body is tied before her chaise: a droll way of being chief mourner."[258]

It took Andrew Stuart another two months to drag himself away from Paris, on December 17th, 1765. Two days later, the order was given in Edinburgh for the evidence to be printed, and the scene was set for the contest.

15

Pleadings and Probabilities

The arguments for and against Archy Douglas's claim would be made before a panel of fifteen Scottish judges, making up the Court of Session in Edinburgh. In those days, it seems that the Scottish legal system was treated by its practitioners like a club whose members had considerable latitude in how they did their job. The judges were a law unto themselves and behaved pretty well however they liked.

For a litigant, receiving a clear and just decision from a judge about some complex legal matter could be jeopardised by all sorts of factors. Drunkenness, for example. A judge called Lord Newton considered that he worked best after six bottles of claret. One day, a client called on him at four in the afternoon and was told by the judge's servant that he was having dinner. When he said to the servant that he thought the judge' dinner time was five, he was told "it is his yesterday's dinner."[259]

Even when sober, some Scottish judges behaved in court as if they weren't. Lord Herman disliked intensely his fellow judge Lord Meadowbank and whenever they were on the bench together he would ask the macer, a court official, to open the court window, knowing that Meadowbank preferred it closed. "Macer, shut that window" Meadowbank would say, and the macer would do so, only to be ordered by Herman to open it again, until one or other of them got tired of it.[260]

This kind of bad behaviour extended to the advocates. One barrister, Henry Erskine, amused himself by making faces at the Principal Clerk of Session, Sir James Colquhoun, who was sitting at a table underneath the judges' bench. Colquhoun became very annoyed and said to the senior judge "My Lord, My Lord, I wish you would speak to Harry, he's aye making faces at me." By this time, of course, Erskine was sitting as sober as – well, as sober as a judge, and the trial continued, only to be interrupted by another cry from Colquhoun of "There, there, my Lord, see, he's at it again."[261]

At the time of the Douglas Cause, there were few rules about judges having to demonstrate impartiality in any case in which they were involved. It is an astonishing fact that several of the fifteen Court of Session judges who heard the case had previously been members either of the Hamilton or the Douglas legal team.

If the Douglas Cause had occurred anywhere else in Great Britain at the time, as a case concerning property it would have been tried by a jury. But Scotland, after the Union with England, had held on to the practice of trying such cases by a bench of judges in the Court of Session. This had a major drawback, as a writer in the *Scots Magazine* pointed out in 1767: "It has been observed that it is next to impossible in so narrow a country as Scotland to find fifteen judges, most of them men of family and fortune, so entirely unconnected with the great causes that come before them, in point of consanguinity, interest or assertion, as to be perfectly indifferent about the event or impartial in the decision."[262]

This was certainly true with the Douglas Cause.

Francis Garden, the pig-lover, who had spent months in Paris preparing the Douglas defence to the Tournelle charges, had by the time of the court hearing been elevated to the bench to become Lord Gardenstoun. David Dalrymple had written several of the intermediate Memorials for the Hamilton side during the various legal skirmishes in France, before becoming Lord Hailes; Lord Justice-Clerk Miller had acted for the Hamilton side before becoming a judge; James Burnet had worked hard for the Douglas team in Paris, where he was detested by James Carnegy, and then when he returned to Scotland he was made a judge, taking the title of Lord Monboddo. In addition, three of the judges, Lords Kames, Coalston and Elliock had all acted as tutors to Archy Douglas.[263]

Such a situation would not be allowed today, when no judge can try a case in which he has any personal interest at all, let alone having been paid by one of the parties to do work to support their case. Indeed, in mediaeval Scottish courts, judges had to 'recuse' or excuse themselves if they had been an advocate for one of the parties.[264] Even in the 18th century, the appointment of Monboddo as one of the judges generated a certain amount of comment from the Hamilton side, but Monboddo's friends and contacts were more powerful and included the Duke of Queensberry, a close relative of Archy's, so Monboddo took his seat on the bench.

Once all the lawyers were back in the country, and the proofs and accompanying paperwork were printed and circulated, the public interest, always high in the case, grew more intense.

"The Attention of the public has of late been much engaged by the important cause between the Duke of Hamilton and Mr. Douglas," one observer wrote. "It has been the prevailing topic of conversation, and has occasioned disputes and wranglings in almost every company. High and low, young and old, male and female, have interested themselves in this cause with a warmth equally unprecedented and unaccountable. The pleasure of society was for a long time imbittered by altercation, and whole evenings dedicated to chearfulness, were spent in ridiculous contest."[265]

"In society every one took a side," said another writer. "Ladies quarrelled over the Douglas Cause at their tea-tables, and gentlemen argued it warmly in the taverns. ... The names of the witnesses and the places were on every one's lips. Nurse Garnier, Mistress Hewit, Godefroi's, and Madame Le Brun's were as well known as Bergami, Majocchi, and the Grotto at the Villa d'Este were at the time of the Queen's Trial."[266]

The lawyers had hoped to put both sets of proofs into the court in January, but the task of printing was so huge, both in the size of each volume and the numbers of copies needed for all the parties, that the job had to be shared between printers in Edinburgh and Paris. Each side printed the testimony and cross-examination of the witnesses it had chosen to call, along with letters and other documents that it had managed to obtain from the other party. Each volume was over a thousand pages, with a total of about 800,000 words between them, including translations into English of the French testimony and documents. The Douglas proof also contained carefully executed engravings, of pages of the Michel books, and of the Pierre La Marre letters.

One indication of the size of the task and the problem of meeting deadlines was a note at the end of the Defender's proof, the account of the testimony of the Douglas witnesses. "As this proof was thrown off in a hurry and in different printing-houses," the harassed lawyer wrote, "mistakes have happened in calculating the number of pages of different parts of it, which were differently printed; for example, it was supposed, that the French proof, as well as the translation of it in English, would have taken up more pages than in fact they have done. ... there are several blanks left in different places, owing to the miscalculation of pages."

It wasn't till the end of February that the volumes were finally handed into the court, but there was then a further delay. Faced with this raw testimony, the Court of Session asked for some kind of analysis of the arguments before they would listen to lawyers' speeches, and it took another three months to prepare these new documents.

Finally, on Tuesday, July 1st, 1766, a lawyer called Andrew Crosbie stood up in the modest room that was the Inner House of the Parliament Hall of Scotland, and addressed the fifteen judges, ranged at the bench in front of a large fireplace. He was the first of four lawyers to speak for the Hamilton side, taking up the rest of the week, including Saturday. Then, the following week, four lawyers spoke for Douglas, from Tuesday till the following Tuesday, with the weekend off. There were then replies by two Hamilton lawyers, and 'duplies' by two Douglas lawyers, taking up another four days.

On July 23rd, as if there hadn't been enough opportunity to spell out the evidence against Archy Douglas, one of the Hamilton lawyers stood up to summarise the case. His 'summary' took up much of the next five days, followed by a mercifully shorter reply – only two days – by one of the Douglas team.

There are no transcripts of these speeches – perhaps mercifully – and indeed, there is not even an exact record of the list of lawyers for each side. There is a suggestion that nine more lawyers were involved in addition to the eight mentioned above.

During the month of pleadings, lasting the whole of July, spectators crowded the narrow gallery that overhung the advocates' tables. The pleadings were, said Sir William Fraser, "the longest, 'tis believed, that ever were before a court of justice."

Long as they were, the pleadings and the associated paperwork were not enough to satisfy the judges, and the court ordered detailed printed arguments for each side, called Memorials, to be prepared and to be handed in by September 27th, less than two months after the end of pleadings.

A week after the due date, Andrew Stuart wrote to his brother about the problems this pressure had caused. When

Stuart realised that it would be very difficult to meet the deadline, he had sent a note to the Douglas lawyers, who hurried to complain to the judges about the proposed delay. Hearing of this, Andrew Stuart decided to rush the Hamilton memorial to print after all, although he wasn't happy about it:

"Sir Adam Ferguson and I are both employed in bringing forward the Memorial as fast as possible. In a matter of this importance every thing must be thoroughly digested and arranged in the best manner before sending abroad to the world a paper on which will depend the opinion of judges and the sentiments of mankind in general. It is evident that this must be the interest of the party which has the merits on their side. As to the party against whom the merits are, their interest is to have the matter as incomplete and indistinct as possible. We are in excellent hands in Sir Adam Ferguson's who understands the Cause thoroughly and will let nothing pass but what is solidly well founded."[267]

The problem with assessing – then or now – the huge amount of evidence for and against the granting of the Duke of Douglas's lands and money to Archibald Douglas is the volume and nature of the testimony gathered over the space of three years, and the lapse of time between taking testimony and the events to which that testimony refers. Both sides adopted the tactic of treating every word of their own witnesses' statements as the gospel truth – unless it failed to support their own case. With these hundreds of statements laid out, they then went into the fine detail of each witness, looking for, and usually finding errors and contradictions. These were then paraded in the Memorials as proof that the other side had primed, bribed and corrupted witnesses.

As usually happens with lawyers, this was partly a tongue-in-cheek process. The adversarial system never allows a lawyer – who may respect and be on good terms with his opponent outside the courtroom – to imply that there exists the slightest jot or tittle of support for the case he is making. There are many examples in the Memorials of righteous indignation at the idea that the other side could believe for a moment the evidence of their own witnesses.

The Hamilton Memorial was written by Sir Adam Ferguson, who drew attention to many inconsistencies in the accounts of witnesses. But, as Robert Richardson pointed out, even the most honest person cannot remember everything that happened to him in fine detail :

"Had these witnesses agreed in every circumstance, every reasonable person would have suspected them of perjury. Errors arising from the defect of memory must be expected at the distance of seventeen years. Sanry's child was taken from him much in the same manner the witnesses have related; it was a transaction only of three days, which deeply interested the persons who saw it; it became the immediate subject of a public inquiry, ... yet in the detail of that short and interesting transaction there are not less than forty mistakes and contradictions in the time, in the number of person, number of visits, and other circumstances. What indulgence then is due to witnesses who are called upon at such a distance of time to recollect trivial circumstances, in which they could never possibly be in any manner interested?"[268]

The oddest example of Adam Ferguson's advocacy was in the extraordinary use he made of the mathematics of probability to 'prove' that Archy and Sholto must have been Jacques Louis Mignon and Joseph Sanry.

In an eight-page section of the Memorial for Hamilton, headed *The Application of these Enlevements [Abductions] illustrated by Calculation* Ferguson wrote:

"It seldom happens in matters of legal discussion, that the facts admitted to proof are ascertained with mathematical certainty ...

The present case, in what relates to the enlevements, is one of those which admit of the application of *numbers*; for it contains *data* upon which a solid calculation can be founded.

The pursuers are sensible, that an attempt of this kind, may, on account of its being unusual, appear at first sight chimerical, or void of solid foundation.

But as they shall state the principles upon which they proceed, and submit to examination every step of the calculation, they flatter themselves, that, when examined, it will appear to proceed upon solid ground; and that this method of viewing the matter may contribute to throw some light upon the subject."

Ferguson starts by asking how likely is it that the crime of abducting someone else's child should take place in Paris just at the time that Colonel Stewart and Lady Jane were staying there, taking a nine day period, and he works that out at 445:1 against.

He also calculates how likely it is that, of all the people in Paris during July it should be another British couple, with the man about fifty-five, who carry out the abduction, and gets the figure of 4500:1 based on the ratio of foreigners to locals.

He then asks: if there were such another couple, how likely is it that they were seeking to replace twins, as opposed to a single baby, and he does some calculations about the frequency of twin births, which he takes as one in ten. (All his estimates are very conservative, taking probabilities that favour the Douglas side, since he knows that the extraordinary method he uses will come up with huge probabilities anyway.)

Combining all these probabilities – 445:1, 500:1, 9:1 and 9:1 he arrives at 22,344,599:1 as the likelihood that Colonel Stewart abducted the Mignon child. But he hasn't finished his impressive mathematical tricks. He now turns to Sanry and, in a similar way, with a few more factors such as the absence of a servant and the fact that there were a man and two ladies involved in the abduction, he comes up with the odds against anyone other than Lady Jane and her husband being involved in the Sanry abduction coming out to be 516,160,259 to 1.

Now, with a final flourish, Ferguson combines the two odds – as he is allowed mathematically to do – and comes up with the following conclusion:

"The result of this is, that there are 11,533,394,545,595,999 to 1 *in favour* of the pursuers application of these enlevements to Sir John Stewart and Lady Jane Douglas, and *against* the defender's hypothesis, of their having been committed by any other persons. ... To give some idea of the immensity of this *odds*, the chance here contended for by the defender is much less than the chance one individual, particularly named, would have of drawing the single prize in a lottery where all the inhabitants upon the globe were equal adventurers."[269] (It's a shame Ferguson chose such a feeble example. If there were four million inhabited planets with as many inhabitants as there are today on earth and all with tickets for a universal lottery, the example would be nearer the truth, and equally pointless.)

Speaking in the House of Lords, Lord Mansfield later dismissed Ferguson's mathematics, saying "such arguments were better suited to certain societies in London, well known to some of their Lordships, than to a court of judicature." Gambling was rife in London at the time.

James Boswell was beginning to take a deeper interest in the case about this time, having become a lawyer himself in July, 1766. He was a friend of Archy, a few years younger than him, and, since he lived in Edinburgh he dropped into the Court of Session from time to time, to hear the pleadings. His father, Lord Auchinleck, was one of the fifteen judges. In a letter to a friend, another of the judges, Boswell wrote: "My Father has been very busy with the Douglas Cause; and as a Relaxation has read Don Quixote. Whether there be any thing allegorical in this, or which of the Parties he takes to be fighting with Windmills, I leave to Your Lordship to judge."[270]

There was much hilarity in legal circles at Ferguson's mathematics and Boswell captured this in one of several sets of verses he wrote about the Cause:

> "Tho' Sages would, with wond'rous strength
> O'erpower him by the force of *Numbers*,
> Think you the gen'rous youth is gone?
> Think you his Counsel will be dumb-bears?
> Since Calculators have advanc'd
> To strike us like a clap of thunder!
> Why don't Astronomers dispute
> The very star he was born under?
> Who e'er denied that Fifty is
> Less giv'n to sport than Five-and-twenty?*
> And who could not from Paris bring
> Blank books and tavern bills a-plenty?
> We've read how children have been owned
> By rings, by bracelets, or by lockets:
> But now, to dispossess an heir,
> Proofs may be found in Falstaff's** pockets.
> Should noble DOUGLAS lose his cause
> Foes may 'gainst all our families dance in,
> And ev'ry egg-shell of a plea
> Become a boat to sail to France in."[271]

There was one other reason why all of Ferguson's calculations might have been beside the point. It was possible – and the writer of the Douglas Memorial said as much – that the Mignons and the Sanrys had merely been bribed to tell stories that, at the very least, were heavily massaged to make them conform to the circumstances of Lady Jane's visit to Paris.

"…That Mignon and his wife have considered themselves as interested in the issue of this process, and that they expected great benefit from it, if the pursuers should prevail, is proved by many witnesses. It appears, that they talked of the cause as their

---

* That a woman arrived at the age of fifty should have a child is much more improbable, than that a woman of twenty-five should have one. HAMILTON *Memorial*, Part 1, p 22

** Boswell compares Godefroi's book of expenses, giving details of many bottles of wine consumed by the party he says were the Stewarts, with Falstaff's consumption of sack "two gallons 5s 8d" in Henry IV Part II Act II last scene.

own, and mentioned themselves as parties. They supposed, they were to get back their pretended son, and were made to believe, that though he should be deprived of his estate, he would still be a rich man, having 25,000 livres of rent independent of the law-suit. Promises appear also to have been made to them, and good deeds done, and offered to be done, to them, and their children. Lest the Monitoire should not be a sufficient instruction, printed papers were given them, by an under-agent for the pursuers, before their examination, containing the whole story of the gentleman and lady, their age, their country, their being in quest of twins, &c. Sensible, however, that if they had acknowledged any of these things upon oath, their credibility would have been suspected, they were pleased roundly to deny every fact of that kind, that was put to them, to assert, that they had always told the story in a uniform manner, and among other things to swear, that they *never read, nor received from any person, any papers with regard to this affair.* – That they have sworn falsely, appears from the following evidence."[272]

The writer of the memorial then quotes the testimony of a police office, M. Loret:

"...she, Mignon, said to the deponent... that Mr. Stuart had promised to do good to her and her husband during the rest of their lives; further, that Mr. Stuart had promised her to cause two of her sons be received guards of the city, (Gardes de la Ville), to give them the privilege of selling wine without buying the freedom; and, as to her youngest son, he would cause teach him the business of cabinet-maker."[273]

Another section of the Douglas Memorial produced evidence that abductions or *enlevements* were not as rare as the Hamilton team made out, and that Paris was rife with child-snatchers during the mid-18th century.

"In the great and populous city of Paris, accidents very frequently happen of children being stole, abstracted, exposed, or missing. Of this there is full proof from the deposition of Mr. Hombron[274], clerk to the hospital of *enfants trouvés*, who, among other things, says, that in the year 1764, there were no less than 5560 children received into the said hospital; and also from the great number of masses which are constantly said for lost children in the different churches of Paris."

This was followed by a few examples:

"A lady from the provinces came to Paris in the year 1755, and lodged in the house of Madame St Martin; she applied to her landlady, telling her, that she would be happy to have the child of some poor person to educate, either boy or girl. It appeared that she had formerly taken and educated the female-child of a poor woman in Burgundy, to the age of seven; after which, being displeased with her, she had returned her to her parents. – Madame de St Martin, the landlady, after some enquiry, procured her a male-child of one Forêt, a gardener at Neuilly Sur Marne; and this child, after having been drest in new cloaths, was put out by the lady to nurse, with a woman called Aubin, at Chaillot near Paris."

Nay, to such a height was this practice of stealing carried some years ago, in Paris, that it occasioned a popular insurrection, for the punishment whereof sundry arrêts of parliament were pronounced. Indeed the many cases of *partus suppositio*, and other questions of filiation, which have been tried in almost every court in France, afford convincing evidence of the frequency of this crime in that country."[275]

A sentence in the Douglas Memorial highlights the one issue above all others that the fifteen Scottish judges would have to decide:

"That a child may have been exposed, sold by, or carried off from, Mignon and his wife, some time in the year 1748, the defender has no occasion to dispute; such accidents happen so often in Paris, that they are not in the least wonderful; but the subject of enquiry, at present, is, whether the pursuers have proved that Sir John Stewart and Lady Jane Douglas did possess themselves of Mignon's child, and whether the defender is that child?"

The whole of Britain — that is to say, the slice of society who mattered — was agog for the answer to that question, which the judges of the Court of Session were to ponder for a further six months before giving their verdict in July, 1767.

16

Neck and Neck

" In the rich and beautiful province of Andalusia lived the prince of Dorando, of the race of the ancient kings of Aragon. His family had long subsisted in splendour, and several branches of it were established in different parts of Europe. But Don Carlos, the last of the male line, having in his youth had some difference with his sovereign, quitted the court, and, taking a disgust at the world, shut himself up in the castle of his ancestors…"

In May of 1767, those words were written down by James Boswell's secretary, at his dictation. They were the opening words of a novella, called *Dorando: A Spanish Tale*, and they were part of Boswell's campaign to get justice for his friend Archy Douglas. He had decided that, in addition to writing verses about the Cause – which he would recite to anyone who would listen in the precincts of the Court of Session – he needed to set out a more expansive and detailed account of the arguments. But because the Court of Session was in the middle of considering the issue, he felt he would be on safer ground if he thinly disguised the case in a work of fiction, and published it anonymously.

They don't come more thinly disguised than *Dorando*. Don Carlos was the Duke of Douglas, with a beautiful sister the lady Maria (Lady Jane). Don Carlos had an evil retainer called Don Stocaccio (Stockbriggs) who adhered to some relatives of the Duke, the Arvidoso family (the Hamiltons). After the lady Maria was married to Don Spiritoso (Colonel John Stewart) they went to Paris for lady Maria to give birth, and the Arvidoso family used Stocaccio to poison Don Carlos's ear with stories of supposititious children.

Boswell painted a flattering portrait of one Donna Eleanora (the Duchess of Douglas), including a dream she had in which the lady Maria visited her to seek her help in getting justice for her son, Don Ferdinand (Archibald Douglas), against the machinations of the Arvidoso's lawyer, Don Pedro Stivalbo (Andrew Stuart).

The climax of the book was the judgement by the "Senate of Seville" on the issue of whether Don Ferdinando was entitled to inherit his uncle's wealth. *Dorando* was published a month before the Court of Session was due to deliver its judgement and in his book Boswell anticipated the result he wanted.

"Never was there a more interesting scene. The judgement-hall was filled with a crowd of spectators, mostly people of rank, who waited in the greatest anxiety and trepidation, to hear the fate of Dorando. When the senators took their places, not a murmur was heard, all was fixed attention. The senators sat for some minutes in awful silence.

The chief justice was a man of great knowledge in the laws of his country; of a clear head and sound understanding. … He at last addressed his brethren – 'I find here before me, a process, the intention of which is to stigmatize with infamy a princess of the noblest blood in Europe. We have the continued acknowledgement of parents. – We have their positive and dying testimony; with the positive and dying testimony of a woman who was present at the birth of the defendant. – I lay my hand upon my heart, and I judge as I would wish to be judged."

In a resounding speech of the sort that Boswell himself would dearly love to have made, if he had achieved his dream of acting for Archibald Douglas, the chief justice wiped the floor with the arguments of Don Pedro. Then in a burst of wishful thinking, Boswell wrote:

"Thus spoke the chief justice, with a warmth of feeling which went to the heart of every spectator. Never did he appear in greater glory. The senators also delivered their sentiments to the same purpose, in various kinds of manly eloquence, which did equal honour to their justice and to their abilities."

Boswell then wrote "The Arvidoso clan gnashed their teeth in rage and despair," and went on to describe an appeal by them "before the grandees of Spain at Madrid." Here, "an illustrious grandee", presciently similar to Lord Mansfield who was to take part two years later in the real Lords appeal, gives an even longer and more eloquent speech in favour of Don Ferdinand than the chief justice. "What have we now before us?" Boswell makes the grandee ask, and he answers his own question: "A daring attempt to render our children uncertain. If adulterers have been thought worthy of death, what punishment do they deserve, who would introduce what is still more dangerous to society? A few wives may be unfaithful; but every wife may be attacked like the princess of Dorando. Have we not here the constant acknowledgement of parents, unredargued, unconcussed, undebilitated; but by vague suspicions mustered up twice seven years after the birth of the prince? And must we then prove the birth of our children? I tremble – I shudder at the consequences."

The book ends with a reconciliation between the prince of Dorando and the prince of Arvidoso, such that "From that time foreward, the greatest intimacy subsisted between the two families. The prince of Dorando married a lady of great beauty and merit, and continued in dignity and in lustre the race of his ancestors."[276]

One reviewer of *Dorando*, clearly a Hamiltonian, wrote: "This is a most contemptible pamphlet, and alludes, though in a very imperfect and unfair manner, to the great cause about the succession of the Douglas estate, which has been so long the object of public expectation."[277]

In spite of, or perhaps because of, such publicity, *Dorando* was a best seller, published in June and going through two more printings in the same month. Clearly this was because people were avid for anything they could get their hands on about the Douglas Cause, rather than because of its literary merit. But it did receive *some* highly favourable comment, accompanied by large extracts from the book. Two days after publication, a review in the *Caledonian Mercury* said "At a time when all ranks are agitated with expectation, and parties have run so high that much ill-will and many unhappy animosities are raised, 'Dorando' comes like old Nestor, to calm the violence, and to diffuse good temper and complacency of disposition."[278]

After the second printing, less than a week later, the same, anonymous, reviewer wrote: "There is here the most perfect poetical justice, while, at the same time, the mind is left to overflow with benevolent sentiments. ... The very favourable reception of a Tale which inculcates the noblest sentiments of virtue and religion does honour to our country..."[279]

The highest praise of all, concise enough to be printed on the dustjacket if they had had such things in those days, was a remark to the effect that "if the hand of M. Rousseau is not there, 'Dorando' is at least the production of no ordinary genius." Unfortunately, the value of these tributes is diminished somewhat by us knowing today, through the scholarship of Frederick Pottle, that they were all the work of James Boswell himself.[280]

Barely a day passed without some newspaper story appearing which we now know was by written by Boswell. He planted an item in the *London Chronicle* saying "a threatening incendiary letter has been lately sent to the Author of *Dorando*, a Spanish Tale, declaring with horrid imprecations, that if he does not retract the speeches and arguments therein contained ... he shall be stabbed in the dark." This took in a friend of Boswell's, who wrote to him in a letter after this item appeared: "I ... expect dayly *Dorando*. I learn by the English prints, that you are threatened to be murdered in the dark for writing it; this is a new way of confuting a book, for the Spanish Inquisition when they put one to death do it in day light."[281]

There was a report that admission tickets to the public gallery in the Court of Session were sold for half a guinea, with the profits going to the Edinburgh Royal Infirmary. Another story described how a party of London stenographers, all acknowledged "to write the shorthand better than any in England," had set out from London to report the speeches.[282] Both of these stories were pure invention, another of Boswell's tricks. So pleased was Boswell with his fictional shorthand writers that he built on the first story, with a report from Berwick of their progress north, including their names. This was followed up three days later with entire biographies of the men, such as "Mr. Noel Burridge", whose "life has been one continued scene of strange adventures ... Cornishman ... went to Pennsylvania ... employed a spy by the government ... with a fountain pen in the shape of a fan..." There was even a letter from Mr. Burridge himself, saying that because of delays in the court hearing he and his friends were about to set off on a jaunt to the Highlands.

On July 7th, 1767, the fifteen judges took their seats in the Inner House of the Scottish parliament. They would take it in turns, in order of seniority, to give their analyses of the case and announce a verdict. Public interest was intense, aroused partly by what one observer has called "that obstetrical flavour which never fails to commend a lawsuit to the public imagination."[283] (This is as true today as it was then.)

They were a colourful lot, these Scottish judges. Many have become a rich source of anecdotes, describing behaviour that suggested a considerable degree of self-confidence, self-importance and lack of concern for the image they portrayed.

Robert Dundas was the Lord President of the Court, and was known as a tyrant. He used to have an hour-glass on the bench to restrict speeches by the other judges. "He had often been seen to shake his old-fashioned chronometer ominously in the faces of his brethren, when their 'ideas upon the subject' began to get vague and windy."[284]

It was said of Lord Pitfour, rather inconsequentially, that "His eyesight was weak, in consequence of which he always wore his hat on the Bench."[285]

Lord Hailes, as Sir David Dalrymple, was known as a historical writer of distinction, with a daughter who was "of dwarfish and deformed figure, while amiable and judicious above the average of her sex." (She remarked to a friend one day: "I can say, for the honour of man, that I never got an offer in my life."[286])

Lord Monboddo was a philosopher, who was roundly mocked at the time for his belief in evolution, and that men and apes were closely related.

And Lord Kames was perhaps the most eccentric of an eccentric bunch. After a witness on a capital trial had concluded his testimony, Kames said, "Sir, I have one question more to ask you, and remember you are on your oath. You say you are from Brechin?" – "Yes, my Lord." – "When do you return thither? " – "To-morrow, my Lord. " – "Do you know Colin Gillies? " – "Yes, my Lord, I know him very well. " – "Then tell him I shall breakfast with him on Tuesday morning."[287]

Kames was noted for his frequent use of the word 'bitch' as a mildly affectionate insult, although when directed at witnesses or the accused it wasn't seen that way. At his last appearance in court, eight days before he died, he looked around the court and said to his fellow judges "Fare ye a' weel, ye bitches!"[288]

Kames once found himself having to try a farmer for smuggling, a man with whom he had occasionally played chess. The poor man was found guilty and Kames sentenced him to death, ending the sentence with the words "The Lord have mercy on your soul." He was then heard to say, *sotto voce,* "and that's check-mate to you."[289]

Dundas, as president, opened the proceedings. As one of the judges in 1761, when Archibald Douglas was served heir to the Douglas estate, he agreed with the decision at the time. But he revealed within the first few minutes that he had now changed his mind. If the other fourteen judges came up with a majority verdict one way or the other, Dundas would not vote, but if there was a tie, he would get the casting vote. Over the next six days, two or three judges a day spoke, sometimes at great length, about what had led them to decide for or against the validity of Archy Douglas's claim.

Each judge was persuaded by different aspects of the case and often in contradictory ways. In his opening speech, Dundas addressed the dying declarations of Lady Jane Douglas and Colonel Stewart.

"The death-bed declarations in this cause do not move me," he said. "When crimes are committed, the committers rarely choose to confess, if by concealing they can escape that infamy which otherwise would pursue them. Lady Jane could not but see, that, when the Rubicon was past, there was no retreating. Had she been tempted to have divulged a secret so important, the consequences would have been infamy on her own memory, and capital punishment on her associates."[290]

Lord Pitfour, in his speech, inferred innocence rather than guilt from the death-bed declarations;

"In the present age, infidelity and scepticism are accounted fashionable; but I will aver, that this is more owing to pride and affectation than to any conviction possible to the mind of man, That there is no future state of rewards and punishments; and I do believe that there are but a very few who are so execrably worthless, and insensibly hardened, as to make a joke of eternity. Some malefactors there may have been, who after having been fully convicted of crimes, may have gone to death publicly denying them. But there was no conviction, nor the least danger of conviction to the parties in the case now before us; and when to this we add, that their characters are proved to have been not at all of the infidel cast; what conclusion can we possibly draw, but that they died asserting the truth?"[291]

And Lord Gardenstoune, too, was entirely convinced by Lady Jane's dying words:

"When I see her in the pangs of death, pouring out her blessings on her then helpless son, the defendant, can humanity allow me to believe that all this is falsehood and hypocrisy? Can we believe that when she was praying with her last breath for the defendant, as her son, she was then, when just going to appear before her Maker, taking Him witness to solemn falsehood?"[292]

Andrew Stuart had – perhaps unwisely – let slip once that he had all the proofs of Lady Jane's pregnancy. For some judges, like Lord Coalston, the pregnancy and her continued avowals were enough to prove that Archy was her son: "Of all the numerous audience now present, there is not, perhaps, one in a hundred able to bring compleat legal evidence of the precise time and place and the other circumstances attending (his birth)."[293]

Lord Strichen asked:

"As Lady Jane Douglas was, at this time, undoubtedly capable of having children, would she be guilty of two such impostures, when the consequence might be to deprive her own children of their birthright? The second child indeed (when they did find him) corresponds exactly to the accounts which they had given of him before they saw him, or knew anything about him. Such is the story as set forth by the pursuers; surely a most improbable one. I own it will not go down with me."[294]

But Lord Kennet was not so sure that Lady Jane had ever been pregnant:

"I think there is a clear proof of the *appearances* of pregnancy; but then I consider, that such appearances are often very deceitful, and that they cannot be well distinguished from an affected pregnancy. Of this we have many instances in that famous title of the Roman pandects, *de ventre inspiciendo.*"[295] (Since its fame has not survived to the 21st century I should say that the phrase refers to the practice that when a woman's claim of pregnancy was important for some legal process – a widow claiming to be pregnant in order to exclude the next heir, or a woman claiming pregnancy to avoid a death sentence – a jury of women was assembled to discover whether she really was pregnant. This was formalised with a writ of *de ventre inspiciendo.*)

Amidst the wealth of detail about the events surrounded the alleged birth, the existence and character of Pierre La Marre was much debated among the judges. Few of the judges doubted that a Pierre La Marre existed, but they couldn't agree on how closely he had been involved with the delivery of children to Lady Jane. Lord Barjarg felt that the La Marre who was a friend of Menager was someone who had had nothing to do with Lady Jane.

"I believe the accounts that Doctor Menager gives of his conversation with La Marre," he said. "I believe that La Marre was for some years in the Hotel Dieu; and that he afterwards practised as a surgeon in a very low sphere, and was a good deal employed in secret services. But then it is clear, that this La Marre cannot be the same one that Sir John Steuart described so particularly. Doctor Menager's friend, La Marre, was not a Walloon, neither could he be a surgeon of a regiment in the year 1721, because he was then but a mere boy. It was very natural for so obscure a man as the La Marre swore to by Doctor Menager, to boast of his great practice, but it would be drawing too strong consequences from the story which he told, about the foreign lady, whom he brought to bed of twins, to fix that foreign lady to be Lady Jane Douglas."[296]

Lord Elliock also felt that Sir John Stewart's La Marre, was too improbable to exist:

"What can be more wonderful … than the account given by Sir John of his accidental meeting with his old friend La Marre, who had come up to Paris upon an affair *en epineuse*. This was a strange security indeed, for the successful delivery of Lady Jane Douglas."

Of course, underlying all the attempts to sort through witness statements and counsels' arguments, was the assumption that what people said to the courts and the Commission was accurate. But since many of the judges and counsel had been closely involved with the gathering and assessing of the evidence they were only too aware of accusations of bribery, threats and corruption made against each side by the other.

For Lord Hailes, the entire Douglas case was riddled with inventions. He felt that neither Mme. Le Brun nor Pierre La Marre existed and compared their creation to "the unparalleled effrontery of the person who termed himself George Psalmanazar. This man invented a description of the island of Formosa, drew up an account of its laws and institutions; made a grammar of its language, and persisted in his fable for many years."

Hailes attacked as another invention a French miniaturist named "Dubois", who, Sir John said, had delivered letters from La Marre to him in London, thus explaining how the letters came to be unstamped. "Anyone who knows London must know that the existence of a painter may be easily proved," Hailes said confidently, "especially the existence of a foreign painter, and of one whose branch of a business is that of painting in miniature, which few painters, comparatively speaking, profess. The defender might have learned any day at Slaughter's coffee-house in St Martin's Lane from the French artists who frequent that coffee-house, whether Dubois existed or not."

The defender might also, had the Internet existed in those days, have discovered that in the latter part of the 18th century a French artist called Frédéric Dubois painted miniatures of society people, which can still be bought today.

Lord Hailes, it was said, had been one of Lady Jane's admirers in his youth, and he clearly felt uncomfortable about attacking her integrity. He said that if his speech required a motto it would be a line from the Aeneid: "Unwillingly, O Queen, I left thy shore."[297]

Lord Stonefield declared for Hamilton, saying that he believed Lady Jane's pregnancy was feigned, that Sir John's La Marre didn't exist, that Godefroi was telling the truth, and that the forgery of the La Marre letters capped everything. The only element of the story that gave him any doubts was the private letters of Lady Jane, but he pointed out – quite rightly – that the proof of her affection for the children, whom she had brought up from infancy, was not necessarily proof that she had given birth to them.

Lord Kames accepted that the La Marre letters were forgeries but couldn't bring himself to use that fact against the Douglas case:

"The forgery of the letters was no doubt an unjustifiable circumstance in the conduct of Sir John, but then I see that these letters were meant as an interim proof to the Duke of Douglas only; for it is clear to me, that there was a La Marre, and that Sir John did, at some time or other, correspond with him. The forgery of the letters then was a circumstance of conduct highly blameable in Sir John Steuart, though I do not think it was much unlike the Tournelle process, which to me seems to have been intended by the plaintiffs to stab the defendant behind his back."[298]

Other Douglas supporters took up the accusations of bad practice against the Hamilton side. Lord Gardenstoune drew a contrast between the villainy of the Hamilton layers and the purity of the Douglas team:

"I see no improper thing, nor ill conduct on the part of the defendant in this cause," he said, which was a bit of a cheek since he had been one of the defendant's lawyers, "whereas on the part of the plaintiffs, I see most improper and most illegal conduct. I see the Tournelle process, the Monitoire, and all their miserable effects. ... I pretend not to be the spirit of prophecy; but it is long since I have said that the plaintiffs will find the Tournelle process to hang about their necks like a millstone, for in vain (as was said in another place) are judges wise and upright, if the channels of justice shall by such means as this be corrupted. ... As to their Monitoire, it was such a one as was never seen but in the case of Calas, which proved fatal to an innocent family, and is a reproach to the annals of justice."[299]

The proceedings had opened on Tuesday, July 7th, and by Saturday July 11th, twelve judges had spoken. Although they had not formally voted, six had made pro-Hamilton speeches and six pro-Douglas. There were two more to be heard, Lord Monboddo and Lord Barskimming. At this point, the hearings adjourned for another piece of court business to be transacted.

Lord Dundas, President of the Court, had been increasingly angry at the anonymous newspaper extracts and reviews of *Dorando*. In his view Boswell's book, not of course identified as his work, was a contempt of court and he hauled the newspaper publishers before the court on Tuesday, July 14th, from the city's Tolbooth prison where they had been incarcerated.

The publishers needed a lawyer to plead for them before the court and of course they chose – James Boswell. The Memorial he wrote for the court in support of John Donaldson, one of the publishers of the Edinburgh Advertiser, should be read with that irony in mind:

"It is with regret that the Memorialist finds himself arraigned before this Supreme Judicature," Boswell wrote on Donaldson's behalf. "He flatters himself that he has hitherto preserved in his news-paper a spirit of impartiality, and of decency, which well becomes the servants of the public: ... (But) such is the playful waggery of many, that they wish for no better sport than to *take in* the publisher of a newspaper, and impose upon him by an appearance of reality, till they have the satisfaction of seeing their own idle fancies circulated through all the corners of the kingdom."[300]

That it was Boswell himself who had 'taken in' the readers as well as the publishers with his own 'idle fancies' must have given him a great sense of pleasure. And since Dundas probably had a pretty good idea of who wrote *Dorando* and the reviews of it, without being able to prove it, he must have listened to the plea with some astonishment.

The newspaper publishers got off with a reprimand and escaped prison, providing Boswell later with the opportunity, again anonymously, to report the decision in a sarcastic piece in the *Advertiser* itself.

Meanwhile, the nation was agog for the final speeches. Both judges had 'form': Lord Monboddo, while still James Burnet, had worked for the Douglas team in Paris, and Lord Barskimming had done some legal work for the Hamilton team. Boswell believed that Barskimming had been swayed by Dundas's opening speech. "We can bring one clerk who wrote for him a speech for Mr. Douglas, and another who wrote for him one for Duke Hamilton," he later told Lord Mansfield. Barskimming chose the speech that supported Hamilton and dismissed criticism of Andrew Stuart and his conduct of the case, and would not accept that the witnesses had been bribed or corrupted.

"I cannot believe that the noble and honourable guardians of the Duke of Hamilton would have either corrupted or concussed the witnesses. To me it is more difficult to believe that these persons would thus wickedly conspire against the young defendant, than that Lady Jane and Sir John should have conspired together to bring in an impostor."[301] His vote, then, would be against Douglas.

Monboddo confirmed that the votes of the fourteen judges would be a tie by saying: "I have a full conviction that the defendant is really the son of Lady Jane Douglas." As a lawyer for Archy Douglas, he could have laid out the pro-Douglas arguments in his sleep, and he now presented a polished *tour d'horizon* of the issues.

Monboddo started by pointing out how the Hamilton lawyers had shifted the grounds of their case with the changing testimony of witnesses.

"At first the whole of their proof was said to be founded, first, upon the books of Michelle; secondly, upon the age of the child brought to her house; thirdly, upon there being no accoucheur in Paris in the year 1748, of the name of La Marre; and, fourthly, upon the suspicions in France at the time. But now we have got a new cause, and there is no vestige remaining of the old one. This new cause is founded, first, on the conduct of the parties themselves; secondly, on the alleged *alibi* in the house of Godefroi; and, thirdly, upon the enlevements. Upon this I would observe that the changing of ground gives at no time a very favourable opinion of a cause."

Monboddo also complained about the delay in questioning the birth, fourteen years after it took place, and put this down to greed rather than a thirst for justice. "When the defendant was a poor man the plaintiffs never attempted to controvert his birth; they have only attempted this when he succeeded to the estate of Douglas."

He refused to countenance the kind of combing of testimony for inconsistencies that the other side had practiced, taking a refreshingly modern view of the fallibility of memory, and pointed out that inconsistencies and contradictions could be seen as reinforcing the genuineness of a story rather than the opposite.

"Mrs. Hewit has indeed fallen into many mistakes in her evidence, but these, instead of proving the imposture, prove against it; for upon the supposition of an imposture she would have been much better prepared to have told her tale. In one of her letters to Isabel Walker, Mrs. Hewit recites the whole circumstances of the affair. What could be the use or intention of this letter, upon the supposition of their both being accomplices together? … Whatever mistakes Mrs. Hewit may have fallen into, is it not absolutely certain that after so long a time most witnesses would have done the same? If the Le Brune had been found out and had been examined as a witness, and had fallen into mistakes, then the plaintiffs would have pleaded that she was perjured likewise."

With a sideswipe at Sir Adam Ferguson's lengthy arithmetic in the Hamilton Memorial, Monboddo said:

"Much has been said about probability and improbability in this cause; but sure I am that the plaintiffs' account of the imposture is of all other things the most improbable. It was surely highly improbable that Lady Jane, who, it is proved, had the capability of having children, should bring in two beggar brats who might cut out her own eventual issue; it was surely highly improbable, too, that they should suppose two at one time, and thereby lay themselves open to so great a danger of detection."

In a statement that revealed how far apart the two sides were, and unabashed at the fact that a year ago he had been in a bitter adversarial relationship with the Hamilton lawyers, Monboddo said:

"I do suspect many bad practices with these witnesses in Paris. By whom these practices were carried on, I am not concerned to enquire, but I have so bad an opinion of the plaintiffs' proof, that although they had proved twice as much, I would have paid no sort of regard to it."

Declaring that "he had not even a suspicion remaining in his mind of the truth of the defendant's birth", Monboddo finished his speech.

It was time to vote. The Lord President asked the court "Sustain or repel the reasons of reduction?" and on getting equal votes for either – 7 against 7 – he used his casting vote to break the balance, saying "As this is a cause of civil property, I think myself bound to give judgment according to my own opinion." Unmoved by Monboddo's oratory, he cast his vote against Archy Douglas and it was all over. Andrew Stuart was triumphant, the Duchess of Douglas was vanquished, and only Archy was uninfected by the strong emotions that swirled around both parties. He wrote to his half-brother: "Our cause is indeed lost here, but there is another Court, where justice and impartiality must prevail. The final decision here is not so great a stroke upon us as I believe upon most of our friends. Every person's character here is pretty well known, as well as their motives for their behaviour, but time and a little patience show every thing and every man in their proper light."[302]

On the evening of July 14th, after a gruelling week of speeches, Lord Dundas, the Lord President of the Court of Session, returned to his home to find a letter waiting for him.

"Dear Bumbo," the letter began. Dundas will have known that the letter was meant for him, since he had been lampooned under the name 'Bumbo' in a satirical pamphlet *Sister Peg*, by David Hume.

"I am surprised at your Beheaviour in Douglas Cause," the letter continued, in a misspelt and unpunctuated style, "you the only person who insethed him into the Estate and caused the Plea to be carried on and then you to turn your back and give the whole Swe to hamelton which I dar say you ar conscious that you are in the Wrong but I hope first that you will Loses your seat in the Parlement House and then as ther is about 350 of in and about Edinr Joined under an head and we shall Burn your Lodgin in Town and then Arnston Lodgins shall go into flames and then your Self, we shall make a Captain Portus of You in the Gras Market as an exampel to all false Judges passing wrong sentence, but I shall think it proper to acquaint you Bumbo to alter your mind a time and not cause any Toumoulous Noise or Mischief. Parhaps you will think me an imprompter Person for ofring to send you such an Epistel but you may Excuse me and if you want to know the writhe they call him Timothy Love Justice.

P.S. You you Great Bubo to speak against the truth and the Clearest Light in false imaginations and false proof that was Taken in France from Persons that would sewar ther Souls to hell for a peny, but I hope you will be sent uter Darkness."

If the style was a true reflection of the education of the writer, even allowing for the generally more haphazard attributes of written English in those days, the contents of the first Bumbo letter show an alert understanding of some of the issues involved in the case. They also give an idea of the strength of partisanship at all levels of society in a dispute between families which most 'low' people can have had no personal reason to support at all.

If this letter spoiled Dundas's supper, his breakfast the following day was also disturbed, by another abusive letter:

"May Lord,

I am not a little surprised you should have Broht on yourself such a Damt Scundruly Law Suite And Sir give me Leav To inform you that in a day or two your Brains will be put up as the Colfine of a Gun may Lord have a care and think on me.

I am Sir yours I mean well otherways you go for

P.S. iff you Don'tVout in Mr. Douglass's Cass may Be Well assured you Will be put to Death on first miting."[303]

In a surprising way, these two semi-literate letters were to generate a considerable amount of activity over the next few weeks. Instead of throwing them into the fire, Dundas reported them to the Court of Session, upon which "the judges, all the members of court, the city, every body were fired with indignation."

Next, more extraordinary still, Dundas packaged up copies of the letters and sent them by courier to London, to the government and the king, along with letters from both parties in the lawsuit, the Hamiltons and the Douglases, saying that, if the king were to consider issuing some kind of proclamation to uncover the writers they begged to be allowed to offer a reward for their apprehension. Sure enough, the king (or his advisers) was outraged enough to publish an advertisement in all the Edinburgh newspapers, on July 23rd. It said, in part, that as a result of two incendiary letters having been sent to the Lord President of the Court of Session "in that part of His Majesty's kingdom of Great Britain called Scotland", the King is pleased to promise a reward of five hundred pounds to anyone "except the person or persons who actually wrote the said letters" who will identify the culprit or culprits. Also published with this letter were further promises of rewards by the Hamilton and Douglas lawyers, to the tune of a further £300 each. Such a huge sum – probably equivalent in total to more than £100,000 in today's money – seems an extraordinary reward to offer to discover the writers of two insulting letters.

In spite of the huge reward for finding the writer of the Bumbo letters, there seems to have been no rush of claimants. The only hint of a resolution to the affair came in a small news item in November,

"As the incendiary letters written and sent to the Lord President of the court of session have made more noise than one would have expected, and a report has been industriously propagated, that this ridiculous insult was instigated by the friends of the family of Douglas, you will be pleased to hear that the real truth is now discovered. The most abusive letter, which begins, *Dear Bumbo*, ... is found to have been written by a poor ragged foolish printer's boy, who has made his escape."[304]

It was clear that, with such a narrow verdict in the Court of Session, the Duchess of Douglas and her team would not let the matter lie where it was, and as the legal system was then, appeals against Scottish decisions were made to the House of Lords in London. Everyone hoped there would be a quick turnaround, perhaps within the next six months, and so the legal teams geared up for more pages of argument about Pierre La Marre, Mme. Le Brun, the Mignons and the Sanrys.

At about this time Andrew Stuart had a couple of letters from Paris about unfinished business from his time there. Aeneas Macdonald, mentioned in Carnegy's journal as one of the Hamilton lawyers at the infamous 'betrayal' meetings, seems to have been charged with arranging the care of a dog Stuart had bought and left behind.

"The Dogg man still plagues us," Macdonald wrote, "and goes to the ambassador to gett your address. If you please, pay him three louis and lett him sell the dogg or do with it what he pleases. For twelve livres a month for all this time he is worthless fellow."[305]

Macdonald also had news of the Mignon family. A Captain Calderwood knew the youngest Mignon boy and was also in touch with his mother. "Young Mignon that was a *garçon marchand du vin* has given us some trouble; for he is a *tres mauvais sujet* and was taken up some days ago as a _filous_* and was very near being sent to the gallys *avec La Marque*** but M. D'Anjou I believe will get him [saved?] for this time."[306]

In November, Boswell produced his edition of the letters of Lady Jane Douglas, to show what a sweet-natured and honest woman she was, and therefore incapable of any wrong-doing. The letters did, indeed, show her love for her children and husband, and the sadness and forbearance in the face of intolerable treatment by her brother. But they also left out a few things. For example, Letter XLIII omits the paragraph: "I'm much afraid that some of our things that are lying out [i.e. in pawn] will be by this time in great danger of never being to be got in, particularly your watch and mine. Pray, dear Mr. Stewart, look to that, by promising them fair till we get money to relieve them."[307]

---

* Rogue

**Branded

Perhaps Boswell couldn't bear to reveal that his beloved Lady Jane and her husband were reduced to pawning their watches, although there are plenty of other references to her poverty in the letters he published. But more understandable is the omission of paragraphs in several letters referring to a mysterious Mr. Lundie, with whom the Colonel appeared to be hatching some kind of money-making scheme, perhaps smuggling. It was an affair "which I cannot explain even to my dearest Lady Jane," the Colonel wrote, "not for want of confidence in her discretion, and all other good qualities, but from the nature of the thing itself."[308]

We hear little of Archy Douglas during these proceedings, swept along in the current of legal activity masterminded by his aunt, the Duchess. But he seems to have been a rather clear-eyed young man when it came to sizing up who his friends were. He had written to his half-brother when the law suits began: "I have resolved steadfastly to regard those who have proved my truest friends in my adversity, and to despise those who have put on a false cloak of friendship since my prosperity, as some people of my acquaintance, and I don't know but relations too, directly as this affair is decided in favour of the Douglases, will fawn like a little dog about them, and at the same time they are wishing then joy at their success, wish them at the devil in their hearts."[309]

His Hamilton relations certainly wished him at the devil in their hearts, as did Andrew Stuart who instead of being able to unwind after a gruelling half-decade was faced with another year at least of service in the cause of the former Duchess of Hamilton. It had all gone so well so far, apart from a few hiccups. None of the things had happened that could have stopped the process in its tracks – an indubitable La Marre or Le Brun; an irreconcilable birth date for Mignon or Sanry – and yet there were those who could scent Hamilton blood in the final furlong. Could victory really be snatched from his hands in the chamber of the House of Lords?

17

The Cause Moves South

As soon as it was clear that there would be an appeal by the Hamilton team against the verdict of the Court of Session, the Douglas lawyers began to plan their campaign. The appeal was to take place before the House of Lords, in London, and the homely Scots lawyers with their broad accents and peculiar legal ways would need the help of more polished, or at least more English, lawyers to argue in front of Britain's most senior law lords.

Although the case had no legal implications for England and its aristocracy, the Douglas and Hamilton families spent so much time in English social circles that the quarrel between them was discussed at length in the drawing rooms of London mansions and English country houses, fuelled by regular newspaper and journal dispatches from Edinburgh. And in the London legal community, the upcoming appeal was a topic of lively dispute over the issues that might be raised and the final arguments that ingenuity could devise for one side or the other.

In November, 1767, four months after the Scottish verdict, lawyers for Douglas went to London to enter an appeal against the judgment. It was not an easy task to find English lawyers familiar with the House of Lords appeal procedure who were willing to read, or even to skim, the formal judgment of the Court of Session, based on ten folio volumes totalling 9,676 pages. During their search for English lawyers to handle the appeal, two Scots law agents took a break in Nando's Coffee House, near Temple Bar, a well-known haunt of London lawyers, who were attracted by the excellent punch and the landlady's younger daughter, Miss Humphreys, "always admired at the bar by the Bar."[310]

On this particular evening, there was a heated discussion going on about the Douglas Cause among a group of lawyers. One advocate applauded the judgment of the Court of Session, while another, Edward Thurlow, forcefully demolished the Hamilton arguments, showing an intimate knowledge of the ins and outs of the Douglas case. It was generally agreed that Thurlow had trounced his fellow-lawyer, and, finishing his flagon of punch, he went home to bed. His success was seen more as a sign of his skill at legal argument than as a particular adherence to the Douglas Cause.

Thurlow was then thirty-six, a lively and successful barrister, seen as a high-flyer. He was pleasure-loving – Miss Humphreys, the bar-maid, was his mistress by whom he had two children. He "occasionally indulged in deep potations"[311] and was an avid reader of novels. He had also spent his time "from morning to night, in giggling, and making others giggle," when he was meant to be studying the law. But even at that stage in his career he had had a number of important briefs in the English courts. He looked so solemn and imposing that it led Charles Fox to say that "it proved him dishonest, since no man could *be* so wise as Thurlow *looked.*"[312]

The following day, the Scottish lawyers deposited at Thurlow's chambers in Fig Tree Court a brief in *Douglas v. The Duke of Hamilton,* along with an immense pile of papers and the offer of a fee that was ten times more than he had ever received. When he met the Scots agents and agreed to take it on, they hinted that his fame had reached the Parliament House at Edinburgh, rather than revealing that they had never heard of him before their night out at Nando's.

Edward Thurlow, in later life as Lord Chancellor

As the work on the appeal proceeded, Boswell's interest in the case continued. He was a close observer of the events, writing to friends about it, approaching lawyers, keeping up his friendship with Archy, and continuing to publish articles and books about the case. He clearly wanted to be involved in the Douglas appeal team, but never was – apart from a minor piece of work after the main verdict – even though his experience of English law might have been useful.

In December, Boswell, eager to know what progress there was in the appeal process at the House of Lords, wrote from Scotland to the Duke of Queensberry, a relative of Archibald Douglas and one of his guardians. In his reply, Queensberry wrote:

"I have done my utmost to prevail with the principal conductors of business in the House of Peers to bring it forward if possible this Session, but have found it impracticable. It is certainly a very disagreable and anxious Situation for our young friend to have a cause of such infinite importance to him hang over his head for a year yet to come; but when I informed him of the necessity of submitting to the delay, I at the same time represented his prospect of success in so favourable, and really, true light, that work'd upon his philosophic and noble mind so as to reconcile him to the unavoidable present disappointment, and he appears to be perfectly easy under it. He knows that people in general here are all favourably inclined to his cause..."[313]

Boswell, with his increasing preoccupation with the Douglas Cause, tried to get Dr. Johnson to give his views on the matter but found that the Great Lexicographer hadn't really given it much thought. Nevertheless Johnson managed to construct a well-rounded comment on the matter:

"I am of opinion that positive proof of fraud should not be required of the plaintiff," Johnson told Boswell, "but that the Judges should decide according as probability shall appear to preponderate, granting to the defendant the presumption of filiation to be strong in his favour. And I think, too, that a good deal of weight should be allowed to the dying declarations, because they were spontaneous. There is a great difference between what is said without our being urged to it, and what is said from a kind of compulsion. If I praise a man's book without being asked my opinion of it, that is honest praise, to which one may trust. But if an authour asks me if I like his book, and I give him something like praise, it must not be taken as my real opinion."[314]

One of the judges who would hear the appeal in the House of Lords was Lord Mansfield, one of the most eminent and influential of all British judges. He was a Scot and before he was elevated to the peerage he was plain William Murray, and the man who had helped Lady Jane get a pension when she "wanted bread." Now, he had been appointed to the highest court in the land and was the Lord Chief Justice, the most powerful legal figure in Britain. Although the Douglas appeal would be voted on by the whole House, it was customary to follow the opinions of the Law Lords, and Mansfield as the chief law lord would clearly be an important voice.

Lord Mansfield

Knowing this, James Boswell decided in May to pay the man a visit, armed with little more than a visiting card, a shared nationality and two years experience in the law courts. But that was Boswell for you, and this got him through the door and into Lord Mansfield's study.

Boswell's journals are full of verbatim accounts of his conversations. These were usually written afterwards so we have to take into account the shaping effect of the memory, particularly in situations where the writer is desperate to be seen in a good light. Boswell's visit to Mansfield to probe his views on the Douglas Cause has been described as "one of the most enticing he ever recorded in his journal."[315]

The visit took place on May 20th, 1768. After the usual pleasantries, Mansfield asked about Boswell's father, Lord Auchinleck, and Boswell remarked on how he and the other Scottish judges had become better-known in London as a result of their Douglas Cause speeches being published.

"I have not read a word of it," said Mansfield.

"These speeches have been read over all here," Boswell said.

"If one thought them authentic, one would like to look at them," replied Mansfield, "Pray, how are they?"

Boswell, with all of his two years court experience, then proceeded to take the Lord Chief Justice through a critique of the talents of the Scottish judges as shown by the speeches they made in the Court of Session. Kames "made a poor figure"; Strichen "spoke like a plain country gentleman"; Alemoor "made a very eloquent speech."

"My father made a solid, sensible speech," Boswell said, "a few sound principles of law and a few reflections on the capital facts, without going into the wide field of circumstance, which is endless."

Mansfield then gave Boswell an insight into his own thoughts on the case, even though he hadn't read the papers.

"I was sorry for the manner in which that cause was decided," he said. "So much time employed in a question of fact, when I should have decided it at a sitting. And such a division. It makes one suspect there was something more in that cause than the cause itself."

Boswell seized on this remark to criticise Dundas, whose casting vote had decided the matter. "It was not well in the president of a court to employ his supposed superior talents in making a violent harangue for the Pursuers. He even says in direct terms that he will not touch on the arguments on the other side. Now, my Lord, that is very dangerous. ... His manner was so violent; and then unluckily his whole speech from beginning to end is without the least foundation in the evidence. He has read it with very little attention and trusted to the Pursuers' memorial, which is a most unfair paper."

"As I told you," said Mansfield, perhaps feeling that Boswell doubted his previous remark, "I have not read a word of the cause."

"I dare say not, my Lord," Boswell said, with a hint of disbelief.

"I have not, upon my honour." Mansfield protested, "I have their great quartos lying here upon my table, but I have been so much employed with other things that I have not had time to open them."

At this point, Mansfield's servant came in to say his carriage was waiting, and Boswell stood up to go. "Sit still, Mr. Boswell," Mansfield apparently said, and Boswell was smugly pleased. "So I thought I would do all I could," he confided to his journal, and plunged deeper into the topic dear to his heart. He now introduced his hobby horse, a point of law he thought would appeal to the ordinary man – or gentleman – in the street. "Your Lordship sees that, although gentlemen without doors are not lawyers, they are still judges of that great principle of law – *filiation* – on which we all depend; and every man is alarmed at the danger of that principle being taken away. ... My Lord, when you deny a man the great privilege of filiation, you are taking the very pavement from under his feet. You are depriving him of half his cause."

"You are so," said Mansfield, failing to share his passion on this point, and so Boswell changed his tack.

"There was now poor Sir John Stewart; why, all the strange suggestions of his wild fancy must be made suspicions against him."

"I did not know Sir John."

"No, my Lord? Your Lordship knew Lady Jane?"

"No, but I was once able to [do] her a piece of service."

This was the pension he helped obtain for her, nearly twenty years beforehand. There were some who thought Mansfield knew her rather more closely that he admitted here, and they were to say so but not till after his death.

Then Boswell returned to the utter confusion that would ensue if every man had to prove where and how he was born.

"I asked my father where I was born. He mentioned a house. I asked an old woman who was in the house at the birth, and she said another house. My Lord, if my birth had been scrutinised, my father and this old woman would have been declared perjured, as contradicting one another."

"Very true," said Mansfield.

"Every man must be alarmed. He runs back in his own mind and sees what difficulties must occur in such questions."

Manfield, probably desperate to change the subject, then said: "You are making great improvements at Edinburgh."

"Yes. We have a Theatre Royal, too."

"I believe you wrote the prologue at the opening of it. I assure you I admired it exceedingly."

Mansfield's praise of Boswell's prologue made his day, if not his week. "I went home and felt myself in most admirable humour," he wrote in his journal that night.

There are signs that the Hamilton party were carrying out further researches in Paris in the summer of 1768, presumably still hoping to dig up new evidence to use in the appeal. Andrew Stuart had a letter from Aeneas Macdonald in June: "One thing is proper to let you know, that Mignon who was putt in prison for picking of pockets has been try'd and sentenced to some corporal punishment as fouetté* and marqué** and three years to [Bicestre]*** or to the gallys.... Perhaps the enemy thinks to *tirer partie* of this misfortune of the Mignon people to tamper with them."[316]

A week later, Macdonald wrote again to Andrew Stuart with some sad news:

"Mignon's son of whom I wrote you last dy'd in the Conciergerie where he was transported after the sentence of the [Chatlet?], as he appealed from it to the Parliament, so that affair is out of the question." [317]

In November, the Reverend Robert Richardson, Prebendary of Lincoln Cathedral, currently at the Hague, opened a letter from his friend James Boswell. Richardson had been writing a book about the Douglas Cause and had asked Boswell some further questions. He was puzzled by what he found in the letter. It was in Italian:

"My dearest friend," Boswell's letter began, "It is truly difficult for me to know how to begin a letter to you after having let so many months go by without replying to the most affectionate one I last had from you. Yet I assure you that this indolence has caused me great pain. I have looked upon myself as ungrateful to a lady of talent, of beauty, and of goodness, to whom I owe more than I can express. Forgive me, dear Momina..."

Since Boswell had never addressed the clergyman as 'Momina' before, and indeed the letter was clearly addressed to a woman, Richardson realised that there was surely some mistake. If he had read on – and we have no way of knowing whether curiosity triumphed over his discretion – he would

---

* flogging

**branding

*** A prison for the mentally ill.

have discovered that Boswell, a concurrent philanderer, was writing to his former mistress, Girolama Piccolomini, to tell her that he was now in love with a beautiful seventeen-year-old Irish girl. "She is sweet and lovable," he wrote, "and has a handsome fortune. But I am too changeable where women are concerned. I ought to be a Turk; I believe I should make a very good sultan."[318]

For a man who led such a life, so busy in mind and body, it was not such a surprising slip-up. Richardson inferred, correctly, that two letters had gone into the wrong envelopes and that 'Momina' had received a long and learned disquisition on some aspects of the Douglas Cause, in English. Richardson wrote to Boswell to tell him of the mishap.

"I cannot but flatter myself that you intended me the favor of a Letter, and sometimes amuse myself with imagining what must happen, if the letter you design'd for me shou'd have gone on to Sienna: Is there any one there who can interpret? With what timidity will the poor Lady confide the unknown secrets of her friend to a third person! And what will be her surprize to find that her Ciceroni* has thought proper to entertain her with an account of a certain Cause, about pregnancies false deliveries and miscarriages...! These or any other affairs may be in that Letter for any concern I have in it, because I hope to hear from you long before it can make its way back to the Hague."[319]

It requires one more letter to complete the story – Signorina Piccolomini's reaction to the letter she received:

"Sir," she wrote to Boswell, "From what seems a blunder, I flatter myself that you still remember me. The blunder is this. I received a letter from you this week clearly addressed to me. But when I saw that it was written in English, I hesitated long whether I could having it read by anyone who

---

* 'Cicerone' (Italian), a word originally applied to a guide to the antiquities of a place, but often used of any guide.

understood English, because of the risk of him in possession of some passage intended only for ourselves. But I concluded that since you knew very well that I did not understand your language, you would have written only generalities. So I found the courage to have it read by a gentleman who knows a little English, and we gathered that you were writing to some gentleman, a friend of yours, and that perhaps you had written also to me and had mistaken the covers and sent my letter to your friend. Tell me if my idea is correct, or whether my hope that you still remember me makes me read matters too much to my own advantage. ... I am afraid that you have forgotten Italian. If so, our correspondence would be a fine thing: I shall not understand your letters and you will not understand mine. Tell me if you love debauchery as you once did; tell me if you are to be married ... I return your letter for you to dispose of as you please."[320]

The Lords appeal was now only two months away. It was expected to start in January, 1769, and the brilliant Edward Thurlow had plunged into the paperwork to produce within a few weeks of his appointment a fiery and very readable account of the Douglas case. Although a slimmer volume than any of the other tomes produced so far, with 'only' 232 pages of text, its thinness was deceptive since the type size was smaller and so there were many more words per page. Although *The Case of Archibald Douglas* was signed by two of the senior advocates who would argue the case, it was written entirely by Thurlow.

"Their case," wrote Andrew Stuart to Baron Mure, "is universally spread in order to create prejudices by the quantity of illiberal abuse that is to be found in it, in every page there are flowers of this kind to be met with, it astonishes people here that either Sir Fletcher Norton or the Advocate but particularly the latter should have allowed their names to be put to it. The fact I am told is that Sir Fletcher had not read a word of it and the Advocate but a few sheets, that however is scarce sufficient apology for allowing such a case to go abroad with their names on it. ...There is a constant mixture of irony which is so jumbled that the reader is at a loss to find out when the author is serious or jocular. ...

By what Mr. Dagg told me to-day of a conversation he had with the sollicitor for the other party, I find they intend to give very high fees to their counsel upon this occasion -- no less than 300 guineas to each for their consultation fees and first day's appearance, and twenty guineas a piece for every other day's appearance. ... we shall be under the necessity of giving the same, or nearly the same fees that they do, which, with so many counsel, will fall heavy...

One comfort is that it is the last expense of this kind, and when we have brought the matter to such a good issue, have weathered out all former difficulties, and are now in sight of land we must not hesitate about doing what is proper and necessary upon this occasion."[321]

Stuart finished his letter to Mure by passing on a comment by one of the Hamilton counsel, Charles Yorke, that he "thinks it impossible that any Judge accustomed to examine evidence can have a doubt of the imposture."

There was not long to wait now to discover how accurate was Charles Yorke's judgement of the judges.

18

The Appeal begins

In January, 1769, Britain experienced an unprecedented spell of cold weather. But the prolific diarist, Lady Mary Coke, tried to keep up with her social engagements, the focus of her life. On the 6th, she called on her friend, the princess Amelia, daughter of George II and aunt of the king, George III. "We talk'd of the Douglass cause," she wrote "which I hear many Lords are determined not to vote in. Lord Hertford said he shou'd attend, but would not vote, but he did not give his reason."[322]

A few days later, at Lady Townsend's, the topic came up again. "Mr. Walpole try'd to make Lady Charlotte Edwin and me dispute about the Douglass cause, but I avoided it by saying I was sure our wishes were the same – that it might be decided according to justice."[323] (Lady Charlotte Edwin was a Hamilton.)

On Sunday, January 15th, it was so cold that Lady Mary decided to give church a miss and read the service at home. And then: "My Servants tell me a duel was fought early this morning just by here; that two or three Post Chaises with four Horses waited; that pistols were fired, & immediately those

279

concerned went into the Chaises that were ready to receive them. They can't tell whether there was any mischief done, but 'tis reported to be the Duke of Grafton and Mr. Beauclerk. To morrow I suppose the truth of this story will be known."[324]

The truth of the story was indeed all over the town within hours. Andrew Stuart, the Hamilton's lawyer, had blown his top.

Two days after her servants told her of the duel, Lady Mary Coke gave her sister more details of the event:

"I was told the duel which was fought near me on Sunday morning was Mr. Stewart and Mr. Thurlow, two of the lawyers concern'd in the famous law suit between the Duke of Hamilton and Mr. Douglas. Stewart chalenged Thurlow, which is thought extraordinary, as the cause is still depending."[325]

We have no insight into Andrew Stuart's state of mind at this time. But after years of hard work on the case, and the shortlived excitement of a victory in the Court of Session, it is possible that the prospect of defeat in the Lords was preying on Stuart's mind, particularly since there were plenty in London who, unlike his own counsel Charles Yorke, predicted that the Hamilton side would lose. But what undoubtedly led to the specific challenge was the masterly case Thurlow had written for Douglas, and in particular the abuse he directed against Andrew Stuart himself.

It must have been a very uncomfortable experience to open *The Case of Archibald Douglas* and read paragraphs such as the following:

"The plan upon which Mr. *Andrew Stuart* set out with in this Expedition to *Paris*, was that of the closest Secrecy; a Plan which, in one and the same Section of his Memorial, he avows as proper, and disclaims as ashamed of. This extraordinary Secrecy looks, at first Sight, as if it could be meant for Nothing but to preoccupy, at least, the Witnesses, and garble their Testimony; as it could lead to no Advantage but that unfair one, to surprize the Defender; to surround him with a long

Case of fraudulent Imputation, and to cut him off from the Opportunity of meeting it with other Evidence.

Mr. *Andrew Stuart* says, he was *conscious* of meaning fairly; and that stands as his Apology for acting as if he meant otherwise. If the Story were true it would not suffer, because he was *conscious* of intending a fair Enquiry. To which it is answered, very calmly and seriously, That Mr. *Andrew Stuart* is not believed upon that Subject; not has he any Right to be believed. For, apart from what actually happened in Consequence of this Secrecy, no Man has a Right to act underhand, and call upon his adverse Party to put Confidence in him. ... He who went over with the Belief that the Story was true, assumes the Falsehood of it as the Justification of his very first Step. And whom did he suspect of supporting this Imposture professedly? Mrs. *Hewit*, who knew nothing of the Country or Language of *France*? Sir *John Stewart*, broken with Infirmity and Age, who never could have weaved or maintained a Plan of Imposture? Wretched Subterfuge! Those were the very People he would have conversed with, if fair Dealing had made any part of his Plan. Whom did he tacitly mean to insult with the Reproach of having less Honour than himself? The Tutors of Mr. *Douglas*? It is dragging down their Names too low, to bring them into comparison with his."[326]

There was paragraph after paragraph attacking Stuart and his employers, the Hamilton family, as well as his father, Archibald Stuart, for his actions in concert with Stockbriggs.

Seizing, for example, on an admission by Stuart that he might have made a few mistakes in understanding French, Thurlow wrote:

"Let Mr. Andrew Stuart have been as inattentive, as forgetful and as ignorant of the French language (that is to say, as unfit for the employment he went upon) as he chooses to have it supposed, so many falsehoods could not have crept upon the meanest of human understanding by accident."

Thurlow's *Case of Archibald Douglas* is a good read as well as a powerful and effective statement of the arguments for one side. Although it wasn't generally published, there were enough copies printed for the many lawyers and interested parties, for the contents to be circulated and enjoyed. And there would be more to come of this sort of stuff, in the pleadings that would be made before the Lords. Stewart clearly had to give vent to his anger. An item in *Town and Country* magazine, not always the most reliable source, gives one account of what happened next:

"A gentleman of the long robe, Mr. T., being concerned in an affair of great consequence, had in his state of the Case particularly traduced a Scotch gentleman of the law, Mr. S., concerned on the other side. On which Mr. S., was so much irritated at finding his character and abilities so freely treated, that he called at Mr. T.'s chambers to know his reasons for such treatment. But finding him gone to Bath, he took post-chaise and went after him; where having met him, he demanded of T. if he wrote the case in question? And upon being answered in the affirmative, S. said he was a scoundrel and must fight him; to which T. very coolly replied he had no objection to fighting him but, as it might possibly endanger his client's cause, declared he would not fight till he knew he should not be called upon as one of the counsel to plead in the matter and that, when he was disengaged, he would let S. know."[327]

You would think it would be a simple matter to discover today whether Thurlow did eventually plead on behalf of Douglas before the House of Lords. But in fact, although several later writers described the excellence of his arguments in the House, I can find no evidence that Thurlow spoke at all. An account of the case published within months of the appeal[328] lists the counsel who actually spoke for both sides and Thurlow does not appear. Indeed, several of the sources who say he did speak, use his 'speech' as the reason for Andrew Stuart's challenge, but in fact the duel took place five days before the Lords hearing began.

The *Scots Magazine* described what happened:

"On Saturday morning, Jan. 14th, the parties met, with swords and pistols, in Hyde park; one of them having for his second his brother Col. S----, and the other having for his, Mr. L----, member for a city in Kent. Both the gentlemen discharged their pistols; which, however, happily did no harm. They then drew their swords, but the seconds interposed, and put an end to the affair."[329]

(While in Paris, as a recreation, Stuart had taken fencing lessons with the famous M. Motet, so perhaps this was a wise move on the part of the seconds.)

Thurlow was said to have stood up to his antagonist "like an elephant." His calmness of mind is shown by the fact that he had stopped on the way to eat an enormous breakfast at a tavern near Hyde Park Corner.[330]

Two days later, January 16th, when the Douglas appeal was due to start, the House of Lords had other matters to deal with. The appeal didn't happen on the 17th either, some preliminary points needing to be settled. The 18th was out because it was the Queen's Birthday, and so it wasn't till the 19th that the hearing began in an atmosphere of heightened public expectation.[331]

Members of the House of Lords, any of whom would be entitled to vote, had been canvassed for weeks beforehand by the two parties. The Duchess of Argyll, formerly Hamilton and mother of Archy's opponent, was said to have solicited the vote of Lord Northington, a former Lord Chancellor, who replied "You are very handsome, by God, Madame, and old as I am I could be wicked with you, but I will not be wicked *for* you."[332]

In spite of the wealth of sparkling oratory that took place over the next few days if we are to believe the diarists and letter-writers, there is no verbatim record of the pleadings. Not only were such accounts not compiled as a matter of official record-keeping, they were sometimes expressly forbidden. Andrew Stuart noted that on the day the Lords gave their opinions, Lord Mansfield banned anyone from taking notes of what was said. [333]

In the Beinecke Library at Yale University, I discovered several pages of notes made by an unidentified reporter, taken down during some of the speeches by the lawyers for each side.[334] Not all speeches are covered and the notes are in very abbreviated form but it is possible to get some sense of the approach of each side.

The first to speak, for Douglas, was the Lord Advocate for Scotland, James Montgomery, a man who was also well known as a farmer, and owned a property called "The Whim", because it was bought on one. His speech lasted thirteen hours and was stretched over three days.

He started with an attack on the motives of Andrew Stuart and the other tutors. "This should never be dropped out of consideration in considering the proofs," he said. He argued strongly on the basis of Archy's filiation and submitted that this could not be taken from him without clear evidence against the possibility of his birth. He said that the pursuers had tried to prove that Lady Jane was never pregnant, had never given birth, and that Archibald Douglas was the son of Mignon and had failed in all three. He warned the Lords not to try the case on the basis of 'impressions', but by the rules of law. Even if there is pretty good evidence in support of the pursuers' allegations, the proofs of birth were so strong as to render that irrelevant. He emphasised the witnesses to Lady Jane's pregnancy, and to the menstruation and miscarriages that proved that she could still conceive, and went on to say that the only witnesses who saw no evidence of Lady Jane's pregnancy had never seen her before and were reporting events from sixteen years beforehand.

Montgomery was scathing about the evidence of Duruisseau, the policeman Andrew Stuart asked to certify the validity of the Godefroi's and Michel's books, before they were hidden away in the Tournelle. "Keep Duruisseau's evidence in view," he said to the assembled lords. "This was one of the worst proceedings in this Cause." If this was the way Andrew Stuart and his team carried on, everything of theirs should be suspected. They examined the Michels without their books on purpose; Godefroi's evidence was worth nothing without his books, which showed that there were huge gaps and it was impossible to argue for or against any specific individual on the basis of the books. Going by the book, there were only two people staying there, at a time when they said the hotel was full. "It would be hard," said Montgomery, "if any right of mankind were to be determined by books kept in this manner."

Another issue in the case dealt with the specifics of the stay of Lady Jane and Colonel Stewart in Rheims in November 1749, when Sanry's child was said to have been abducted in Paris. There had been a constant back and forth on this issue between the two sides. Now, like a rabbit from a hat, a document was produced by Montgomery before the House of Lords, a document no one had seen before, showing that Colonel Stewart had paid a sum of money to a merchant in Rheims on the 14th November, 1749. It was important for the Hamilton side to show that the couple were in Paris for a period from the middle of November, when the abduction was said to have taken place. The Douglas lawyers said the couple went to Paris in the first half of November and were back in Rheims with Sholto at the time of the abduction.

"Sir John paid a merchant on the 14th and there are three separate books to prove that," Montgomery said.

At this point Lord Mansfield interrupted and queried this point, since this was a new discovery not set out in the previous paperwork.

"Two nights ago," said Montgomery, "a clerk arrived with the books. If Sir John was at Rheims on the 14th it blows up the whole of this enlèvement."

I found one of the thousands of documents that are scattered around the world in connection with this case in the archives of Louisiana State University. It is a solitary document in French, written by one of the Hamilton lawyers in London while the pleadings were taking place. It shows how, in the face of Montgomery's eleventh hour claim, they were determined, even at this late stage, to make every effort to disprove it.

The document is a brief to one of the French members of the Hamilton team to carry out certain researches in Rheims.

"On Mr. Douglas's side they have just produced in the House of Lords here an extract taken from the books of M. Benoit showing that on the 14th November he had received from Mr. John Stewart 22 livres 10 sols from which one argues on the part of Mr. Douglas that this is a proof that this sum was paid by Mr. Stewart in person and that it is also a proof that he had already made the journey to Paris and had returned to Rheims on the 14th November."[335]

The Hamilton lawyers tried to persuade themselves that this piece of evidence was not conclusive support for the Douglas side. Perhaps it hadn't been Colonel Stewart personally who paid, or perhaps the journey to Paris began after this date and still allowed for the abduction. The brief to the French agent, therefore, was to try to pin down more firmly the exact date of departure from Paris. If Colonel Stewart was paying bills in Rheims before the family set off to England in December, perhaps by canvassing the various merchants in Rheims it would be possible to find out which dates they were paid and by whom.

"If one could find some evidence in writing in the books of their creditors in Rheims which would show payments made by Colonel Stewart or Lady Jane on one of the days between the 2nd and 14th November that would destroy at a blow the argument drawn by Mr. Douglas of the item of the 14th November which is found in the books of M. Benoit, thus the principle objective of the research which needs to be done is to discover payments made on one of the days between 2nd and 14th November or some other unwritten evidence if it exists which could show that Colonel Stewart and Lady Jane were at Rheims on one of the days between the 2nd and the 14th November."[336]

I find it astonishing that, within days of what would have to be the final settlement of the case one way or the other, there are still lawyers for the Hamiltons scurrying around Rheims, talking to wine merchants and grocers about the dates on which their bills might have been paid, twenty years beforehand, and that there was a belief that some of them might actually have the answers.

There were many more hours of Montgomery's opening speech on behalf of Douglas, dealing with Pierre La Marre and Mme. Le Brun; the forged letters; the correspondence between Lady Jane and her husband; and the credibility of M. Menager. Montgomery finished by saying that he would leave his colleague Sir Fletcher Norton to deal with the Tournelle and related matters.

The following day it was the turn of another Hamilton counsel to plead, Mr. Charles Yorke, who spoke for a total of six hours over the next two days. He was somewhat of a turncoat. Having originally agreed to plead for Douglas, he had then changed sides and appeared for Hamilton. Furious, the Duchess of Douglas confronted him with this – not a pretty sight – and when he could not deny his change of allegiance, she said "Then, sir, in the next world whose will you be, for we have all had you?"[337]

Londoners crowded the Lords, often for days at a time. One of Boswell's correspondents, Isabella Strange, wrote to him on January 24th: "...We are much emerg'd in the Douglass cause which for these 4 days has wore a smiling Face before all the Nobles of the Land."[338]

Lady Mary Coke, an ardent Douglas supporter, wrote to her sister that same evening: "Mr. York, one of the Council on the Duke of Hamilton's side, pleaded to day, but I'm glad to find he made little or no impression on the Lords."[339] She was also pleased to hear the following day, from the wife of one of the peers who might eventually vote, that "the pleading of the Council for Mr. Douglass had made great impression on many of the Lords. I feared Lady Gower's influence [a friend of the Duchess of Hamilton] wd have carried all that party against Mr. Douglass, but Lady Waldegrave told me that Lord Waldegrave was determined not to vote."

On the 26th, Alexander Wedderburn rose to speak for Hamilton. Known for his oratory, he was said by Charles Fox to have given the best speech he had ever heard. Hundreds were turned away from the public gallery and Wedderburn's pleading was greeted with "greater applause than was almost ever known."[340]

He spoke over two days, with an adjournment of almost a week in the middle of his pleading. At the end of his first day, a Thursday, the Douglas camp was plunged into gloom by the brilliance of his arguments, as Lady Mary Coke reported to her sister:

"At seven O'clock made a visit to the Duchess of Douglas: the anxiety She is in made my heart acke. She said the cause was just, & She hoped the House of Lords thought so, but still, till it was over, She cou'd injoy no peace. Mr. Douglass came up stairs. He behaves with the utmost composure: God send he may have justice done him. I was engaged to Lady George Sackville, where I found a great deal of company. I observed Lady Gower, Duchess Hamilton, etc., much inliven'd by the praises which Mr. Wedderburn's fine Oratory had procured him in the House of Lords, but I flatter myself, tho' his pleading was admired, it has not so blinded the judgements of the Lords, but they will be able to distinguish between reason and oratory."[341]

At this stage in the proceedings, the Duchess of Hamilton was wielding her legendary beauty in the service of her son, by soliciting votes from members of the Lords. And Lady Mary Coke was alert to every such move.

"I went to Lady Holland," she wrote on Friday, January 27th. "The Duchess of Bedford ask'd me to play with her at Lu. Duchess Hamilton & Lady Holdernesse came in. The Duchess of Bedford said Mr. Walpole being there we might then sit down, upon which the two Ladys whisper'd, got up, & went out of the room. Lady Holland said for them, that the Duchess of Hamilton, having heard Lord Holland was favourable to her cause, was gone to make him a visit to desire he wou'd attend the House of Lords..."[342]

Three days later, another Hamilton supporter lobbied for support right under the nose of the King at his 'drawing room', a regular social occasion when the monarch was at home to selected members of the upper classes.

"The Drawing room was very full," wrote Lady Mary Coke. "The King and Queen were very civil. ... Lady Gower was very busy and made Lord Egmount to sit down by her, in hopes of gaining him over to the Duke of Hamilton's side; but I'm persuaded Lord Egmount will act from the conviction of his own conscience, and not be influenced by anybody. I wish for the sake of Mr. Douglass that the whole House of Lords were composed of Men like him."[343]

Wedderburn resumed his pleadings on Wednesday, February 1st. He had some difficulty with the new evidence produced by Montgomery that placed Colonel Stewart in Rheims on November 14th, 1749, and had to fall back on the possibility that the merchant's books were not accurate. He summed up by saying that the accumulation of so many coincidences between the dates and places of the two abductions and the movements of Lady Jane and the Colonel meant that it was overwhelmingly likely that they had acquired their two children in that illicit way. And as for the motives for such a crime, there were two: "present penury and future hope of a better condition."

With gaps in the process, it was now nearly a month since the pleadings had begun, Those lords who had attended the appeal had already had to listen to about thirty-two hours of speeches, going over ground which had also been spelt out in the four thousand pages or more of the Memorials and Proofs.

Now, the biggest gun of all was wheeled in to earn his keep – Sir Fletcher Norton, known to satirists as "Sir Bullface Doublefee."

Norton had been Attorney General and the following year was to become Speaker of the House of Commons. He was a man known for his wit in argument, although like most examples of the wit of previous eras, it doesn't always travel well. In response to George Grenville who had been shaking his head as Norton spoke in the House of Commons, he said: "I wish the honourable gentlemen, instead of shaking his head, would shake a good argument out of it." This was quoted by the anonymous satirist, Junius, who went on: "If to the elegance, novelty, and bitterness of this ingenious sarcasm, we add the natural melody of the amiable Sir Fletcher Norton's pipe, we shall not be surprised that Mr. Grenville was unable to make him any reply."[344]

Ever alert to possible disaster for Douglas, Lady Mary Coke had been concerned that Norton might not be available for this all-important speech:

"'Tis a cold, disagreeable day," she wrote. "Lady Betty Mackenzie & Lady Lichfield made me a visit. Lady Betty alarmed me by saying that Sir Fletcher Norton being obliged to go to Guildford, where he was opposed in his Election, 'twas fear'd he wou'd not be able to make the reply in the House of Lords. 'Twou'd be a great detriment to Mr. Douglass'es cause if that shou'd be the case."[345]

But it wasn't the case, and on February 20th, he got up to reply to the Hamilton charges. The chamber was filled to suffocation, said one observer, and young Archy was among the spectators. Once again, we have only the very abbreviated notes of the anonymous reporter to go by.

Norton started by addressing the question of filiation and giving three reasons why this applied in Archibald Douglas's case – his baptism, the reputation that he was son of Lady Jane for his entire childhood, and his treatment by his parents. He made the point – a favourite of Boswell's – that if any ordinary person were required to produce the sort of evidence of his birth that the Hamiltons required of Archibald Douglas, most people would fall short. "I have read foreign authors till my head is giddy," Norton said, and they all supported this view of the matter. "Did his parents ever *not* treat him as their child?" Norton asked. "I can see no safety if after fifteen years, evidence of the sort brought forward by the Pursuers is admitted. We can accept nothing but *irrefragable* proof."

At this point, the reporter appears to make fun of Norton. In dealing with the way Andrew Stuart used the Tournelle to charge Sir John Stewart with crimes, the reporter writes "crraimes" as if to mock Norton's accent. This use of the French court was an impropriety, said Norton. "Impropriety, did I say? Iniquity is more like it! And to use the Monitoire was infamous and illegal!"

At times the combination of brevity and legal Latin in the reporter's notes descends into incomprehensibility – to me anyway. "In this Cause evidence *per Fas & Refas* Examination Sir Jo. St. *nobile officium.*" the reporter writes.

Having fired off his salvo in favour of filiation and against the Tournelle, Norton got down to the task of examining the evidence. In an ungainly choice of words Norton said "If Lady Jane was pregnant I cannot conceive of her issue being spurious." Her capacity to conceive was proved by twelve witnesses, her pregnancy by about twenty. If she was pregnant, she must have been delivered. The Pursuers said that there was no delivery at Le Brun's by La Marre. But this does not affect the *fact* of delivery. And in trying to prove that Lady Jane and Colonel Stewart were somewhere else when they claimed Lady Jane was giving birth, the Hamilton lawyers had relied on fabricated evidence by Godefroi and other Tournelle witnesses.

At half past four, Sir Fletcher Norton sat down, half way through his argument, and the House adjourned. That night, Lady Mary Coke was very pleased with how things were going. "He was thought to have acquitted himself extremely well, & had turn'd all the arguments of the Council on the other side against themselves. 'Tis everybody's opinion Mr. Douglas will certainly carry his cause."[346]

The following day, Norton spoke for another hour and a half. "There were three witnesses to the actual birth," he said. "The Pursuers object that there is no La Marre and no Le Brun, but in fact Menager and Gilles produced a La Marre, and so did a Mme. Fountaine, *before* she was examined. There is also evidence of *three* Le Bruns. The Mignon story, said Norton "is the fruit of the Monitoire."

In dealing with the abduction of Sanry's child, Norton brought up the evidence just in from the books of the merchant, suggesting that Sir John was in Rheims when he was alleged to have been in Paris.

In summing up and considering whether there was a plot to deceive, Norton said "I will avail myself of the tenderness in the correspondence between Sir John and Lady Jane." And his final words were: "If Mrs. Hewit and Isabel Walker were not perjured, Archibald Douglas has proved his title to the state of possession."

The House of Lords adjourned on February 21st, a Tuesday, and resolved to meet again the following Monday, the 27th, for final speeches and the expected announcement of the verdict.

Although time was running out, Lady Mary Coke noted a couple of days later how the Duchess of Hamilton had not given up her efforts to influence the lords:

"Went to Lady Hertford's before ten O'clock, & play'd at

Lu till twelve: won seventeen guineas*. Ld Hertford say'd the Duchess of Hamilton had sent more papers to all the Peers; that he did not intend to vote, but that if he did, he was very well determined on which side it would be. The Duchess of Douglas has never gone out of her House, or solicited any of the Peers for their votes. How different and how much more decent is her conduct than that of the Duchess of Hamilton."[347]

Whatever his employer might think, Andrew Stuart had suddenly become very worried. It was not that he had changed his mind about the guilt of Lady Jane and Sir John, but he had heard something – it is not clear what – about Lord Mansfield's opinion of the case. As the senior Law Lord, Mansfield's views would be listened to by many of the uncommitted peers, who would defer to his knowledge of the law and his study of the papers and vote the way he voted. On Friday, February 24th, Stuart sat down to write a letter to Baron Mure.

"Monday is the day appointed for deciding our fate. By what I hear there is a very respectable part of the House of opinion with us, at the same time I think it incumbent on me to acquaint you of my real sentiments that the cause of truth will not prevail. Notwithstanding all the reports we had heard of the partiality of certain persons neither I nor our counsel thought it possible there would be depravity and boldness enough to venture upon a reversal of the Decree of the Court of Session, but symptoms which appeared to me infallible on the last day of the pleading joined with other reports convince me now that one man whom you will easily guess is determined against us and several others who either wish to take him for a leader or have not confidence enough in themselves or activity to strike against him. It is yet by no means clear that we are to lose it but I choose to prepare you for the worst. If a victory comes it will be so much the

---

* About £1700 in today's money.

more agreeable but do not depend on it."[348]

That weekend, as William Murray, Lord Mansfield, Lord Chief Justice of England, put the finishing touches to his speech, he held in his hand not only the future of Archibald Douglas, but that of Andrew Stuart. If Stuart lost the case, after all these years of effort, he could be a ruined man.

19

"Omni Exceptione Major"

O n February 27th, the House of Lords was the focus of an enormous amount of public interest. It must have been frustrating for those Scots connected with the case who had been unable to get to London for the climax of years and years of effort. The scene was set for the absent Scots in a dispatch to the *Scots Magazine* from a correspondent in London:

"It is impossible to convey to you an adequate idea of the striking solemnity and dignity with which the cause was conducted yesterday. The profound silence and anxious attention which every Lord, and indeed every creature, in the house, listened to the debate, was as extraordinary, as it was satisfactory, to all who had a just sense of the importance of it."[349]

Anyone with a friend in the Lords solicited a seat – or even a standing place – at the event. The Rev. Alexander Carlyle wrote:

"On the 27th I attended the House of Peers on the Douglas Cause. The Duke of B[uccleuch] had promised to carry me down to the House; but as I was going into Grosvenor Square to meet him at ten o'clock, I met the Duke of Montague, who was coming from his house, and took me into his chariot, saying that the Duke of B. was not yet ready. He put me in by the side of the throne, where I found two or three of my friends, among them Thomas Bell. The business did not begin till eleven, and from that time I stood, with now and then a lean on the edge of a deal board, till nine in the evening, without any refreshment but a small roll and two oranges."[350]

Also among the spectators was another Scot, Robert Strange, who wrote to a friend: "No cause I believe was ever brought before the Parliament of Great Britain so much attended to as this has been. I was present at the pleadings at the bar for the last two days by Sir Fletcher Norton, in favour of Mr. Douglas, and I again was there yesterday, being the day of decision. They began at 11 in the morning, and continued without intermission till 9 at night."[351]

There were a hundred and five peers, including the bishops, assembled in the main body of the hall, with the crowd of spectators packed in a dense mass around the walls.

At 11.28 a.m., according to the meticulous note-taking of the anonymous reporter, after some routine business of the House, the Duke of Newcastle rose to speak. His speech was brief, twelve minutes or so, and according to Horace Walpole, he spoke "very poorly."[352] The *Scots Magazine* correspondent thought differently. After the unsurprising admission that he had read the cases on both sides, Newcastle "made a short, but strong, speech, in favour of Mr. Douglas; not as a lawyer, but breathing those truly noble sentiments which became his high rank, and delivered with great dignity." The difference in reactions to his speech was not unconnected with the allegiances of the writers. Walpole was a Hamiltonian and the *Scots Magazine* correspondent was clearly a supporter of Douglas. Partisanship was to colour all public reactions to the speeches.

The Duke of Bedford, a Hamilton supporter, rose next. "His speech," said Robert Strange, "was short, nor was it much attended to." This may be because of its inaudibility. The *Scots*

Magazine correspondent said "I did not hear him distinctly enough to give you any account of his arguments."

One report says that Lord Gower spoke next, on the same side as Bedford,[353] and then came the first speech of the day to create a stir in the crowded House.

John Montagu, 4th Earl of Sandwich, was a man who trailed publicity and scandal in his wake. He is generally acknowledged to be the inventor of the sandwich. This is not an urban legend, as the origin of such eponyms sometimes turns out to be, although one of his descendants has dismissed the story that it was invented in order to allow him to gamble for twenty-four hours without stopping for meals. It seems that, more prosaically, he used to put slices of salt beef between bread when he was working long hours in the admiralty where he was First Lord. He made major contributions to the rebuilding of the English navy, and was also responsible for bring the music of Handel to a wide public.

He was known to be a libertine, a member of an aristocratic circle of men who regularly frequented the brothels of Soho and St James. At the time of the Douglas Cause he was living with his mistress, Martha Ray, an Eliza Doolittle-like figure with whom the Earl took up after his much-loved wife became insane.

Sandwich's speech for Hamilton[354] lasted three and a quarter hours, in a house where, in spite of the winter weather, the heat was oppressive as a result of the crush of bodies. According to Robert Strange "The speech was wearisome and full of digressions, which served no purpose but an attempt to illustrate the arguments he adduced."[355] But it seems to have been rather a lively speech and "made the most of the obstetrical aspects of the cause and put the Bishops to the blush."[356]

We're fortunate to have a detailed transcript of Sandwich's speech, in a handwritten journal in the library of the Earl's descendant, the current Earl of Sandwich.

Near the beginning, Sandwich addressed the argument that the genteel and virtuous Lady Jane could never have taken part in such a deception, by pointing out the inherent wickedness of the human race, as he of all people would be very aware.

"Take it in high or low life," he said, "Mankind is so much depraved that every argument is founded in absurdity that supposes any thing too horrid for their perpetration. But the tender hearted matrons and others whose compassion leads them to be imposed upon by plausible appearances will tell you that Lady Jane was too virtuous, too good, too religious, to be concerted in so wicked a scheme. I shall say the same if the contrary was not proved in evidence against her. And I think no woman at the Old Bailey was ever more palpably convicted of a crime with many persons to appear to her character (according to the custom of that Place) than this virtuous Lady Jane; whose failings I must in support of my argument be obliged to lay upon your Lordships in the course of this debate."[357]

Sandwich had no time for Norton's attack on Andrew Stuart and his conduct of the case, suggesting that he took that tack only because the facts of the case were weak. Then, in spite of never having met Stuart in his life, he told the House of Lords that: "I may fairly give him the description which the Council on the other side have most grossly misapplied in allotting to their hero Sir John Stewart. My Lords, all persons who are acquainted with Mr. Andrew Stuart will concur with me in testifying that he is a man *omni exceptione major*."*
Sandwich had one witness to Andrew Stuart's character in his friend, the Duke of Bedford, who had been British ambassador in Paris at the time Andrew Stuart was carrying out his research.

"This great personage was an eye witness of Mr. Stuart's behaviour when he was in France. I know he thinks his

---

* Beyond contradiction

conduct there was unexceptionable, and after this testimony, I believe I shall meet with no farther contradiction when I declare that Mr. Stuart bears as irreproachable a character as any one of his majesty's subjects."[358]

It's difficult to know which parts of Sandwich's speech gave the greatest offence to the bishops. They may have been affronted by his account of one of his relatives, Edward Wortley Montagu, brought out as an example of the problems that could arise from strict adherence to the attribution of parentage by 'habite and repute.'

"The person that succeeds to my children is Mr. Wortley Montague," Sandwich said. "He has lived at Grand Cairo and Jerusalem and God knows where – he is all over the world. I know Mr. Wortley very well – he is a man of gallantry* – he has a particular affection for matrimonial women for in many places there has generally been a Mrs. Wortley, I dare say every one of them very fairly married. Well, my Lords, now we may suppose if my branch of the family should be extinct and a son of Mr. Wortley's born at Alleppo come to your Lordships' bar and claims the peerage, the Turks will cry 'O Lord, here is the habit and repute, there is nothing on earth so clear, he must be the earl of Sandwich.' A great many people lived with Mr. Wortley and a great many women knew Mr. Wortley. Will your Lordships admit him upon that claim?"[359]

The Bishops might also have been offended by Sandwich's description of the symptoms of pregnancy as laid out by the doctors who were witnesses for the Douglas side. He didn't have much time for doctors and brought up an example of an extraordinary story that would have been familiar to many of the peers, of a woman who, it was certified by some distinguished doctors, had given birth to a clutch of rabbits:

"I fear I am old enough to remember a controversy that took up the attention of all the physical gentlemen in this

---

* The word was generally used at the time to mean promiscuity.

town for a considerable time. I mean the case of Mary Toft of Godalming in Surrey. For in consequence of her delivery, great and warm factions arose among the faculty and pamphlets were wrote to prove that it was very possible for a woman to be brought to bed of rabbits; tho' indeed at last the Writers on the other side gained a complete victory, for in dissecting some of these rabbits they found in their stomachs a pretty large quantity of cabbage and turnip tops, which the learned very wisely concluded they could not have found in the place from which they last came."[360]

Sandwich then addressed the recently proffered evidence seeking to strengthen Colonel Stewart's alibi in Rheims at the time the Sanry child was kidnapped in Paris.

"This circumstance was mentioned with such a degree of exultation," he said, "and ushered in with so much solemnity at the bar, as decisive in the Cause, that I thought they were going to produce the actual Le Brun or La Marre, which would indeed have at once put an end to the contest, but *parturient montes nascetur rediculus mus**. Never was a mountain delivered of a more pitiful mouse indeed than this. They produce the books of Mr. Benoit, a merchant at Rheims, to prove that the balance of a debt amounting, I think, to about 25 shillings and sixpence was paid by Sir John Steuart. Does this say that he was there to pay it himself? And if my Steward was to pay in Money for me to my Banker at London when I was at York would it not stand exactly in the same manner in the Banker's books; 'money received from the Earl of Sandwich' but would that prove me to be at that time in town? My Lords this is too ridiculous to deserve any farther answer."[361]

In closing, he made the remark that "A woman seldom forgets the circumstances that attend the birth of her first child," and said that Lady Jane's vagueness about most of the

---

* "The mountain laboured and brought forth a mouse."

details of the births persuaded him that they had not occurred as described, and therefore, Archibald Douglas was not her son.

The next to speak was the Lord Chancellor, Lord Camden. He was unusually nervous, sensing how important his speech would be in influencing the other peers. That morning, on the way to the House of Lords, one of his colleagues, John, Lord Campbell, who later became Lord Chancellor himself, observed Camden's demeanour.

"Though I knew him to be anxious," Campbell wrote, "I never had seen him so tremulous and flurried. He was afraid of the demand upon him, which fear he told me had induced him to write, not the whole of his argument, but the heads of it. He had shown them to me in his own hand, fairly written, upon seven or eight pages of folio paper. He said he was afraid of not using them, and was afraid of using them too – but as it was not his habit in such an assembly to look at a paper it should throw his thoughts into confusion."[362]

Camden need not have worried. His speech was generally acclaimed. As he began there was such a silence "that a handkerchief might have been heard to drop,"[363] in spite of the huge crowds who were present. Robert Strange wrote: "In my life was I never so entertained. Eloquence itself seemed to flow from his lips."[364]

"My Lords," Camden began, "the cause before us is, perhaps, the most solemn and important ever heard at this bar. ... I come to consider this cause with the most perfect indifference. I am happy, my lords, in having no connection whatever with any party on either side. I confess I never was so much perplexed in fixing my judgment in any question as in this cause, I was long in forming any opinion but this opinion being now formed, your lordships will find it is, indeed, very positive, very clear. In order to obtain this clearness, I have waded through more intricacy and doubt than I ever before met with in my life. ... We have one short question before us, — Is the appellant the son of the late Lady Jane Douglas, or not? I am of the mind that he is; and own that a more ample and positive proof of the child's being the son of a mother never appeared in a court of justice, or before any assize whatever."

Horace Bleackley, never at a loss for hyperbole, says of this moment:

"In an instant the great news had flashed from the chamber and was on a thousand lips. 'The Chancellor is speaking strongly for Mr. Douglas!' Until this moment the views of the great jurist had been kept secret, and no one had known which party he favoured."[365]

As Camden got into his stride, John, Lord Campbell, was fascinated to see what had happened to the notes Camden had shown him in the carriage:

"When he began to address the House, my attention was fixed upon this paper which he had rolled up. Not having at first any other occasion for it, he waved it as a kind of truncheon. From one topic he was led on to another, and through a very long – as well as able and impressive – argument he never unfolded the paper nor was at a loss for a single fact."[366]

Camden was entirely convinced by the evidence of Lady Jane's pregnancy and of the birth of twins, from the testimony of a number of witnesses in Rheims and of Mrs. Hewit that "she received them into her lap as they came from Lady Jane's body."

But that wasn't all. He did not share Sandwich's belief in the "depravity of mankind" and was perfectly willing to believe in the honesty of Colonel Stewart and Lady Jane as shown by their behaviour towards the children:

"'Tis in proof that, on every occasion, she showed all the fondness of a mother; when he casually hit his head against a table she screamed out and fainted away; when her husband, the Colonel, was in prison she never wrote to him without making mention of her sons; She recommended them to clergymen for the benefit of their prayers, is disconsolate for the death of the youngest; takes the sacrament, owns her surviving son; does everything in her power to convince the world of him being hers; blesses and acknowledges him in her dying moments; and leaves him such things as she had. Sir John likewise shows the same tenderness in effect. He leaves him 50,000 merks by a bond in September, 1763, ten years after the death of Lady Jane; and on his death-bed solemnly declares, before God, that the appellant is the son of Lady Jane. 'I make this declaration,' said he, 'as stepping into eternity.' A man that is a thief may disguise himself in publick, but he has no occasion for any mask when in private by himself."[367]

With such overwhelming evidence in favour of the birth, how on earth could it ever have been doubted? Camden had the answer. It had all been the fault of the Duke of Hamilton's tutor:

"How unfortunate for the Duke of Hamilton to be under the direction of such a man! One who has involved him in such an immensity of expenses, and this by examining a multitude of witnesses upon articles really foreign to the cause, which, indeed, is not the Duke of Hamilton's; it is the cause of Andrew Stuart ... I now mention his name for the first time. ... I really do not know who this Mr. Andrew Stuart is. I observe a marvellous attachment to this gentleman, a most unaccountable anxiety for any things that may touch his character. I observed an anxiety of the counsel at the bar to vindicate him, forgetting their client's cause for two hours together. I don't know what sacredness there is about this gentleman. This I know very well; that whenever a cause requires it, Mr. Andrew Stuart must be content to hear such observations as the evidence in the case makes it necessary for the judges or the counsel to throw out. I shall not, from any misguided lenity or indulgence, spare the least reflection that I find necessary upon him or any other person in this cause."

At one point in Camden's speech, possibly this passage, Andrew Stuart, who had been sitting on the left of the throne, "seemed much affected and left the House."[368] He wasn't the only one to be affected by the strength of Camden's abuse. Robert Strange felt pretty uncomfortable: "He treated Andrew Stuart in a manner I would not have been brought upon the carpet, not for the estate of Hamilton itself."[369]

Camden went on to look at the various tactics adopted by the Hamilton lawyers. He hadn't been able to understand at first why they had devoted so much effort to disputing the pregnancy, but then he realised why:

"Suppose the birth itself is dark or doubtful," he said, "and the evidence of it not so clear as could be wished, will any person say that a clear proof of the pregnancy does not supply the defect in the proof of the birth? Does not the delivery presuppose the pregnancy? Are all marks of pregnancy to be slighted because once in ten thousand, or perhaps once in a million of times, appearances may be set up to counterfeit pregnancy, or because it is barely possible in nature that there may be a false conception? Is this any ground or foundation for your lordships to reject the whole evidence of the pregnancy? ... Upon the whole of this evidence, my lords, I can no more doubt of the pregnancy than I can of my own existence. ... I say, my lords, it was a million to one if she was not pregnant. And the unavoidable consequence of this pregnancy must be either a miscarriage or delivery, for the preconception must somehow or other be disposed of. Give me leave to say, my lords, that the *onus probandi*[*] lies upon the respondents in this particular. The respondents' counsel saw this, and they knew that nothing less than evidence amounting almost to demonstration could overthrow so solid a proof of pregnancy."

Camden was impressed by the fact that Menager, at one of his earliest meetings with Andrew Stuart, had told a story that had much in common with Sir John's account of the birth.

---

[*] Burden of proof

"Are both the tales invention? It is impossible, my lords, to say that this man would invent a story so punctually alike, and that no part of the same story thus invented in different parts of the world should prove true. Nothing less than omniscience could do this. The consideration of this has stilled my mind more than any other; that when I see a credible witness in France, without tampering in any sort, give the same historical account of the birth that Sir John and Lady Jane have done, then I throw aside a thousand particulars related by Sir John. I care not whether they be true or no in every particular circumstance; the solid foundation, the main substance is true; and I don't weigh slight circumstances when the most material are confirmed by such credible evidence."

Camden was clearly uninfluenced by the abuse that had been heaped on the shifty Menager by the Hamilton lawyers and some of the Scottish judges.

"Mons. Menager, the single credit of whose testimony I dare venture to affirm, stands fairer than any other that has been examined in this cause; nor is there a witness in the whole list of them whose credit is so pure, so untainted, so free from reproach, so much *omni exceptione major*. ... He told Mr. Andrew Stuart that he was well acquainted with Monsieur La Marre, that Mons. La Marre acquainted him, in the year 1748, that he had brought a foreign lady to bed of twins; that the lady was advanced in years, and came last from Rheims. ... This was unlucky evidence for Mr. Andrew Stuart's cause for it cut up his whole hypothesis by the root. It produces a La Marre; it produces a Le Brune; it brings two persons into existence to whom he had denied any existence whatsoever. I had understood from Mr. Andrew Stuart, and his counsel averred it, that when he went to France he went in search of truth, that truth was his object, and whenever he found her she was to be taken up; that he even wished to find truth in favour of Lady Jane. But if this was really the case, if character was to be preserved, why conceal the evidence of Mons. Menager and Gilles?"

There were other witnesses, ignored, dismissed or possibly corrupted by Andrew Stuart, who in Camden's view supplied some of the missing facts.

"Madame Le Brune, in St. Germain, knew a Madame Fountain, who told her of a delivery in the house of one Le Brune, in the Rue de la Comédie. She had a conversation concerning this in presence of several gentlemen, and four days after she denied every word she had said. My lords, I do not like this; I have a right to say, as a judge, I do not like it. It speaks strongly of some improper management on that side of the question; an endeavour, if possible, to suppress the truth."

Reading the enormous amount of witness testimony today, and the fine and detailed arguments that were based on it, it is difficult not to agree with Camden's next point, that far too much reliance was being placed – by both sides, one might say – on the specific wording of memories dredged up from the cerebral mists of more than a decade ago.

"My lords, examine yourselves touching any material fact twelve years back; was it this month? in such a company? was it in that place? before Christmas? or after Christmas? Is there a man living, let his memory be ever so retentive, let the images of things be ever so strong, that can recollect every fact at that distance of time, with all its concomitant circumstances?"

Camden had been speaking for more than two hours, and he finished on a note which probably had more weight then than it would have today – the question of Lady Jane's piety.

"Lady Jane was religious, it is said, almost to a degree of enthusiasm," Camden said, "but I believe not to too great a degree. If religion is ever to be depended up [sic], it is under misfortunes. Her trials were great, and she bore them with true resignation. After engaging in the most solemn act of devotion, in her last dying hours she poured blessings upon her son. I shall never believe, my lords, this lady died with a lie in her mouth. In her life she was perfectly blameless in every respect.

I do therefore, upon my honour and conscience, pronounce that I believe that the appellant is the genuine son of Lady Jane Douglas, and that the judgment of the Court of Session ought to be reversed."

The *Scots Magazine* described the Lord Chancellor's speech as "one of the ablest speeches, that perhaps was ever heard in that, or any other house." Its reporter believed that, by the end, "there was not a doubt remained on any one's mind, of Mr. Douglas's being truly the son of Lady Jane. He [Camden] has not only gained great honour to himself, but really added dignity to the high office he bears."[370]

Unlike some of the other members of the House, Camden formed his views entirely by considering the evidence. He told a friend later that "he himself, on first beginning to consider the subject, felt the strongest prepossession that he should find it all an imposture. 'But,' said he, 'we lawyers have a method of threading and disentangling evidence, which I could not easily explain to anybody not of the profession, and when I gave my mind seriously to study the case, new light broke in upon me. I do assure you, I never was more clearly convinced of any fact in my life, than that this young man is Lady Jane Douglas's son.'"[371]

It was two minutes to six when Camden sat down and Lord Mansfield rose to speak. Camden's speech had the ring of sincerity and integrity about it. But expectations were different for Mansfield. To some, he was often economical with the truth. "Like the generality of the Scotch" said Lord Shelburne, "he had no regard for truth whatsoever." And the Master of the Rolls remarked to an acquaintance: "You and I have lived long in the world and of course have met a great many liars, but did you ever know such a liar as Will Murray, whom we have seen capable of lying before twelve people, every one of whom, he knows, knows that he lies."[372]

What more could Lord Mansfield possibly contribute to the growing swell of pro-Douglas opinion?

20

"Let Justice be Done..."

I n August 1958, a child was born in China to a married couple whom we will call R and W. R was an American man living in Hawaii, and W was a Chinese woman living in Hong Kong. Their child, C, had been conceived during a visit by R to Hong Kong, one of only five occasions the couple spent together. An application was then made to the courts in Hawaii for insurance benefits for C.

So far so boring.

What happened next was an example of the endurability of legal decisions in circumstances that can never have been envisaged at the time the decision was made. The courts in Hawaii were asked to consider a challenge to the right of the child to receive benefits, in the light of the fact that a blood test had shown that the child could not have been fathered by R.

This is what the court said: "This depends upon whether the Lord Mansfield Rule preclude the admission of the blood grouping test results as proof of the illegitimacy of C under the laws of Hawaii, the State of R's domicile."

More than a hundred and fifty years after Lord Mansfield's

death, his name was still being invoked in a modern law court, as a result of a presumption he articulated, that the child of a married woman should be treated in law as the child of her husband.

At the time Mansfield gave this ruling, it was a useful guideline to follow, and the only exception was if the husband was "beyond the four seas during the whole of his wife's pregnancy."[373] It's surprising that even in the 20th century – and the case above was plucked at random from many that still invoke the rule – an 18th century legal dictum retains its usefulness in a much-changed world.

Mansfield's was a formative voice in 18th century law. He played a part in streamlining the legal process as well as helping to decide most major legal questions during his time on the bench.

He was, according to Dr. Johnson "not a mere lawyer: he drank champagne with the wits."[374] One of the wits was Alexander Pope. In one of his couplets he wrote of Mansfield:

"Graced as thou art with all the power of words,
So known so honoured at the House of Lords."[375]

Colley Cibber, actor and versifier, parodied these lines by writing:

"Persuasion tips his tongue whene'er he talks,
And he has chambers in the King's Bench Walks."[376]

For thirty years, as advocate, judge and finally Lord Chief Justice, Mansfield had been an influential voice in shaping the law in numerous *causes célèbres* and leading cases, and the Douglas Cause was another. The speech he made in the last hours of the Appeal made it virtually impossible for any peer to vote in contradiction to his arguments.

What we can discover today of what he said at the time of the Douglas appeal is rather disappointing. The only printed text[377] certainly doesn't sparkle with legal acumen or deal a destructive blow to the carefully assembled cage of fact and inference that the Hamilton side felt was impossible for the defender to escape. And yet, for some observers he was on top form. The *Scots Magazine* said:

"To say that he was great, pathetic, and eloquent, is saying nothing. There was such music in his speech, such elegance in his diction, such irresistible force in his reasoning, that it was impossible to hear him without raptures."[378] On the other hand, another writer describes him as making "the worst speech he ever delivered."[379]

I have used the version that is printed in the *Notable Scottish Trials* series, along with some quotes from a manuscript in the National Library of Scotland that was written by someone having trouble hearing what Mansfield was saying, since it is riddled with gaps. But there are two reasons for thinking the printed version is very imperfect. First, it deals with hardly any of the legal arguments that we might have expected from the report of his speech in the *Scots Magazine*, which said: "…he demonstrated, with the utmost clearness and precision, that the most material proofs which the agents on the Hamilton side had produced, disproved themselves, and could not possibly, in the nature of things, have happened to Sir John and Lady Jane; he cleared his ground constantly as he went on; and unravelled all the intricacies of the cause with the utmost perspicuity; he illustrated all his arguments with parallel instances in other trials…" Second, as we shall see, Andrew Stuart responded later to Mansfield's speech, and referred to several points made by Mansfield against the Hamilton case that were not in the printed version.

The most striking thing about the speech we do have is that the burden of Mansfield's argument is derived less from the evidence brought forward by the Hamilton team and more from the impossibility of Lady Jane having been party to such a deception. For a man who had seen and passed judgement on the most important cases of the last twelve years, he began with a remarkable statement:

"My Lords," he said, "I must own that this cause before us

is the greatest and most important that occurs to me. It is no less than an attack upon the virtue and honour of a lady of the first quality, in order to dispossess a young man of an eminent fortune, reduce him to beggary, strip him of his birthright, declare him an alien and a foundling. I have slept and waked upon this subject, considered it upon my pillow, to the losing of my natural rest, and with all the judgment I was capable of, have considered the various articles that made up this long and voluminous cause, upon which I am now to give my opinion before your Lordships."

(He had clearly come a long way since he told Boswell "I have not read a word of it.")

"I apprehend that, in the matter before us, three things are to be considered. The situation of Lady Jane before her delivery, at her delivery, and after it was over: to all which the Chancellor has spoken with great propriety. It is proved beyond a doubt that she became pregnant in October, 1747, at the age of forty-nine years, a thing far from being uncommon, as is attested by physicians of the first rank and confirmed by daily experience; and that in the month of July she was delivered of twins, one of whom died, the other is still alive; he has been presented to the world by Sir John Steuart and Lady Jane Douglas as their son; nor can he be wrested from the hands of his parents unless some other hand in their lifetime claimed him as their child in a legal and a justifiable way.

This action, my Lords, did not lie against the appellant as an impostor, for an impostor, in the sense of the law, is a person who wilfully and knowingly 'pretends to be different from what he really is, in order to defraud another, and to impose under a fictitious name upon the publick.' If any be an impostor, it must have been Lady Jane whom they ought to have prosecuted in her lifetime, and not at the distance of nine years after her death."

Mansfield relied on his personal assessment of Lady Jane's character to dismiss the years of work Andrew Stuart and his team had put into assembling their multifaceted case. For the next section of the speech I have used both the printed version and the hand-written notes from the National Library of Scotland archives, which adds some detail. In this version, Mansfield picks on the fact that the lawyers for Hamilton had apparently mentioned his own association with Lady Jane as a possible confounding factor in his objectivity. Although the text is garbled, he appears to have denied any close association with her, but brings up the fact that she applied to him for help in getting a pension from the King:

"My Lords, the Respondents' case mentions my name … I will tell your Lordships all that I know with respect to Lady Jane Douglas and as her life was a life of adventure this perhaps is no less adventurous than the rest … All that I know of My Lady Jane is as an absolute stranger to her and all her family. My Lords, she sent to my house and desired to be allowed to talk with me. She came a second time and went away without saying one syllable for what she came. She came again a third time. I thought she might have some particular emergency. She told me she was married to Sir John Stewart, that he had been in the army in the year 1715. She said she had applied to Lord Marischal & he would do nothing for her. I was vastly moved; I thought to have given her money and supposing she would have said something to me. But she went away & said nothing at all."

Mansfield's next statement contained an incongruous choice of words, at least to a modern eye: "The distress of her appearance," he said, "seemed to me absolutely literally starving without a morsell of bread, tho I do remember her to have been a famous toast, as a great character of a woman."*

"Her visage and appearance were more powerful advocates than her voice," Mansfield said, "and yet I was afraid to offer her

---

* Words which might have been even more appropriate if spoken by the Earl of Sandwich.

relief, for fear of being constructed to proffer her an indignity. In this manner she came twice to my house, before I knew her real necessities; to relieve which now was my aim. I spoke to Mr. Pelham in her favour, told him of her situation with regard to her brother the Duke of Douglas, and of her present straits and difficulties. Mr. Pelham without delay laid the matter before the King; the Duke of Newcastle, being then at Hanover, was wrote to; he seconded the solicitations of his brother: His Majesty immediately granted her £300 per annum out of his privy purse; and Mr. Pelham was so generous as to offer £150 of the money to be instantly paid. I can assure your Lordships that I never did trouble His Majesty for any other. Lady Jane Douglas was the first and the last who ever had a pension by my means."

Mansfield quoted from accounts of Lady Jane's attachment to her children, her distress at Sholto's death and her near-death declaration:

"She declared that the children Archy and Sholto were born of her body, and that there was one blessing of which her enemies could not deprive her, which was her innocency, and that she could pray to Almighty God for the life of her other son, that she was not afraid for him, for that God Almighty would take care of him."

Onward and upward, Mansfield's oratory – or at least the printed version – praised the saintly Lady Jane in pseudo-Biblical mode.

"Would she, my Lords, have blessed her surviving child on her death-bed? Would she have died with a lie in her mouth and perjury on her right hand? Charity that thinketh no evil, will not suffer me for a moment to harbour an opinion so cruel and preposterous. Or can we suppose that two people who had not wherewith to support themselves would be solicitous and show all the tenderness of parents towards the children of creatures, who, forgetting the first principles of instinct and humanity, had sold their children to people whom they did not even as much as know by their names? The act of Joseph's brethren in selling him is represented as wicked and unnatural, but indeed the crime of Madam Mignon and Madam Sanry is still more black and atrocious!"

When I first read Lord Mansfield's speech and his reasons for dismissing the case against Lady Jane, I couldn't help remembering a more recent case in which allegations about the credibility of a certain Lady Mary were also dismissed by a judge on the grounds of her personal charms and conjugal bliss, in these words:

"Your vision of her will probably never disappear. Has she elegance? Has she fragrance? Would she have… radiance? What is she like in physical features, in presentation, in appearance, how would she appeal? Has she had a happy married life? Has she been able to enjoy rather than endure her husband?"[380]

This was, of course, Lady Mary Archer, whose evidence in support of her husband, Lord Archer, who had been suing a newspaper for libel, was accepted, perhaps partly as a result of the judge's account of her charms.*

There was clearly more to the Mansfield/Lady Jane connection than being total strangers. Although he said in his speech that all he knew was "as an absolute stranger to her and all her family", he went on to reveal slightly closer contact:

"And here we see Sir John as much a parent to the appellant as Lady Jane; he was every way fond of him! it is in evidence. I know it to be true. My sister and I have been frequently at Mrs. Murray's with them [Archy and Sholto] and were always delighted with the care we observed. No mortal harboured any thoughts of their being false children at that time, I mean in 1750 and 1751. Every person looked upon them as the children of Lady Jane Douglas and of Colonel Steuart."

---

* It later emerged that Lord Archer had committed perjury in that trial, and he was imprisoned in 2002 for the offence.

At some point in the middle of his speech, in a packed and sweltering House of Lords, Mansfield showed signs of illness. One of the crowd of spectators, Alexander Carlyle, reported: "Lord Mansfield, overcome with heat, was about to faint in the middle of his speech, and was obliged to stop. The side-doors were immediately thrown open, and the Chancellor rushing out, returned soon with a servant, who followed him with a bottle and glasses. Lord Mansfield drank two glasses of the wine, and after some time revived, and proceeded in his speech. We, who had no wine, were nearly as much recruited by the fresh air which rushed in at the open doors as his lordship by the wine."[381]

Fortified by Lord Camden's offering, Mansfield resumed his speech.

"I always rejoice to hear truth," he said, "which is the ornament of criticism and the polished gem that decorates a bar. The scrutiny in France, followed by an action in Scotland … brought forth a striking acknowledgment of the appellant by his father, Sir John Steuart (who) openly acknowledged him before the Court of Session in the midst of a crowded multitude and when labouring under a load of anguish and pain.

If Sir John Steuart, the most artless of mankind, was actor in the *enlèvement* of Mignon and Sanry's children, he did in a few days what the acutest genius could not accomplish for years. He found two children, the one the finished model of himself, and the other the exact picture in miniature of Lady Jane. It seems Nature had implanted in the children what is not in the parents; for it appears in proof that in size, complexion, stature, attitude, colour of the hair and eyes, nay, in every other thing, Mignon and his wife, Sanry and his spouse, were *toto caelo* different from and unlike to Sir John Steuart and Lady Jane Douglas. Among eleven black rabbits there will scarce be found one to produce a white one."

At some point in the speech, when discussing Sir John Stewart's part in the story, Mansfield had to explain away the issue of the forged La Marre letters, which he called 'supposed letters', and he did this with reference to a strange case that had been reported by the eminent legal historian, Sir Edward Coke, in the middle of the previous century. Mansfield had decided that he could not argue that the letters from Pierre La Marre were genuine – the evidence of Diderot and less eminent French speakers made that impossible. But he argued that, because someone does wrong in order to strengthen his case, it does not invalidate the case.

"Being accused of forgery and examined as with a rope about his neck [Sir John] lies backward and forward, therefore neither party can take him as a witness. But all the circumstances are predicting a La Mar. … It is not an uncommon thing for a man to defend a good cause by foul means, that is by false pretences."[382]

Mansfield then quoted the report in Coke of a man who brought up his brother's daughter after his brother died. When she was about eight or nine years old, her uncle corrected her for some misdeed, and she was heard to say, "Oh! Good Uncle, kill me not!" Shortly after this, the niece disappeared and a search failed to find her. Since the uncle stood to inherit his brother's money and estates he was suspected of her murder, and arrested. When he denied the crime, he was allowed to go free in order to find her and produce her to the court. In fact, he returned to the court at the next assizes accompanied by a child he said was his niece. When witnesses proved that she was not, the man was tried, found guilty and hanged. Eight years later, the niece reappeared, having run away at the time of her argument with her uncle, been taken in and educated by a stranger, and now returned at the age of sixteen to claim her inheritance.[383] (In 1886, the author Wilkie Collins used this case as the basis for a short story, published in the *Boy's Own Paper.*)

Andrew Stuart later described this case as the result of Mansfield ransacking his memory to find instances of innocent forgeries "to give an antidote with the poison", i.e. to cancel out any harm done by the undoubted fact of La Marre forgeries.

In his closing words, Mansfield returned yet again — in case the Lords hadn't yet got the point — to the intrinsic and undeniable virtue of his heroine.

"How is it possible to credit the witnesses, some of them of a sacred character, when they speak of Lady Jane's virtues, provided we can believe her to have been a woman of such abandoned principles as to make a mock of religion, a jest of the sacrament, a scoff of the most solemn oaths, and rush with a lie in her mouth and perjury in her right hand into the presence of the Judge of All, who at once sees the whole heart of man, and from whose all discerning eye no secrecy can screen, before whom neither craft nor artifice can avail, nor yet the ingenuity and wit of lawyers can lessen or exculpate. On all which accounts I am finding the appellant to be the son of Lady Jane Douglas."[384]

After just over three hours, Mansfield sat down at about nine o'clock in the evening. No one now doubted what the outcome would be. The two senior Law Lords having spoken on the same side, it would have been very unusual for the House of Lords to have voted against them. The vote began at ten, and with hands on their breasts the lords reversed the decision of the Scottish court and declared that they believed the appellant to be legitimate son of Lady Jane Douglas.

But there were strong feelings on the other side, among the peers who supported the Hamiltons. Although it was theoretically permissible for peers to object to a verdict arrived at by the law lords, it was frowned upon, and had not happened for fifty years. But the Duke of Bedford, the Earls of Sandwich, Bristol, and Dunmore and Lord Milton, caused a stir by registering strong disagreement with the verdict. Lady Mary Coke wrote in her journal:

"Lord Sandwich, having no character to lose, suprised nobody. Lord Milton, being all violence, was easily induced to an act of this nature. Lord Dunmore, being a very worthless man, it signified very little what he did; but the Duke of Bedford and Lord Bristol surprised everybody, tho' it has often been his Grace's fate to be governed by those who have not half his worth or understanding. Lord Bristol's conduct is still more unaccountable, unless one resolves it to proceed from the great influence Lady Charlotte Edwine [a Hamilton relation] is thought to have over him; however, it is the general Opinion they have done themselves much more injury than they could do Mr. Douglass."[385]

The news that the great Cause was finally over spread quickly round the town. Horace Walpole had mixed reactions. He thought that the verdict was "conformable to equity, as the child was owned by both parents; and the imposture not absolutely proved; yet in my opinion not awarded in favour of truth – a declaration I should not be so arrogant as to make, if many very able men were not as much persuaded as I am of the child being supposititious."[386]

Archy Douglas was not in the House. "The Duchess of Queensberry had carried him in the morning to Kew, by way of diverting his anxiety" but apparently he received the news of his success with great composure. "Thank God," he cried, "my anxiety is now over!"[387]

Percy Fitzgerald, a Hamilton supporter to the last, commented more than a century later on this reaction of the man he still believed to be the son of M. Nicholas Mignon:

"Is it straining a point to say this behaviour is more characteristic of a Frenchman than an Englishman, as the former always knows well how to play his part with due effect in such a situation?"[388]

Well, Percy, since you ask, I would say that the answer to your question is probably 'Yes'.

The Reverend Alexander Carlyle, after standing or leaning for twelve hours in the fetid heat of the House of Lords was in need of a drink.

"After the decision," he wrote, "I persuaded my friends, as there was no coach to be had, not to attempt rushing into any of the neighbouring taverns, but to follow me to the Crown and Anchor in the Strand, where we arrived, Thos. Bell, Alderman Crichton, Robert Bogle, junior, and I, in time enough to get into a snug room, where we wrote some letters for Scotland, the post then not departing till twelve; and after a good supper, Bell and I got home to Aldermanbury about one o'clock, where our wives were waiting, though not uninformed of the event, as I had despatched a porter with a note to them immediately on our arrival in the tavern."[389]

Lady Mary Coke, out and about at the Spanish Ambassadress, heard the news late that night. "It gave me great pleasure, but I kept it to myself, for fear there might be somebody present that it might offend, tho' I believe there never was an event that gave more general satisfaction."[390]

And what of Andrew Stuart, meanwhile? There cannot have been a more depressed man in London at the news. The following day, February 28th, 1769, he wrote a grim – almost suicidal – letter to his patron and friend, Baron Mure:

"My Dear Sir,

Last night our fate was decided, and agreeable to the prediction I sent you; but I may venture safely to say, not agreeable to the dictates either of common sense or of equity. There is no help for it; we cannot command events, we can only deserve success and surely if ever there was a cause where truth and justice were entitled to success, that is the Cause we have been embark'd in.

The Law Lords decided the fate of the day without a division though there were many Peers of opinion with us; but the talents of Law Lords for public speaking dazzles and bamboozles others. I never before, nor ever shall again, wish so much to be a Peer as I did yesterday; for I am sure there was not a thing said by either, but what was either without foundation in fact, or fallacious in argument; and any man, possest fully of the cause, might easily have answered both. ... Such agitations as I have felt in the course of the pleadings and decision of this cause, is more than I believe I could possibly undergo again for any object whatever. I feel myself quite exhausted, and sick of every thing that relates to Courts of judicature; I had almost said sick of a world where such injustice can be committed.

Were it not for ... the consciousness of having acted uprightly, the iniquity and injustice I have met with in this Cause even in the last stages of it would almost be enough to deprive a man of his senses."[391]

Stuart's depression was assuaged a little when on the day after the verdict he received a bond for £400 a year for life, about £40,000 in today's money, from an M.P. friend, "in consideration of the cruel treatment he had met with."[392]

There were various estimates of what the whole business had cost both sides over the previous eight years. The Duchess of Douglas faced a bill for £23,000 (£2,300,000 in today's money) and one estimate for what the Duke of Hamilton had to pay came out very precisely at £31,154 0s. 72d (£3,115,403).[393] Another estimate gives the total costs as about £100,000 (£10,000,000).[394]

In the years that followed, the most widely discussed issue concerning the verdict focussed on the conduct of Lord Mansfield, the villain of the piece in the eyes of Andrew Stuart, although from all that we can discover of the speeches, it was Camden's that dealt the most wounding blows. There were three unworthy motives ascribed to Mansfield for his partisan and sentimental speech. The first and least outrageous was that he argued against Hamilton to prevent the Hamilton family from acquiring too much power in the land through the acquisition of all the Douglas estates. This was apparently one of the rumours believed in Scotland.

The second rumoured motive was bribery. This accusation was levelled at Mansfield in the early 19th century by Philip Francis, a rather malicious M.P. whom some believed to be the pseudonymous essayist Junius. Robert Malcolm, writing later in the century, relayed the story:

"... He (Mansfield) pleaded the cause of the defendant with all the earnestness and zeal of a hired advocate, and he did so not only in disregard of the evidence of facts but in defiance of established law, as often laid down by himself in other causes. That such a man should have pursued such a course was often the subject of wonder and astonishment to professional men, both in England and Scotland, till at length, after many dark hints, conveyed to the public, at various intervals of time, the damning fact was broadly promulgated, even in the House of Commons, that, in this celebrated cause, the ermine of justice had been stained indelibly by his Lordship's acceptance of an enormous bribe, – not less, it is said, than a Hundred Thousand Pounds! This unexampled instance of corruption in an English judge was repeatedly alluded to in the speeches of the celebrated Sir Philip Francis, a man of great talents and high honour, who would certainly never have made such a charge had he not been thoroughly satisfied of its truth. The last notice taken of it by Sir Philip was in 1817, in reply to a member of the House of Commons who had ... eulogised Lord Mansfield. 'Never, while you live, sir' exclaimed Sir Philip indignantly, 'say a word in favour of that corrupt judge. *Lord Mansfield was sold in the Douglas Cause* and the parties are known through whom the money was paid.'"[395]

Mansfield certainly died a rich man. He left a vast fortune, with the interest alone on his mortgages amounting to £26,000 p.a. (£2,600,000). But then he was well-paid when he lived, and it is difficult to see how his head would be turned in one particular case even by such a large sum. Not to mention the fact there there is no evidence, other than Francis's malignant barbs at a man he already hated. He was said to have a "violent prejudice" against Lord Mansfield.

The third ascribed motive, which in its extreme form is improbable but may have an element of truth in it, is to be found in a footnote to the published letters of Charles Kirkpatrick Sharpe, an antiquary and artist.

"Lady Jane Douglas is mentioned in Mrs. Heywood's 'Utopia' in no very favourable terms. She was suspected of being prone to gallantry; and it was said that she had a child by Lord Mansfield, who afterwards proved so favourable to the cause of her son. There is a picture of her at Newbattle – pale, slight-looking, with blue eyes, and not pretty."[396]

This would be extraordinary if true, although I have found no reference anywhere else to this putative child. But the terms in which Mansfield spoke of Lady Jane in his speech were little short of adoring. In spite of trying to distance himself from any connection with her, he had admitted he had met her several times and indeed spent time with her children. His sister, Miss Nicky Murray, was a leading light in Edinburgh social circles and certainly knew Lady Jane. And there is one intriguing reference, probably irrelevant, in a biography of Mansfield to a mysterious romantic encounter when Mansfield was thirty one.

"By 1736 his prospects were sufficiently encouraging to explain, if not to justify, an indulgence in romance. The object of his passion is unknown; but female perversity or parental prudence rejected his advances, and he was left to seek consolation in the generous indignation of Pope.

> *"Shall one whom nature, learning, birth, conspired*
> *To form, not to admire, but be admired,*
> *Sigh while his Chloe, blind to wit and worth,*
> *Weds the rich dulness of some son of earth?"*[397]

Could William Murray, Lord Mansfield, have been another of the younger men who seemed to cluster round Lady Jane at various stages in her life? She was thirty-eight at the time but looked much younger.

What is more likely is that Mansfield just had a soft spot for ladies of the aristocracy. There is a famous case in which he was involved which occurred five years later, involving the alleged bigamy of the Duchess of Kingston. Described at the time of her trial by a newspaper as "a stout lady of fifty or thereabouts, not without traces of former charm," Elizabeth Chudleigh had married the Duke of Kingston some years before, although some alleged that she had been previously secretly married to a Lieutenant John Hervey. Since Hervey became Earl of Bristol, Miss Chudleigh was either a duchess or a countess, and Mansfield seems to have treated her with astonishing sympathy when she applied to his court for bail. She was freed, even though Mansfield later said that no person to be tried by the House of Lords on a felony had ever been let out on bail. It came out later that Mansfield had befriended Elizabeth and met her privately, telling her that she was in no danger of punishment for bigamy, even if she were to be found guilty.[398]

Whatever the reasons for Lord Mansfield's passionate defence of the legitimacy of Archibald Douglas's birth – and we have to accept that it was probably due to the fact that he accepted the Douglas lawyers' arguments – it was the end of the road for the Hamilton cause and for Andrew Stuart's role in it. The verdict was final, but all of Scotland had to wait for two days to find out what it was.

21

Celebrations

From London to Edinburgh is about four hundred miles. There was keen interest in Scotland in the result of the House of Lords decision, but while one side was celebrating and the other licking its wounds in London, there was no conceivable way the Scots could find out which was doing which. In the mid-to-late 17th century, animal motion, either human or horse, was the only means to transport information over distances of more than a few miles.

The *Caledonian Mercury* on March 1st, the day after the verdict, had to announce that "We are sorry we have it not in our power to satisfy the anxiety of our readers with regard to the decision of the Douglas Cause, no account having yet arrived of that event."[399] In an age of instant communication, it is difficult to put ourselves in the place of people for whom, however important the message, there was no way to reduce its transmission time from an agonisingly long period of several days.

At eight o'clock in the evening of Thursday, March 2nd, seventy hours after the vote in the House of Lords, the news finally arrived in Edinburgh. It had travelled at nearly six miles an hour, much faster than the usual journey by stage coach which took up to eight days.

The message was carried by Ilay Campbell, one of the Douglas counsel and a relative of the Scottish judge, Lord Kames. He rode from the Duchess of Douglas's house in Piccadilly to the Mercat Cross in the centre of Edinburgh, changing horses to travel as fast as possible. Shortly before eight o'clock on the evening of March 2nd, 1769, Campbell halted at the Cross, waved his hat in the air and shouted "Douglas for ever!"

There was clearly popular support for Archibald Douglas among the ordinary people of Scotland. Someone once asked Boswell why all the people of extraordinary sense were Hamiltonians. "I cannot tell." he answered, "but I am sure all persons of common sense are Douglassians."[400]

The news of the Douglas victory led to rejoicing in the cities and towns of Scotland, and attacks on the houses of people known to favour the Hamilton side. There were bonfires in the streets and the ships in Leith harbour displayed their flags. In Glasgow twenty cartloads of coals were heaped on a bonfire before the *Saracen's Head* in the centre of town.

The judges who had originally voted for Hamilton in the Court of Session were particular targets of mob anger. One surprising participant in the rioting was James Boswell. As the mob's stones shattered the glass of the judges' windows, he is alleged to have said "These honest fellows in their turn are giving their casting votes." He even went so far as to stone the windows of his own father, Lord Auchinleck, who had voted for Douglas in the Court of Session but failed to put a light in his windows on the news of a Douglas victory.[401]

The violence continued for several days, and the *Scots Magazine* reported that the Edinburgh magistrates had published a handbill offering a reward of fifty pounds for the uncovering of those who had attacked the judges, and recommending to "all sober honest citizens, householders, tradesmen, and others ... that they use the proper means to hinder their apprentice-boys, and servants, from going abroad from their houses without proper errands, or when they have ground to suspect that they may, from their own levity, or the instigation of other disorderly people, be in danger of engaging in such lawless proceedings."

The article went on to lend its general support to the celebrations:

"The satisfaction expressed on this event in all the corners of Scotland, has, it is believed, been more general than ever happened in any case before. Our news-papers are crouded with accounts of the rejoicings, and yet they say it is impossible to find room for all those that are sent them."[402]

Archy's half-brother, Sir John Steuart of Grandtully, heard the news in a letter from a friend in Edinburgh: "Your brother has carried his cause unanimously: no division of the House. God make us all thankful... This is glorious. The joy here is beyond description ..."[403]

Two leading Scottish intellectuals, David Hume and Adam Smith, were appalled by the verdict and by Camden and Mansfield's formative roles in swaying the peers. Smith wrote that Lord Camden had "always run after the applause of the mob," while Mansfield had "followed his fears and inclinations!" Hume wrote from Paris that he felt "very sensible indignation at the decision, though I foresaw It for some time. It was abominable with regard to poor Andrew Stewart, who had conducted the Cause with singular ability and integrity: and was at last exposed to reproach which unfortunately can never be wiped off. For the Cause, though not in the least intricate, is so complicated, *that it will never be reviewed by the public:* who are besides perfectly pleased with the sentence: being swayed by compassion and a few popular topics. To one who understands the Cause as I do, nothing could appear more scandalous than the pleadings of the two law lords. Such gross misrepresentation, such impudent assertions, such groundless assertions never came from that place. But all was good enough for their audience…"[404]

One tiny consolation for Andrew Stuart – too little and too late – was an apology from Thurlow, his duelling opponent, who wrote to Stuart's brother within ten days of the verdict.

"After what passed between us in January last," he wrote, "I have wished to take an early occasion of expressing my sense of Mr. Stuart. The final decision of the Douglas Cause gives me this opportunity and I lay hold on it to explain to you that I think him a man of honour. When the case in that cause was compiled I was unacquainted with Mr. Stuart's general character. I have now heard him spoken of by very respectable persons in terms which induce me to think of him in this manner. The terms of esteem in which such persons who have known or conversed with him, speak of his character, may seem to render any attestation of mine of little use; but I have thought it right to express myself thus, that I may not be imagined to entertain a different opinion of him."[405]

Meanwhile, Londoners who had had a head start for their celebrations were equally delighted with the verdict. On the night of the Lords vote, the Duchess of Douglas went with the Duchess of Queensberry and Archy to the theatre to a benefit performance of *The Albion Queens* for the actress, Mrs. Bellamy. At some point in the performance their presence was noted and the audience applauded. The Duchess of Douglas stood up and curtseyed several times until the Duchess of Queensberry leant across Archy and cried "Sit down, Peg!" so loudly that Mrs. Bellamy heard and missed her entrance. The Douglas trio were in high spirits and Mrs. Bellamy's problems were not over. She was playing Mary, Queen of Scots, and her concentration must have been badly disrupted by the continuing cries of "Well said, Mary! Bravo, Mary!" from the Duchesses' box, "'nearly turning the play into a tragi-comedy,' as Mrs. Bellamy later said."[406]

One of the other plays in London at the time was *The Fatal Discovery* by John Home, Scots author of the play *Douglas*. Anti-Scots feeling was running high at the time, and Home was advised by Garrick to conceal the fact that he was the author. But it slipped out – perhaps leaked by Home himself – and audiences dropped. Alexander Carlyle, a friend of Home's, wrote: "Home, in his way, ascribed this to the attention of the public, and especially of the Scotch, being drawn off by the Douglas Cause, which was decided in the House of Lords on the 27th, forgetting that this took up only one night, and that any slackness derived from that cause could not affect other nights."[407]

Lady Mary Coke, ever deferential to royalty, gave a hint in her journal that the King himself was rather pleased with the verdict. The day after the decision, she was summoned to see her friend Princess Amelia, the King's aunt.

"She seem'd to be very much pleased with the unanimity of the House of Lords in their decision on Monday night, tho' H.R.H. had been very cautious in every thing She had said upon that subject; tho' She told me She cou'd not help thinking the King had wish'd for Mr. Douglass. My Answer was that their Majesty's were too great Names to be mention'd on that, or other subjects, but that I was inclined to be of H.R.H.'s opinion."[408]

While the Duchess of Douglas was parading around town, receiving the plaudits of the crowds, the Duchess of Hamilton was nursing her wounds in private. It took her three weeks to summon up enough composure to write to Baron Mure, the lead instigator with Andrew Stuart of the suit.

"Dear Sir," she wrote on March 21st, "I should sooner have thanked you for your kind letter upon the late division, if I could have trusted myself to write upon a subject that has made me more uneasy – I might say unhappy – than I can express. It is impossible for me now ever to have a good opinion of many of whom I have endeavoured to think well. ...

Andrew Stuart will not let me ask for anything for him…
I have no inclination to write about these affairs. I hope when
we meet in Scotland I shall think more coolly. Something
ought certainly to be done for Mr. Stuart, but I suppose the
tutors will choose to have a meeting upon this subject, as soon
as they can after I come to Scotland.

E. Hamilton"

This is how the letter is printed in the collected papers of
Baron Mure of Caldwell.[409] But there is a significant omission.
The original letter is in the archives of the National Library
of Scotland, and before the last paragraph there is another
sentence, one that shows there were people who guarded
the reputation for charm and sweetness of the former Miss
Gunning as solicitously as Boswell with Lady Jane when he
edited out passages in her letters.

"My only comfort," wrote the furious duchess, "is the
thoughts of somehow or other having it in my [power] to hurt
those who have hurt me."[410] (The word 'power' is omitted in
error, but the sense requires some such word.)

Meanwhile, Boswell was receiving congratulations from
his friends as if the Douglas victory was solely his.

"…I congratulate you very sincerely on Mr. Douglas's
success," wrote his friend, George Dempster. "You know the
Young man, think him Lady Jean's, and that he has been hardly
dealt with, and therefore the fortunate Issue of his Cause must
be highly agreeable and Gratifying to You. Never was a case
that admitted of such diversity of honest Opinion. I suspect I
may be under the Influence of prejudice and as it is not to the
humane side I regret it. But I own my doubts are very strong
on all those points. In so much that I took my Horse to day
and came out of Dundee in the Midst of Bone fires, ringing
of Bells, firing of Cannon etc. etc. Chusing to decline Lord
Gray's invitation to a grand Entertainment and to expose my
self to the whole Tempest of the D. of D's wrath rather than
mix in a Company with whom my heart was not at unison.

For woman and Child are mad with joy."[411]

Another friend rejoiced on hearing of Boswell's activities in Edinburgh after the verdict:

"I am highly delighted with your behaviour in the Douglas cause, *Finis coronat Opus*, you broke, I am told, your father's windows because they were not enough illuminate. Bravo, Bravissimo! I am of your opinion, that Mr. Douglas should imediatly marry, I wish much to live to hear he has sons."[412]

In early March, the Duchess of Douglas and Archy were presented at Court, at one of the King's Drawing Rooms. Lady Mary Coke was there, with her sister, Lady Greenwich. It was an opportunity to see how the Duchess of Hamilton behaved. She had an official position at court as one of the Queen's Ladies in Waiting.

"Their Majesties were very civil. ... The Duchess of Queensberry said the Duchess of Hamilton was a mighty steady Lady; She wou'd not curtsey to her. I did not expect Her Grace wou'd have been in the Drawing room, but She came with the rest of the Ladys of the Bed Chamber, & did not look gracious upon those who were with the Duchess of Douglass."[413]

Never mind. The Duchess of Douglas was in her element and a snub by the Duchess of Hamilton was merely another indication of how absolute was her victory, which she marked by bequeathing an estate to Archy, to be called The Lands of Douglas-Support, and a coat of arms of a woman trampling on a snake and bearing a child crowned with laurel.[414]

Two days later the Duchess of Queensberry gave a Ball at her London residence, Northumberland House, in honour of Archy Douglas. Several members of the royal family were there, along with the Lord Chancellor and his family. Lady Mary Coke was also invited, a little out of sorts, since she had been told by the hostess she shouldn't wear a hoop, a wide framework of whalebone underneath the fabric of a dress. She wrote in an aggrieved tone in her journal that the Duchess of Queensberry "would not have a Bone -- not even in her Chickings; they were to be boned before they came to table."[415]

The month of July, 1769, found the Hamilton family in the depths of despair, while Archy Douglas and his aunt celebrated the culmination of their good fortune.

On July 14th, Lady Mary Coke noted in her journal: "The Weather continues fine & my Hay all got in. The news papers mention the death of Duke Hamilton; I hope it is not true, but I've seen Nobody, so can't tell a thing more about it."

It was true. On July 7th, George-James, seventh Duke of Hamilton died, aged fourteen. He was five feet eight inches tall and was said to have "outgrown his strength." His father had died at thirty-three and his grandfather at forty. The *Scots Magazine* reported:

"The death of this young Nobleman, who was possessed of parts and dispositions of the happiest nature, is to be lamented, not less by the public, than by the nearest connections of his illustrious family. He shewed, in the early period of life, warm and constant affections, a genius and quickness of apprehension, together with an insatiable desire of knowledge; and had attained to a judgement and penetration greatly beyond what is common at his years."[416]

If one is to believe the *Scots Magazine*, very few noblemen in those days, particularly those who died young, were mean, ugly, ill-natured, or stupid.

A few days later, Lady Mary Coke wrote again about the Duke's death, including a sidelight on the peculiar practice of a friend of hers.

"So it seems it is but too true that poor Duke Hamilton is dead, I really pity the Duchess, as I cannot help feeling for all who suffer, tho' like her Grace they may have most unworthily treated me. I'm told the Dowager Waldegrave wou'd arrive there just about the time the Duke dyed; I shou'd think a visitor at such time must be very troublesome. I fancy you may remember the time when She used to force her way into

any House, where She cou'd see a dead body. Your Neighbour
Lord Rockingham must recollect an extraordinary instance of
this inclination, when She came to Kensington after the death
of the King & insisted upon seeing him; Lord Rockingham
was in waiting & refused her, not thinking the King's Body
was to be made a sight of."[417]

It must have been a devastating time for the Duchess of
Argyll, whose only crime in the whole matter was to agree
to put the Cause in the hands of Andrew Stuart. Compared
with the grotesque antics of the Duchess of Douglas, Elizabeth
Gunning's behaviour was only what was expected of a young
woman of twenty-eight who was advised that her young
son was about to have his inheritance snatched away by an
impostor. Her grief can only have been deepened by the
events three days after her son's death, when Archy Douglas
celebrated his twenty-first birthday and came into his fortune.

There was a big party at Bothwell Castle, one of the
Douglas stately homes, with a magnificent dinner, live music,
and a series of toasts, listed by the *Scots Magazine*:

"The King, Queen, and Royal Family.

Archibald Douglas of Douglas, Chief of the Name.

The Duchess of Douglas, and the Duke of Queensberry,
the late worthy guardians, to whom the family of Douglas
owes so much.

The family of Douglas, and to its increase.

The House of Peers.

The Glorious 25th of February, 1769.

With many other suitable toasts."

With each toast a cannon was fired and the local people
gathered around, caps no doubt in hand, and cheered. Later
in the evening there were fireworks, a large bonfire, and a
ball, opened by the Duke of Queensberry and the Duchess
of Douglas.

Five days later, George-James Duke of Hamilton and
Brandon was buried in the family mausoleum at Hamilton.

In late April, Andrew Stuart had written again to Baron Mure. It was nearly two months since the verdict, and he had had time to collect his thoughts. But his anger was unabated, as we can see from paragraphs that were omitted from the published correspondence:

"It is impossible to view with tranquillity such a scene of cruel injustice as that which we and our pupils have met with. I never can reflect upon it without being filled with indignation against the Authors of it but in fact we ought to feel ourselves greatly superior to those who have been thus capable of perverting truth and justice, and should leave to them all uneasy reflections and regrets.

We have ... this comfort, that the truth was discovered and made manifest to the impartial and most intelligent part of mankind and in spite of the torrent of prejudice a Decree obtained in our own country from intelligent judges much better acquainted with the merits of the case and the character of persons than those who overturned that judgement. In short there was on our side every thing that could entitle us to justice.

The first shock was so violent and my mind at that time as little prepared for an event which till within a few days of the decision appeared to me impossible that fatigued and exhausted as I then was it preyed upon me too much. I found it necessary to exclude the subject from my thoughts as much as possible and was advised to withdraw myself from all manner of business and occupation for some time to divide my time between town and country and to endeavour to pass my time agreeably in the company of friends. ...

I have had many letters from all quarters with such demonstrations of kindness and friendship as are sufficient to overbalance the injustice, blindness or barbarity of the less valuable part of mankind."[418]

It was beginning to look as if bygones would never be bygones with Andrew Stuart, and that any dogs trying to get some sleep in his vicinity would be continually prodded by his sturdy boot. This proud Scotsman felt he had thrown away years of his life, and it would be several more years before he gained peace of mind by launching an intemperate and injudicious attack on the man he most blamed for his misfortunes.

In January 1770, we find an unaccustomed glimpse of the dour Scot enjoying himself – although with painful consequences – in a letter to a friend:

"At present I am tied to the house by the foot having sprained my foot some days ago in what you will think a very idle manner dancing in slippers in a family party with sisters and nieces upon Lord Cochrane's birthday. André in his hurry of getting away my baggage to London so as to ensure my speedy departure had sent off my dancing shoes and the company having insisted on my performing in slippers I sprained my foot in such a manner is likely to confine me some days having gone out too often and made it worse."[419]

In June, 1770, Stuart was appointed to the post of King's Remembrancer in Scotland, an administrative post, presumably granted through the intercession of friends in high places, and this led to protests by Douglas supporters. A "Constant Reader" wrote in high dudgeon to the *Public Advertiser*:

"I read with the utmost astonishment in your paper of the 7th instant, that an office of trust and confidence in Scotland is conferred on a man who was judicially stigmatized for iniquitous practices by the Lord Chancellor, and my Lord Chief Justice Mansfield, at the decision of a great cause brought before the House of Lords no longer ago than last year..."[420]

A few days later there was a spirited defence of Stuart from another anonymous writer:

"[Mr. St---t's] character came out like gold from the furnace, in the opinion of every good and impartial man, purer from being tried; and even his opponents, on more occasions than one, have done justice to it, and declared his conduct, through all the mazes of so tedious and intricate an affair, to have been irreproachable."[421]

Such an ecomium could almost have been written by Andrew Stuart himself. But if it wasn't, it may have been a sign that the tide was turning in his favour.

His friend Lord Stair had had an interview with Lord Camden and persuaded him that he had been wrong to attack Stuart so vehemently in the House of Lords. Camden agreed to see Stuart to apologise and the meeting is described in a memorandum prepared the following day.

"Mr. Stuart," Camden said, "I am very happy to have an opportunity of being acquainted with you, as I have a very great esteem for your character. If any thing in the heat of argument escaped from me in the Douglas cause, I hope it will be forgot; perhaps things may have escaped me at that time, which, in talking coolly over a matter in a private company, would not have happened. I am sure I do not recollect what I may have said, but, from all I saw in that affair, I conceived a very high opinion of your ability, and thought you had done great duty to your pupils, and acted with great fidelity and attention. ... No man enjoys a better reputation, and I declare to you that I have a very high opinion both of your integrity and ability, and will be very happy in every opportunity of cultivating your acquaintance."

Stuart must have been astonished to hear of such tergiversation, but in his reply he resisted the temptation to score off Camden by reminding him of his actual words in the Lords.

"What your Lordship has now said makes up to me for the distress I suffered from some things which passed that day in the House of Lords," he said to Camden, "for I will own to your Lordship, that, though conscious of the purity of my own intentions and conduct, it did distress me to have any reflection thrown out against, me in such an assembly, and from such a height."

"Mr. Stuart," Camden replied, "you were quite a stranger to me at that time; the cause and the persons concerned in it were quite new to me that year. I am thoroughly convinced of the integrity of your conduct; and if any thing was said that gave you uneasiness, it does not remain with me, and I hope you will forget it."[422]

Brimming with glee, Stuart sent the memorandum to Baron Mure with an letter in which he wrote: "What [Camden] said there, and his manner of saying it, amounted to as complete an atonement for what had formerly past as the circumstances of the case could now admit of."

Although the surviving transcripts of the Law Lords' speeches show Lord Camden's criticism of Andrew Stuart as much harsher than Lord Mansfield's, it was Mansfield whom Stuart blamed for the verdict. He had taken, or arranged to be taken, detailed notes of the speeches, and in the months following the appeal he began to put together an indictment of Mansfield's guidance to the other peers, based on a point by point rebuttal of the arguments Mansfield put forward. It was not a wise thing to do, but even before it saw the light of day it must have helped to take some of the steam out of his anger.

Mansfield, meanwhile, probably thinking he had heard the last of Andrew Stuart, continued to be a major figure in British law, participating in a number of important hearings. His best-known decision, which led to Jane Austen choosing the title 'Mansfield Park' for one of her novels, was in the law respecting slavery. Mansfield himself had a tolerant attitude to black people and much has since been made of the fact that he had a coloured great-niece, called Dido Elizabeth Lindsay, who lived with the childless Mansfield and his wife at Kenwood, with a status that was half-relative, half-servant.

In 1772 the case of Somersett v. Knowles came before the courts. Somersett was a slave who had been brought to England and some time later ran away from his master.

He was recaptured and clapped in irons in a ship awaiting passage to Jamaica.

Mansfield decided that the slave must be freed, on the grounds that English law did not recognise slavery and that slavery was so odious that nothing but a positive law in its favour could support it. It was in this case that he became well-known for applying the old Latin tag *fiat justitia, ruat coelum.* "Let justice be done though the heavens fall." This decision did not, of course, bar Englishmen from owning slaves abroad. Nevertheless, it sent a frisson of fear through those who used slaves in the colonies, as Sir Thomas does in *Mansfield Park*, and was the beginning of the end for slavery in the British Empire and America. Even though it took several more decades for it to be formally abolished, Mansfield's decision in Somersett's case was one of the decisions quoted in the arguments for abolition.

By December, 1772, Andrew Stuart had completed a literary work which he hoped would put Lord Mansfield in his place. In spite of the fact that for many Mansfield was the greatest English judge of the age, Stuart proposed to expose him as shallow, wayward and self-serving by analysing his behaviour in the Douglas Cause. He had written *Letters to Lord Mansfield*, a book-length polemic, and he now planned to launch it onto the literary and legal world of England and Scotland.

22

"...Though the Heavens Fall"

On January 23rd, 1773, four years after the Hamilton defeat in the lords, Baron Mure received a letter and a package from Andrew Stuart which showed that the injustice of the appeal verdict still burned fiercely in his bosom.

The package contained the printed version of *Letters to the Right Honourable Lord Mansfield*, along with a letter apologising for not consulting the baron or any of his friends about the wisdom of writing the book at all. Stuart was so clearly determined to have his say that he saw no point in allowing his friends to dissuade him from what would have seemed a very unwise course for someone who wanted to be of some influence in society. But his desire for revenge overrode prudence:

"My whole attention has been given to the completion of a work I have long had at heart," he wrote to Mure, "an address to Lord Mansfield, on the subject of the Douglas cause, and the injuries sustained by the Duke of Hamilton's guardians, and myself in particular, at the decision of that contest.

... [A]s I had found from experience that it was requisite to my own happiness thus to unload my mind, and on that account was determined on the measure at this time, I thought it better to acquaint my friends of it after it was done, than to ask their advice upon a point already unalterably fixed in my own breast."

The package included a second copy of the book to be passed to David Hume. "I need not desire you to recommend him a carefull perusal of these Letters," Stuart went on, "the name at the bottom of them will sufficiently secure that point; but if he can spare so much time, either from his whist partys or from his entertainments, I expect that he will send me his criticisms and observations."

Lord Mansfield would have received his copy a few days beforehand, along with a letter of icy politeness.

"My Lord," Stuart wrote, "The printed Letters addrest to your lordship, which I have now the honour to send to you, are not the result of any sudden thought or precipitate resolution. They would have been presented to your Lordship before this time, if it had been in my power to have completed them sooner.

The object of these few lines is merely to express to your Lordship, that the same principle which has ever made me disapprove of anonymous publications in cases of this nature, has determined me to present to you the first complete copy of these Letters. It seems to me highly proper that your Lordship should be possessed of the facts contained in them before they are given to the public, which will be in a few days. I have the honour to be, with respect,

Your Lordship's most obedient and most humble servant, Andrew Stuart."[423]

Since much of the satisfaction of writing these intemperate letters must have come from imagining Mansfield's fury at reading them, it would have been a great disappointment to Stuart to know that Mansfield never read them, if we are to believe his niece. She revealed this many years later, when she was nearly a hundred, and said that it was Mansfield's practice never to read attacks made upon him, lest they should disturb his equanimity in judgment.[424]

The book was privately printed in January 1773, a month after Stuart had tried without success to persuade four publishers in turn to take it on. But the fact that there are at least two formats – quarto and octavo – with that date, and a later version with a Dublin imprint, suggests that there was such a demand for the letters, once the word had spread, that it was finally properly published. The smaller version has a vignette on the title page of two cherubs, one with a sword and one with a bow and arrows, perhaps representing Archy and Sholto, although that seems rather more frivolous than we have come to expect of Stuart.

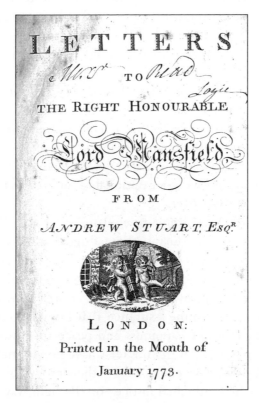

The frontispiece to Andrew Stuart's attack on Lord Mansfield

While *Letters to Lord Mansfield* is partly a final chance for Stuart to go over – yet again – the points of evidence in favour of his client, its main purpose is to launch a series of apparently restrained but nevertheless *ad hominem* remarks about Mansfield's own conduct in the case.

Stuart starts with a frank admission of the effects of Mansfield's speech on his emotional state:

"You have not been absent from my thoughts," he writes, "during any one compleat day, for more than three years past; but the subject on which I meant to address your Lordship, was too interesting, and agitated me too strongly, to admit of my commencing this correspondence sooner."[425]

He explains that his statement of the case "may sometimes produce a little warmth, but, I hope, will never carry me beyond the bounds of good manners."[426] In this hope he was mistaken.

It is difficult to take Stuart entirely seriously when he says how unwillingly he has approached the task:

"Without any tincture of that restless disposition, which makes some men so readily engage in scenes of contention, animosity, or adventure, it has been my fate to be thus embarked, contrary to my wishes or inclination; and, after being once unwillingly engaged in a situation of the greatest anxiety and contention, it was no longer optional to me to quit my station, until the storm was over."[427]

His motive was simple to explain:

"It is this: That during these three years I have made every effort to reconcile myself to the fate and incidents of this cause, or at least to blot them from my remembrance; but from experience, I have found these efforts vain: The same experience has given me assurance, that I never could be able to regain my former happiness and peace of mind, without unloading my breast in the matter I have now done."[428]

Stuart – the lawyer for hire – then proceeds to lecture Mansfield – the Lord Chief Justice –on the right way to behave in court:

"A Lord Chief Justice, when making an attack upon a private man, in presence of the most illustrious assembly in the world, in a place where no defence could be made, in a place too, where that Judge enjoys the highest degree of confidence, (especially in questions of appeal from the Northern part of this island) ought to be perfectly sure, that he has truth and justice on his side, before he ventures to throw his poisoned darts: The advantage of the situation from whence they are thrown is such, that they can seldom fail to prove mortal to those against whom they are directed, whether they be deserving of that fate, or guiltless..."[429]

It was no secret to the world, and your Lordship must have been conscious of it, that if there was ever a cause, where it was in your power to make either scale preponderate, it was in this: If you did not feel the sacredness of the trust that was reposed in you, you must at least have felt that the balance was placed in your hands: and you ought to have foreseen, that the judgement you that day gave, would be rejudged, even in this world, by the great tribunal of the public."[430]

Stuart was particularly angry at the time of the appeal that so much credence should have been placed on the testimony of Pierre Menager.

"...I believe your Lordship's scales were the first, in which such a feather of evidence as that of Menager, could have outweighed such mountains of proof as were produced on the other side..."[431]

As we might expect with such a proud man, Stuart uses the *Letters* to suggest that he is as entitled as Mansfield to make an *ad hominem* attack :

"If I had been capable of the conduct thus directly or indirectly imputed to me, I shall readily agree, that I deserved, not only to be despised as a fool, for thinking it practicable to disprove the reality of a delivery which really had happened, but to be abhorred as a monster of wickedness, capable of acting such a part, in opposition to his own internal conviction;

I should have been guilty of such a complication of crimes as is rarely to be met with...[432]

In vain will you wrap yourself up in silence, covered with the false appearance of disdain: In vain will you affect scorn towards this expostulation from a private Gentleman; and, though I am proud only of my conscious innocence and integrity, I shall add, One whose birth intitles him, when provoked by injury, to feel no inferiority to your Lordship; and One possessed of as fair a fame as you yourself enjoyed, even before the decision of this cause – I throw out this defiance in my own name before the world; and if no answer is given to it, (as I am confident none satisfactory ever can) the person whose reputation you attempted publickly to murder, though then obliged to keep an indignant silence, will not go unlamented and unrevenged to his grave."[433]

Letters to Lord Mansfield is about 60,000 words long – half the length of this book. Writing the book was like closing the stable door after the horse had died of old age. And since Mansfield almost certainly didn't read it, its main value was to soothe Stuart's own pride. But for people who had followed the case fitfully and read the newspaper stories and garbled versions of the speeches, it was a spirited read in which issues which might have seemed muddled and clouded at the time were now simplified and clarified through the Hamilton prism of Stuart's elegant and forceful prose.

Andrew Stuart gave away two hundred and forty copies of the book, and the recipients included Pitt and Fox, Edmund Burke and Horace Walpole, David Garrick and Allan Ramsey.

Horace Walpole described it as "a prodigy of abilities, reasoning and severity, yet observing a show of tenderness and decorum, that did not abate the edge of the satire."

If he had proposed a second edition, Stuart could have put a fine selection of quotes in any advertisement:

"Truth, persuasion, and superior Dignity of soul appear like sunshine thro' the whole of these letters." (Mrs. Binning)

"We do not understand the reason why your letters were never sold. We do not doubt but you had a good reason. I only say we do not understand it. We wish you had not stop'd short halfway; nor would scruple to give a second edition." (David Hume)

"I am extremely rejoiced to find that there is a man in this vile town who has virtue enough to revenge an injury, when the person who offers it is in the highest situation in this country." (Baron Mure)

"In none of the demonstrations of Euclid is there more satisfying proof, than what you have brought for setting aside what this scoundrel has so scandalously sworn to." (John Nisbet)

Andrew Stuart was pleased with the reception of the book, copies of which were much in demand. John Moore, the Duke of Hamilton's tutor, who was touring the continent with his charge, wrote to ask for a copy for the Duc de Rochefoucault, who "has all the Douglas Cause papers."

Having failed to get a publisher to consider the book two months beforehand, he was now pressured to publish as a result of the weight of public interest:

"A few days ago," he write, "I was most earnestly solicited by (a publisher) to let his name be in the title page, and to let him have the publication of them; he gave me, as a reason for it, that every hour of the day he had messages at his shop for these letters."

In March, Stuart wrote to Mure again, to deny the persistent rumours that he was to be prosecuted for libel:

"…To remove that uneasiness I can assure them that hitherto there has not been any step taken towards prosecution or persecution and tho'it is frequently rumoured here that such things are to happen yet I do not think it probable.

I must now dismiss this subject, least you should think me too full of it, which in reality is not the case; tho' it would be affectation in me to deny that I am very happy at what has passed, and enjoy a satisfaction and tranquillity which it would have been difficult for me to have attained, if I had left undone what I have done."[434]

In fact to modern eyes, and in modern terminology, Andrew Stuart can sometimes seem to be "full of it," but I suppose having experienced his sufferings, even though brought on somewhat by his own ambition, he should be allowed to luxuriate in a brief period of public approval and private warmth.

There were, of course, dissenting voices. When a friend of Baron Mure praised the book in front of the Duchess of Douglas and asked her what she thought, "she just tapt her forehead with her forefinger, but did not utter a syllable."

Mure himself offered to take a copy of the *Letters* to Dr. Johnson, and Boswell wrote about his reaction to them in his *Life of Johnson*. Boswell described the *Letters* as "elegant and plausible", which was surprising coming from a Douglas supporter. Johnson, however, was less impressed:

"'They have not answered the end," he said. "They have not been talked of; I have never heard of them. This is owing to their not being sold. People seldom read a book which is given to them; and few are given. The way to spread a work is to sell it at a low price. No man will send to buy a thing that costs even sixpence, without intention to read it."

The *Life* continues:"BOSWELL:'May it not be doubted, Sir, whether it be proper to publish letters, arraigning the ultimate decision of an important cause by the supreme judicature of the nation?' JOHNSON. 'No, Sir, I do not think it was wrong to publish these letters. If they are thought to do harm, why not answer them? But they will do no harm. If Mr. Douglas be indeed the son of Lady Jane, he cannot be hurt: if he be not her son, and yet has the great estate of the family of Douglas, he may well submit to have a pamphlet against him by Andrew Stuart. Sir, I think such a publication does good, as it does good to show us the possibilities of human life. And Sir, you will not say that the Douglas cause was a cause of easy decision, when it divided your Court as much as it could do to be determined at all. When your Judges were seven and seven, the casting vote of the President must be given on one side or other: no matter, for my argument, on which; one or the other *must* be taken: as when I am to move there is no matter which leg I move first. And then, Sir, it was otherwise determined here. No, Sir, a more dubious determination of any question cannot be imagined."[435]

Boswell added in a footnote:

"I regretted that Dr. Johnson never took the trouble to study a question which interested nations. He would not even read a pamphlet which I wrote upon it, entitled *The Essence of the Douglas Cause*; which, I have reason to flatter myself, had considerable effect in favour of Mr. Douglas; of whose legitimate filiation I was then, and am still, firmly convinced."[436]

On a later occasion Johnson said, "Andrew Stuart's *Letters* could not give Lord Mansfield any uneasiness, for either he acted honestly, or he meant to do injustice. If he acted honestly, his own conscience would protect him. If he meant to do injustice, he would be glad to see Stuart so much vexed. His letters were the wailing of a dog that had been licked."

"But, Sir," said Boswell, "a dog may bite."[437]

We have a glimpse of Lord Mansfield in the aftermath of the book when Boswell, ever curious, visited him in April, 1773. On discussing another lawsuit, Boswell rather daringly brought up the subject of Stuart's book:

"Boswell: 'This is as good reasoning as Andrew Stuart's *Letters*. They are very well written. I got your sister Mrs. Murray to promise to read them. I told her she'd be very angry, but that they were worth reading' (or words to that purpose).

Mansfield says nothing.

Boswell: 'Tis a cruel thing on poor Douglas now that he's settled and the question over so long ago.'

Mansfield: 'Twill do him no harm. 'Twill not take the estate from him.'"[438]

Another great literary figure gave his reaction to the book in May. John Moore, the tutor to the Duke of Hamilton, in a letter to Andrew Stuart, wrote: "The Duke and me went to Fernay lately but had the misfortune to miss M. Voltaire. I left a copy of your *Letters*." A short while later he returned to Fernay and this time Voltaire was at home.

"He had read your Book with great attention," Moore wrote, "was master of most of the great facts in the Cause, and expressed the utmost astonishment at the decision.... It appeared to him that every circumstance attending the pretended fact carryd falsehood on its forehead, and he was amazed that any man of sense could give the smallest weight to the vague rambling evidence of Menager, contradictory to the acct given by Sir John Steuart himself. He added that he had a very bad opinion of that man, on acct of his conduct in some late affair in which this same Menager has been engaged."[439]

In fact, the late affair was at that time reaching its final stages in the French courts. As if to vindicate everything Andrew Stuart had said about the man, Menager had been accused of perjury in a lawsuit in which the Count of Morangiés sued the Widow Veron for the shortfall in a loan of 100,000 écus which she claimed to have handed over in full. For reasons which are time-consuming to explain, the money had to be delivered in wheelbarrowloads, many of them, through the streets between their two houses. The widow claimed that her grandson had made these deliveries, and she produced a witness who said he had spoken to the grandson while he was moving the money. However, in support of Morangiés, a doctor came forward to say that this witness had actually been under treatment by him at the time he claimed to have spoken to the grandson, and was not allowed to leave his house. This doctor was, of course, M. Menager.

It didn't take long to establish that Menager was lying. The treatment had indeed occurred but at an entirely different time and, in any case, there was no question of the patient being confined to Menager's house. It was only the intervention of the Prince de Turenne, the man who first brought Menager to the attention of the Duchess of Douglas, that led to the charge against Morangiés being toned down so that he could get off with a fine and Menager escape being charged with perjury.

In a letter to Baron Mure, George Jardine, who was supervising Mure's sons on a tour of France, described the dénouement of the case and concluded:

"There is nobody I have ever conversed with on the subject, who doubts of Menager's villainy and who does not also see the reason why he has escaped. In short I don't believe there is anybody but Lord Mansfield and those who have occasion for it that would give one farthing for his testimony."[440]

1773 was the last year in which the Cause made ripples in English and Scottish circles. For the two families involved, the battle was over. During that year, on his way to the Hebrides, Dr. Johnson met Peggy, Duchess of Douglas, at dinner in Boswell's house in Edinburgh and described her as an "old lady who talks broad Scotch with a paralytic voice, and is scarcely understood by her own countrymen." In October, Boswell and Johnson stayed at an inn near Inveraray Castle, the seat of the Duke and Duchess of Argyll – the Duchess being the former Duchess of Hamilton. The Duke was a very tall strong man, of whom it was said:

> *"When Campbell walks the street*
> *The paviours cry*
> *'God bless your legs!'*
> *And lay their rammers by."*[441]

He was perfectly friendly to Boswell, but his wife was less likely to be, in the light of Boswell's support for Douglas. So Boswell asked Johnson whether they should go to pay their respects to the duke or not.

"Dr Johnson … was clear that I ought," Boswell wrote, "but I mentioned, that I was afraid my company might be disagreeable to the duchess. He treated this objection with a manly disdain: 'THAT, sir, he must settle with his wife.' I went to the castle just about the time when I supposed the ladies would be retired from dinner. I sent in my name; and, being shewn in, found the amiable duke sitting at the head of his table with several gentlemen. I was most politely received … As I was going away, the duke said, 'Mr. Boswell, won't you have some tea?' I thought it best to get over the meeting with the duchess this night; so respectfully agreed. I was conducted to the drawing-room by the duke, who announced my name; but the duchess, who was sitting with her daughter, Lady Betty Hamilton, and some other ladies, took not the least notice of me. I should have been mortified at being thus coldly received by a lady of whom I, with the rest of the world, have always entertained a very high admiration, had I not been consoled by the obliging attention of the duke."

When Boswell and Johnson returned the following day for dinner, the Duchess made her displeasure known in a more obvious way:

"Her grace made Dr Johnson come and sit by her, and asked him why he made his journey so late in the year. 'Why, madam,' said he, 'you know Mr. Boswell must attend the Court of Session, and it does not rise till the twelfth of August.' She said, with some sharpness, 'I KNOW NOTHING of Mr. Boswell.' … I had that kind of consolation which a man would feel who is strangled by a SILKEN CORD."[442]

23

Life Resumes

I n 1771, Archibald Douglas, now aged twenty-three and in possession of the Duke of Douglas's fortune, had married Lady Lucy Graham, only daughter of the Duke of Montrose. We know little about Archy at this stage, apart from the fact that the Duchess of Queensberry worried that "he would grow too fatt for such a young person."[443] He clearly had no need to work for a living but seems to have become involved in the affairs of a Scottish bank which got into trouble and this led to large losses for a number of people. The bank was Douglas, Heron & Co, and the collapse of a London bank had led to a run on the Scottish bank's funds. Alexander Makonochie, still involved in the Douglas family affairs, wrote to Lady Lucy with some reassurance. '…The Dss (of Queensberry) was very happy at hearing the prospect we have of getting clear of the Bank, but would scarcely believe it possible. She said, if the Duke, the Duke of Buccleugh & Mr. Douglas gett out, it will be as great a miracle as Shadrach, Mechech, & Abednego getting out of the furnace, and calls the Duke of Queensberry Duke Shadrach. She is in excellent spirits…"[444]

Three years after Archy's marriage, in 1774, his aunt, the formidable Duchess of Douglas, died at Bothwell Castle, her dower house. Without her unceasing efforts on his behalf, many would have considered him to be Jacques-Louis Mignon, stolen son of a poor French glassblower, even if he was accepted by some as the true Douglas heir deprived of his inheritance. He would also have had only a modest income, instead of being one of the richest men in Scotland. Some Hamilton relatives rejoiced at Peggy's death, but the Duchess of Argyll's reaction was more muted. She just said that nobody would believe her if she expressed any concern.

Lady Lucy had a friend, Lady Frances Dalkeith, who was short and dumpy but with a charming disposition, a sense of humour and a cultivated mind.[445] When Lucy had her first daughter, Frances came to be with her. For some time after the birth, Lucy was unwell, without any specific illness being diagnosed. One day, as she lay on a couch and Frances sat near her, Lucy said: "If I should die, I wish to God you and Mr. Douglas would marry, for I am sure you would be kind to my poor children — Aye you may laugh; but I tell you once again I wish it." Archy came into the room at this point and Lucy said to him "Do you hear!" and told him what she had just said. "Well" said Frances to Archy, "what say you! Had not we better agree upon it!" — "By all means," he said, "I think there cannot be a better scheme."[446]

Within a few weeks, Lady Lucy Douglas was dead.

Frances Dalkeith was about thirty when Lady Lucy suggested that Archy take her as his second wife. The couple didn't meet again for a year or so after Lucy's death. Then, on a Scottish trip, Frances bumped unexpectedly into Archy at a house in Edinburgh. He was much affected and soon he was a regular visitor to Dalkeith, the family country seat.

Archy seemed to be a man in search of a role. He wanted to be an M.P. and stood against Andrew Stuart for one seat, but was beaten. It was one Hamilton v. Douglas match that Archy lost. A Sir John Douglas commented on Stuart's impudence, having been condemned so roundly by senior legal figures, in standing for a seat in parliament. "What think you of this fellow? He has brass indeed! why, you may make ten dozen of tea-kettles out of his forehead."

But in 1782, Archibald Douglas became M.P. for Forfarshire, having been Lord Lieutenant of that county. As was the custom in those days, this was less a tribute to his merits by local voters and more a job arranged for him by his relatives. "No speech of his is recorded," says the official history of the House of Commons.[447] Having to attend parliament in London meant that he was a regular visitor at Lady Greenwich's London house, where Frances lived. In an excess of delicacy, Archy arranged for the Duchess of Montrose, his late wife's mother, to approach Lady Greenwich to see whether she would agree to him marrying Frances.

While, of course, agreeing, Lady Greenwich confided to her friends that "though delighted at dear Frances's wonderful good-luck, she owned she could not understand Mr. Douglas's having so soon forgotten that charming woman." Aunts and siblings spoke meanly behind Frances back, wondering how anybody, let alone Archy, could marry her.

Nevertheless, the couple did marry, in May 1783, and after a sweltering summer in a small house in Kew, they set off for Scotland, and for a painful return to Bothwell, the house where Frances had last seen her dear friend, Lady Lucy.

Exactly nine months after the wedding, Frances gave birth to a daughter. She had been worried that she was too old to have a child – she was thirty-three at the time – and had intended to spend her life looking after her stepchildren. Indeed, she was so concerned about not giving her own child special treatment that she didn't suckle her baby, although she wanted to very much.

Apart from some blazing rows with the nanny who looked after the older Douglas children, Frances settled into an enjoyable married life at a time when she had expected to be an old maid. Archy seems to have been a good, if unexciting, husband. "He is a safe man, and what is more, a comfortable man," Frances said to her cousin, Lady Louisa Stuart. In her care for Archy's children by Lady Lucy Graham, Frances provided an interesting counterargument to those who cited Lady Jane Douglas's displays of affection for her children as evidence for the fact that she must have given birth to them. While walking in Hyde Park with Lucy's two children, Frances turned to Lady Louisa Stuart and said: "Oh! you have little conception what a soft balmy feel it is that those creatures will belong to me, that they are mine!"[448]

Meanwhile, in the Hamilton family, matters were less comfortable. The Duke of Hamilton, younger brother of the plaintiff in the Cause, was a source of heartache to his mother in the years following the Hamilton defeat. He was uncontrollable as he went on jaunts round the continent, in spite of the efforts of his tutor, Dr Moore, and the archives of Baron Mure and Andrew Stuart are full of reports from Moore about his wayward behaviour. Moore had taken his own son, also John, along on the tour as a companion for the Duke, but this nearly cost the son his life. One day, the Duke playfully drew his sword and fenced with his swordless companion. As the Duke forced the young Moore to skip from side to side, the sword penetrated his chest. The boy's father, a medical doctor, was soon on the spot and his son eventually recovered. "The incident," wrote one biographer, "led to the formation of a lasting friendship between the penitent and his almost victim."[449]

The Duke's mother procured a commission in the army for the fifteen-year-old John Moore and he went on to become a British hero at the battle of Corunna in 1823. His burial was celebrated in the poem by Charles Wolfe, learnt by heart by generations of English schoolchildren, beginning "Not a drum was heard, not a funeral note, As his corse to the rampart we hurried..."

The Duke's behaviour on the continent showed how much he took after his dissolute father, particularly in the matter of 'gallantry.' One day, the Duke and his entourage were visiting Geneva when he fell in love. "His whole soul was engross'd, every thing was neglected," Moore wrote in a letter to Baron Mure. The tutor persuaded the Duke that it might be wise to move on, but just at that time, the new lady friend was visited by a married woman from Lausanne, who, Moore wrote, "without scruple or ceremony snatched the morsel out of her friend's mouth and put it in her own."[450]

Mure passed this letter and similar ones to Andrew Stuart who replied in January, 1775, "I showed them to the Duke of Argyle with whom I have had many conversations on the subject. We agreed it was better not to show these letters to the Duchess at present. Some parts of them are not very fit to be shown to a lady and others would only serve to give uneasiness."

"That the Duke should have a disposition for gallantry," Stuart wrote to Mure, "is not to be wondered at at his age. It would rather be unnatural if he had not a great degree of sensibility for the ladies. It is to prevent that passion carrying him too far that the efforts of his friends must be employed."[451]

In 1777, the young Duke settled down and married the sister of one of his friends. But his continued wildness, including a devotion to the prize-ring and the cockpit, and the absence of any legitimate heirs, eventually led to a divorce. A few years later, aged forty-three, the Duke continued the tradition of Hamilton males dying before their time, often as a result of dissipation.

The Duchess of Argyll had lost her elder Hamilton son, and been disappointed by the dissipation of the younger. Now, consumption took hold of her, and she went often to France and Italy, accompanied by her husband and daughters. During the last couple of years of her life, she stayed in Naples and spent time with a relation of her first husband, Sir William

Hamilton, whose marriage to Emma, future mistress of Horatio Nelson, she encouraged. She died in 1790, aged fifty-seven.

For Andrew Stuart, his interests had finally turned away from the Douglas Cause. Boswell, quoting Virgil, had said to Wilkes "He is exhausted, like a bee after stinging."[452] In spite of the memories the place must have held, Stuart returned to Paris in 1789 to research his own family history, and the book which resulted from these researches was later criticised for distorting the facts to prove that Stuart's own branch of the family was more senior to another.

James Boswell met Andrew Stuart from time to time and on one occasion Stuart said to him: "You once asked Lord Mansfield if he had read – Something." Boswell replied "Your *Letters* – It is not true. I did not, upon my honour. But since you have mentioned the subject, I will tell you. I introduced them – observed if he winced – if he was hurt. He did not wince. He was not hurt. They were *telum imbelle* (an unwarlike weapon)."[453]

In 1790, at the age of about sixty, Stuart married "a buxom young lass," and Boswell, never short of inspiration, wrote a poem to him:

"Andrew you struggled right or wrong
To prove the heir of Douglas – Mignion
But now, if you're not dev'lish strong,
You'll struggle worse in my opinion

As your young spouse will kissing want
The Lords* ex nobile officio
Letters of Supplement must grant
To save a partus suppositio."[454]

In the same year as Andrew Stuart married, Archibald Douglas was elevated to the peerage and made Baron Douglas of Douglas.

---

* The Court of Session in which he was formerly an eminent Writer, or Attorney

He had hankered after a peerage for some time, and tried at one stage to establish his right to be Earl of Angus. Boswell noted also that "He has flattered himself with being created Earl of Douglas."[455]

His later life seems to have been uneventful, apart from one odd episode in 1814 when we suddenly find him on the isle of Elba, visiting Napoleon in exile. Lady Lucy Barry and her husband had entertained Archibald Douglas to dinner in Cannes after he had returned from the island, and in a letter to a friend she relayed his account of his experience.

"On his arrival in the Island he went to Gen'l Bertrand (who is a sort of chamberlain) to state that he was a member of the English Parl't and to request permission to pay his respects to the Emperor. He was received accordingly introduced & received with courtesy."

The two men discussed the general state of European affairs and Napoleon lamented the fact that France had not given up the slave trade, which he said he would have done, if he had remained in power.

He said the Bourbons would repent if they gave up Belgium ... France would not bear to be confined to her ancient limits. He compared her to air compressed, within so small a compass the explosion of which is like thunder."

Napoleon then said, as reported in French in the letter: "Cursed be the Bourbons if they ever make peace without holding on to their conquests. There is in France a seething mass of 100,000 young men who have become accustomed to the profession of war."

"He was here evidently carried away by his subject," Lady Lucy wrote, "and suddenly recollecting himself he said 'mais ce n'est pas mon affaire. Je suis mort.' ... He said he understood the world expected him to put a pistol to his head, but no – he had been bred a soldier, had found the throne of France vacant, circumstances had placed him on it, that he had remained there 14 years, had been obliged to descend from it.

Having done this 'ce serait un lâche qui ne pourroit pas soutenir l'existence.*'"

Archy ... says Buonaparte is in excellent health, not so fat as he had been told, he was very dirty and vulgar in his appearance and manner of speaking. He is certainly poor, the French government not having paid him his pension and in consequence he has been obliged to reduce his household one half. ... Mr. D. says his apparent want of feeling is beyond anything he could have conceived."

Finally, Archy described to Lady Barry and her husband some gossip he heard about a felucca which landed on one of the most barren points of the island and deposited a messenger who summoned Napoleon:

"He came down, was unattended by any servant and received a lady; whom he conducted to a country house of his. She remained there for two days, at the end of which time he reconducted her in the same manner. They embraced often at parting, the Elbese think it was Maria Louisa [the Empress, his second wife] but it is generally supposed to have been a Polish lady to whom he was attached. Mr. D. in the course of conversation two or three times mentioned the Empress, whom he had seen in Switzerland but Buonaparte took no notice of it, and seemed extreamly anxious to avoid the subject."[456]

Then, out of the blue, in September, 1816, forty-seven years after the Douglas victory in the House of Lords, Lord Douglas received a letter from someone he didn't know, William Playfair, offering to sell him some "curious papers." What could these papers be? Lord Douglas replied to Playfair:

"... before I can give any answer to the purport you have in view in writing (I) must beg leave to know from you the subject of the papers alluded to and the compensation expected for them. ... Are the papers still in Paris or have they been brought to England?"

---

* 'It would be cowardice not to put up with life.'

Playfair said in his reply:

"...the papers concerning which I wrote relate to the time and manner in which a child was obtained from its parents in 1748 by English people in Paris, and some curious enquiries that were made some years afterwards. ...

To the second question about compensation, I cannot say exactly but a few hundred pounds certainly not more than Five.

To the third question the answer is, 'the Papers are in Paris'."

Playfair then put on the pressure to get Douglas to pay up quickly:

"...there are so many English in Paris, many of them intriguing adventurers that they may get out of the reach of this person who is in Paris to recover some papers for me."

It was, of course, possible that some document turned up that had escaped the army of lawyers who combed Paris for such papers in the early 1760s. Possible but extremely unlikely. On the other hand, the Memorials and Proofs prepared by lawyers for the Duke of Hamilton are full of quotations from papers which "relate to the time and manner in which a child was obtained from its parents in 1748 by English people in Paris," any one of which might persuade someone who hadn't followed the Cause closely that he had stumbled on a clinching piece of evidence. Douglas must have been a little reassured by this because he wrote a robust reply:

"From the contents of (your letter) I am satisfied the papers you allude to can be of no consequence to any person and therefore must request you will give yourself no further trouble about them."

Douglas then sent the correspondence to his solicitor, David Wemyss. "Possibly on inquiry," he wrote, "you may be able to find out in Edinburgh what this man's real character and conduct in life is, or has been, and be able to form an opinion. ... I do not conceive it possible after what has passed that any question can be brought before a court of law upon the subject to which these French papers are stated to relate, or that the old law suit can be renewed, but I certainly do not wish to see advertisements or paragraphs in the newspapers relating to it. I do not mean by this to propose paying for his silence, but to be prepared, in case he should proceed, to repel the attack in the most serious way the law will permit."

Wemyss replied: "It now appears from Playfair's letters, that his object has been to extort money from your Lordship, and I am happy to think that your Lordship has expressed yourself so guardedly. I have heard of four brothers of the name of Playfair. John, Professor of Natural Philosophy in the University of Edinburgh, James who built your Lordship's house of Bothwell Castle, Robert a Writer here who has never been in much repute; and I think I have heard of another brother in London who I presume is your correspondent; and I think that I have heard, although I cannot at present recollect the source from which I derived my information, that this brother in London was a person held in no respect. His letters upon this occasion I think show, that like many others in London he wishes to live upon his shifts."*

William Playfair may have been held in no respect then, but he is someone who, in spite of various disreputable or shifty activities, is now recognised as having made an important contribution to the graphic display of numerical information. He published the first bar chart, for example. He was an inventor, and after inferring from various hints the mechanism by which telegraphy worked in France, he adapted it to British use, along with his own method of transmitting the alphabet.

Playfair was a prolific pamphleteer, frequently attacking the French Revolution, and was imprisoned in France for doing so. With a Mr. Joel Barlow, he ran a scheme to colonise the banks of the River Scioto in America and sold plots of land for five shillings an acre. Eventually, two shiploads of colonists set sail to take up their residence there, only to find

---

* "Shifts" meant tricks or expedients—this usage is uncommon now, but c.f. shifty.

a very confusing situation when they tried to take possession of the land they had bought from the Scioto Land Company, which, in the view of one judge at the time, "has been the subject of considerable mystery and the cause of much misrepresentation."[457]

Playfair seems to have been a man who loved money-making schemes, and perhaps he rashly assumed that documents someone tried to sell him would be another way of making money. But Douglas, although worried, conducted the matter calmly and with good sense.

Some weeks later, not having achieved his aims, Playfair stepped up the pressure with a prospectus for a scheme to publish and sell the "curious papers," which he sent to Douglas.

It was headed "Proposals for Publishing by Subscription

Price one guinea to be paid on delivery of the work

The Douglas Cause Elucidated by the papers lately produced in Paris

Relative to the Children said to be borne by Lady Jane Sister of the last Duke of Douglas and Wife of Sir John Stewart Baronet of Grandtully."

The prospectus then went on to describe a 'new light' in which the story could be seen, which in fact was the 'old light' of the Hamilton case, and concluded:

"Nothing is more curious or interesting than to trace the schemes and practices of persons bent on some great object of deceit. Perkin Warbeck, Lambert Simnel and many others whose pretensions were high and their birth disputed have always excited a lively interest and such characters ever will; in the present instance immense sums of money were expended and no ordinary sympathy excited in favour of a child in opposition to a powerful and unpopular Duke; but now comes out the most important fact of all – first that the child really was bought; and secondly that it would have been proved at the time, had it not been for the active exertions that were made to suppress the information."

On receiving the prospectus, one of Douglas's sons, Charles, consulted the Attorney General about possibly prosecuting Playfair. He then wrote to his father, passing on the lawyer's advice: "He admits the <u>possibility</u> of a Prosecution for what has passed, but doubts the <u>prudence</u> of such a step at present. ... I trust you will in no way have occasion to repent adopting the advice he gives for the future; <u>I</u> do not think that Playfair will give you much more trouble. His lies betray their object too plainly, and cannot impose on any one; in his efforts to annoy, he must, I am afraid, if he chuses, be indulged, till he is ripe, and then, I trust, you will find the Attorney General very ready to give him a squeeze."

This is the last we hear of the matter, suggesting that Playfair never 'ripened' beyond drafting the Prospectus to frighten money out of Lord Douglas.[458]

In his later years, Archy was noted for very little. The few references there are to his middle age suggest that he was dignified and benign. A correspondent in the *Glasgow Gazette* later wrote: "When he came into Glasgow, as he did frequently, from Bothwell Castle, in his elegant carriage, and four high mettled blood horses, with their handsome outriders in their cockades, he received the most polite attention from gentle and simple, young and old. He was a hale hearty old man down to the day of his death."[459]

By his two wives Archy had twelve children, eight boys and four girls. Four of the boys died before their father and the other four came into the title of Lord Douglas one by one but had no children of their own. Only one of the girls had any children. Jane Margaret married a Buccleuch and inherited all the Douglas estates when her father died. She had four daughters, the eldest of which married the eleventh Earl of Home, and the Douglas name was then attached so that the family became Douglas-Home. In reporting this chapter of failed Douglas heirs, Lady Louisa Stuart wrote "In this way the property so bitterly fought for through the courts, the occasion of so much abuse, character assassination and contrivance, passed from the apparently secure twelve pronged possession of Lord Douglas, first to the Buccleuchs and then to the Homes in so short a space of time that the devout saw the dreadful hand of the Almighty moving."[460]

24

Whatever Happened to Lady Jane?

I n December, 2003, I was visiting California and decided to look up an old friend whom I hadn't seen for some time. When I rang her number, I spoke to her teenage daughter who said "Mum's had some important changes in her life recently. She's now got more children, *many* more children." In fact this was a slight exaggeration, as I found out when I visited my friend. She had been the mother of two daughters, now in their teens, and in the previous month she had given birth to twins.

Deirdre, as I shall call her, was forty-nine, the same age as Lady Jane Douglas when *she* gave birth to twins. My friend had not had fertility treatment and, indeed, had thought that she might be going through the menopause when she first noticed the signs of pregnancy.

The story of the Douglas Cause began with the real or pretended incredulity of the Hamilton side that a woman could give birth at the age of forty-nine. In fact, this incredulity was unjustified, as shown by my friend's story and many other examples. There was also the belief that giving birth to twins was more improbable as women got older. We now know that the frequency of the birth of twins *increases* with age. And it turns out that Sir John Stewart came from a family that had produced twins in the past, another factor that increases the likelihood of his wife having twins.

Most people hearing nowadays about the central issue of the Douglas Cause have remarked on the fact that if such an issue arose nowadays the matter could be settled with a simple DNA test. There have even been some who wondered whether by digging up Lady Jane and Archibald Douglas such tests could still be carried out to settle the matter once and for all.

In this book, I have not tried to settle the matter, for several reasons.

First, if the Scottish judges, who gave most consideration to the evidence, were so evenly divided it is unlikely that I, reading through four thousand pages of Proofs and Memorials, could find anything that had escaped them which would bring the matter down more firmly on one side than the other. The 'facts' that were assembled by both sides were sufficient, it seems to me, to prove both sides' arguments – if they were correct. Clearly they weren't all correct since they were contradictory, but even at the time it was impossible to know who was lying or mistaken. In the end, making a decision nowadays – if we are really kept awake at night by the matter – comes down to the question of motive.

Lady Louisa Stuart, whose lively memoir of Frances Douglas is full of good sense, wrote "To judge fairly of those who lived long before us, or of foreigners, we should put quite apart both the usages and the notions of our own age or country, and strive to adopt for the moment such as prevailed in theirs."[461]

This can work both ways, of course. We know more about human behaviour and psychology today than we did then. Perhaps the participants at the time would have got nearer to the truth if they had "put quite apart both the usages and the notions of (their) own age or country." But of course only we can apply 21ˢᵗ century knowledge to 18ᵗʰ century people.

In earlier centuries there was a belief – which now seems naïve – that if someone made a statement about the past, based on his or her own personal experience, and that that statement was full of sharp, well-described detail, then it was likely to be true. And if it turned out not to be true, the person making the statement was considered to be a liar. The lengths to which lawyers from both sides went to gather thousands of words of such statements and then to argue from the tiniest details, shows how much weight was placed on human memory. There was also great weight placed on negative testimony, the *failure* to remember certain things. Robert Richardson, in his well-reasoned assessment of the evidence, picked on the Hamilton use of this negative evidence to discount Lady Jane's pregnancy, and turned it on its head to disprove the kidnapping of Jacques-Louis Mignon:

"If one was to have recourse to the negative testimony of persons, who were in the way to know the circumstances of the enlevement, and yet did not know them, it might be alledged, that neither Mad. Baudoin, Mad. Mignon's sister; nor Eugene, Mr. Mignon's son; nor Mad. Flon, who lent her child to be suckled by Mad. Mignon, and saw her during that period five times a day; nor Mad. Edouard, in whose house the child was drest; nor Mad. Odeneau, in whose house Mignon then lived; ever heard of lending the child, or of the twins. This is a stronger negative testimony than any of those, of which the Pursuers make such frequent use."⁴⁶²

Richardson was also good at attacking the Hamilton use of discrepancies in testimony to discredit witnesses. They had taken this approach with Mrs. Hewit, and Richardson pointed out that: "These, and other little differences, are of such a nature as cannot but be expected. They are indeed rather a proof of the artless integrity of the witnesses, than a ground for supposing they do not mean the same thing.

By such criticisms as one may read in the pursuers' memorial, the writer of these papers (Richardson) would undertake to prove, that Sanry never lost his child, and that sir John Stewart was never at Michel's."[463]

Attitudes to hearsay evidence were much more relaxed in 18th century courts, and Richardson analysed the way in which second- and third-hand accounts were used to bolster an argument.

"The writer of these papers is sensible of the necessity of admitting a second-hand kind of evidence in this cause, which came on so many years after the facts, on which it depends, had passed, and when many important witnesses were dead. But a witness at third-hand, who comes to tell us what was told by a dead person, who was present, seems hardly to be admissible. Circumstances vary so much in passing through different hands, that were the whole of this cause related by such persons, the whole would be discredited, and we should never see any one point on which we could fix."

One point the Hamilton lawyers hammered home time and again was the unfortunate statement by the failing Sir John Stewart that the male midwife, Pierre La Marre, who attended Lady Jane was a Walloon he had encountered in Liége in 1721. By pointing out that this couldn't be the Pierre La Marre whom several witnesses knew in Paris – indeed, this La Marre's wife was discovered still alive – Andrew Stuart succeeded for a time in deflecting attention away from the fact that there *was* a Pierre La Marre in Paris in 1748 and that this fact, combined with a confused memory of forty years earlier by Sir John, was a much more likely explanation than that Sir John had plucked a name out of the air and created an entire figment, helped by the perjury of the shady doctor, Menager.

Among the 21st century knowledge that might have been helpful to 18th century lawyers is an understanding of human memory and its almost limitless capacity to deceive.

Professor Elizabeth Loftus of the University of California at Irvine has spent many years devising experiments that demonstrate unambiguously that there is little or no correlation between the truth of a memory and its vividness or subjective "feeling" of veracity to the rememberer. She and her colleagues have done this by planting false memories in volunteers that they later were convinced were true. One of these was the memory of seeing and being hugged by a person in a Bugs Bunny outfit at Disneyland. "Bugs is a Warner Brothers character. He wouldn't be allowed on Disney premises," Loftus says. Nevertheless, thirty-six percent of her volunteers when questioned after she and her researchers 'planted' the memories were convinced that they had had the experience. Similar work on people who claimed to have been abducted by aliens showed that in remembering their experiences they showed all the physical responses that people do who are remembering a real and traumatic event. (I am making the assumption – which seems to me reasonable – that they had not really ever been abducted by aliens.)

The unreliability of memory is a result of several factors. First, there is the role of *attention* at the time the events first take place. If you don't think much about whether a woman might be pregnant, if you are a man in a society where you don't in any case stare at someone, particularly if she has a title or is clearly your superior, then it might have been easy to miss the fact that Lady Jane was pregnant. And even if you are motivated or in the right frame of mind to consider some factor, competing stimuli can blank out a memory, or influence your interpretation of it.

Second, there is the way in which memory changes over time. There seems to be an active process by which the brain 'works on' existing memories and smoothes out inconsistencies or oddities, reinterpreting what was seen or perceived in the light of what is known or believed. This must have been a particularly important factor in the months and years of questioning and requestioning that took place in Paris.

By the time the witnesses came before the Tournelle, they had often heard new details of the story it was hoped they would tell, and could well have incorporated such details unwittingly into their testimony, forgetting whether they were told them by Andrew Stuart or Alexander Makonochie, or by their neighbours, or had actually experienced them for themselves. And then, when they were asked to tell their stories again in front of the Commission arranged by the Court of Session, there was a further layer of uncertainty since they might well have been remembering or misremembering what they said to the Tournelle rather than what actually happened.

None of this is to suggest that there were no 'facts of the matter', merely that fifteen or more years after the events it was unlikely that a process that placed such weight on the testimony of witnesses would be able to ascertain them, and that, two hundred and fifty years later, a similar process would succeed in doing so.

In the end, since the evidence didn't – and perhaps can't – settle this issue, it was the assessment of Lady Jane's likely intentions and motivation that influenced the view people took one way or another. If she did it, why did she do it?

It is certainly not unheard of for a titled lady to be accused of obtaining children illicitly in order to secure an inheritance. We've seen that Lady Kinnaird was accused of doing just that. And in 1903, newspaper readers in Europe were given daily accounts of a trial in which the following allegations were laid before the court:

An aristocratic lady, desperate for a male heir to inherit the family estates, had travelled to a foreign capital with an old servant, and pretended to have a baby which she had actually purchased from a peasant woman. She said she had gone to the foreign capital to get better medical attention but actually employed an obscure midwife for the birth. Cousins of the woman's family, who would have inherited if she had not produced a boy, claimed that as she was fifty years old she was too old to have given birth, and they produced a woman who claimed to have sold her son shortly after birth to an aristocratic lady from another country. The woman's lawyers alleged that the peasant had been bribed to give false evidence that she had sold her baby.

In this case, the aristocrat was a Pole, Countess Isabella Kwilecki, and it was to Berlin that she went to have the baby. Her husband's cousins were the people who set lawyers investigating the events, and they found a Silesian peasant, Cecelia Meyer, who claimed to have sold or given the baby to a Polish countess.

As in the Douglas Cause, there was an initial decision that was overturned on appeal, but in this case the child was first declared to be the heir, and then, on appeal, having lived as a Count for some years, the boy was ordered to be returned to 'his rightful mother, the peasant woman.'[464]

And later in the 20th century I came across the odd story of Margaret, Duchess of Argyll, married to a descendant of Duchess of Hamilton's second husband, who contemplated something similar.

"…Margaret wanted nothing more than to have a son of her own who would become heir to the Duke of Argyll, and benefit from all the money she had invested in Inveraray and secure her future as dowager. Then she would have it all: a duchess herself, having a daughter who was also a duchess, a son who would be a duke, and also grandsons who would be dukes in the future.

In order to fulfil her bizarre scheme, having failed to become pregnant she decided to plan a fake pregnancy, in an effort to have her stepsons disinherited and replace them with her own child. Thus, Margaret summoned her long-standing friend Diana Napier to luncheon and said to her, 'Darling, I want you to go to Venice at my expense. I would like you to use your Polish contacts to adopt a newborn child or get a newborn child over from Poland to Venice.' Pressed by Diana for an explanation, Margaret said, 'I have padded my tummy with a cushion and put it about that I am pregnant. I want to fake a pregnancy and go to Venice and bring back the Polish child as the Duke's son.'"[465] There is no evidence that this scheme was ever brought to fruition.

Colonel Stewart and Lady Jane were married in August 1746. It would be evident to the couple from the existence of Lady Jane's periods that she could conceive. The date of coinception was inferred to be October 1747. Would Sir John and Lady Jane have given up after just over a year of trying and decided that the only way to have children would be by this drastic scheme? Perhaps, if the pressure was great enough. But why would the pressure be so great? Lady Jane had had thirty years in which some of the most eligible suitors had sought her hand, and we know from many accounts and from portraits that she looked younger than her age and was very attractive. She could have produced heirs legitimately at any time if such had been her strong desire.

So where does the truth lie?

Over the years, various writers have attempted not only to tell the story of the case but also to support one or other side.

Two of the authors who wrote popular books that told the story of the Cause, Horace Bleackley and Percy Fitzgerald, did little more than the Hamilton counsel, rolling out all the characters and statements that cast suspicion on Sir John Stewart and Lady Jane and not trying very hard to counteract them with an equivalent amount of pro-Lady Jane testimony.

Lillian de la Torre, whose book *The Heir of Douglas* came out in 1953, took a different approach. She was a writer of true history detective stories and prided herself on taking some mystery from the past and solving it. In the files she left to Brigham Young University in Utah, there are hundreds and hundreds of pages of research notes and a first draft of her manuscript which is four times the length of the book she finally published.

In fact, Lilian de la Torre did solve the mystery, to her own satisfaction at least. She applied to the Douglas Cause what she defined as 'de la Torre's law': "If in spite of evidence, a mystery remains unsolved, then the truth has never been suspected and neither side is right. *The solution lies somewhere down the middle.*"

De la Torre found her answer in the account by Mme. Guynette of the mysterious stranger who approached her. "My wife," he said to her, "has lain in of twins, and they are dead. She will be so afflicted should she find it out, that there is reason to fear for her life if we do not present her with living children, and make her think they are hers, until she is quite recovered. Or if two cannot be found, one would keep her happy, and I will tell her the other is too feeble to be brought to her."[466]

Without diverging too much from the story, it's worth pointing out that de la Torre had a very creative writing style. She often tried to write in the style of the period she was writing about and also, as in this case, was quite free with the way she used quotations.

She describes the quote above as 'the confession, by the plotter, of the nature of the plot.' In fact, the nearest text to the quote she gives comes from the deposition of Mme. Guynette's daughter, since Mme, Guynette had died by the time the Cause was in process. The daughter's testimony is given in indirect speech and is as follows:

"That a gentleman spoke two or three times to the deponent's said mother, and asked her, if she could find for him two children or one, having blue eyes, because his wife was delivered of two male children but they were dead, and that he wanted to present her with two children or at least one until she should be recovered."[467]

Not only is this hearsay, Mme. Guynette's daughter is relaying something she says elsewhere she "heard more than a hundred times from her mother." Now, of course, hearing something a hundred times may emphasise its truth. But *telling* someone something a hundred times may well lead to an account of events that has 'drifted' from the original circumstances.

Nevertheless, a stranger who was Sir John Stewart may have said something like this to Mme. Guynette. Does the account derived from 'de la Torre's law' hold up? It's certainly a possibility, although as I try to think of the minute by minute events of the day of the birth, the hypothesis raises a number of queries:

Why would Colonel Stuart, dazed and dismayed by the death of his twins, think that he could walk out into the streets of Paris and find a replacement child, of exactly the right age and colouring, just like that?

What were Lady Jane and Mrs. Hewit doing while two dead babies lay somewhere in the house of Mme. Le Brun? Presumably, by this account, Mrs. Hewit was a conspirator.

How could Lady Jane be persuaded to accept that her second son had been immediately sent off to another part of Paris without her seeing him at all?

Why would Colonel Stewart wait another seventeen months before trying to procure another child? If the Mignon enlèvement worked so well, wouldn't he have been able quickly to find another?

Could Colonel Stewart and Mrs. Hewit keep this secret to themselves for the rest of Lady Jane's life? And if not, would she then go along with the deception, once it was revealed?

And this hypothesis still leaves unexplained various elements of the Hamilton case against Douglas – the absence of Mme. Le Brun and her house, the two conflicting Pierre La Marres and so on.

I decided not to add my own hypothesis to the pile. In spite of the fact that I have read much of the existing material, my research has not been exhaustive. But as I thought about the case, I came to believe in Lady Jane and in the improbability of her taking part in the complex deception alleged by the Hamiltons. There was one overriding reason for forming this judgement and that was her devoutness. Throughout her life, she was a very religious person. She attended church services, she spoke openly about her faith, she prayed. The afterlife, hell and damnation seemed real. Punishment for mortal sins was eternal. In today's society, where an Anglican bishop can doubt the reality of the resurrection, we can sometimes forget about the powerful hold that Christianity had over its adherents,.

How could Lady Jane Douglas have lived easily with deception for the rest of her life? And the lies would mount. This was not just one bad deed. She would have had to sin every time she avowed that the children were hers. Was the end worth the means – the loss of her eternal soul?

Of course, the de la Torre theory, provided the secret was kept from Lady Jane by Colonel Stewart and Mrs. Hewit, might take care of that. (While it would raise similar problems for the two conspirators, I suspect it would only be Mrs. Hewit who would be afraid for her soul.) Mrs. Hepburn, who knew Sir John Stewart very well, was asked whether she thought he could keep the secret if the children had not been Lady Jane's and she said "From the violence and heat of his temper I do not think he could have carried through a thing of that kind, without blundering in some shape or other."[468]

One of the most thought-provoking speeches among the various attempts to arrive at a fair verdict, was by Lord Strichen in the Court of Session:

"Is it credible," Lord Strichen said, "that when Lady Jane and Sir John were so poor, that it is proved they could scarcely maintain themselves, is it credible, I say, that they should add to this poverty, by bringing upon themselves the burden of maintaining other people's children, and that too, with the danger of so much guilt as that of committing the crime of *partus suppositio?* Is it credible, that when one child would have served their purpose, they would have burdened themselves with two? Is it credible, that they would go to Paris, without any person to assist them in the commission of so dangerous a crime? And what is stronger than all this, is it credible, that after they had got the imposture of the first child accomplished, and knew what a dreadful punishment they must suffer, if detected; is it credible, I say, that they would have remained so long in Paris, where they might be easily found out by those who might be in search of them?"[469]

Each time I read that paragraph, I feel for a moment that I know that Lady Jane and her husband were innocent, and then somehow the certainty fades as I read the legal papers and explore more archives. There is in fact no natural end-point to researching the story of an event as complex as the Douglas Cause. You may get ever nearer to the point where you feel you have read every scrap of paper that may cast light on the story, but you will never reach that point.

Some years ago the Scottish National Archive Service produced a catalogue of the Earl of Home's papers and they e-mailed it to me. There were a hundred or more pages covering the entire history of the Home family, along with papers relating to the Douglases. There was enough, it seemed, to justify a trip to Lord Home's home, the Hirsel, near Coldstream, just by the Scots-English border.

The Hirsel is a large 17th century house, much altered over the centuries, and the Earl of Home keeps his family papers in three rooms in the south wing. The archivist who had compiled the catalogue had done a good job. The papers were organised into large acid-free cardboard file-boxes, and in each box papers were tied into numbered bundles. It was easy to find any item mentioned – the official House of Lord verdict, for example, was written in fine copperplate writing on a sheet of paper in Bundle N in Box M. I spent the morning working my way through the items I thought might refer to the Douglas Cause. There was a narrative of Lady Jane's life which I had hoped might be in her own hand but turned out to be assembled from a number of sources I'd already seen — letters, legal documents and so on. But there were also original letters written by Lady Jane to her husband, some which I had read in transcript and one or two which I hadn't seen before. There were letters from Sir John, and in spite of his reputation towards the end of his life as a rambling, incoherent old man, his writing was surprisingly firm.

Over lunch Lord Home told me that he didn't think he was descended from Mignon the French glass-grinder. "My sister and I have talked about this from time to time," he said, " and we don't think it very likely. After all," he went on, "neither of us is any good at languages."

In the afternoon I returned to the archives. Box 60, Bundle 3, was said to contain "Letters to Sir John Stewart from John Cockburn, William Mackewan and others concerning Sir John's financial straits and the Duke of Douglas's treatment of Lady Jane. Also a few minor personal letters between Lady Jane and Sir John Stewart, and 2 household accounts for Lady Jane at Aix-la-Chapelle, 1747."

Some of the individual items were folded into long thin strips, about two inches by six, usually with a description written on the outside. Others were notepaper-sized sheets folded in half. In those days most letters didn't have envelopes and so a sheet of about A5-size paper would be folded and refolded to produce a small packet with the addressee's named written on the outside, and a blob of sealing wax to stop it being unfolded. They were all layered with grime on the outside. I opened each item one by one, trying to work out who had written it and why.

Then in the middle of Bundle 3 I came across an item that was different from the others. It wasn't a neatly written and folded letter or legal document and the paper was flimsier than the other items. It was six sides of scrawl, written with large flourishes and overlapping lines, in a handwriting that I had come to know as Lady Jane's. Her writing was never neat at the best of times, but this was untidy even for her, and seemed to degenerate over successive pages. It didn't seem to be a letter. There was no address, no Dear So and So and no signature. As I deciphered the writing it was clear that it was a prayer, a prayer written to God for forgiveness. From its writing and its passion it was written by a woman in the throes of anguish, a woman who was convinced she was a sinner, and could scarcely believe that the sins she had committed were forgiveable, but was pleading nevertheless with her God in the hope that He would look kindly on her.

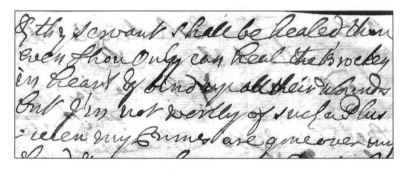

Part of the prayer written in haste or distress by Lady Jane Douglas

Some of the writing was so scrawled as to be illegible but the following extracts from the six-page document leave no doubt that Lady Jane Douglas was deeply ashamed of things she had done:

"Oh most Adorable & ever Great and Glorious Lord God Almighty the Gracious and ever Living God the Least & Most unworthy of thy Servants takes upon her to address her self to thy Devine Majesty imploring pardon and remission of all her many and mighty transgressions and sins for the sake of my Great Lord and redeemer Jesus Christ beseeching his perfect forgiveness to be sent upon me to deliver me from the ruin of sin & from the punishment I so justly deserve by my repeated crimes and doings which have not been good from my earliest childhood even until now for which I repent before thy divine Majesty in dust and in ashes …

O bless me for the lord Jesus sake with a humble and contrite frame of mind sutable to my exceeding great offences which I am guilty of in thy sight. O most Holy most pure & perfect excellence & sutable to the calamitous distressful painful state I am reduced to by my repeated Crimes and dreadful iniquity by which I have done evil against the Most Glorious God Almighty…

O Lord of Infinite Mercy and Great Compassion this is a day of great Perplexity with me and of great trouble & distress therefore I come to thee say thou the word and thy servant shall be healed thou even thou only can heal the brocken in heart and bind up all their wounds but I'm not worthy of such as this when my crimes are gone over my head and are a heavy burden too heavy for me to bear …

Cleanse me from all my vileness and wickedness and make this guilty heart yet a sacrefise of Praise unto thee …

Jesus Christ to whom I commite my soul acept of me in mercy for the Lord Jesus Christ take [Jane Douglas] & dedecate my self to the O Holy Glorious Family Three persons & one essence: For the lord sake pardon mine [sins?] for they are great accept of me for the Sake of my Great Lord and Redeemer My Lord and My God Jesus Christ."[470]

Even allowing for the greater sense of sinfulness that 18th century Christians might feel after small transgressions, this seems altogether more serious. The problem is that we have no idea when it was written. Perhaps she wrote it when she was in deep distress at the time Sholto died, seeing the death as some kind of punishment for unspecified sins she had committed. Perhaps it came from even earlier in her life, when she was rejected by her brother or jilted by a suitor.

But if she wrote it near the end of her life it could form, perhaps, a fitting epitaph to the Douglas Cause. Because of course, this prayer achieves the remarkable feat of confirming whichever view you take of the truth about the birth of Archy and Sholto.

If you believe that Lady Jane was innocent, the prayer would merely confirm her devoutness by showing how even the burden of 'normal' sins was heavy for someone who believed what she believed, and therefore she would be unlikely to contemplate anything as serious as the crime she had been accused of.

If, on the other hand, you believe that Lady Jane colluded in the faking of the birth, it has always been difficult to see how a religiously devout woman such as Lady Jane could do such a thing. But if she *did* do it nevertheless, it would leave such a burden on her conscience that this is just the sort of prayer she would write to her saviour, particularly if she was near death – intense, pleading, desperate.

Lady Jane Douglas now lies buried in the chapel of Holyrood House in Edinburgh. A story from Boswell's *Journal of a Tour to the Hebrides* allows us to hear last words on the matter from the best-known partisan of the Douglas Cause and his wise friend:

"I spoke with peculiar feeling to the miserable neglect of the chapel belonging to the palace of Holyrood House, in which are deposited the remains of many of the kings of Scotland, and of many of our nobility. I said, it was a disgrace to the country that it was not repaired: and particularly complained that my friend Douglas, the representative of a great house, and proprietor of a vast estate, should suffer the sacred spot where his mother lies interred, to be unroofed, and exposed to all the inclemencies of the weather. Dr Johnson, who, I know not how, had formed an opinion on the Hamilton side, in the Douglas cause, slily answered, 'Sir, sir, don't be too severe upon the gentleman; don't accuse him of want of filial piety! Lady Jane Douglas was not HIS mother.' He roused my zeal so much that I took the liberty to tell him he knew nothing of the cause; which I do most seriously believe was the case."

Acknowledgments

F irst, of course, I owe thanks to the two ancient families whose intimate histories I have tried to unravel in the research for this book.

The Earl of Home, descended on the female side from Lady Jane via one of Archie's daughters, opened up the Douglas-Home archives at the Hirsel and gave me free rein. It was here that I found, among other useful material, two of the most illuminating documents, James Carnegy's journal and Lady Jane's hand-written prayer.

Then there are the Hamiltons, who for better or worse, put their entire case in the hands of Andrew Stuart, with the results we have seen. The late Duke of Hamilton, Angus, and his wife Kay, the Duchess, gave me help and encouragement, and showed me paintings and documents that have helped me understand their side of the story.

Henry Steuart Fothringham, a descendant of Sir John Stewart, Lady Jane's husband, discussed the Cause with me in some detail, and showed me round the Stewart family seat of Murthly.

John Montagu allowed me to peruse the handwritten

journal of his ancestor, the 4th Earl of Sandwich, covering the House of Lords hearing in which the 4th Earl participated so entertainingly.

I have made much use of several libraries and archives, to all of whom I am grateful for permission to quote from materials they hold:

> Beinecke Rare Book and Manuscript Library,
> Yale University
>
> National Archives of Scotland
>
> National Library of Scotland
>
> Lewis Walpole Library
>
> Harold B. Lee Library, Brigham Young University,
> Provo, Utah
>
> Archives Nationales, Paris

Sources

The main sources of lawyers' and witnesses' statements are four large volumes called Proofs and Memorials, printed for the use of the numerous lawyers in the main case and the appeal. I have used the following abbreviations in the Endnotes:

PM = "Pursuers Memorial", *Memorial for George-James Duke of Hamilton*, printed 24th January, 1767

DM = "Defender's Memorial", *Memorial for Archibald Douglas of Douglas, Esq, etc*, 1766

PP = "Pursuers' Proof", *Proof in the Conjoined Processes, George-James Duke of Hamilton, etc,* printed for the Lords of Session, dated December 19, 1765 and February 5, 1766

DP = "Defender's Proof", *Proof for Archibald Douglas*, 28th January, 1766

Service = *Service of Archibald Douglas as Heir of Provision*, 9th September, 1761. [Bound in with DP]

Case = *The Case of Archibald Douglas and his Guardians*, [London 1768]

Richardson = Robert Richardson, D.D *A State of the Evidence in the Cause between His Grace the Duke of Hamilton and Archibald Douglas of Douglas Esquire*, London MDCCLXIX

Stuart = *Letters to the Right Honourable Lord Mansfield from Andrew Stuart, Esq.* London, January 1773

Other abbreviations used in the notes include:

NLS = National Library of Scotland

BYU = Lillian de la Torre Collection, L. Tom Perry Special Collections Library, Harold B. Lee Library, Brigham Young Univeristy, Provo, Utah

Beinecke = Yale University Beinecke Rare Book and Manuscript Library, New Haven, CT

Hirsel = the archives of the Earl of Home at the Hirsel.

Farmington = The Lewis Walpole Library, department of Yale University Library, Farmington, MA

NBT = *Notable British Trials: The Douglas Cause*, by A. Francis Steuart

LMC = *The letters and journals of Lady Mary Coke*, 4 vols, first published 1889-96, Kingsmead Reprints, Bath, 1970

DLT = *The Heir of Douglas*, by Lilian de la Torre, Michael Joseph, 1953

Endnotes

Prologue:

1 PP, p. 340
2 James Boswell, *Letters of the Right Honourable Lady Jane Douglas,* London, 1767, p. 9

Chapter 1:

3 *Case,* Part 1, Book 1, p. 2
4 *Case.* Part 1, Book 1, p. 4
5 *The Letters of Horace Walpole,* Project Gutenberg Etext, Volume www2. cddc.vt.edu/ gutenberg/ etext03/ lthw110.txt
6 *Memoir of Lady Jane Douglas Stewart.* n.d. Anonymous, handwritten. (Douglas-Home Archives: Box 187, Bundle 4)
7 *The Living Age,* Vol 172 issue 2228 (March 5 1887) p 591 ff
8 *Memoir of Lady Jane Douglas Stewart. n.d.* Anonymous, handwritten. (Douglas-Home Archives: Box 187, Bundle 4),
9 *Ibid*
10 *Memoir of Lady Jane Douglas Stewart.* n.d. Anonymous, handwritten. (Douglas-Home Archives: Box 187, Bundle 4)
11 *Ibid*
12 James Ferguson, *Select Mechanical Exercises,* Introduction, London, 1773
13 PM p. 3
14 Percy Fitzgerald, *Lady Jean, the Romance of the Great Douglas Cause,* London, T. Fisher Unwin, 1904, p.9
15 Lady Louisa Stuart, *Selections from her manuscripts,* (ed. Hon. James A. Home), David Douglas, Edinburgh, 1899 p. 28-9
16 *Memoir of Lady Jane Douglas Stewart.* n.d. Anonymous, handwritten. (Douglas-Home Archives: Box 187, Bundle 4)
17 William Fraser, C.B. LL.D *The Douglas Book,* Edinburgh MDCCCLXXXVI, p. 1-8
18 *Ibid*
19 Horace Bleackley, *The Story of A Beautiful Duchess,* Archibald Constable & Co. Ltd, 1907, p. 63
20 William Fraser, C.B. LL.D *The Douglas Book,* Edinburgh MDCCCLXXXVI, p. 1-8

21 Alexander Allardyce, ed. *Letters from & to Charles Kirkpatrick Sharpe, Esq.,* William Blackwood 1888, p. 200, n. 1

22 *Memoir of Lady Jane Douglas Stewart.* n.d. Anonymous, handwritten. (Douglas-Home Archives: Box 187, Bundle 4), p. 13-14

23 Quoted in Lillian de la Torre draft MS, BYU MSS 2167 Box 13 Folder 8, letters from Stuart-Stevenson papers IV

24 *Ibid*

25 DP 896-899

Chapter 2:

26 Violet Biddulph, *Kitty, Duchess of Queensberry,* Ivor Nicholson and Watson, London, 1935, p. 18

27 Robert Chambers, *Traditions of Edinburgh,* W&R Chambers, London and Edinburgh, 1869, p. 75

28 Lady Constance Russell, *Three Generations of Fascinating Women,* Longmans, Green, and Co, 1904, Pp. 272-77

29 John Macdonald, *Memoirs of an Eighteenth Century Footman,* Century Publishing, 1985 p. 93

30 Horace Bleackley, *The Story of A Beautiful Duchess,* Archibald Constable & Co. Ltd, *1907* P. 36

31 Duke of Douglas anecdotes, Hirsel, Box 187, Bundle 4

32 Ibid

33 Ibid

34 Hirsel papers, Box 187 Bundle 4

35 *Case.* Part I, Book I, p. 9

36 PP p. 63.

37 DP pp. 896-899

38 *Memoir of Lady Jane Douglas Stewart.* n.d. Anonymous, handwritten. (Douglas-Home Archives: Box 187, Bundle 4), p. 14-15

39 Francis Douglas, *Observations on the Douglas Cause in General in a Letter to a Noble Lord* 1768 pp. 35-7

40 Duke of Douglas anecdotes, Hirsel, Box 187, Bundle 4, p. 2

41 Case, Part 1, Book 1, p. 7

42 *Ibid*

43 *Ibid*

44 Francis Douglas, *Observations on the Douglas Cause in General in a Letter to a Noble Lord* ,1768 pp. 35-7

45 John Hill Burton, ed. T*he Autobiography of Dr. Alexander Carlyle of Inveresk,* T.N. Foulis, London & Edinburgh 1910, p. 239

46 *Case.* Part 1, Book 1, p. 7

47 Francis Douglas, *Observations on the Douglas Cause in General in a Letter to a Noble Lord,* 1768 pp. 35-7

48 Ibid

49 *Memoir of Lady Jane Douglas Stewart.* n.d. Anonymous, handwritten. (Douglas-Home Archives: Box 187, Bundle 4), p. 20

50 PP p. 331

51 Percy Fitzgerald, *Lady Jean, the Romance of the Great Douglas Cause,* London, T. Fisher Unwin, 1904, p.11

52 DP 896-899

53 *Memoir of Lady Jane Douglas Stewart.* n.d. Anonymous, handwritten. (Douglas-Home Archives: Box 187, Bundle 4), p. 16-19

54 Percy Fitzgerald, *Lady Jean, the Romance of the Great Douglas Cause,* London, T. Fisher Unwin, 1904, p. 22

55 *Memoir of Lady Jane Douglas Stewart.* n.d. Anonymous, handwritten. (Douglas-Home Archives: Box 187, Bundle 4), p. 21-23

56 Ibid

57 PP, p. 376

58 *The Living Age,* Vol 172 issue 2228 (March 5 1887) p 591 ff

59 William Fraser, C.B. LL.D *The Douglas Book,* Edinburgh MDCCCLXXXVI, p. 13-21

60 *Memoir of Lady Jane Douglas Stewart.* n.d. Anonymous, handwritten. (Douglas-Home Archives: Box 187, Bundle 4), p. 19-20

Endnotes

Chapter 3:

61 http://www2.lib.uoguelph.ca/ resources/ebooks/Literary_Life/v1/ Literary_Life_v1b_text.htm

62 Richardson, p. 129

63 DP, p. 385

64 DP, p. 387

65 PP, p. 31

66 Service p. 6

67 PP, p. 29

68 PP, p. 45

69 PP, p. 29

70 PP, p 35-7

71 PP, p 35-7

72 Percy Fitzgerald, *Lady Jean, the Romance of the Great Douglas Cause*, London, T. Fisher Unwin, 1904, p. 34

73 DP p. 162

74 PP, p. 40

75 PM, appendix, p. 37-8

76 Defender's Service, p.9

77 Richardson, p 144, quoting DP p. 35

78 PP, p. 50

79 Defender's Service and DP, pp 3-4

80 Richardson, p. 138

81 DP, p. 963

82 PP p. 327-8

83 *Memoir of Lady Jane Douglas Stewart*. n.d. Anonymous, handwritten. (Douglas-Home Archives: Box 187, Bundle 4), p. 24

84 *Ibid*

85 Richardson, p. 156

86 PP, p. 339

87 Defender's Service and DP, pp 3-4

88 *Memoir of Lady Jane Douglas Stewart*. n.d. Anonymous, handwritten. (Douglas-Home Archives: Box 187, Bundle 4), p. 25

Chapter 4:

89 Richardson, p 64 (Richardson's translation of letter in French)

90 DP, p. 163

91 James Boswell, *Letters of Lady Jane Douglas*, Printed for J. Wilkie, London 1767, p. 9

92 DP, p. 428

93 Stuart, Letter I, p. 11

94 Quoted in *Notes and Queries*, 1863, December 26, p. 522

95 *Scots Magazine*, Vol 31, Dec. 1769, p. 671

96 Defender's Service, p. 68

97 DP, p. 996

98 Case, p 59

99 Robert Gore-Brown, *Chancellor Thurlow*, Hamish Hamilton, London 1953, p. 48

100 Richardson, p. 307

101 Ibid

102 Service, p. 69

103 Richardson, p. 329

Chapter 5:

104 Edward Walford, *Old and New London*, Vol. VI, p. 65, Cassell Petter and Galpin, n.d.

105 NST 24 and DLT 36

106 Philip Mansel, *Paris Between the Empires*, Phoenix, 2001, p. 179

107 PP, p. 812

108 DP, p. 970.

109 DP, p. 840-1

110 Andrew Henderson, *A Letter to a Noble Lord*, pp. 10-11

111 Hirsel Box 60 Bundle 3

112 *Notes and Queries*, 1860, March 10, p. 183

113 Hirsel papers Box 60 Folder 3

114 DP, p. 841.

115 Percy Fitzgerald, *Lady Jean, the Romance of the Great Douglas Cause*, London, T. Fisher Unwin, 1904, p. 124-5

116 Abraham Hayward, ed. *Autobiography, Letters and Literary Remains of Mrs. Piozzi*, 2 vol. London, 1861. ii. 81- 2

117 Lady Constance Russell, *Three Generations of Fascinating Women*, Longmans, Green, and Co, 1904, p. 102-3

118 *The Letters of Horace Walpole*, Project Gutenberg Etext, Volume www2.

cddc.vt.edu/ gutenberg/etext03/
lthw110.txt

[119] Lady Constance Russell, *Three Generations of Fascinating Women*, Longmans, Green, and Co, 1904, p. 135

[120] James Boswell, *Letters of Lady Jane Douglas*, Printed for J. Wilkie, London 1767, p. 82

[121] LMC Vol II, p. 367

[122] Horace Bleackley, *The Story of A Beautiful Duchess*, Archibald Constable & Co. Ltd, 1907p. 52

[123] DP pp 886-7

[124] DP. pp. 864-5

[125] Serv. p. 25

[126] DP p. 41

[127] *Memoir of Lady Jane Douglas Stewart.* n.d. Anonymous, handwritten. (Douglas-Home Archives: Box 187, Bundle 4)

[128] DP pp. 896-899

[129] PP, p 374

[130] PP, p. 319.

[131] PP p. 329

[132] Case, p. 13

Chapter 6:

[133] DP (Service) p. 63

[134] DP 859

[135] DP p. 951

[136] DP p. 401

[137] PP, p 305

[138] The Project Gutenberg Etext of *The Letters of Horace Walpole*, Volume 1 by Horace Walpole. Letter 66 To Sir Horace Mann. Strawberry Hill, Oct. 28, N. S. 1752. www2.cddc.vt.edu/ gutenberg/etext03/lthw110.txt

[139] Ibid

[140] DP, p.939

[141] DP, p. 939

[142] DP, p. 994.

[143] *Memoir of Lady Jane Douglas Stewart.* n.d. Anonymous, handwritten. (Douglas-Home Archives: Box 187, Bundle 4), p. 31-32

[144] James Boswell, *Letters of Lady Jane Douglas*, Printed for J. Wilkie, London 1767, p. 154.

[145] *Memoir of Lady Jane Douglas Stewart.* n.d. Anonymous, handwritten. (Douglas-Home Archives: Box 187, Bundle 4), p. 2-3

[146] *Ibid*

[147] DP, p. 713

[148] PP, p. 304-5.

[149] Case, p. 14

[150] PP pp 3-4

[151] John Hill Burton, ed. T*he Autobiography of Dr. Alexander Carlyle of Inveresk*, T.N. Foulis, London & Edinburgh 1910, p. 116

[152] Hirsel, Box 187, Bundle 4

[153] Hirsel, Box 187, Bundle 4

[154] C.K. Sharpe, p. 170

[155] PP, p 307

[156] PP, p. 324

[157] PP, p. 324

[158] PP, p 312

[159] National Library of Scotland, Andrew Stuart papers, Item 973 P. 62

Chapter 7:

[160] http://www.canalmuseum.org.uk/ history/ukcanals.htm

[161] *The Letters of Horace Walpole*, Project Gutenberg Etext, Volume www2. cddc.vt.edu/ gutenberg/etext03/ lthw110.txt

[162] Percy Fitzgerald, *Lady Jean, the Romance of the Great Douglas Cause*, London, T. Fisher Unwin, 1904, p. 181

[163] James Boswell, *Letters of Lady Jane Douglas*, Printed for J. Wilkie, London 1767. p. 144; William Fraser, *The Red Book of Grandtully*, vol. i. p. ccvi.

[164] DP pp. 896-899

[165] Case, p. 20

[166] Edmund George Petty Fitzmaurice. Baron Fitzmaurice, *Life of William, Earl of Shelburne, afterwards first*

Marquess of Lansdowne.., 3 vol. Macmillan & Co.: London, 1875, Vol. ii., p. 470

167 DP, pp. 896-899

168 DP, p. 429.

169 Ibid. pp. 430, 431.

170 John Macdonald, *Travels in Various Parts of Europe, Asia and Africa* published by J. Forbes, Covent-garden. 1790. Reprinted as *Memoirs of an Eighteenth Century Footman*, by Century Publishing, London, 1985, p 51

171 Robert Chambers, *Traditions of Edinburgh*, , W&R Chambers, London and Edinburgh, 1869, p. 261

172 James Boswell, *Letters of Lady Jane Douglas*, Printed for J. Wilkie, London 1767 p. 96, 18th November 1752.

173 Colonel Hon. Arthur C. Murray CMG DSO, *The Five Sons of "Bare Betty"*, John Murray, London 1936, p 142

174 *Letters to the Right Honourable Lord Mansfield from Andrew Stuart, Esq.* London 1773, Letter IV, p. 8-9

175 DM Appendix, p. 27

176 Stuart, Letter IV, p. 8-9

177 Ibid, p. 11

Chapter 8:

178 Lady Louisa Stuart, *Gleanings from an Old Portfolio*, i, 218, 225.

179 Case, Part 1, Book 1, p. 9

180 Stuart, Letter IV, p. 10

181 DM Appendix, p. 25-35 (All quotes from this document translated by the author.)

182 *Scots Magazine*, Vol. XXV, p. 308

183 Stuart, Letter III, p. 19

184 DM Appendix, p. 25-35

185 DM Appendix, p. 25-35

186 PP p. 888

187 Mure Collection NLS MS 4944 f. 193

188 ANSWERS for Duke of Hamilton to Petition of Archibald Douglas, dated 1st December 1763, p. 23

189 DP p. 164

190 NLS Stuart-Stevenson papers, Box VII

Chapter 9:

191 Case, p. 97

192 DP, p. 435

193 DP, p. 452

194 PP, p. 297

195 Defender's Service, p. 12

196 William Fraser, C.B. LL.D *The Douglas Book,* Edinburgh MDCCCLXXXVI p. 64

197 PP p. 1-17

198 William Fraser, C.B. LL.D *The Douglas Book*, Edinburgh MDCCCLXXXVI, p. 64

199 NLS 5371 11/3/1765 Letter from AS

200 NLS 5371 11/3/1765 Letter from AS

201 www.electricscotland.com/history/other/garden_francis.htm

202 Robert Chambers, *Traditions of Edinburgh*, , W&R Chambers, London and Edinburgh, 1869, p. 146

203 Quoted in Ian Simpson-Ross, *Lord Kames and the Scotland of his Day*, Oxford, 1972

204 LMC Vol IV, p. 116

205 PP p. 183

206 DP p. 1031

207 DP p. 448

Chapter 10:

208 Carnegy Journal, Hirsel papers, Vol 282 p. 7

209 Ibid, p.12

210 Quoted in DLT, p. 134-5

211 Carnegy Journal, Hirsel papers, Vol 282 p.26

212 PP, pp. 1071-2

213 PP p. 273

214 CP 20

215 Percy Fitzgerald, *Lady Jean, the Romance of the Great Douglas Cause*, London, T. Fisher Unwin, 1904, pp200-208

216 DP p. 1028

217 PP, p. 1107
218 http://mss.library.nottingham. ac.uk/cats/port_3rdduke17cat.html, Pw F 8714

Chapter 11:
219 http://www.site-magister.com/ afcal.htm «Ces Visigoths ont pour maxime que quatre quarts de preuve, et huit huitièmes, font deux preuves complètes, et ils donnent à des ouï-dire le nom de quarts de preuve et de huitièmes. Que dites-vous de cette manière de raisonner et de juger ? Est-il possible que la vie des hommes dépende de gens aussi absurdes ?» (Author's translation)
220 Carnegy Journal, Hirsel papers, Douglas-Home volumes Vol 282 p. 24
221 Ibid, p. 26
222 Carnegy Journal 16
223 Carnegy Journal, Hirsel papers, Douglas-Home volumes Vol 282, loose sheet
224 DP p. 723ff
225 DP p. 723ff
226 Farmington, Douglas Cause 77 pieces, Vol 2, Item 4
227 PP p. 728
228 PP, pp. 596-7
229 PP p. 1097 ff (author's translation)
230 PP p. 1097 ff

Chapter 12:
231 James Boswell, *The Essence of the Douglas Cause*, London: J. Wilkie, 1767, p. 15-16
232 Case, Introduction, p. 1
233 *Scots Magazine*, Vol XXV, July 1763, p372
234 NLS MS 4942 f. 252
235 PP p. 737-8
236 E-mail to author from E.A. Smith, Archivist, Westminster School
237 NLS MS 4942 f. 252

238 *Edinburgh Courant*, April 23rd, 1764, quoted in DP, p. 894-5

Chapter 13:
239 Peter Martin, *A Life of James Boswell*, Weidenfeld and Nicolson, 1999, p. 122
240 Robert Chambers, *Traditions of Edinburgh*, W&R Chambers, London and Edinburgh, 1869, p. 74
241 Frederick A. Pottle, *James Boswell: The Earlier Years, 1740-1769*, New York and London, 1966, , p 314
242 BYU – LDLT papers
243 James Boswell, *The Essence of the Douglas Cause*, London: J. Wilkie, 1767
244 Frederick Pottle, *Judiciary Review*, Nebraska, xxxvii (1925)
245 DP, p. 447; *Scots Magazine*, vol. xxvi. p. 350.
246 James Boswell, *Letters of Lady Jane Douglas*, Printed for J. Wilkie, London 1767, Epilogue
247 *Selections from the Family papers preserved at Caldwell*, Part II. Vol I, The Maitland Club, Glasgow MDCCCLIV, p. 253
248 Horace Bleackley, *The Story of A Beautiful Duchess*, Archibald Constable & Co. Ltd, 1907, p. 139
249 Sir William Fraser, *History of the Carnegie Family*, n.d.

Chapter 14:
250 Stuart, Letter III, p. 19
251 P.N. Furbank, *Diderot*, Minerva, London, 1992
252 Denis Diderot, *Correspondance*, Vol V (Janvier 1765 – Fevrier 1766), edited by Georges Roth, Les Editions de MinuitLettre 368. To Sophie Volland [20 décembre 1765]
253 PP, p. 887
254 Richardson, p. 56
255 Robert Colville, *Considerations on the Douglas Cause* 1767, p. 8
256 Richardson, p. 76
257 Ibid, p. 80

258 The Project Gutenberg Etext of *The Letters of Horace Walpole*, Volume 1, by Horace Walpole. www2.cddc. vt.edu/gutenberg/etext03/lthw110. txt Letter 267 To The Hon. H. S. Conway. Amiens, Wednesday, Sept. 11, 1765. (page 421)

Chapter 15:

259 Robert Chambers, *Traditions of Edinburgh*, W&R Chambers, London and Edinburgh, 1869, p. 154

260 James Maidment, ed., *The Court of Session Garland*, London: Hamilton, Adams & Co, 1888, p.76

261 Ibid

262 *Scots Magazine*, Vol xxix, Aug. 1767, p. 428

263 Ian Simpson-Ross, *Lord Kames and the Scotland of his Day*, , Oxford, 1972

264 Lord Cooper (ed), *Regiam Majestatem and Quoniam Attachiamenta*, , 1947, pp. 324-5

265 Robert Colville, *Considerations on the Douglas Cause* 1767, p. 1

266 George W. T. Omond, *The Lord Advocates of Scotland*. Edinburgh, David Douglas 1883, p. 62

267 NLS MS 4943 f. 240

268 Richardson, p. 181

269 PM p. 302-11

270 Richard C. Cole, *The General Correspondence of James Boswell, 1766-1769*, Vol. 1: 1766-1767, Edinburgh University Press, Yale University Press. 1997, p. 148

271 MS Douce 193 (f.70), Bodleian Library

272 DM P 430-1

273 DM P 653

274 DP p.707

275 DM P 424

Chapter 16:

276 James Boswell, *Dorando*, a Spanish Tale, J. Wilkie, London, 1767

277 *Scots Magazine*, Vol xxix, p. 338

278 *Caledonian Mercury*, 17th June, 1767

279 *Caledonian Mercury*, 22nd June, 1767

280 *Blackwood's Magazine*, No. MCCCXVIII, Vol CCXVIII, August 1925 , pp 149-165

281 Richard C. Cole, *The General Correspondence of James Boswell, 1766-1769*, Vol. 1: 1766-1767, Edinburgh University Press, Yale University Press. 1997, p. 244

282 *Edinburgh Advertiser*, June 16, 19, 26; July 7, 1767

283 Andrew Dewar Gibb, *Law from Over the Border*, quoted in Ian Simpson-Ross, *Lord Kames and the Scotland of his Day*, , Oxford, 1972. p. 134

284 Robert Chambers, *Traditions of Edinburgh*, W&R Chambers, London and Edinburgh, 1869, p. 147

285 James Maidment, ed., *The Court of Session Garland*, London: Hamilton, Adams & Co, 1888, p. 71

286 Robert Chambers, *Traditions of Edinburgh*, , W&R Chambers, London and Edinburgh, 1869, p. 146

287 James Maidment, ed., *The Court of Session Garland*, London: Hamilton, Adams & Co, 1888, p. 63

288 Robert Chambers, *Traditions of Edinburgh*, , W&R Chambers, London and Edinburgh, 1869, p. 145

289 *Selections from the Family papers preserved at Caldwell*, Part II. Vol II, The Maitland Club, Glasgow MDCCCLIV, p. 128

290 George W. T. Omond, *The Lord Advocates of Scotland*. Edinburgh, David Douglas 1883, p. 64

291 A. Francis Steuart, ed. *The Douglas Cause*, Glasgow and Edinburgh, William Hodge and Co., 1909, p. 91

292 Ibid, p. 95

293 Ibid, p. 66

294 *The Speeches and Judgement of the Court of Session...* taken down and published by William Anderson,

Balfour, Auld and Smellie, Edinburgh, 1768, p. 49

295 A. Francis Steuart, ed. *The Douglas Cause,* Glasgow and Edinburgh, William Hodge and Co., 1909, p. 100

296 Ibid, p. 70

297 Ian Simpson-Ross, *Lord Kames and the Scotland of his Day,* , Oxford, 1972

298 A. Francis Steuart, ed. *The Douglas Cause,* Glasgow and Edinburgh, William Hodge and Co., 1909, p. 57

299 Ibid, p. 94

300 *Memorial for John Donaldson,* 1767, p2

301 A. Francis Steuart, ed. *The Douglas Cause,* Glasgow and Edinburgh, William Hodge and Co., 1909, p. 118

302 William Fraser, C.B. H.D., *The Douglas Book,* by Edinburgh – MDCCCLXXXVI, p. 56-57

303 *Scots Magazine,* Vol 29, July 1767, p. 388

304 *Scots Magazine,* Vol 29, Appendix 1767, p. 702

305 NLS 148 26/10/1767

306 NLS 148 3/12/1767 Aeneas Macdonald to AS

307 DP p. 861, cf. *Letters* p. 93

308 DP 869

309 William Fraser, C.B. LL.D *The Douglas Book,* Edinburgh MDCCCLXXXVI, p. 56

Chapter 17:

310 Cradock's memoirs, quoted in Ben Weinreb and Christopher Hibbert, eds., *The London Encyclopaedia,* Macmillan, 1983

311 John Lord Campbell, *Lives of the Lord Chancellors,* Vol V, London, John Murray 1846, p. 485-6

312 Ibid, p. 661

313 Richard C. Cole, *The General Correspondence of James Boswell, 1766-1769,* Vol. 1: 1766-1767, Edinburgh University Press, Yale University Press. 1997, p. 2

314 James Boswell, *Life of Johnson,* Oxford University Press, World's

Classics, 1998, p 390

315 Peter Martin, *A Life of James Boswell,* Weidenfeld and Nicolson, 1999, p. 233

316 NLS 5371 p 169

317 NLS 5371 p 169

318 Richard C. Cole, *The General Correspondence of James Boswell, 1766-1769,* Vol. 1: 1766-1767, Edinburgh University Press, Yale University Press. 1997, p. 119

319 Ibid, p. 122-3

320 Ibid

321 NLS MS 4944 f. 178

Chapter 18:

322 *The Letters and Journals of Lady Mary Coke,* Volume Third 1769-1771, first published 1889-96, Kingsmead Reprints, Bath, 1970, p. 3

323 Ibid, p. 7

324 Ibid, p. 8

325 Ibid, p. 9

326 Case, Part 1, Book 1, p. 28-9

327 Quoted in Robert Gore-Brown, *Chancellor Thurlow,* Hamish Hamilton, London 1953, p. 50

328 *A Letter to a Noble Lord, or a Faithful Representation of the Douglas Cause,* 1769, Printed for A. Henderson and sold at his house in College St. Westminster, p. 39

329 *Scots Magazine,* vol xxxi. pp 107-110

330 John Lord Campbell, *Lives of the Chancellors,* vol. 1. pp. 500, 501; *Scots Magazine* for 1769, vol. xxxi. p. 107; *Edinburgh Evening Courant,* 23d January 1769.

331 *Scots Magazine,* vol xxxi. Pp 107-110

332 *Letters to and from Lord Malmesbury,* i. 173;

333 Stuart, Letter III, p. 2

334 Beinecke, Documents and Manuscripts, BBb44 150

335 Mss. 1691. French-Language Manuscript Materials in the Louisiana and Lower Mississippi

Valley Collections, Special Collections, LSU Libraries

336 Ibid

337 Horace Walpole, Derek Jarrett, ed., *Memoirs of the Reign of King George III*, ,Yale University Press, New Haven and London, 2000

338 Richard C. Cole, ed., *The General Correspondence of James Boswell, 1766-1769*,Vol. 2: 1766-1767, Edinburgh University Press,Yale University Press. 1997, p. 139

339 *The Letters and Journals of Lady Mary Coke*,Volume Third 1769-1771, first published 1889-96, Kingsmead Reprints, Bath, 1970, p. 12

340 Horace Walpole, Derek Jarrett, ed., *Memoirs of the Reign of King George III*, ,Yale University Press, New Haven and London, 2000

341 *The Letters and Journals of Lady Mary Coke*,Volume Third 1769-1771, first published 1889-96, Kingsmead Reprints, Bath, 1970, p. 12

342 Ibid, p. 13

343 Ibid, p 14.

344 *Letters of Junius*,Vol. 1, p.120

345 *The Letters and Journals of Lady Mary Coke*,Volume Third 1769-1771, first published 1889-96, Kingsmead Reprints, Bath, 1970, p. 19

346 Ibid, p. 28

347 Ibid, p. 30

348 NLS MS 4944 f. 184

Chapter 19:

349 *Scots Magazine*, vol xxxi. Pp 107-110

350 John Hill Burton, ed.T*he Autobiography of Dr. Alexander Carlyle of Inveresk*, T.N. Foulis, London & Edinburgh 1910, p. 537-9

351 James Dennistoun, *Memoirs of Sir Robert Strange, Knt*,Vol II, London, Longman, Brown, Green, and Longmans, 1855, Letter from Robert Strange to Andrew Lumisden, Feb. 28, 1769

352 Horace Walpole, Derek Jarrett, ed., *Memoirs of the Reign of King George III*, ,Yale University Press, New Haven and London, 2000

353 Robert Gore-Brown, *Chancellor Thurlow*, Hamish Hamilton, London 1953, pp 51-2

354 Mapperton library, *The Douglas Cause,* handwriten journal

355 James Dennistoun, *Memoirs of Sir Robert Strange, Knt*,Vol II, London, Longman, Brown, Green, and Longmans, 1855, Letter from Robert Strange to Andrew Lumisden, Feb. 28, 1769

356 John Lord Campbell, *The Lives of the Lord Chancellors of England,* vii. 172-3, 387-9; Holdsworth, *A History of English Law*, xii. 309-10.

357 NLS 5361 p. A8

358 NLS 5361 p. A16

359 NLS 5361 p. B29

360 NLS 5361 p. A53

361 NLS 5361 p. A75

362 John Lord Campbell, *Lives of the Lord Chancellors,* Vol V, London, John Murray 1846, p. 363

363 Ibid, p. 288

364 James Dennistoun, *Memoirs of Sir Robert Strange, Knt*Vol II, London, Longman, Brown, Green, and Longmans, 1855, Letter from Robert Strange to Andrew Lumisden, Feb. 28, 1769

365 Horace Bleackley, *The Story of A Beautiful Duchess*,Archibald Constable & Co. Ltd, 1907 , p. 163-5

366 John Lord Campbell, *Lives of the Lord Chancellors, Vol V,* London, John Murray 1846, p. 363

367 A. Francis Steuart, ed. *The Douglas Cause,* Glasgow and Edinburgh, William Hodge and Co., 1909, p. 137

368 Robert Gore-Brown, *Chancellor Thurlow*, Hamish Hamilton, London 1953, pp 51-2

369 James Dennistoun, *Memoirs of*

Sir Robert Strange, Knt Vol II, London, Longman, Brown, Green, and Longmans, 1855, Letter from Robert Strange to Andrew Lumisden, Feb. 28, 1769

[370] *Scots Magazine*, vol xxxi. Pp 107-110

[371] *The Letters and Journals of Lady Mary Coke*, Volume Third 1769-1771, first published 1889-96, Kingsmead Reprints, Bath, 1970, p. 32-3

[372] From LdlT unpublished chapter in BYU

Chapter 20:

[373] C.K.Davis, *The Law in Shakespeare*, St. Paul: West Publishing Co.1884, p. 144.

[374] Quoted in C.H.S. Fifoot, *Lord Mansfield*, reprint of Oxford Edition 1936, Scientia Verlag Aalen, 1977, p. 30

[375] Alexander Pope, *The Sixth Epistle of the First Book of Horace,*

[376] C.H.S. Fifoot, *Lord Mansfield*, by, reprint of Oxford Edition 1936, Scientia Verlag Aalen, 1977, p. 32

[377] In A. Francis Steuart, ed. *The Douglas Cause,* Glasgow and Edinburgh, William Hodge and Co., 1909

[378] *Scots Magazine*, vol xxxi. Pp 107-110

[379] John Lord Campbell, *Lives of the Lord Chancellors, Vol V*, London, John Murray 1846, p. 288

[380] David Hooper, *Reputations Under Fire,* Little, Brown and Company, 2000, p. 127

[381] John Hill Burton, *The Autobiography of Dr. Alexander Carlyle of Inveresk,* T.N. Foulis, London & Edinburgh 1910, p. 537-9

[382] NLS 5361, p. 163

[383] S.M. Phillips, *Famous Cases of Circumstantial Evidence*, Frederick D. Linn & Co, Jersey City, 1879

[384] A. Francis Steuart, ed. *The Douglas Cause,* Glasgow and Edinburgh, William Hodge and Co., 1909, p. 142-150

[385] *The Letters and Journals of Lady Mary Coke*, Volume Third 1769-1771, first published 1889-96, Kingsmead Reprints, Bath, 1970, p. 33-4

[386] Horace Walpole, Derek Jarrett, ed., *Memoirs of the Reign of King George III,* Yale University Press, New Haven and London, 2000

[387] W. Fraser, *Red Book of Grandtully,* ii. 370

[388] Percy Fitzgerald, *Lady Jean, the Romance of the Great Douglas Cause*, London, T. Fisher Unwin, 1904, p. 256

[389] John Hill Burton, ed.. *The Autobiography of Dr. Alexander Carlyle of Inveresk,* T.N. Foulis, London & Edinburgh 1910, p. 537-9

[390] *The Letters and Journals of Lady Mary Coke*, Volume Third 1769-1771, first published 1889-96, Kingsmead Reprints, Bath, 1970, p. 32-3

[391] NLS MS 4944

[392] Horace Walpole, Derek Jarrett, ed., *Memoirs of the Reign of King George III,* , Yale University Press, New Haven and London, 2000

[393] Ian Simpson-Ross, *Lord Kames and the Scotland of his Day,* , Oxford, 1972

[394] *The Living Age*, Vol 172 issue 2228 (March 5 1887) p 591 ff

[395] Robert Malcolm Kerr, *Literary Gleanings*, Glasgow, 1850, Note E, Notes, p. 35 ff

[396] Alexander Allardyce, ed., *Letters from & to Charles Kirkpatrick Sharpe, Esq.*, William Blackwood 1888, p. 200, n. 1

[397] Alexander Pope, *Sixth Epistle of the First Book of Horace*, quoted in C.H.S. Fifoot, *Lord Mansfield*, reprint of Oxford Edition 1936, Scientia Verlag Aalen, 1977, p. 35

[398] Norman S. Poser, *Lord Mansfield, Justice in the Age of Reason,* McGill-Queen's University Press, 2013, pp341-3

Chapter 21:

[399] *Caledonian Mercury,* 1st March 1769

[400] Ramsay's *Scotland and Scotsman,* quoted in John Hill Burton, ed., *The Autobiography of Dr. Alexander Carlyle of Inveresk,* T.N. Foulis, London & Edinburgh 1910, p. 537-9

[401] Ian Simpson-Ross, *Lord Kames and the Scotland of his Day,* , Oxford, 1972

[402] *Scots Magazine,* vol xxxi. Pp 107-110

[403] Letter, 2d March 1769. Original at Murthly, quoted in William Fraser C.B. H.D., *The Douglas Book,* Edinburgh – MDCCCLXXXVI, p. 59

[404] J. H. Burton, *Life of Hume,* ii. 423

[405] Robert Gore-Brown *Chancellor Thurlow,* Hamish Hamilton, London 1953, p. 53

[406] Violet Biddulph, *Kitty, Duchess of Queensberry,* by Ivor Nicholson and Watson, London, 1935, p. 245

[407] John Hill Burton, ed., *The Autobiography of Dr. Alexander Carlyle of Inveresk,* Edited by T.N. Foulis, London & Edinburgh 1910, p. 534-5

[408] *The Letters and Journals of Lady Mary Coke,* Volume Third 1769-1771, first published 1889-96, Kingsmead Reprints, Bath, 1970, p. 33-4

[409] *Selections from the Family papers preserved at Caldwell,* Part II. Vol II, The Maitland Club, Glasgow MDCCCLIV p.153

[410] NLS MS 4944 f. 193

[411] Richard C. Cole, *The General Correspondence of James Boswell, 1766-1769,* Vol. 1: 1766-1767, Edinburgh University Press, Yale University Press. 1997, p. 153

[412] Ibid, p. 226

[413] *The Letters and Journals of Lady Mary Coke,* Volume Third 1769-1771, first published 1889-96, Kingsmead Reprints, Bath, 1970, p. 37-8

[414] Percy Fitzgerald, *Lady Jean, the Romance of the Great Douglas Cause,* London, T. Fisher Unwin, 1904 , p. 257

[415] *The Letters and Journals of Lady Mary Coke,* Volume Third 1769-1771, first published 1889-96, Kingsmead Reprints, Bath, 1970, p. 39

[416] *Scots Magazine,* July 1769 p 389

[417] *The Letters and Journals of Lady Mary Coke,* Volume Third 1769-1771, first published 1889-96, Kingsmead Reprints, Bath, 1970, p. 114-5

[418] *Selections from the Family papers preserved at Caldwell,* Part II. Vol II, The Maitland Club, Glasgow MDCCCLIV, p. 154 plus sections of Mure Collection NLS MS 4944 f. 193

[419] NLS MS 4945 f. 3

[420] Quoted in *Scots Magazine,* vol. xxxii, p314

[421] Quoted in *Scots Magazine,* vol. xxxii, p314

[422] *Selections from the Family papers preserved at Caldwell,* Part II. Vol II, The Maitland Club, Glasgow MDCCCLIV, Item CCLXVI, p 184

Chapter 22:

[423] *Selections from the Family papers preserved at Caldwell,* Part II. Vol II, The Maitland Club, Glasgow MDCCCLIV, p. 211-12

[424] Robert Chambers, *Traditions of Edinburgh,* W&R Chambers, London and Edinburgh, 1869, p. viii

[425] Stuart, Letter I, p. 1

[426] Ibid, Letter I, p. 4

[427] Ibid, Letter IV, p. 6

[428] Ibid, Ltter IV, p. 37

[429] Ibid, Letter III, p. 42

[430] Ibid, Letter IV, p. 27

[431] Ibid, Letter II, p. 10

[432] Ibid, Letter III, p. 36

[433] Ibid, Letter III, p. 43

[434] NLS MS 4946 f. 51

[435] James Boswell, *Life of Johnson,* Oxford University Press, World's Classics, 1998, p 522-3

[436] Ibid

437 LdlT papers, Q p. 25 Malahide xi 213

438 LdlT papers *Q p. 23* Malahide VI 107

439 Quoted in LdlT papers, ref. given Gray, *Letters*, p. 78-9

440 LdlT Q + SS Letters

441 Lady Constance Russell, *Three Generations of Fascinating Women*, Longmans, Green, and Co, 1904, p. 182

442 James Boswell, *The Journal of a Tour to the Hebrides with Samuel Johnson, LL.D.*, Charles Dilly: London, 1785

Chapter 23:

443 Violet Biddulph, *Kitty, Duchess of Queensberry*, Ivor Nicholson and Watson, London, 1935, p. 254

444 LMC Vol IV, p. 116

445 Violet Biddulph, *Kitty, Duchess of Queensberry*, Ivor Nicholson and Watson, London, 1935, p. 231

446 Lady Louisa Stuart, (Jill Rubinstein, ed.) *Memoire of Frances, Lady Douglas*, Scottish Academic Press, Edinburgh and London 1985, p.81

447 Sir Lewis Namier and John Brooke, *The House of Commons, 1754-1790;*, London, HMSO Publications, Vol II, p. 330

448 Lady Louisa Stuart, (Jill Rubinstein, ed.) *Memoire of Frances, Lady Douglas*, Scottish Academic Press, Edinburgh and London 1985, p. 87

449 Lady Constance Russell, *Three Generations of Fascinating Women*, Longmans, Green, and Co, 1904, p. 125-6

450 NLS MS 4946 f. 181

451 NLS MS 4946, f. 4

452 LdlT papers Q p. 29

453 LdlT references to Malahide xvi 83

454 Quoted in LdlT Q last page, from "New Boswell 6"

455 Sir Lewis Namier and John Brooke, *The House of Commons, 1754-1790*; London, HMSO Publications, Vol II, p. 330

456 Letter from Lady Lucy Barry, Hirsel archives, Box 34, Folder 1

457 ftp://ftp.rootsweb.com/pub/usgenweb/oh/history/1884/chapt1.txt

458 The correspondence between Playfair and Archy Douglas is in the National Register of Archives (Scotland), Survey 859, Box 217, Bundle 2, and has been described by Ian Spence, http://psych.utoronto.ca/users/spence/personal.html

459 *Glasgow Gazette*, 17th January 1863.

460 Lady Louisa Stuart, (Jill Rubinstein, ed.) *Memoire of Frances, Lady Douglas*, Scottish Academic Press, Edinburgh and London 1985, p.xx

Chapter 24:

461 Hon. James A. Home, *Lady Louisa Stuart: Selections from her manuscripts*, Edinburgh, David Douglas 1899 p. 29

462 Richardson, p. 44

463 Ibid p. 124

464 *North Western Advocate and the Emu Bay Times, May 19, 1911*, p. 1

465 Charles Castle, *The Duchess who Dared*, Sidgwick and Jackson, 1994, pp. 65-6

466 Lillian de la Torre, *The Heir of Douglas*, Michael Joseph, 1953, p228.

467 PP p. 705-6

468 PP p. 340

469 *The Speeches and Judgement of the Court of Session...* taken down and published by William Anderson, Balfour, Auld and Smellie, Edinburgh, 1768, p. 48

470 Hirsel Box 60 Bundle 3

Index

Hamilton, James, sixth duke, 30, 83, 84, 93, 101
Hamilton, Lady Mary, 38
Hamilton, Lord Anne, 30
Hamilton, Sir William, 355
Hamilton, Thomas, 104
Hamilton, William, 38, 57, 89, 102, 103, 106
Handel, George Frederick, 297
Hanover, royal family of, 17
Hay, John, 159, 191, 192, 197, 212, 214
Hédouard, Mme., 174, 179, 187
Henry VII, King, 15
Henry VIII, King, 15
Hepburn, Mrs., 54, 55, 59, 108, 116, 375
Herman, Lord, 233
Hertford, Lady, 292
Hertford, Lord, 293
Hervey, Lieutenant John, 324
Hewit, Mrs. Helen, Lady Jane Douglas' maid, 10, 24, 45, 55, 61, 64, 65, 74, 97, 140, 145, 148, 160, 184, 261, 292, 374
Heywood, Mrs., 323
Hibert, Abbé, 154
Hibert, Mr. and Mrs., 60
Holdernesse, Lady, 289
Holland, Lady, 289
Home, Earl of, 362, 376
Home, John, 114, 329
Hume, David, 7, 189, 225, 327, 345
Humphreys, Miss, barmaid, 268
Jacobitism, 5, 12, 31, 43
James II, exiled King of Scotland, 12, 17
James Erskine, Lord Grange, judge of Court of Session, 29
Jardine, George, 349
Johnson, Dr. Samuel, 270, 310, 346, 349, 350, 380
Johnston, James, Chevalier, 48–50
Johnstone, William, 137
Junius, pseudonym of campaigning journalist, 290

Kames, Lord, Scottish judge, 235, 252, 257, 272, 326,
Keith, Rev. Robert, 46
Kennet, Lord, 255
Ker, Mally, 50, 66
Ker, Mark, Lord, (also Kerr) 25, 27, 51, 70, 74
Ker, Mark, Lord, 51
Kerr, Lady Mary, 16
Kerr, Lady Mary, Marchioness of Douglas, 25
"King of Corsica", aka Theodore, Baron Neuhoff, 78-79
King's Bench prison, 73
Kingston, Duchess of, 324
Kingston, Duke of, 324
Kinnaird, Charles, fifth lord , 54
Kinnaird, Lady Magdalene, 54, 370
Kwilecki, Countess Isabella 370-371
La Marre, François, 149
La Marre, Mme., 162, 208
La Marre, Mme., 208
La Marre, Pierre, 70
La Marre, Pierre, man midwife, 65, 75, 86, 119, 126, 143, 144, 146, 162, 190, 196, 221, 222, 226, 255, 300, 317, 368, 374
Le Brun, Mme., 64, 86, 128, 131, 142, 149, 185, 190, 191, 210, 261, 292, 300, 306, 374
Lichfield, Lady, 290
Loch, William, 86
Loftus, Prof. Elizabeth, 369
Loret, M., 243
Lorne, Lord, 173
Lothian, Lady, 108
Lothian, Marquess of, 108
Louis XV, 127
Lovat, Lady, 119
Lundie, Mr., 266
M'Crabbie, Mary, 92
Macdonald, Aeneas, aka Angus , 195, 208, 265, 274
Macdonald, John, 117
Macelligot, Baron, 68